# AI and Blockchain Applications in the Oil and Gas Industry

Shashi Bhushan
*School of Computing Science and Engineering, Galgotias University, Greater Noida, India*

Fasee Ullah
https://orcid.org/0000-0001-6167-5253
*Department of Computing, Faculty of Science, Management and Computing, Universiti Teknologi Petronas, Malaysia*

Hilmi Hasan
*Department of Computing, Faculty of Science, Management and Computing, Universiti Teknologi Petronas, Malaysia*

IGI Global Scientific Publishing
Publishing Tomorrow's Research Today

Published in the United States of America by
IGI Global Scientific Publishing
701 East Chocolate Avenue
Hershey, PA, 17033, USA
Tel: 717-533-8845 | Fax: 717-533-7115
Website: https://www.igi-global.com E-mail: cust@igi-global.com



Library of Congress Cataloging-in-Publication Data

Names: Bhushan, Shashi, 1988- editor | Ullah, Fasee, 1983- editor | Hasan, Hilmi (Mohd Hilmi), 1979- editor
Title: AI and blockchain applications in the oil and gas industry / edited by: Shashi Bhushan, Fasee Ullah, Hilmi Hasan.
Description: Hershey PA : IGI Global Scientific Publishing, [2026] | Includes bibliographical references. | Summary: "This book explores the strategic and operational implications of integrating AI and blockchain in the oil and gas industry"-- Provided by publisher.
Identifiers: LCCN 2025032050 (print) | LCCN 2025032051 (ebook) | ISBN 9798337354576 hardcover | ISBN 9798337354583 paperback | ISBN 9798337354590 ebook
Subjects: LCSH: Petroleum industry and trade--Data processing | Artificial intelligence--Industrial applications | Blockchains (Databases)--Industrial applications
Classification: LCC HD9560.5 .A455 2026 (print) | LCC HD9560.5 (ebook)
LC record available at https://lccn.loc.gov/2025032050
LC ebook record available at https://lccn.loc.gov/2025032051

British Cataloguing in Publication Data
A Cataloguing in Publication record for this book is available from the British Library.

# Table of Contents

# Detailed Table of Contents



Fake news is a critical threat in the information age of today, and identifying it is essential to prevent misinformation and uninformed decision-making. In the oil and gas sector, where market stability, investment choices, and public perception are all extremely sensitive to news, the diffusion of false information has critical monetary and operational repercussions. Spurious news of oil spills, political unrest, or incorrect reserve calculations can lead to market panic or supply chain disruption. Detection of such disinformation guarantee sensible policymaking, investor confidence, and the industry's credibility. The sector's integrity and resilience, thus, require enhanced mechanisms to identify and combating of false news. This study performs a comprehensive comparative analysis of various Machine Learning models for the detection of fake news using two different news domains, i.e., general and sector-specific content related to oil and gas.

Due to growing energy demand and unconventional source issues in the world, the oil and gas trade are going through a digitalized change with AI as the central technology. This transformation is based on ML, DL, NLP, and big data analytics to increase operations, decision-making, and efficiency of the energy value chain. It describes AI and how it is being revolutionarily applied in the upstream oil and gas, the most capital intensive and erratic industry. The main causes of this digital revolution are analyzed, and in particular AI technologies improving upstream operations such as exploration, drilling, production and reservoir management. The oil and gas industry are where AI helps to solve the engineering process that was time-consuming and inefficient, as well as enhancing efficiency and safety. It covers regression analysis, classification models, clustering methods, artificial neural networks and state-of-art NLP frameworks in oil and gas. Final chapter reports about the experiments of AI in the upstream processes, especially exploration and reservoir characterization.

This chapter shows how blockchain improves transparency, efficiency, and trust in oil and gas. Supply chains and trade finance are slowed by fragmented systems, manual handoffs, delays, and fraud risk. A decentralized, tamper-evident ledger enables shared real-time data, end-to-end traceability, and secure records across operators, suppliers, shippers, banks, and regulators. Smart contracts automate terms, cut intermediaries, speed settlements, and improve liquidity. We map use cases in procurement, logistics tracking, asset integrity, and financial clearing, and pair blockchain with IoT telemetry for live monitoring and tokenization of commodities for digital trade. We also address regulatory uncertainty, scalability, and interoperability, and propose a stepwise framework for end-to-end rollout aligned to the oil and gas value chain. Uniting technology, operations, and governance, the chapter positions blockchain as a pillar of Industry 4.0 in energy, enabling secure, transparent, efficient global commerce.

In this chapter, the transformative power behind AI-blockchain convergence in energy systems is explored. It investigates the use of AI-enhanced technologies to assist with load forecasting, predictive maintenance as well as energy efficiency, how blockchain can be used to enable verifying transactions, participating in a decentralized market and having tamper-proof records in areas like peer-to-peer energy trading or managing a micro-grid. The combination of the two technologies leads to a paradigm, in which energy systems may become both intelligent and trustless, both decentralised and coordinated.



The upstream oil and gas industry is being significantly revolutionized by new digital technology. Merging Artificial Intelligence (AI) with blockchain is an empowering way to improve the industry, especially in predicting when equipment will break down and making the supply chain transparent. AI helps track equipment in real time and feeds data to predict when something is likely to break, thereby minimizing the chances of sudden shutdowns and optimizing equipment performance. Blockchain ensures integrity by logging how equipment is used, when it is serviced, and what happens in the supply chain; these logs cannot be altered. The combination of Blockchain and AI results in a smart and sound system that enhances business, making it easier, cheaper, and more compliant with regulations. The AI models performed better when they operated on data that were secure and verified by the blockchain. Smart contracts can also be used to automate maintenance and supply purchases.

Growing operational complexity, ageing infrastructure, and rising demands for efficiency and sustainability are all contributing factors to the oil and gas industry's current dramatic transformation. To improve operations in offshore facilities, this chapter investigates the combination of two innovative digital technologies: blockchain and large language models (LLMs). LLMs offer sophisticated features for handling unstructured technical data, automating documentation, enhancing decision-making, and assisting with predictive maintenance. Blockchain guarantees trust, transparency, and safe, decentralised data management throughout the value chain. Applications like smart contract automation, secure data exchange, real-time compliance, and intelligent asset monitoring are made possible by these technologies working together. The chapter also discusses issues with workforce development, data quality assurance, integration, and compatibility with legacy systems.

This chapter aims to bring out the integration between Artificial Intelligence and blockchain. While AI helps systems learn from data and produce insights, Blockchain ensures that the data remains clear, secure and traceable. The integration of these technologies results in hybrid intelligent systems. Such systems are leveraged to deliver secure and accountable outputs. This chapter covers integration models, technical foundations, and real-world applications in multidisciplinary areas. The chapter further addresses the substantial challenges in terms of scalability, data privacy, ethical responsibility and allied issues. The chapter concludes by addressing policy issues and research pathways related to the adoption of these hybrid systems. The chapter would offer great insights to researchers, policymakers, and practitioners. The aim of the chapter is to present the information in a manner that helps provide clarity and practical understanding regarding the integration of Artificial Intelligence and blockchain technologies and how they combine to create intelligent hybrid systems.



Distributed Acoustic Sensing (DAS) is a rapidly advancing technology in the oil and gas industry, enabling remote field operations monitoring in harsh and inaccessible environments. Utilizing laser-based optical fiber cables, DAS provides high-resolution, real-time spatiotemporal data over long distances. It generates massive volumes of data, necessitating advanced preprocessing methods. Integrating edge intelligence, including machine learning and AI, enables automated analysis, event detection (e.g., fluid leakage), and predictive capabilities such as $CO_2$ flux estimation. DAS supports applications like wellbore, caprock, reservoir, and pipeline monitoring, offering advantages over conventional sensors like geophones. Its use extends beyond oil and gas to marine, traffic, infrastructure, and seismic monitoring. Combining DAS with Edge Intelligence and IoT technologies delivers a cost-effective, sustainable, and autonomous solution for continuous surveillance, marking a significant shift toward smarter and safer operations in various industries.

# Preface

The oil and gas industry is undergoing one of the most profound transformations in its history. Driven by rising operational complexity, volatile markets, stricter regulatory frameworks, and mounting pressure for efficiency, safety, and sustainability, the sector is increasingly turning to advanced digital technologies for solutions. Among these, Artificial Intelligence (AI) and Blockchain have emerged as two of the most influential and disruptive forces reshaping how energy systems are designed, managed, and governed.

## ABOUT THIS BOOK

This book, *AI and Blockchain Applications in the Oil and Gas Industry*, brings together cutting-edge research, practical frameworks, and real-world use cases that illustrate how these technologies are redefining the energy value chain, from exploration and production to supply chain management, workforce identity, and digital trade. The chapters collectively demonstrate that AI and Blockchain are not merely incremental improvements, but foundational enablers of a new, data-driven, transparent, and intelligent energy ecosystem.

The opening chapters focus on the growing role of AI in managing information integrity and operational intelligence. Issues such as misinformation and fake news, which can significantly impact investor confidence, market stability, and public perception, are addressed through machine learning–based detection techniques tailored to both general and oil-and-gas-specific data domains. These discussions highlight the importance of trustworthy data as a prerequisite for effective decision-making in energy markets.

Subsequent chapters explore the synergy between AI and Blockchain across upstream, midstream, and downstream operations. From seismic interpretation, drilling optimization, and predictive maintenance to decentralized supply chains and automated trade finance, the book illustrates how AI-driven analytics gain reliability and scalability when combined with blockchain's secure, immutable, and transparent data infrastructure. Together, these technologies enable real-time monitoring, automated execution through smart contracts, and improved coordination among diverse stakeholders.

Several contributions emphasize digital transformation in upstream operations, showcasing how machine learning, deep learning, natural language processing, and big data analytics are revolutionizing exploration, reservoir characterization, and production management. These chapters underscore how intelligent systems can reduce operational risk, enhance safety, and unlock efficiencies in one of the most capital-intensive segments of the energy industry.

The book further extends its scope to emerging paradigms such as hybrid intelligent systems, large language models, edge intelligence, IoT-enabled monitoring, and self-sovereign identity. These chapters present forward-looking perspectives on decentralized identity management, workforce mobility, real-time field surveillance, and the integration of unstructured data into operational workflows. Together, they reflect the industry's shift toward autonomous, human-centered, and trust-enabled digital infrastructures.

Beyond technical innovation, the chapters also address critical challenges related to scalability, interoperability, data quality, governance, privacy, and regulatory compliance. By combining theoretical foundations with applied case studies and implementation frameworks, this volume offers balanced insights for researchers, engineers, technology developers, policymakers, and industry leaders.

In summary, this book aims to serve as a comprehensive reference on the convergence of AI and Blockchain in the oil and gas industry. It captures the current state of innovation while pointing toward future research directions and practical adoption pathways. As the energy sector continues its digital evolution, the ideas and solutions presented here seek to contribute to building a more resilient, transparent, efficient, and sustainable global energy system.

Chapter 1

# A Machine Learning-Based Fake News Classification for the Oil and Gas Industry Using Diverse News Datasets

**Muhammad Hamza**
https://orcid.org/0009-0006-1854-0525
*Qurtuba University of Science and Information Technology, Pakistan*

**Shahab Haider**
https://orcid.org/0000-0001-6802-6133
*Ghulam Ishaq Khan Institute of Engineering Sciences and Technology, Pakistan*

**Abdur Rashid Khan**
*Qurtuba University of Science and Information Technology, Pakistan*

**Fasee Ullah**
https://orcid.org/0000-0001-6167-5253
*Department of Computing, Faculty ty of Science, Management and Computing, Universiti Teknologi Petronas, Malaysia*

**Ambreen Zahra**
*Qurtuba University of Science and Information Technology, Pakistan*

**Faizan Ahmad**
*Qurtuba University of Science and Information Technology, Pakistan*

**Muhammad Ismail**
*Qurtuba University of Science and Information Technology, Pakistan*

## ABSTRACT

*Fake news is a critical threat in the information age of today, and identifying it is essential to prevent misinformation and uninformed decision-making. In the oil and gas sector, where market stability, investment choices, and public perception are*

DOI: 10.4018/979-8-3373-5457-6.ch001

*all extremely sensitive to news, the diffusion of false information has critical monetary and operational repercussions. Spurious news of oil spills, political unrest, or incorrect reserve calculations can lead to market panic or supply chain disruption. Detection of such disinformation guarantee sensible policymaking, investor confidence, and the industry's credibility. The sector's integrity and resilience, thus, require enhanced mechanisms to identify and combating of false news. This study performs a comprehensive comparative analysis of various Machine Learning models for the detection of fake news using two different news domains, i.e., general and sector-specific content related to oil and gas.*

## I. INTRODUCTION

The spread of fake information has raised serious issues globally, as it distorts public perceptions (Ghinadya & Suyanto, 2020). Fake news refers to intentionally fabricated content that mimics credible news sources to deceive audiences (Vogel & Meghana, 2020). In an era marked by rapid digital advancement, dissemination of information has transformed drastically. Traditional sources, such as newspapers, radio, and television have been overtaken by digital channels, like online news portals, social media platforms, and interactive websites. This shift has dramatically improved access to information, allowing users to consume news in real time and engage with content globally. However, this technological democratization has also led to the widespread diffusion of misinformation and disinformation phenomena that threaten public understanding, institutional credibility, and societal cohesion. Its purpose may range from political manipulation and economic disruption to social unrest or character defamation (Khanam et al., 2021). Fake information can even defame individuals, political parties, organizations, firms, and countries, leading to conflicts and societal instability (Liu & Wu, 2018). Despite significant progress, existing approaches still face limitations in generalizability across domains, handling low-resource languages, and detecting contextually nuanced misinformation. As highlighted by Jolly and Kumar (2022), future research must focus on cross-lingual adaptability, model interpretability, and hybrid frameworks that combine social, linguistic, and network-level signals (Jolly & Kumar, 2022). Modern approaches, such as supervised machine learning methods, allow the development of automated detection systems that can process vast amounts of content more efficiently than manual verification (Periodicals of Engineering and Natural Sciences, n.d.). Among these, advanced deep learning models, such as Recurrent Neural Networks (RNNs) and particularly Long Short-Term Memory (LSTM) networks have shown strong potential in recognizing fake news (Trueman et al., 2021). Furthermore, Natural

Language Processing (NLP) techniques enhance these systems by analyzing linguistic and contextual cues within news content (Imbwaga et al., 2022).

Despite these advancements, challenges remain significant. Fake news spreads rapidly during crises, such as the COVID-19 pandemic, highlighting the limitations of current detection tools (Jehad & Yousif, 2020). Political campaigns often weaponize fake news, making it difficult to differentiate between opinion, satire, and deception (Sahoo & Gupta, 2021). Similarly, economic misinformation, such as exaggerated statistics or rumors about stock markets and currency values can trigger public panic (Kaliyar, 2020). The emergence of deepfake videos has further complicated the issue, as synthetic media is increasingly difficult to distinguish from authentic content (Okoro et al., 2018). The detection of fake news is particularly difficult because of its dynamic nature, linguistic variety, and intentional manipulation. Zhou and Zafarani (2020) presented a comprehensive survey of fake news detection methods, categorizing approaches into knowledge-based, style-based, and propagation-based techniques (Zhou & Zafarani, 2020).

Fake news has emerged as a critical challenge in the digital era, particularly with the rise of social media platforms that enable rapid information dissemination. It not only misleads the public, but also influences political outcomes, social trust, and public health debates. Allcott and Gentzkow (2017) highlighted how fake news played a significant role in shaping public opinion during the 2016 United States of America presidential election, illustrating its wide-reaching societal consequences (Allcott & Gentzkow, 2017). Similarly, Lazer et al. (2018) defined fake news as 'fabricated information that mimics news media content in form but not in organizational process or intent,' emphasizing the need for scientific frameworks to combat its spread (Lazer et al., 2018).In addition the author examined rumor detection and resolution, showing how early intervention can mitigate the viral spread of misinformation on social media (Asudeh et al., 2020). These works demonstrate that fake news detection is not only a technical challenge but also a socio-behavioral problem. Given these challenges, this study performs a comprehensive comparative analysis of various Machine Learning (ML) models for fake news detection, with a special emphasis on oil and gas industry–related news. The approach leverages supervised learning algorithms and evaluates them across both general and domain-specific datasets. These models were assessed in terms of accuracy, precision, F1 score, and recall providing deeper insights into the effectiveness of fake news detection approaches.

The rest of the chapter is structured as follows. Section II reviews the existing literature on fake news detection technologies and domain-specific applications. Following this, the research methodology includes dataset preparation, model training, and evaluation strategies. The results and analysis section provides a comparative overview of the aforementioned models' performances. Finally, the study concludes with a summary of findings, limitations, and recommendations for future work.

## II. LITERATURE REVIEW

In this part, various sources are referenced and examined from the literature and are being thoroughly analyzed. In the literature review, we have studied existing systems related to fake news detection, which may provide background knowledge to aid in creating a new fake news detection model.

Supervised learning is a type of learning that applies labeled data points to train models (Zubiaga et al., 2018). The K-Nearest Neighbor (KNN) algorithm is effectively applied in various areas, such as anomaly detection (e.g., fraud), regression problems, and identifying false information on social media platforms. KNN is straightforward for creating classification models that allocate class labels to occasions. It is frequently applied in recommendation systems, semantic searches, and detecting anomalies. KNN's popularity in the industry stems from its interpretability, efficiency in processing time, and ability to manage noisy data effectively (Luger, 2022). Similarly, they compared four types of features—message-based, user-based, topic-based, and propagation-based—to classify the credibility of tweets. Jin et al. analyzed conflicting user viewpoints about news articles to verify news. News content-based features, derived from linguistic and visual cues, were utilized. Ott et al. introduced an approach for identifying unreliable spam reviews, while Feng et al. investigated ambiguous reviews using Context-Free Grammar (CFG) fundamentals (Tyagi, ). Social networking platforms have changed the way information is disseminated. Tacchini et al. analyzed a dataset of 15,500 Facebook posts, employing logistic regression and a crowdsourcing algorithm, achieving 99% accuracy,utilized a Support Vector Machine (SVM) model to evaluate 360 news articles, achieving 90% precision, 84% recall, and an F1 score of 87%. These efforts demonstrate the effectiveness of machine learning in analyzing social media content and news articles (Das et al., 2023).

Natural Language Processing (NLP) and Computer Vision focus on understanding language and interpreting images using machine learning for analysis and understanding (Ling, 2023). This motivates the present study to explore machine learning approaches for improving fake news detection, particularly within the context of supervised learning methods (Nasteski, 2019), Following the U.S. presidential elections, fake news and misinformation dominated the news cycle. Social media platforms produce and spread information for various reasons, often to enforce political agendas, harm reputations, or gain attention. Fake news erodes public trust and instills fear, destabilizing society. Researchers explore text-based and social media-based detection approaches (Rokach & Maimon, 2018). Fake news deliberately incorporates inaccuracies and aims to deceive. Misleading content on online platforms can harm individuals, organizations, and societal stability. Researchers use datasets like word-based (processing text for reports), categorical data (using machine learning to classify fake and real news), and numerical data (measurable information). Preprocessing involves cleaning, stemming, and encoding text into numerical vectors (Jurafsky & Martin, 2024). AI-based fake news detectors enable organizations to identify and prevent misinformation effectively. Metrics for evaluating multi-class classification models help ensure their reliability and accuracy (Mitchell, 2015).

The use of ML models in oil and gas operations offers a compelling parallel to its application in fake news classification, particularly within industry-specific domains. The article demonstrates how algorithms such as gradient boosting machines (GBM), random forests, and deep learning architectures outperform traditional regression models in forecasting oil well production using synthetic reservoir data. Notably, GBM achieved the lowest prediction error, highlighting its robustness in handling noisy, high-dimensional datasets. This mirrors the demands of domain-specific fake news detection, such as oil and gas misinformation, where nuanced, non-linear patterns often evade traditional text classification techniques (Logistic regression in medical research, 2021). In the context of the oil and gas industry, misinformation can significantly impact economic stability, investor confidence, and public perception. As highlighted by author that fake news related to pipeline explosions and oil price manipulation can distort markets and cause widespread misinformation (Kesarwani et al., 2020). In this paper the author observes that predictive maintenance models, while effective in one setting, often struggle when transferred to other equipment types or operational environments. This mirrors the difficulty of applying a fake news classifier trained on general political news to oil and gas news, which may feature domain-specific terminology and narrative structures. The article advocates for domain-aware modeling strategies, such as tailored training datasets and feature selection informed by expert knowledge. Incorporating this approach into fake news classification could improve the adaptability and accuracy of models across diverse domains, reinforcing the comparative framework of your study (Kaplan & Haenlein, 2019).

They emphasize the role of long short-term memory (LSTM) networks and ARIMA models in capturing temporal dependencies and anomaly patterns that are used to detect fake news, especially when misinformation spreads in a sequence, such as during crisis events or regulatory updates. Just as LSTM can anticipate machinery degradation based on historical trends, it can also identify linguistic and stylistic signals that precede fake news dissemination. Furthermore, the combination of IoT and real-time monitoring with machine learning highlights the value of adaptable systems, a feature that is becoming more and more pertinent in thwarting changing disinformation strategies in quickly expanding fields like the energy markets (Smitha & Bharath, 2020).

## III. RESEARCH METHODOLOGY

This section provides a comprehensive comparative analysis of the various ML models in detection of fake news including data pre-processing, models selection, and models implementation. The selected models are evaluated based on accuracy, precision, F1-Score and Recall. As mentioned in literature review, misleading content on online platforms can harm individuals, organizations, and societal stability. Researchers use datasets like Word-Based (processing text for reports), Categorical Data (using machine learning to classify fake and real news), and Numerical Data (measurable information). Pre-processing involves cleaning, stemming, and encoding text into numerical vectors. In the existing system K-Nearest Neighbor (KNN) algorithm is effectively applied in various areas, such as anomaly detection (e.g., fraud), regression problems, and identifying false information on social media platforms (Ogunsuyi & Ojo, 2022). KNN is a classification model that allocate class labels to occasions. It is frequently applied in recommendation systems, semantic searches, and detecting anomalies. Social networking platforms have changed the way information is disseminated. In this paper they analyzed a dataset of 15,500 Facebook posts, employing logistic regression and a crowd sourcing algorithm, achieving 99% accuracy (Rubin et al., 2016). Rubin et al. utilized a Support Vector Machine (SVM) model to evaluate 360 news articles, achieving 90% precision, 84% recall, and an F1 score of 87%. These efforts demonstrate the effectiveness of machine learning in analyzing social media content and news articles (Tacchini et al., 2017).

*Figure 1. Procedural Flowchart of our research methodology*

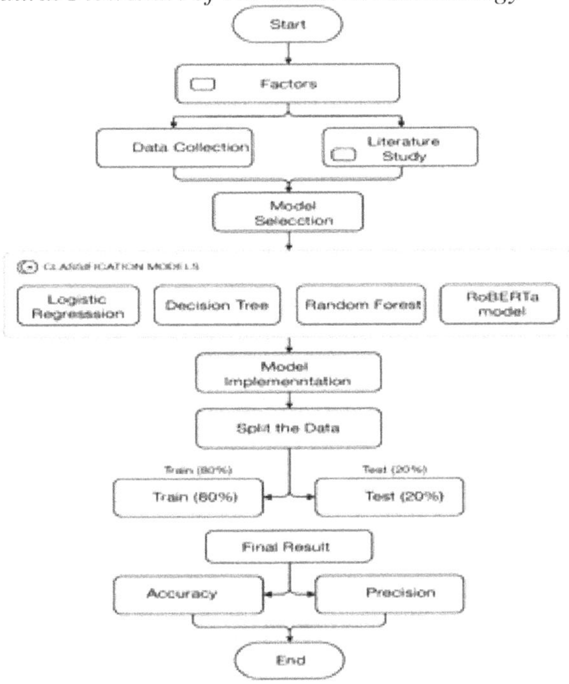


This work uses Logistic Regression, Decision Tree, Gradient Boosting, Random Forest, and RobERTa to analyze their effectiveness in fake news detection. While previous studies examined factors contributing to misinformation, this method combines classical considerations with machine learning to provide both technical insights and a foundation for policy recommendations grounded in statistical and ethical evaluation. Data pre-processing corrects errors in the collected data through cleaning techniques, including managing missing values while preserving data integrity. The raw text contains inconsistencies that could affect model accuracy; therefore, pre-processing steps include eliminating URLs if present in the dataset, text tokenization, removing stop words (if necessary), eliminating punctuation, converting labels to binary classes, etc. Label conversion is performed based on classifications, such as True, Partly True, Half True, True (Real), and all others as Fake (False). The exploratory data analysis includes reading, inspecting, and visualizing the data to uncover patterns. This involves reading the dataset, analyzing the data, identifying and removing duplicates, and calculating missing values. Considering the model selection, the dataset consists of categorical labels and numeric features, and based on these features, the following models were selected.

Logistic Regression, a classification algorithm used to determine the probability of an event based on input features; Decision Tree, a supervised learning model using conditional rules to classify data; and Random Forest, an ensemble method that builds multiple trees to improve prediction accuracy (Hosmer, Lemeshow, & Sturdivant, 2013). The methodology includes data preprocessing (e.g., tokenization), model selection, model implementation, and evaluation. Python, with libraries like scikit-learn and tools like VS Code and Google Colab, was used to implement and validate the models. The approach emphasizes the use of multiple ML models for improved reliability and insight.

## IV. RESULTS AND DISCUSSION

This section provides a comprehensive depiction of the outcomes derived. The dataset, initially in an Excel spreadsheet format, was converted into a *.csv* file using Python's pandas library for further processing. The data was divided into training and testing subsets, with 80% allocated for training and 20% for testing. The aforementioned ML models were trained to determine the one yielding the best results. The dataset underwent a thorough pre-processing phase, including cleaning and exploratory data analysis, to ensure integrity. Key steps included cleaning missing values; tokenization and vectorization, where text data was transformed using *TF-IDF* for feature extraction; and result consolidation, in which results from various models were saved in a unified result file for analysis. The dataset selection process involved choosing from publicly available repositories on Kaggle, including both a general fake news dataset and a domain-specific oil and gas news dataset. Following selection, the data underwent pre-processing to remove inconsistencies, followed by exploratory data analysis (EDA) to identify patterns and prepare the data for modeling.

The dataset consists of 44,088 observations and 4 variables, including three text variables and one categorical variable. It is well-structured, with no missing values and a minimal percentage (0.4%) of duplicate rows, totaling 196 duplicates. The dataset occupies approximately 1.4 MB of memory, with an average record size of 320 bytes. This clean and compact structure ensures efficient processing and analysis, making it suitable for machine learning applications such as fake news detection. The general fake news dataset included news articles across categories such as world news, politics, and entertainment. It was divided into "fake" and "real" categories after merging data from multiple sources. A similar cleaning and structuring procedure was followed for the oil and gas dataset. The language chosen was Python, selected for its simplicity and robust ecosystem, which is particularly well-suited for data sciences and ML tasks. Several essential Python libraries were utilized, including pandas, numpy, matplotlib, and scikit-learn, to handle data manipulation, numerical operations, visualization, and machine learning processes respectively.

The model implementation followed a structured workflow. First, the environment and necessary libraries were configured. Then, preprocessed data was prepared and fed into the models. Following this, the models were trained using the training subset of the data. After training, model validation was performed on the test data to assess generalization capability. Finally, performance was evaluated using standard metrics, such as accuracy, precision, recall, and F1-score.

The Decision Tree model performed well by utilizing hierarchical splitting to classify the data effectively and achieving high accuracy in its predictions (Quinlan, 1993). Logistic Regression was applied for binary classification with satisfactory outcomes (Hosmer, Lemeshow, & Sturdivant, 2013). Gradient Boosting achieved the highest accuracy among all the models evaluated. The performance assessment included accuracy, precision, recall, and F1-score as key evaluation metrics (Natekin & Knoll, 2013). Together, these metrics provided a comprehensive framework for evaluating and comparing the performance of the models. The evaluation of ML models for fake news detection reveals that Gradient Boosting achieved the highest accuracy, while Random Forest performed comparatively lower among the selected models. Nevertheless, all models demonstrated strong predictive ability with accuracies above 97%, reflecting the robustness of supervised learning approaches for this task. Gradient Boosting and Decision Tree achieved the highest accuracies, followed closely by Logistic Regression, while Random Forest showed relatively lower performance. Overall, all models demonstrated strong predictive ability, with most exceeding 97% accuracy, as shown in Table II.

*Table 1. Models Insights for General News Dataset*

| Model | Accuracy | Performance Insight |
|---|---|---|
| **Gradient Boosting** | **99.56%** | Best performing model, showing superior predictive power and handling of complex patterns. |
| **Decision Tree** | 99.41% | Strong accuracy with interpretability, but slightly less robust than Gradient Boosting. |
| **Logistic Regression** | 98.56% | Simple and efficient, still achieved very competitive accuracy. |
| **Random Forest** | 97.92% | Lowest among the models tested, yet still a strong performer above 97%. |

*Table 2. Models Insights for Oil and Gas Industries Dataset*

| Model | Accuracy | Performance Insight |
|---|---|---|
| **Decision Tree** | 92.93% | Best performing model, showing superior predictive power and handling of complex patterns. |
| **Gradient Boosting** | 92.54% | Strong accuracy with interpretability, but slightly less robust than decision tree. |
| **Logistic Regression** | 92.40% | Simple and efficient, still achieved very competitive accuracy. |
| **Random Forest** | 92.28% | Lowest among the models tested |

Furthermore, we present the evaluation of the same ML models trained on the oil and gas dataset for fake news classification. The dataset includes attributes such as news headlines, content, publication dates, and binary labels (real or fake). Among the models trained on the oil and gas dataset, Gradient Boosting and Decision Tree consistently delivered the highest performance, followed closely by Logistic Regression and Random Forest. The confusion matrix highlights the classification strengths and common misclassifications made by the best-performing models. It also points toward potential areas of refinement for higher predictive accuracy. Table III shows comparison for all the models tested in terms of the aforementioned evaluation metrics.

*Table 3. Comparative Performance of ML Models on Oil & Gas and General News Datasets*

| Model | Accuracy (General) | Accuracy (Oil & Gas) | Precision (General) | Precision (Oil & Gas) | Recall (General) | Recall (Oil & Gas) | F1 (General) | F1 (Oil & Gas) |
|---|---|---|---|---|---|---|---|---|
| Logistic Regression | 0.985652 | 0.924030 | 0.985727 | 0.925013 | 0.985652 | 0.924030 | 0.985642 | 0.924094 |
| Decision Tree | 0.994107 | 0.929389 | 0.994107 | 0.929904 | 0.994107 | 0.929389 | 0.994107 | 0.929437 |
| Random Forest | 0.979247 | 0.922871 | 0.979459 | 0.923540 | 0.979247 | 0.922871 | 0.979221 | 0.922929 |
| Gradient Boosting | 0.995516 | 0.925478 | 0.995519 | 0.932985 | 0.995516 | 0.925478 | 0.995516 | 0.925465 |

The results highlight that all four machine learning models performed consistently well on both the oil & gas dataset and the general news dataset. Among them, Gradient Boosting achieved the highest accuracy on the general news dataset, followed closely by Decision Tree. While the oil & gas dataset showed slightly lower accuracies across all models, the performance remained above 92%, indicating strong generalization capabilities. Overall, Gradient Boosting and Decision Tree outperformed the other models, confirming their robustness in both domain-specific and general contexts.

The comparative evaluation across general and oil and gas datasets highlights the adaptability and effectiveness of machine learning in domain-specific fake news detection. Models such as Gradient Boosting and Decision Tree achieved excellent results on both datasets, with the oil and gas dataset reaching accuracies as high as 99.5%, proving that specialized datasets can enhance classification performance when carefully curated and modeled. However, challenges remain in extending such systems to real-time and multilingual scenarios, which require more advanced approaches.

## V. CONCLUSION

Fake news has become one of the biggest challenges of our time and spotting it quickly is essential to stop misinformation from shaping poor decisions. This problem is especially serious in the oil and gas industry, where even small pieces of news can shake market stability, influence investments, and shape public opinion. False reports, such as claims of oil spills, political unrest, or wrong reserve estimates can cause unnecessary panic and even disrupt supply chains. This is why, being able to detect and correct fake news isn't just about protecting facts; it's about supporting smart policies, maintaining investor trust, and safeguarding the reputation of the industry. The sector's strength and resilience depend upon having reliable ways to identify and fight misinformation. Hence, our study investigated how different Machine Learning models perform when it comes to detecting fake news. We tested four popular supervised learning algorithms, i.e., Logistic Regression, Decision Tree, Random Forest, and Gradient Boosting on various datasets that included features like the article's title, body text, subject, and publication date. Among these, Gradient Boosting stood out, delivering the best results with an impressive accuracy of 99.56%. Future extension of this work may focus on multimodal fake news detection. Moreover, real-time multilingual and regional fake news detection can also be considered in future.

## REFERENCES


Allcott, H., & Gentzkow, M. (2017). Social media and fake news in the 2016 election. *The Journal of Economic Perspectives, 31*(2), 211–236. DOI: 10.1257/jep.31.2.211

Asudeh, A., Jin, Z., & Jagadish, H. V. (2020). Assessing and remedying coverage for a given dataset. In *Proceedings of the 2020 ACM SIGMOD International Conference on Management of Data* (pp. 377–392). DOI: 10.1145/3318464.3380598

Das, S., Dey, A., Pal, A., & Roy, N. (2023). Applications of Artificial Intelligence in Machine Learning: Review and prospect. *International Journal of Computer Applications, 115*(9), 31–41. DOI: 10.5120/20182-2402

Ghinadya, N., & Suyanto, S. (2020). Synonyms-Based Augmentation to Improve Fake News Detection using Bidirectional LSTM. DOI: 10.1109/ICoICT49345.2020.9166230

Hosmer, D. W., Lemeshow, S., & Sturdivant, R. X. (2013). *Applied logistic regression* (3rd ed.). Wiley., DOI: 10.1002/9781118548387

Imbwaga, J. L., Chittaragi, N., & Koolagudi, S. G. (2022). Fake news detection using machine learning algorithms. In *Proceedings of the 2022 Fourteenth International Conference on Contemporary Computing*. DOI: 10.1145/3549206.3549256

Jehad, R., & Yousif, S. A. (2020). Fake news classification using random forest and decision tree (J48). *Al-Nahrain Journal of Science, 23*, 49–55. DOI: 10.22401/ANJS.23.4.09

Jolly, A., & Kumar, S. (2022). Fake news detection in different applications: State-of-the-art and future directions. *Research Square*. DOI: 10.21203/rs.3.rs-2024922/v1

Jurafsky, D., & Martin, J. H. (2024). Speech and language processing (3rd ed. draft). Retrieved from https://web.stanford.edu/ jurafsky/slp3/

Kaliyar, R. K. (2020). Fake News Detection Using A Deep. *Neural Networks*. Advance online publication. DOI: 10.1109/CCAA.2020.8777343

Kaplan, A., & Haenlein, M. (2019). Siri, Siri, in my hand: Who's the fairest in the land? On the interpretations, illustrations, and implications of artificial intelligence. *Business Horizons, 62*(1), 15–25. DOI: 10.1016/j.bushor.2018.08.004

Kesarwani, S., Chauhan, S. S., & Nair, A. R. (2020). Fake News Detection on Social Media using K-Nearest Neighbor Classifier. DOI: 10.1109/ICACCE49060.2020.9154997

Khanam, Z., Alwasel, B. N., Sirafi, H., & Rashid, M. (2021). Fake news detection using machine learning approaches. *IOP Conference Series. Materials Science and Engineering*, *1099*(1), 012040. DOI: 10.1088/1757-899X/1099/1/012040

Lazer, D. M., Baum, M. A., Benkler, Y., Berinsky, A. J., Greenhill, K. M., Menczer, F., Metzger, M. J., Nyhan, B., Pennycook, G., Rothschild, D., Schudson, M., Sloman, S. A., Sunstein, C. R., Thorson, E. A., Watts, D. J., & Zittrain, J. L. (2018). The science of fake news. *Science*, *359*(6380), 1094–1096. DOI: 10.1126/science.aao2998 PMID: 29590025

Ling, Q. (2023). Machine learning algorithms review. *Applied and Computational Engineering*, *4*(1), 91–98. DOI: 10.54254/2755-2721/4/20230355

Liu, Y. P., & Wu, Y. F. B. (2018). Early detection of fake news on social media through propagation path classification with recurrent and convolutional networks. *AAAI Conference Proceedings*. DOI: 10.1609/aaai.v32i1.11268

Logistic regression in medical research. (2021). Retrieved from https://www.anesthesia-analgesia.org

Luger, G. F. (2022). Artificial Intelligence (Structure and strategies for complex problem solving) (6th ed.).

Mitchell, T. (2015). *Machine Learning*. McGraw Hill.

Nasteski, V. (2019). An overview of the supervised machine learning methods. Horizonti. *Serija B*, *4*, 51–62. DOI: 10.20544/HORIZONS.B.04.1.17.P05

Natekin, A., & Knoll, A. (2013). Gradient boosting machines, a tutorial. *Frontiers in Neurorobotics*, *7*, 21. DOI: 10.3389/fnbot.2013.00021 PMID: 24409142

Ogunsuyi, O. J., & Ojo, K. O. (2022). K-nearest neighbors Bayesian approach to false news detection from text on social media. *International Journal of Education and Management Engineering, 12*(4), 22–32. . Manzoor, S. I., Singla, J., & Nikita, N. (2019). Fake News Detection Using Machine Learning approaches: A systematic Review. In 2019 3rd International Conference on Trends in Electronics and Informatics (ICOEI). https://doi.org/DOI: 10.5815/ijeme.2022.04.03

Okoro, E., Abara, B. A., Umagba, A. O., Ajonye, A. A., & Isa, Z. S. (2018). A hybrid approach to fake news detection on social media. *Nigerian Journal of Technology*, *37*(2), 454. DOI: 10.4314/njt.v37i2.22

Periodicals of Engineering and Natural Sciences. (n.d.). Retrieved from https://pen.ius.edu.ba/

Quinlan, J. R. (1993). *C4.5: Programs for machine learning*. Morgan Kaufmann., DOI: 10.1016/C2009-0-06116-2

Rokach, L., & Maimon, O. Z. (2018). Data Mining with Decision Trees: Theory and Applications.

Rubin, V. L., Conroy, N. J., Chen, Y., & Cornwell, S. (2016). Fake news or truth? Using satirical cues to detect potentially misleading news. *Proceedings of the Second Workshop on Computational Approaches to Deception Detection*, 7–17. DOI: 10.18653/v1/W16-0802

Sahoo, S. R., & Gupta, B. B. (2021). Multiple features based approach for automatic fake news detection on social networks using deep learning. *Applied Soft Computing*, *100*, 106983. DOI: 10.1016/j.asoc.2020.106983

Smitha, & Bharath, R. (2020). Performance comparison of machine learning classifiers for fake news detection. In 2020 Second International Conference on Inventive Research in Computing Applications (ICIRCA). DOI: 10.1109/ICIRCA48905.2020.9183072

Tacchini, E., Ballarin, G., Della Vedova, M. L., Moret, S., & de Alfaro, L. (2017). *Some like it hoax: Automated fake news detection in social networks*. arXiv preprint arXiv:1704.07506. https://doi.org//arXiv.1704.07506.DOI: 10.48550

Trueman, T. E., Kumar, A., Narayanasamy, P., & Vidya, J. (2021). Attention-based C-BiLSTM for fake news detection. *Applied Soft Computing*, *110*, 107600. DOI: 10.1016/j.asoc.2021.107600

Tyagi, N. (n.d.). 6 Major Branches of Artificial intelligence (AI) — Analytics Steps. Retrieved from https://www.analyticssteps.com/blogs/6-major- branches-artificial-intelligence-ai

Vogel, I., & Meghana, M. (2020). Detecting Fake News Spreaders on Twitter from a Multilingual Perspective. DOI: 10.1109/DSAA49011.2020.00084

Zhou, X., & Zafarani, R. (2020). A survey of fake news. *ACM Computing Surveys*, *53*(5), 1–40. DOI: 10.1145/3395046

Zubiaga, A., Liakata, M., Procter, R., Hoi, G. W. S., & Tolmie, P. (2018). Detection and resolution of rumours in social media: A survey. *ACM Computing Surveys*, *51*(2), 1–36. DOI: 10.1145/3161603

# Chapter 2
# Digital Transformation in Oil and Gas: AI Fundamentals and Applications in Energy Upstream Operations

**Damodharan Palaniappan**
https://orcid.org/0009-0003-0721-3068
*Marwadi University, India*

**T. Premavathi**
https://orcid.org/0009-0003-0172-2021
*Marwadi University, India*

## ABSTRACT

*Due to growing energy demand and unconventional source issues in the world, the oil and gas trade are going through a digitalized change with AI as the central technology. This transformation is based on ML, DL, NLP, and big data analytics to increase operations, decision-making, and efficiency of the energy value chain. It describes AI and how it is being revolutionarily applied in the upstream oil and gas, the most capital intensive and erratic industry. The main causes of this digital revolution are analyzed, and in particular AI technologies improving upstream operations such as exploration, drilling, production and reservoir management. The oil and gas industry are where AI helps to solve the engineering process that was time-consuming and inefficient, as well as enhancing efficiency and safety. It covers regression analysis, classification models, clustering methods, artificial neural networks and state-of-art NLP frameworks in oil and gas. Final chapter reports about the experiments of AI in the upstream processes, especially exploration and reservoir characterization.*

DOI: 10.4018/979-8-3373-5457-6.ch002

# 1. INTRODUCTION

Artificial Intelligence implementation has unleashed a revolutionary change into the oil and gas industry, offering optimization of production, minimization of downtimes, improved safety requirements, and new forms of exploration and drilling (Li et al., 2024). The context that has led to the emergence of digital technologies, especially AI and ML, is reflected in their implementation in different spheres, including health care, finances, and transport. Figure.1 demonstrates that AI promotes a cascade of enhancements of an oil and gas industry starting with production and continuing with automation.

## 1.1 Overview of the Global Energy Landscape

Energy dynamics clearly show that the world is becoming complicated, changing, and it depends on population increases, economic growth, technology, and the environment. However, there has been a certain trend towards the use of renewable energy sources which is noticeable currently because fossil fuels contribute to a significant proportion of the energy mix in the world yet they are intended to be the cause of climate change and thus there is a trend towards resolving the same through adoption of renewable energy sources. The shift will require new strategies that are meant to maximize the current hydrocarbon reserves and at the same time engage in investing in sustainable energy resources. The oil and gas sector are part of this changing scenario as it meets the demand of energy consumption and deals with the challenge of minimizing its environmental footprints and increasing efficiency.

## 1.2 Need for Digital Transformation in Oil & Gas

The rationale behind digital transformation in oil and gas sector is a complex combination of factors such as the growing industry complexity, the reduction of oil and gas production on stuck fields, the requirement of exploring and developing unconventional reserves, and the rising environmental awareness. Traditional techniques have a hard time efficiently handling huge data sets created throughout the energy value chain of exploration to refining. AI and ML applications allow drawing important information out of such datasets making it easier to make data-driven decisions and automate complex operations. All data show that the oil and gas sector has accepted the necessity of taking up digital solutions as a matter of routine, rather than a choice of staying competitive, sustainable, and adaptable to meet the changing demand of world power (Wang et al., 2025). The growing popularity of digital metamorphosis can be explained by the radical increase in technologies, AI, in particular, and the constantly expanding amount of digital data (Murroni et al.,

2023). The use of AI and ML has developed a new trajectory of intelligent library systems due to enhanced communication between different technologies as well as between the technologies and people, which boosts the performance of different libraries.

*Figure 1. Digital Transformation in Oil & Gas*

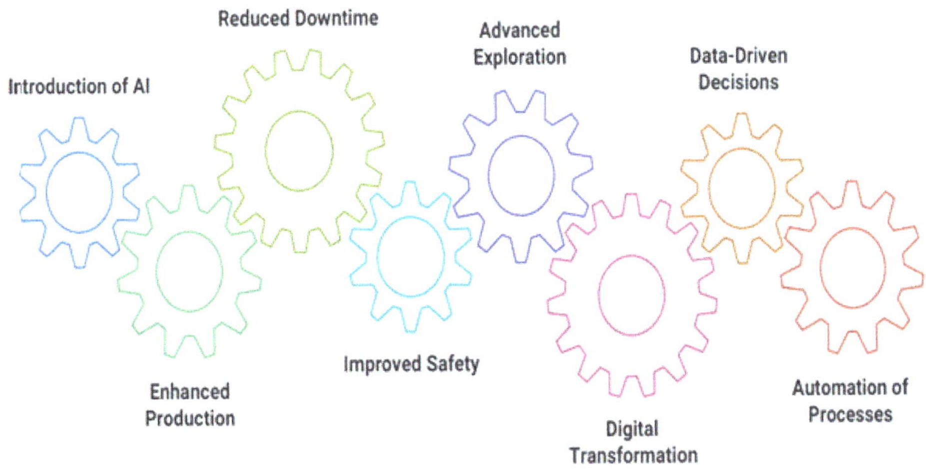


## 1.3 Role of Artificial Intelligence in Meeting Energy Demands

AI plays a crucial role in addressing energy requirements, as it provides instruments of enhancing efficiency, reducing losses, and enhancing sustainability along the energy value chain. Analytics powered by Artificial Intelligence can make production processes optimized by making correct predictions of equipment failure, by optimizing energy intake, and by streamlining maintenance. All of these solutions, i.e., energy consumption optimization, predictive maintenance, and streamlined maintenance schedules, have positive outcomes when using AI (Pandey et al., 2020). Also, AI will allow including renewable sources of energy into the work of the existing grids and will facilitate the process of transition to the low-carbon energy system, making it safer and more predictable.

Only the oil and gas business has benefited through the increasing application of artificial intelligence and artificial intelligence is promising in the oil and gas business, its exploration and drilling, production and distribution (Waqar et al., 2023). The ability of AI to process large amounts of information, identify patterns and automated processes, is changing the ways in which oil and gas companies operate, leading to significant gains in efficiency, cost effective savings, and safety. This includes better decision making, automation of complex tasks and ability to draw meaningful knowledge out of large data sets. The need to improve the productivity, sustainable practices, and the need to respond to the dynamics of the changing world energy demands are some of the issues which drive this change.

## 2. DRIVERS OF DIGITAL TRANSFORMATION IN UPSTREAM OIL & GAS

Upstream Oil and gas industry is experiencing profound digitalization which is being spurred by a set of factors. These are the growing complexity of operations, diminishing production in mature fields, imperative to explore and develop the unconventional resources as well as emerging environmental issues. It is also driven by the exponentially growing technologies, especially AI, and the availability of more and more digital data. The industry agrees that adoption of digital solution is no longer a choice, but a requirement in order to stay competitive, sustainable and flexible amid a changing global energy landscape.

### 2.1 Operational Efficiency and Performance Demands

The demands of efficiency and performance in operations drive the industry to maximize all parts of upstream valued chain. As stated above, the urgent need in optimization is due to the fact that the production rates in the mature fields are decreasing and the organizations are becoming more complex in their nature. Predictive maintenance, real-time drilling parameter optimization and optimized reservoir management are some of the solutions provided by the AI and ML methods that can be applied in the oil and gas industry, providing an increased production rate with minimized downtime and operating expenses. The goal of the industry to achieve operational excellence requires it to adopt AI-based solutions so that new heights of efficiency and performance can become a reality (Boukredera et al., 2025).

The range of opportunities offered by AI to optimize workflow, reduce costs, and increase outputs in the oil and gas industry is negligibly small. It is implemented to identify the points of improvement in drilling, production and refining activities, decrease the downtime, increase decision-making (Chen et al., 2025). Businesses are keen on applications of such advanced technologies but they are unable to apply their models, obtain actual outcomes and have a nice payback on those investments. Moreover, intelligent technologies may utterly alter the safety process in the oil and gas sector due to the fact that they observe the functioning of equipment's and employee conduct to identify possible threats and prevent accidents in the real-time mode (Li et al., 2024).

## 2.2 Cost Reduction Imperatives

The imperatives of cost reduction are also important, and digital transformation provides the means of reducing operating costs. The document points to the fact that the analytics with AI can optimize the production process by predicting breaks in the operation of equipment in advance, the optimal use of energy, and the smoothing of tight maintenance costs, which reduces costs. Moreover, the AI algorithms will help examine huge volumes of seismic data and detect the prospects of drilling more precisely, lower exploration expenditures, and the possibility of drilling drills.

AI also plays a stellar role in organizing data, and it is necessary to assist in real-time data analysis and make effective decisions (Alghamedy et al., 2024). There is also the automation, control, and optimization of processes; that leads to reduced total costs and enhanced compatibility of the actions made. Consequently, the application of the AI technologies to facilitate streamlined operations and resulting cost reductions is slowly becoming a mandatory step to ensure the profitability of oil and gas companies in ruthless markets.

## 2.3 Health, Safety, and Environment Considerations

Digital technologies can positively influence the aspects of health, safety, and a positive environmental impact through the real-time tracking of the processes and the predetermination of hazards. Systems powered by AI, will be able to monitor the data fed by sensors, cameras and so on, and detect leaks, spills and other environmental hazards so that remedial action can be initiated in time causing the least harm to the environment. Since there is increased emphasis on the environment, sustainability has become a priority in the oil and gas industry and the application of AI in order to enhance environmental performance (Wang et al., 2025). AI comes in to improve energy management systems, minimize emissions of greenhouse gases, track environmental effects, and promote moral and sustainable actives. Besides, AI was used to enhance safety standards, construct a barrier between workers and accidents, and reduce the risk of accidents. By working with AI technologies to reduce its impact on the environment and enhance safety, the oil and gas companies will have a chance to show their stakeholders that they are willing to continue working sustainably and take proper care of the environment, which will increase the reputation of such companies and make the stakeholders feel better about working with this company (Waqar et al., 2023).

## 2.4 Regulatory Pressures and Compliance

Regulatory challenges and compulsions are also contributing to phasing digital transformation around regarding the oil and gas sector being under pressure in the light of its environmental performance and the integrity of its operations. Digital solutions provide an opportunity to monitor emissions, waste management, and environmental regulations compliance practices. Besides, AI algorithms can help forecast and avoid accidents making people and workers safe. AI assists in reinforcing compliance functions, regulating regulatory reporting, and ensuring that industry regulations are followed which are fundamental to maintaining teamwork integrity and prevention of penalties (Khurram et al., 2025). The technologies that utilize AI can provide real-time insights into the data regarding the operations which allows determining the potential compliance issues more easily and prevent them. Using AI allows oil and gas companies to increase their reputation among regulators and stakeholders because it can automate their compliance processes, allow them to monitor the impacts of their operations to the environment, and ensure their operations and facilities are safe in a way that promotes their culture of responsibility and transparency.

## 2.5 Complexity of Unconventional Resource Development

The design of unconventional resources implies the need to analyze a huge amount of data, and AI and ML are key technologies to analyze the large volumes of data produced in the course of exploration, drilling, and production. The process of extracting the hydrocarbons like shale gas, tight oil, and oil sands is complex and it involves working with actual significant amounts of data which have been generated over many sources. With the help of AI algorithms, it is possible to analyze them and optimize drilling strategies and predict production rates and reduce the impact on the environment (Alghamedy et al., 2024). In the non-conventional resource development, The AI has an important role to play in combing multisource data to model dynamically and to optimize enhanced oil recovery approaches. Regression and forecasting models, classification algorithms, and clustering, are only some of the AI techniques to deal with the data-intensity of unconventional resource development. The technologies can be used to handle high dimension/nonlinear reservoir data that the industry is able to handle.

# 3. FUNDAMENTALS OF ARTIFICIAL INTELLIGENCE AND RELATED TECHNOLOGIES

In the oil and gas industry, the role of artificial intelligence is getting more and more significant as now it is possible to automate operations, raise the effectiveness of decision making and overall efficiency.

## 3.1 Artificial Intelligence: Definitions and History

Artificial Intelligence can be defined as a simulation of human Intelligence on machines which are actually programmed to think like and act like human beings. AI is the various methods used by machines to complete tasks that involve intelligence which is normally accomplished by a human being thereby incorporating AI in those tasks. AI is a history that could be traced back to the mid-20th century, where the works of pioneers like Alan Turing could be traced. There are a series of different stages that the field has gone through in its quest to reach the current level in this field, including, but not limited to the use of symbolic AI and expert systems, as well as more recent stages of machine and deep learning (Shah et al., 2025). The purpose of AI systems is to analyze complex data, learn by patterns, and either give a decision or a prediction on the basis of the available information. There are numerous methods and methods of AI such as machine learning, deep learning, natural language processing, and computer vision (Kostadimas et al., 2025) (Shah et al., 2025).

## 3.2 Machine Learning: Principles and Types

Machine Learning is a form of the AI when it allows computers to use data and learn without explicit programming. The algorithms of the ML learn and progress as a result of experience automatically (Revelou et al., 2025). There are some important types such as: Supervised Learning: Training a model with labeled data to learn how to input and how to output. Unsupervised learning: Teaching a machine through unlabelled data to determine patterns or structures. Reinforcement Learning: Education of a machine to make decisions in a world to maximize a signal-rewarding exercise. There are numerous algorithms in machine learning such as regression, classification and clustering.

## 3.3 Deep Learning: Architectures and Use Cases

Deep Learning falls under the category of machine learning, together with artificial neural networks characterized by multiple layers (deep neural networks) to process data. Such networks are able to get pattern and representation of complex data using large volume of data. Such typical architectures are Convolutional Neural Networks, recurrent neural networks, and Transformers (Gao et al., 2025). Some of the fields where deep learning has been used are image recognition and natural language processing among others. It has proved to have enormous potential in computer visions, speech recognition and natural-language processing. The deep learning models are the geometric transformations across numerous layers, and were recently successfully used in drug discovery.

### 3.4 Natural Language Processing

Applications in Knowledge Management Natural Language Processing is an area in AI, which concerns the computer and human language communication. With NLP techniques computers are allowed to comprehend, analyze and produce a human language. NLP finds its applications in document analysis, operational knowledge mining, and text mining in the oil and gas line. As an illustration of the application of NLP, one can mention analyzing technical reports, reviewing customer feedback, or automating the processes by conducting compliance. Natural language processing endows computers with the capabilities to gain and interpret the human language, as well as create it (Raza et al., 2025). When searching the library catalogs and search engines, NLP is used to enhance the accuracy of the search results.

### 3.5 Big Data Analytics in Oil & Gas

Big Data Analytics refers to the strategy of gathering, storing, processing and analyzing large, complex data collections in order to extract useful knowledge. Oil and gas Industries The data generated in oil and gas industries, both during exploration, drilling, production and refining is huge and has to be managed and analyzed using big data analytics. Data mining, statistical analysis, and machine learning techniques were used to detect trends, patterns and anomalies in data, that can be utilized to make decisions as well as to streamline operations (Wang et al., 2025). The current document points out that the oil and gas industry is a very good management of high-dimensional and non-linear reservoir data.

## 4. CORE AI TECHNIQUES APPLICABLE TO UPSTREAM OPERATIONS

Artificial intelligence has transformed the oil and gas fabric through automation, decision-making, and efficiency of operations in the upstream part of the oil and gas industry. The use of AI methods in the upstream processes is disrupting processes through which companies generate and drill in products, and the management of the reservoirs. These Forte techniques take advantage of data-driven intelligence to maximize processes, minimize cost and enhance safety.

## 4.1 Regression and Forecasting Models

The most valuable and basic AI techniques when it comes to upstream operations include regression and forecasting models. Since these models yield continuous results in regard to input variables, they are very useful in forecasting production rates, estimation of equipment failures and ideal working parameter (Boukredera et al., 2025). According to Figure.2, the applications are explained, including: production forecasting, forecasting equipment failure, and estimation of reservoir parameters based on the data-driven models.

Production forecasting: The regression models (e.g., linear regression, polynomial regression, and support vector regression) are applied to predict the needs of a specific production rate of oil and gas. These models are used to examine the previous production indicators, the features of the reservoir, and operation conditions in order to determine future production behaviour (Gandhi et al., 2024). As an example, a time-series forecasting model, e.g., ARIMA, could be used to predict the curves of production decline, and thus operators could plan corrective actions and develop effective production plans. Equipment Failure Forecasting: Sensor data, maintenance history and operating conditions of specific pieces of equipment can be used to determine the remaining useful life of this critical equipment through the use of regression modelling. These models allow performing predictive maintenance, minimize downtimes and maintenance costs due to the identification of the key indicators of equipment degradation (Tsallis et al., 2025).

*Figure 2. AI in Upstream Operations*

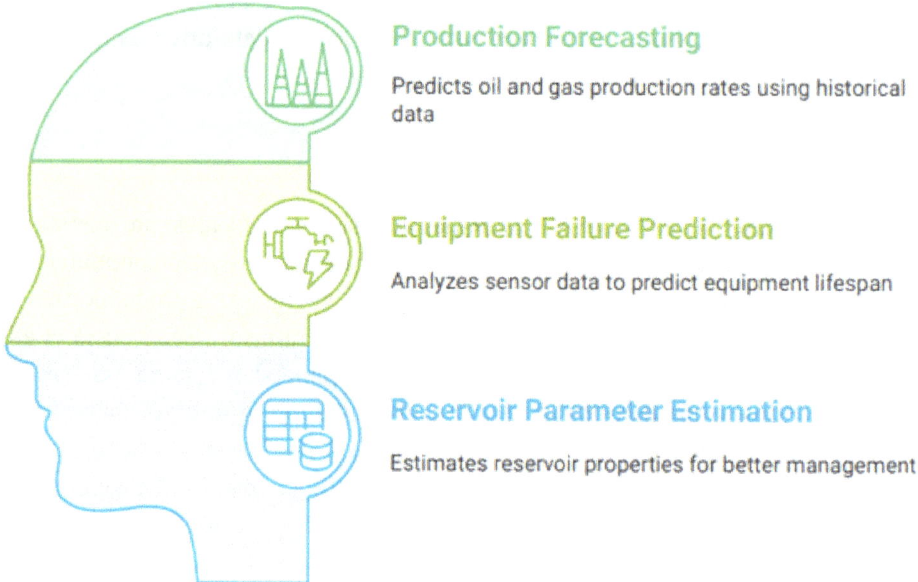


Reservoir Parameter Estimation: Reservoir parameters (permeability, porosity, and saturation) regression models are calculated based on well logs, seismic estimates and well core analysis. The estimations are critical in reservoir modeling and simulation that can be used in making decisions on reservoir management and enhanced oil recovery methods (Dong et al., 2025). The regression models will also be central in terms of predicting the continuous outcomes, thus enabling enhanced production predictions as well as equipment maintenance. Machine learning can be used with statistical methods to improve predictions.

## 4.2 Classification Algorithms for Pattern Recognition

Pattern recognition and taking decisions in upstream operations requires the installation of classification algorithms. Such algorithms divide data into previously specified classes or groups of features, thus allowing finding anomalies, predicting the occurrence of events, and the classification of geological formations. The Applications are, Anomaly Detection: The procedure of identifying anomalies in operational data makes use of the classification algorithms e.g., support vector machine, decision tree, random forest. Large-scale anomaly detection is essential in detecting the equipment breakdowns, detecting fraud and maintaining the quality of the data (Fejjari et al., 2025). Event Prediction: The classification models involved use the real-time data of the sensors, monitoring systems, and even the past records to predict events, like the impact of a well kick, blowout, pipeline leakage, etc. This prediction helps the operators to implement proactive steps in order to avoid accidents and minimize the risks (Liu et al., 2025). Geological Formation Classification: Classification of geological formations occurs by use of classification algorithms on well logs, seismic and core samples. Such a division is critical to the development of geological models and discoveries of hydrocarbon reserves and the perfection of drilling plans (Zhao et al., 2025). Classification algorithms help in grouping data, forecasting occurrences and spot anomalies, thus making operations safer and efficient.

## 4.3 Clustering for Geological Data Grouping

Clustering algorithms were applied in order to segment similar data points that will be characterized by their respective features. Clustering in upstream will be used in the grouping of geological data, zonation of reservoirs and also in customer segmentation (Padhy et al., 2024). Applications include the following: Geological Data Grouping Clustering algorithms are applied to classify geological data into groups depending on the lithology, mineral composition and petrophysical characteristics using k-means clustering, hierarchical clustering and DBSCAN. Such grouping assists the geologists in determining the geological trends, mapping of the reservoir facies and construction of geological models. Reservoir Zonation: Clustering algorithms, i.e. algorithms which group together similar reservoirs based on their properties, say permeability, porosity and fluid saturation, are applied to partition a reservoir into zones with homogenous behaviour. Important applications of zonation in reservoir simulation, optimization of production and EOR planning. Customer Segmentation: Cluster algorithms are employed to group customers on the basis of water-temperature preferences, energy-consumption patterns and their demographics. This kind of segmentation will assist energy firms to customize their goods and services to satisfy the needs of various customers (Gonen et al., 2024).

## 4.4 Artificial Neural Networks and Reservoir Modeling

Included in powerful machine learning models are the Artificial Neural Networks, which resemble the structure and operations of the human brain. ANNs, in up-stream operations, apply in reservoir modeling, production optimization as well as smart well controls. The apps are Reservoir Modeling: ANNs are utilised in creating reservoir simulations that model the fluid alterations, pressure and settlement in reservoirs. These models were allowed to learn on past production, well logs, seismic and core analysis. Production Optimization: ANNs are applied to optimize production parameters which include well head pressure control, flow rates and choke settings and maximize oil and gas production. These models examine data provided in real-time of the sensors and monitoring systems to determine the best operating conditions. Smart Well Control: ANNs control smart wells through adjustment of the downhole valves and flow control devices in order to maximize production assigned zones in reservoirs. These modellers are based on downhole sensors to give automated decision about the well control based on real time information. ANNs were applied to carrying out regression and classification. ANN models grasp the context of an issue where multiple feature space transformations are done, and nonlinearity is followed to generate simplified representations (Rouf et al., 2021).

### 4.5 NLP Models for Document Analysis and Operational Text Mining

Unstructured textual data is analyzed and text is retrieved using the Natural Language Processing models. NLP has been used in upstream operations, in document analysis, operational text mining and knowledge management. The applications are the following: Document Analysis: NLP models are applied to review technical reports, well logs and regulatory documents to capture important data pertaining to reservoir characteristics, operational processes and regulation. It is applied in the creation of knowledge bases, in better decision making, and guaranteeing regulatory compliance. Operational Text Mining: Operational text mining uses NLP-derived models to search operational text data (e.g. maintenance logs, incident reports, and operator notes) to capture trends, patterns, and anomalies. It is a piece of information that improves efficiency of operations, safety and downtimes. Knowledge Management: There are NLP models to develop and manage knowledge bases to record shared information in an organization. Employees can access the information which they require to make proper decisions and solve complicated challenges using such knowledge bases. The use of NLP in search engines and library catalog is in order to enhance the accuracy of the search results. Using these fundamental AI processes, the oil and gas upstream industry can achieve huge operational advantages, enhance safety, and reduce environmental effects, as well as innovation. Further development and implementation of AI will largely predetermine the future of the industry (Wang et al., 2025).

## 5. AI IN EXPLORATION ACTIVITIES

A superior analysis of AI when applied to exploration based on the ability of machine learning to deduce patterns and perceptions even when dealing with massive data restructured the way geoscientists conduct their search of new hydrocarbon reserves (Kuang et al., 2021). AI can be deployed in exploration in four important ways, shown in Figure.3, seismic interpretation, geospatial targeting, hydrocarbon prediction and geological-uncertainty management.

*Figure 3. AI Applications in Hydrocarbon Exploration*

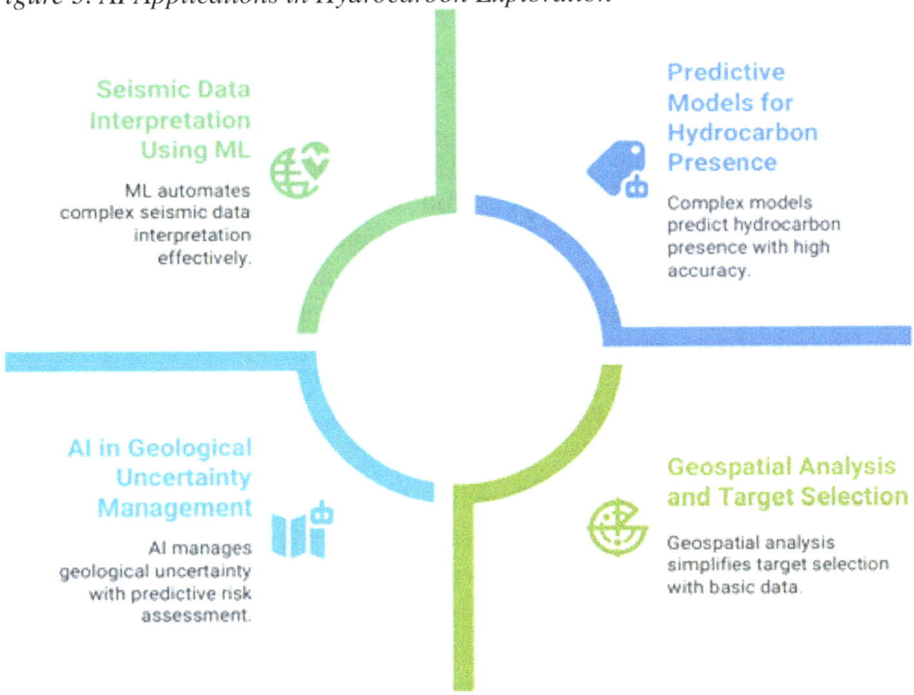


## 5.1 Seismic Data Interpretation Using ML

Machine learning constitutes a shift in interpretation of seismic data and an automation of detection of underground structures and geologic features. Anomaly detection is important; seismic occurrences, indicating an anomaly, may identify a hydrocarbon reservoir or other geological feature of interest, and can be detected via machine learning, e.g. via a neural network. Combining anomaly detection and conventional seismic interpretation methods has enhanced efforts to explore (Abd-Elfattah et al., 2025). Seismic data interpretation is of essence in the process of recognizing possible hydrocarbon reservoirs. With traditional methods, expert geoscientists never fail to analyze seismic images manually, a process that consumes a lot of time and is subjective. Machine learning simplifies this technique by training algorithms to identify the subsurface features like faults, folds, and stratigraphic traps (Kuang et al., 2021).

## 5.2 Geospatial Analysis and Target Selection

Geospatial analysis with the help of AI automates multisource data integration and makes the target selection accurate. Predictive models are used in order to identify possible exploration target analyzing geospatial information and combining geological trends, structural characteristics and geochemical anomalies being able to determine the probability of the occurrence of hydrocarbons (Zhao et al., 2025). The AI models evaluate the geological risks, environmental risks of exploration projects based on the combination of the following data: characteristics of the reservoirs, environmental regulations, and market conditions to help to make better decisions. Geospatial analysis is important in exploration since it entails compilation and combination of data gathered through different channels, including satellite imagery, geological maps, or geochemical surveys.

## 5.3 Predictive Models for Hydrocarbon Presence

Machine-learning algorithms are applied through predictive model to estimate the likelihood of the presence of hydrocarbons. Reservoir models are created with the help of Artificial Neural Networks which helps to estimate the flow of fluids, pressure distribution and changes in saturation. These models were trained using historical production logs, well logs, seismic, and core analysis, a better prediction of whether hydrocarbons would be present could be made (Ramy et al., 2025). Drilling, completion, and surface facility engineering have also been done with data mining that leads to intelligent equipment and integrated software (Kuang et al., 2021). The prospect of the AI advancement in the petroleum exploration and development is intelligent equipment in the production stage, automatic processing and interpretation, and professional software platforms.

## 5.4 AI in Geological Uncertainty Management

Geological uncertainties are quantified and controlled by means of AI procedures. AI algorithms combine the data sources and develop scenarios and evaluate the degree to which uncertainty can affect the results of the exploration. By facilitating the comprehension of the variety of possible underground conditions and producing more solid decisions, such an integration can aid (Zhu et al., 2025). AI is able to optimize the EOR approach taking into account the role of the uncertainty in the project economics. Such algorithms can determine the exploration that maximises the expectation of a project with minimum risk of failing. Application of these AI techniques is a welcome concept that can immensely enhance efficiency and the success of new hydrocarbon resources discoveries in the oil and gas sector. Gradual further development and introduction of AI will be of vital importance in increasing the supply of energy globally and cutting down the environmental impacts and exploration risks (Chen et al., 2025).

## 6. AI APPLICATIONS IN DRILLING AND PRODUCTION

Artificial intelligence is revolutionizing the drilling and the production process of the oil and gas sector because it has increased efficiency, safety, and decision-making. Examples of AI application in such locations all the way up to real-time optimization of drilling parameters, as well as the prediction of equipment failure and automated production processes (Wang et al., 2025). Embarkation of AI technologies aids corporations in realizing operational benefits, reducing environmental effects, and enhancing general productivity.

### 6.1 Real-Time Drilling Optimization

The drilling optimization considered in real-time is the optimization where the AI is trained to read data provided by the sensors and drilling equipment to optimize the drilling parameters on the fly. This process is able to help improve penetration rate, lower drilling cost, and stability of wellbore (Yu et al., 2025). The optimization of the development of the waterflooding system and prediction of the oil and gas production can be achieved in real time with the help of deep learning and optimization technology applied to reservoir engineering.

Predictive Modeling of ROP: Machine learning models review the data on past and real time drilling and forecast the best ROP. Through factors like type of rock drilling fluid, equipment performance, and drilling fluid characteristics, these models give advises on what to change in the drilling parameters to make it as efficient as possible. Drilling Parameter Adjustment: AI algorithms are used to monitor drilling parameters, namely the weight on bit, rotary speed and mud flow rate and make real time adjustments to detect anomalies. This is to avoid occurrence of drilling dysfunctions, which include use of stick-slip, bit whirl and borehole instability.

Automated Decision-Making: AI-enabled systems may automate decision making in drilling operations and eliminate the operational skill of people in drilling operations and also increase the uniformity of drilling operations. These systems have the ability to collect the information of various sources and give recommendations to optimizing drilling parameters in real time.

Real-time drilling optimization allows the companies to minimize chances of drilling incidents, minimize drilling costs and also minimize the time spent in drilling.

## 6.2 Anomaly Detection and Predictive Maintenance

With the help of AI, anomaly detection and predictive maintenance enable the identification of strange patterns and the prediction of a machinery failure before a breakage actually happens. This aids it in minimizing downtimes, saving maintenance expenses, and the dependability of drilling and production gear. In the oil and gas industry, AI technologies are changing the way it operates, as they predict the equipment failures and prevent them by stopping the disruption of operations and minimizing maintenance expenses (Waqar et al., 2023). The list of AI techniques in drilling and completion engineering offers the basics of machine learning and deep learning, key algorithms, and process of AI in drilling and completion engineering, where data are gathered, and technology is implemented and optimized (Yang et al., 2023). The main peculiarities of anomaly detection and predictive maintenance are the following. Figure.4 directs the practitioners to AI for Industrial Efficiency the module to minimize costs by monitoring and checking equipment status, predictive maintenance, root cause analysis and NLP-based insights.

*Figure 4. Enhancing Operations with AI*

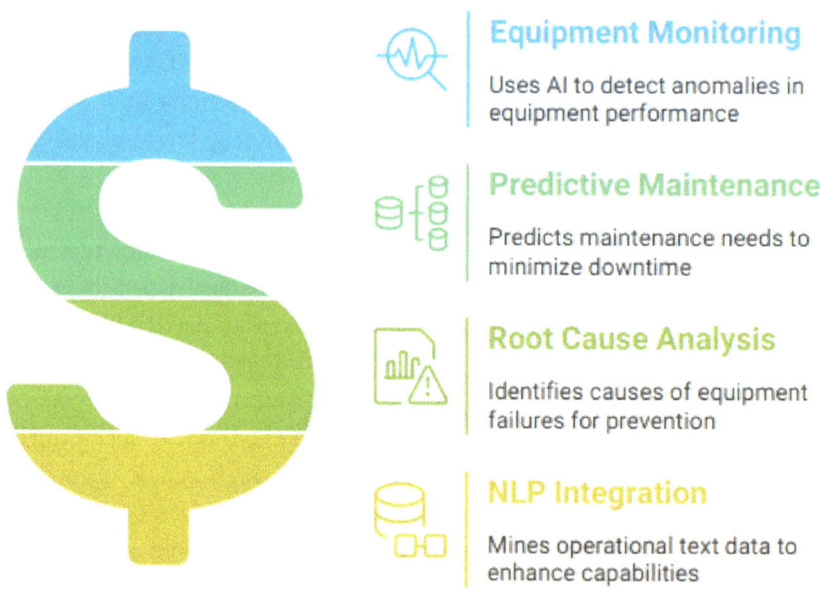

Equipment Monitoring: AI algorithms are used to analyze data collected by sensors and other monitoring systems to spot an anomaly in the working performance of the equipment. These algorithms can raise early alarms before devices fail by determining anomalies with their typical working conditions. Predictive Maintenance: It is a machine learning-based approach where the prediction of maintenance is done using previous maintenance records, sensor data and device specification. This assists in scheduling the maintenance programs in advance and reduce the times of disrupted operations and keeps the physical equipment longer. Root Cause Analysis: AI systems are able to undertake root cause analysis of instances when equipment malfunctions are recorded, determine the root causes of the issues and propose their solution. This limits future breakdowns and enhance the quality of the whole machine reliability.

Through anomaly detection and predictive maintenance services, organizations will save their maintenance expenses, increase reliability of their equipment, and their drilling and productions will be safer. The editor document notes that NLP models can be used to mine working text data set, e.g. maintenance log sets, incident reports, to identify data tendencies and trends and further extend these capabilities (Bub hek et al., 2025).

## 6.3 Smart Drilling Automation and Robotics

Smart drilling automation/robotics Smart drilling automation and robotics have been introduced where the principle has been to use AI to automate the drilling processes as well as to improve on the capabilities of the drilling equipment. This assists in enhancing drilling efficiency, minimizing human-error, and maximising safety. Use of robotics in waste management and infrastructure maintenance is also another critical thing that was used in automating the waste collection and maintenance of infrastructure systems (Fatorachian et al., 2025). The applications are, Automated Drilling Systems: other drilling activities can be automated based on IA systems: pipe-handling, makeup connection and drilling fluids. Some of these systems employ sensors, robotics and algorithms based on machine learning to do work automatically, thus eliminating the need of human interaction. Robotic Drilling Equipment: Robots could be used to do operations in the dangerous or inapt localities like inspection of wellbores, repair of casing, and deployment of downhole tools. These robots have sensors, cameras, and artificial intelligence (AI) code to run and work through them. Remote Drilling Operation: One can operate drilling remotely using AI powered solution, where a remote control reduces the number of operators and you can control the drilling equipment by staying at a central place. This will assist in getting fewer people physically present, enhancing and safeguarding security as well as cutting operation expenses. The automated drilling will help companies to enhance the efficiency of drilling, minimize the risk of human error and improve the safety of the drilling process by incorporating smart drilling automation and robotics (Boukredera et al., 2025).

## 6.4 Intelligent Production Monitoring Systems

AI is employed through intelligent systems of production monitoring which combines data gathered by sensors and monitoring systems to optimize the production process by enhancing reservoir management. This can assist in maximizing the rate of production as well as operating at reduced cost and increasing the life of oil and gas reserviors (Rojas et al., 2025). The applications used were the following, Production Optimization: AI algorithms compare the data provided by sensors and monitoring tool to find out the most efficient working conditions. Based on the parameters like the reservoir pressure, the amount of fluid moved through the pipe and equipment efficiency, these algorithms make the recommendations related to the alteration of the parameters of the production in order to maximize the result. Smart Well Control: As it is mentioned in the editor document, smart wells are tackled through the Artificial Neural Networks that regulate the downhole valves and flow-controlling-devices to maximize production of various reservoir zones. The models are autonomous in that they take real-time information provided by downhole sensors and decides on the well control.

Reservoir Monitoring: Artificial Intelligence Systems are used to monitor performance of reservoirs being able to notice variation in the reservoir pressure, saturation of fluids, as well as patterns of fluid flow. This assists to detect possible issues like water breakthroughs, gas coning, and reservoir depletion. However, through the use of smart production monitoring systems, businesses are able to maximize production rates, minimize operation costs and maximize the life of the oil and gas reservoirs. An example is the potential of optimising production of various reservoir zones using real-time data and autonomous decisions as demonstrated in the incorporation of AI technologies such as smart well control using ANNs. Artificial intelligence apps are shaking the oil and gas sector as they improve efficiency, safety and decision-making (Boukredera et al., 2025). Real-time drilling modification and predictive maintenance, smart drilling automation, and intelligent production monitoring are examples of AI solutions that assist companies when unlocking operational benefits, reducing environmental consequences, and boosting performance altogether.

# 7. AI FOR RESERVOIR CHARACTERIZATION AND MANAGEMENT

AI is changing the knowledge and operations in oil and gas reservoirs. It can be done to construct a more realistic picture of the reservoir with the help of machine learning, neural networks, and advanced data analytics, which further will allow optimizing enhanced oil recovery procedures and manage complicated data (Boukredera et al., 2025).

## 7.1 Reservoir Modeling With Neural Networks

Neural networks are best suited in developing reservoir representations via learning of complex patterns in past history information. In a common situation, traditional reservoir modeling usually includes simplistic assumptions, but neural networks have the potential to identify nonlinear effects and complex geological characters (Qiu et al., 2025). Some Key applications would be as follows, Static Reservoir Properties: Neural networks used to give important static properties, i.e. porosity, permeability, or lithology, trained on well logs, cores data, and seismic attributes. Such models provide better copies of subsurface conditions.

Dynamic Reservoir behaviour They are trained up on historic production data, well test, and simulation output to predict dynamic behaviours of fluid flow, pressure distribution and changes in saturation. They also perform Uncertainty Quantification: Using multiple equiprobable realizations, neural networks evaluate uncertainty in reservoir model to help quantify the uncertainty in decision, and have a range of possibilities. During geological exploration, the application of AI in the identification of fractures, classification of lithology, and prediction of reservoir parameters enhance exploration efficiency and accuracy substantially (Chen et al., 2025).

## 7.2 Integration of Multi-Source Data for Dynamic Modeling

Dynamic modeling needs to combine various types of information about reservoirs to ensure effective management. AI enables the integration of information contained in different sources to develop extensive and trustworthy models (Zhao et al., 2025). The aspects are,

Data Structuring Techniques: Artificial intelligence algorithms combine information on geological surveys, seismic data, well logs, the history of production, and experimental information to construct quality models of the reservoirs. Real-time Data integration: AI allows integrating real-time data (sensor, smart well, and monitoring data) into reservoir models continuously and consequently makes the models more accurate. Enhanced Decision-Making: Integrated models can provide a complete picture of the reservoir dynamics, and thus enhance decision-making on issues that pertain to production optimization, injection, and surveillance of the reservoir. With multisource data combined with AI, a more comprehensive picture of the behavior of the reservoir can be obtained, which, in its turn, allows more effective management of the reservoir and higher oil and gas recovery (Zhao et al., 2025).

## 7.3 Enhanced Oil Recovery Strategy Optimization

AI can improve EOR screens through its ability to determine the effectiveness of various techniques and parameters that could be changed to provide the best results, in terms of the amount of oil recovered as well as economic gains (Li et al., 2025). The Key strategies are as follows, Selection of Means of EOR: Machine learning models analysis the applicability of various EOR techniques (e.g., chemical flooding, gas injection, and thermal) depending on the nature and nature of the reservoir, the nature of the fluids, and the economics. Parameter Optimization: AI algorithms can optimize oil recovery by optimizing the rates and the pressure of the injection and the fluid to reduce the overall cost and environmental impact.

Real-Time Optimization: AI tracked the EOR performance and updated parameters in real time to respond to changing the conditions of the reservoir and optimize oil extraction. The use of AI can improve oil recovery and making decisions, as its applications enabled more accurate and efficient characterization and management of the reservoir. AI has augmented effectiveness in responding to emergencies and ensuring the safety of the population to a great extent (Acemoğlu et al., 2022). There is the implementation of AI systems processing meteorological and geological data and predicting floods, earthquakes, and wild covered land fires in advance, ensuring early warnings and effective planning of resources.

## 7.4 Managing High-Dimensional and Non-Linear Reservoir Data

The data that considers reservoir are mostly in many dimensions hence non-linear making them a problem to the common analysis methods (Wang et al., 2025). Artificial intelligence methods are ideally applicable in processing and mining of complex data. The Key techniques are, Dimensionality Reduction and Feature Extraction: AI algorithms, including Principal Component Analysis, autoencoders, and t-distributed Stochastic Neighbor Embedding (t-SNE) are used in order to find the reduced dimensionality of reservoir data, but with the necessary preservation of information and feature extraction (Choudhary et al., 2025; Zhao et al., 2025). Dimensionality Reduction: The AI algorithms simplify the development of the models by tidying up the reservoir data on the dimensionality, which simplifies the extraction of the key variables and features. Non-Linear Modeling: The non-linearity between the properties of the reservoir and the production performance are captured on machine learning models, hence enhancing the accuracy of the models. Pattern Recognition: AI detects both tendencies and abnormalities in reservoir data that might not be noticed during regular analyses, to provide the insights into the behavior of the reservoir and possible risks. The approach used by the oil and gas industry, such as applying AI, has the potential to characterize and manage the reservoir, increase the knowledge of the reservoir and optimize production plans as well as provide overall better performance of the operations (Boukredera et al., 2025). Intelligent transformation of the drilling engineering has been spurred by the formulation and implementation of AI technologies (Kuang et al., 2021). Intelligent transformation of drilling engineering is promoted by the advancement and usage of AI technologies.

## 8. BENEFITS AND CHALLENGES OF AI INTEGRATION

AI in oil and gas would have significant benefits and significant challenges. An in-depth knowledge of these niches is most important in the successful deployment and achievement of the intended results. The following paragraphs will delve deeper into the twofold character of AI integration by thoroughly discussing the possible advantages and unavoidable obstacles that companies will have to overcome in order to utilize the transformative potential of the given innovation at best (Popa et al., 2025).

### 8.1 Operational Gains and Efficiency Improvements

Automation, optimization, and predictive analytics are the ways through which AI improves operational efficiency. Such enhancements result in high-cost reductions and profitability and the main advantages are as follows: Automation of Reoccurring Tasks: Owing to the repetitive nature of human-reoccurrence, AI handles automation of processing Routine tasks, production of reports, and monitoring of equipment. Process optimization: AI algorithms process optimization can optimize processes like drilling, production, and maintenance through massive dataset analysis, and parameter identification. In the document you have edited it is said that the smart wells are controlled by the Artificial Neural Networks to regulate the downhole valves and the flow control equipment to maximize the production of various zones in the reservoir. Predictive Maintenance: AI forecasts equipment failures and maintenance requirements, and thus diminishes downtime and costs of maintenance.

## 8.2 Safety Enhancements and Risk Reduction

AI enhances safety because it identifies possible risks, forecasts faulty equipment and expands real-time tracking. Key Aspects - Hazard Detection: The AI systems process data collected by sensors and cameras in real-time to identify possible hazards, including leaks, fires, and malfunctioning of equipment. Predictive Maintenance: AI forecasts the equipment malfunctioning and minimizes the chance of accidents and enhances the whole safety. Real-Time Tracking: AI would be used to boost real-time tracking of operations to provide instant responses to the possible safety-related concerns. In the document you have edited it has been stated that the AI-powered systems are used to monitor the performance of reservoirs, which in turn helps to discern the changes in pressure, saturation of fluids as well as fluid flow patterns in the reservoirs that can allow identifying the issues which may be faced like the issue of water breakthrough, the problem of gassing cones and the problem of reservoir depletion.

## 8.3 Environmental Impact Minimization

AI can be used to reduce the environmental footprint of oil and gas activities: use of resources, emissions and garbage management. Certain ways in which AI leads to environmental stewardship entail the following. Emissions Reduction: AI helps optimize the consumption of energy and decrease the level of greenhouse gas emissions by finding areas of inefficiency and making changes in terms of operational parameters. Waste Management AI can solve the problems of waste management, forecasting waste production and more efficient disposal techniques. Resource Optimization: AI makes the best use of water, chemicals, and other resources and, in that way, minimizes environment impact and cost.

## 8.4 Barriers: Data Quality, Talent Gap, Integration Costs

Although AI has the potential to transform the oil and gas industry, it has various obstacles that make it impossible to adopt its extensive use in the industry. The quality of data, the lack of talent in the field of AI, and the price of incorporating AI technologies to the current infrastructure are the main issues that impede the mass implementation of AI in the oil and gas field. The inaccuracy of data could compromise the accuracy and reliability of the AI models, and one should pay much attention to the fact that the data should be precise, fulfilled, and uniform. The gap between the AI professionals is a binding factor which affects capacity of firms to produce develop and sustain AI solutions. The current structure of a company may demand considerable financial investments in the hardware, software, and training when it comes to introducing AI technologies into the system.

## 8.5 Change Management and Organizational Culture

The key to successful AI integration is an efficient change management and favourable organizational culture. This needs to be planned and communicated thoroughly so that the employees are aware of the advantages and get ready with the changes in their positions. In addition, an innovation-culture, teamwork, and lifelong learning culture are critical in effective implementation of AI. Training and development of the needed employees to operate AI technologies are essential in the smooth integration (Qi et al., 2025).

# 9. CASE STUDIES AND REAL-WORLD IMPLEMENTATIONS

AI is not an abstract idea; indeed, its practical use is actively taking place in the oil and gas industry to produce real results. Some of these ways of demonstrating the same are as follows - The success story of AI-Based Exploration: With AI, exploration has been able to transform because geological models have been made more accurate and the location of possible drilling sites have been made better. AI Algorithms follow seismic data to determine characteristic patterns and abnormalities indicating the existence of hydrocarbon, as they process large masses of data quicker and higher quality than the conventional means, with the discovery of formerly unknown deposits as a result. Machine learning models combine the geological, geophysical and geochemical data into a better prospect map, and lowers the chance of drilling dry wells. Predicting Drilling Performance to Enhance Drilling Performance: Artificial intelligence-based predictive analytics streamlines the drilling process, providing a clear vision of the looming problems and enhancing the general performance. As one case in point, the drilling machines have a set of sensors whose data AI algorithms use to predict malfunctions and arrange it so that maintenance would be conducted preventively, reducing downtime and cost and optimizing the drilling parameters like the rate of penetration, drill string rotation, and mud weight to increase the rate at which the drilling is being conducted and, thereby, minimize the time of running into complications. NLP in Digitizing and Compliance of Documents: Document management and compliance activities are simplified through Natural Language Processing, as they facilitate the unstructured data that automate the extraction and analysis of information on the papers.

Example: Automated Document Processing: NLP models can automatically retrieve important data in well logs, contracts and regulatory documents by converting unstructured data to structured data, saving time and manual work. Compliance monitoring: AI systems also check compliance with regulatory issues and absence of fines and penalties because operations adhere to the requirements of environmental and safety standards.

## 9.1 Intelligent Reservoir Management Applications

Comprehensive information on how AI can be used to improve reservoir management is provided in, mainly through optimizing production strategies and increasing the accuracy of reservoir models. To illustrate, AI algorithms compare production data to discover the potential of optimizing the performance of wells and maximize recoveries of oil and gas. In the edited document, the document says that AI algorithms will optimize rates of injection, pressure as well as mix of fluids to recover maximum oil at the lowest possible cost and most of all the least impact on the environment. Machine learning models forecast the effectiveness of various elements of EOR and maximize the injection parameters to better the oil extraction figures (Yin et al., 2025).

# 10. FUTURE TRENDS AND RESEARCH DIRECTIONS

The art of AI is fast paced and a number of recent trends have defined its new applications in the oil and gas industry. Rising AI Capability (e.g. Generative AI, Edge AI): Generative AI models are unique in the sense that they are able to generate novel data, designs and solutions, which can be used in an application that is related to reservoir modeling, equipment design and other aspects of scenarios. Edge AI also implies local data processing on edge devices and not processing by sending data to the cloud, which has fewer delays, better security, and allows making decisions in real time in remote areas. By combining AI with the IoT devices, all oil and gas operations may be monitored, and controlled in real-time, which increases efficiency, safety, and reliability (Miller et al., 2025). Integration of AI and Internet of Things - AI and the IoT open up the potential of monitoring, predictive maintenance, and autonomous processes in real-time. AS-enabling sensors Traffic management: Smart sensors powered by AI to monitor equipment and infrastructure and collect and analyze data on performance and possible issues Autonomous inspection/ maintenance: AI algorithms guide autonomous vehicles, robots, and drones to perform such functions as inspection/ maintenance of EM systems and carry out emergencies. Simulation-Based Operations and Digital Twins: Digital twins are a virtual representation of physical assets and systems available to simulate, optimize, and perform predictive maintenance, allowing real-time visibility into the performance of assets and systems, pro-actively identifying the potential issues, and virtualizing different operating scenarios to support companies optimize their work and prepare contingencies (Bubuni et al. 2025). The Purpose of Free Data and Crowdsourcing Places

Innovation and speed of adoption of AI in the oil and gas sector occurs due to open data projects and collaborative platforms. Open data programs grant access to large data sets that can be trained to build AI models and create new applications, and shared platforms allow businesses, scientists, and developers to exchange knowledge, code, and hardware, boosting the rate at which AI products and solutions are created and put to use.

## CONCLUSION

Some of the major ways artificial intelligence is transforming the oil and gas industry is by increasing the operational efficiency of the industry through automation and more efficient operations; boosting safety by predicting and preventing accidents; decreasing its impact on the environment by more efficient use of resources and monitoring emissions; and accelerating the speed of innovation in exploration, production, and refining. Other AI algorithms are used to analyze large volumes of data to simplify operations, anticipate machine failures, and enhance decision making throughout the value chain. With the progress of the AI technologies, the adoption of the AI-powered solutions along the value chain will be even higher in the industry. Addressing challenges, including quality of data, skills shortages, and cost of integration, is paramount in developing full potential of AI use in the oil and gas industry. An important strategy at this time is to make strategic investments in artificial intelligence infrastructure, training and partnerships to enable innovation and long-term success.

## REFERENCES


Abd-Elfattah, N., Dahroug, A., Kammar, M. E., & Fahmy, R. (2025). Machine learning and AVO class II workflow for hydrocarbon prospectivity in the Messinian offshore Nile Delta Egypt. *Scientific Reports*, *15*(1), 3566. Advance online publication. DOI: 10.1038/s41598-025-86765-7 PMID: 39875438

Acemoğlu, D., Autor, D., Hazell, J., & Restrepo, P. (2022). Artificial Intelligence and Jobs: Evidence from Online Vacancies. *Journal of Labor Economics*, *40*(S1), S293–S340. Advance online publication. DOI: 10.1086/718327

Alghamedy, F., El-Haggar, N., Alsumayt, A., Alfawaer, Z. M., Alshammari, M., Amouri, L., Aljameel, S. S., & Al-Bassam, S. (2024). Unlocking a Promising Future: Integrating Blockchain Technology and FL-IoT in the Journey to 6G. *IEEE Access : Practical Innovations, Open Solutions*, *1*, 115411–115447. Advance online publication. DOI: 10.1109/ACCESS.2024.3435968

Boukredera, F. S., Hadjadj, A., Youcefi, M. R., & Ouadi, H. (2025). AI-Driven Optimization of Drilling Performance Through Torque Management Using Machine Learning and Differential Evolution. *Processes (Basel, Switzerland)*, *13*(5), 1472. DOI: 10.3390/pr13051472

Chen, F., Sun, L., Jian, S., Huo, X., Pan, X., Feng, C., & Zhang, Z. (2025). A Review of AI Applications in Unconventional Oil and Gas Exploration and Development [Review of A Review of AI Applications in Unconventional Oil and Gas Exploration and Development]. Energies, 18(2), 391. Multidisciplinary Digital Publishing Institute. DOI: 10.3390/en18020391

Choudhary, A., Pawar, S., & Haribhakta, Y. (2025). Efficient Malware Detection with Optimized Learning on High-Dimensional Features. DOI: 10.1109/ISAC364032.2025.11156575

Dong, Z., Yan, X., Zhang, J., Chen, Z., & Ma, H. (2025). Reservoir Characterization of Tight Sandstone Gas Reservoirs: A Case Study from the He 8 Member of the Shihezi Formation, Tianhuan Depression, Ordos Basin. *Processes (Basel, Switzerland)*, *13*(5), 1355. DOI: 10.3390/pr13051355

Fatorachian, H., Kazemi, H., & Pawar, K. S. (2025). Digital Technologies in Food Supply Chain Waste Management: A Case Study on Sustainable Practices in Smart Cities. *Sustainability (Basel)*, *17*(5), 1996. DOI: 10.3390/su17051996

Fejjari, A., Delavault, A., Camilleri, R., & Valentino, G. (2025). A Review of Anomaly Detection in Spacecraft Telemetry Data [Review of A Review of Anomaly Detection in Spacecraft Telemetry Data]. Applied Sciences, 15(10), 5653. Multidisciplinary Digital Publishing Institute. DOI: 10.3390/app15105653

Gandhi, Y., Zheng, K., Jha, B., Nomura, K., Nakano, A., Vashishta, P., & Kalia, R. K. (2024). Generative AI-driven forecasting of oil production. arXiv (Cornell University). /arxiv.2409.16482DOI: 10.48550

Gao, S., Wang, X., Xia, Z., Zhang, H., Yu, J., & Yang, F. (2025). Artificial Intelligence in Dentistry: A Narrative Review of Diagnostic and Therapeutic Applications [Review of Artificial Intelligence in Dentistry: A Narrative Review of Diagnostic and Therapeutic Applications]. Medical Science Monitor, 31. International Scientific Information Inc. DOI: 10.12659/MSM.946676

Gonen, L. D., Tavor, T., & Spiegel, U. (2024). Unlocking Market Potential: Strategic Consumer Segmentation and Dynamic Pricing for Balancing Loyalty and Deal Seeking. *Mathematics*, *12*(21), 3364. DOI: 10.3390/math12213364

Khurram, M., Wu, C., Muhammad, S. M., Kishnani, H., An, K. R., Abeywardena, K., Chadha, U., & Behdinan, K. (2025). Artificial Intelligence in Manufacturing Industry Worker Safety: A New Paradigm for Hazard Prevention and Mitigation. *Processes (Basel, Switzerland)*, *13*(5), 1312. DOI: 10.3390/pr13051312

Kostadimas, D., Kasapakis, V., & Kotis, K. (2025). A Systematic Review on the Combination of VR, IoT and AI Technologies, and Their Integration in Applications [Review of A Systematic Review on the Combination of VR, IoT and AI Technologies, and Their Integration in Applications]. Future Internet, 17(4), 163. Multidisciplinary Digital Publishing Institute. DOI: 10.3390/fi17040163

Kuang, L., Liu, H., Ren, Y., Luo, K., Shi, M., Su, J., & Li, X. (2021). Application and development trend of artificial intelligence in petroleum exploration and development. *Petroleum Exploration and Development*, *48*(1), 1–14. DOI: 10.1016/S1876-3804(21)60001-0

Li, J. X., Zhang, T., Zhu, Y., & Chen, Z. (2024a). Artificial General Intelligence (AGI) for the oil and gas industry: a review [Review of Artificial General Intelligence (AGI) for the oil and gas industry: a review]. arXiv (Cornell University). Cornell University. /arxiv.2406.00594DOI: 10.48550

Li, J. X., Zhang, T., Zhu, Y., & Chen, Z. (2024b). Artificial General Intelligence (AGI) for the oil and gas industry: a review [Review of Artificial General Intelligence (AGI) for the oil and gas industry: a review]. arXiv (Cornell University). Cornell University. /arXiv.2406.00594DOI: 10.48550

Li, X., Li, J., Zhao, P., Feng, G., & Lei, Z. (2025). Overview of the Progress in Practice and Experimental Research in Petroleum and Natural Gas Engineering. *Energies, 18*(11), 2738. DOI: 10.3390/en18112738

Liu, Y. M., Xie, W., Guo, Q., & Wang, S. (2025). Enhancing Pipeline Leakage Detection Through Multi-Algorithm Fusion with Machine Learning. *Processes (Basel, Switzerland), 13*(5), 1519. DOI: 10.3390/pr13051519

Miller, T., Durlik, I., Kostecka, E., Kozlovska, P., Łobodzińska, A., Sokołowska, S., & Nowy, A. (2025). Integrating Artificial Intelligence Agents with the Internet of Things for Enhanced Environmental Monitoring: Applications in Water Quality and Climate Data. *Electronics (Basel), 14*(4), 696. DOI: 10.3390/electronics14040696

Murroni, M., Anedda, M., Fadda, M., Ruiu, P., Popescu, V., Zaharia, C., & Giusto, D. (2023). 6G—Enabling the New Smart City: A Survey [Review of 6G—Enabling the New Smart City: A Survey]. Sensors, 23(17), 7528. Multidisciplinary Digital Publishing Institute. DOI: 10.3390/s23177528

Padhy, N., Suman, S., Priyadarshini, T. S., & Mallick, S. (2024). A Recommendation System for E-Commerce Products Using Collaborative Filtering Approaches. 50. DOI: 10.3390/engproc2024067050

Pandey, Y. N., Rastogi, A., Kainkaryam, S., Bhattacharya, S., & Saputelli, L. (2020). Opportunities, Challenges, and Future Trends. In Apress eBooks (p. 259). DOI: 10.1007/978-1-4842-6094-4_8

Popa, I., tefan, S. C., Josan, A., Mircioiu, C.-E., & Căruceru, N. (2025). Artificial Intelligence as a Catalyst for Management System Adaptability, Agility and Resilience: Mapping the Research Agenda. *Systems, 13*(1), 47. DOI: 10.3390/systems13010047

Qi, M., Wu, T., Duan, W., & Li, S. (2025). Effects of Employee–Artificial Intelligence (AI) Collaboration on Counterproductive Work Behaviors (CWBs): Leader Emotional Support as a Moderator. *Behavioral Sciences (Basel, Switzerland), 15*(5), 696. DOI: 10.3390/bs15050696 PMID: 40426473

Qiu, Z., Kownatzki, C., Scalzo, F., & Sang, E. (2025). Historical Perspectives in Volatility Forecasting Methods with Machine Learning. *Risks, 13*(5), 98. DOI: 10.3390/risks13050098

Ramy, C., Rîpeanu, R. G., Nassreddine, S., Tănase, M., Zouein, E. Y., Dini ă, A., & Muresan, C. C. (2025). Recent Advances in Stimulation Techniques for Unconventional Oil Reservoir and Simulation of Fluid Dynamics Using Predictive Model of Flow Production. *Processes (Basel, Switzerland), 13*(4), 1138. DOI: 10.3390/pr13041138

Raza, M., Jahangir, Z., Riaz, M. B., Saeed, M. J., & Sattar, M. A. (2025). Industrial applications of large language models. *Scientific Reports*, *15*(1), 13755. Advance online publication. DOI: 10.1038/s41598-025-98483-1 PMID: 40258923

Revelou, P., Tsakali, E., Batrinou, A., & Strati, I. F. (2025). Applications of Machine Learning in Food Safety and HACCP Monitoring of Animal-Source Foods [Review of Applications of Machine Learning in Food Safety and HACCP Monitoring of Animal-Source Foods]. Foods, 14(6), 922. Multidisciplinary Digital Publishing Institute. DOI: 10.3390/foods14060922

Rojas, L., Peña, Á., & García, J. (2025). AI-Driven Predictive Maintenance in Mining: A Systematic Literature Review on Fault Detection, Digital Twins, and Intelligent Asset Management. *Applied Sciences (Basel, Switzerland)*, *15*(6), 3337. DOI: 10.3390/app15063337

Rouf, N., Malik, M. B., Arif, T., Sharma, S., Singh, S., Aich, S., & Kim, H. (2021). Stock Market Prediction Using Machine Learning Techniques: A Decade Survey on Methodologies, Recent Developments, and Future Directions. *Electronics (Basel)*, *10*(21), 2717. DOI: 10.3390/electronics10212717

Shah, M., Wever, M., & Espig, M. (2025). A Framework for Assessing the Potential of Artificial Intelligence in the Circular Bioeconomy. *Sustainability (Basel)*, *17*(8), 3535. DOI: 10.3390/su17083535

Tsallis, C., Papageorgas, P., Piromalis, D., & Munteanu, R. (2025). Application-Wise Review of Machine Learning-Based Predictive Maintenance: Trends, Challenges, and Future Directions. *Applied Sciences (Basel, Switzerland)*, *15*(9), 4898. DOI: 10.3390/app15094898

Wang, H., Chen, J., Zheng, Y., & Song, X. (2025). Accelerating flood warnings by 10 hours: The power of river network topology in AI-enhanced flood forecasting. *Npj Natural Hazards*, *2*(1), 45. Advance online publication. DOI: 10.1038/s44304-025-00083-6

Wang, J., Luo, X., Zhang, X., & Du, S. (2025). Artificial General Intelligence (AGI) Applications and Prospect in Oil and Gas Reservoir Development. *Processes (Basel, Switzerland)*, *13*(5), 1413. DOI: 10.3390/pr13051413

Waqar, A., Othman, I., Shafiq, N., & Mansoor, M. S. (2023). Applications of AI in oil and gas projects towards sustainable development: A systematic literature review. *Artificial Intelligence Review*, *56*(11), 12771–12798. DOI: 10.1007/s10462-023-10467-7 PMID: 37362898

Yang, H., Shang, G., Li, X., & Feng, Y. (2023). Application of Artificial Intelligence in Drilling and Completion. In *IntechOpen eBooks*. IntechOpen., DOI: 10.5772/intechopen.112298

Yin, H., Yu, J., Qu, H., & Siqi, Y. (2025). A Novel Approach to Waterflooding Optimization in Irregular Well Patterns Using Streamline Simulation and 3D Visualization. *Processes (Basel, Switzerland), 13*(4), 1114. DOI: 10.3390/pr13041114

Yu, S., Wang, K., Dong, H., Tai, Y., Chen, Z., Zhou, D., & Sun, S. (2025). Optimized Economic Evaluation Model for Intensive Drilling in Unconventional Oil and Gas Development. *Processes (Basel, Switzerland), 13*(5), 1579. DOI: 10.3390/pr13051579

Zhao, A., Yu, Y., Wang, B., Liu, Y., Liu, J., Fu, X., Zheng, W. J., & Tian, F. (2025). Real-Time Intelligent Recognition and Precise Drilling in Strongly Heterogeneous Formations Based on Multi-Parameter Logging While Drilling and Drilling Engineering. *Applied Sciences (Basel, Switzerland), 15*(10), 5536. DOI: 10.3390/app15105536

Zhu, L., Han, R., Zhang, Y., Fu, H., Luo, J., & Luo, Y. (2025). Enhancing Prospecting Target Prediction Precision: A Multi-Source Data Mining Approach in Gansu's Beishan Area. *Applied Sciences (Basel, Switzerland), 15*(10), 5430. DOI: 10.3390/app15105430

# Chapter 3
# Enhancing Transparency and Efficiency:
## Blockchain-Based Supply Chain Management and Automated Trade Finance in Oil and Gas

**Md Tahmid Ashraf Chowdhury**
https://orcid.org/0009-0003-8886-1138
*Department of Computing, Faculty ty of Science, Management and Computing, Universiti Teknologi Petronas, Malaysia*

**Shamsu Abdullahi**
https://orcid.org/0009-0003-2498-5078
*Department of Computing, Faculty ty of Science, Management and Computing, Universiti Teknologi Petronas, Malaysia*

**Fasee Ullah**
https://orcid.org/0000-0001-6167-5253
*Department of Computing, Faculty ty of Science, Management and Computing, Universiti Teknologi Petronas, Malaysia*

**Shoaib Ul Hassan**
*Department of Computing, Faculty ty of Science, Management and Computing, Universiti Teknologi Petronas, Malaysia*

**Mujeeb Ur Rehman Shaikh**
*Department of Computing, Faculty ty of Science, Management and Computing, Universiti Teknologi Petronas, Malaysia*

**Md Mohibul Alam**
*Department of Computing, Faculty ty of Science, Management and Computing, Universiti Teknologi Petronas, Malaysia*

## ABSTRACT

*This chapter shows how blockchain improves transparency, efficiency, and trust in oil and gas. Supply chains and trade finance are slowed by fragmented systems, manual handoffs, delays, and fraud risk. A decentralized, tamper-evident ledger enables shared real-time data, end-to-end traceability, and secure records across operators, suppliers, shippers, banks, and regulators. Smart contracts automate terms, cut intermediaries, speed settlements, and improve liquidity. We map use*

DOI: 10.4018/979-8-3373-5457-6.ch003

*cases in procurement, logistics tracking, asset integrity, and financial clearing, and pair blockchain with IoT telemetry for live monitoring and tokenization of commodities for digital trade. We also address regulatory uncertainty, scalability, and interoperability, and propose a stepwise framework for end-to-end rollout aligned to the oil and gas value chain. Uniting technology, operations, and governance, the chapter positions blockchain as a pillar of Industry 4.0 in energy, enabling secure, transparent, efficient global commerce.*

## 1. INTRODUCTION

The oil and gas industry are a cornerstone of the global economy, providing essential energy resources for transportation, industrial manufacturing, and power generation (Cynthia Onukwulu et al., 2025). With its vast operations and intricate global supply chains, the industry faces numerous challenges that hinder operational efficiency and transparency. Traditional supply chain management and trade finance practices, often reliant on paper-based systems and manual processes, are prone to delays, errors, and fraud. However, the emergence of blockchain technology presents a promising solution to address these issues (Ioannou & Demirel, 2022). By enabling real-time data sharing, secure record-keeping, and the automation of processes, blockchain offers the potential to revolutionize the way the oil and gas sector manages its operations, ensuring greater transparency, efficiency, and trust across all stakeholders (Okoh & Odorikpe, 2025).

### 1.1 Overview of Oil and Gas Sector Operations

The oil and gas sector operates within a highly complex ecosystem that involves a multitude of stages, from exploration and production to transportation, refining, and distribution (Cordes et al., 2016). Companies in the industry must manage diverse assets, including offshore platforms, drilling rigs, pipelines, storage facilities, and refineries. The supply chain spans multiple continents, involving an array of suppliers, contractors, logistics providers, and regulatory authorities (Abdullahi, Qabasiyu, et al., 2025). Each stage of the value chain is governed by strict regulations, safety standards, and environmental considerations. The sector is also highly capital-intensive, requiring significant investment in technology, infrastructure, and human resources to maintain operational efficiency(Campanella et al., 2023).

In addition to the technical and logistical challenges, the oil and gas industry also operates in an environment marked by volatility, as fluctuating commodity prices and geopolitical factors can significantly impact profitability and production decisions (Ibrahim Shelash et al., 2025). As companies strive to meet growing global energy demands, they must also navigate increasingly stringent environmental and sustainability requirements. The industry is under constant pressure to optimize operations, reduce costs, and enhance the efficiency of supply chains to remain competitive. These factors highlight the need for a transformative solution that can improve transparency, reduce operational risks, and enable better decision-making throughout the entire value chain (Rauniyar et al., n.d.).

## 1.2 Challenges in Supply Chain and Trade Finance

One of the major challenges in oil and gas supply chain management is the fragmented nature of existing systems (Ebrahimi et al., 2018). The industry relies on disparate, often incompatible software platforms for procurement, logistics, and asset management (Adamu et al., 2025). These siloed systems make it difficult for stakeholders to access real-time data, track the movement of goods, or verify the authenticity of transactions. As a result, the supply chain is prone to delays, miscommunication, and a lack of traceability, all of which can lead to costly inefficiencies and risks. The use of paper-based documentation further exacerbates these issues, making it harder to maintain a transparent and auditable record of transactions and assets (Kaluvakuri & Amin, 2018).

Trade finance in the oil and gas sector faces similar inefficiencies, as traditional processes for settling payments and securing financing remain slow and cumbersome (Okah Elumah & Sopelola, 2025). The involvement of multiple intermediaries, such as banks, brokers, and insurers, leads to increased transaction costs and delays in payment processing (Abdullahi, Usman Danyaro, et al., 2025). Moreover, the risk of fraud and disputes is heightened due to the lack of transparency and accountability within the system. Letters of credit, which are commonly used to guarantee payments in international trade, can be slow to process and subject to errors, further adding to the complexity of global oil and gas transactions. These challenges highlight the need for a more efficient, secure, and automated solution for both supply chain management and trade finance (Hassija et al., 2021). Table 1 highlights the challenges faced in traditional oil and gas supply chain and trade finance systems and compares them with the solutions provided by blockchain technology. Figure 1 shows Traditional pain points vs blockchain levers in oil and gas.

*Table 1. Challenges in Oil and Gas Supply Chain and Trade Finance vs Blockchain Solutions*

| Challenge | Traditional System Issues | Blockchain Solution |
|---|---|---|
| **Fragmented Systems** | Disparate software platforms, incompatible systems | Unified platform with real-time data sharing |
| **Lack of Transparency** | Limited visibility, prone to fraud | Transparent, immutable ledger with real-time tracking |
| **Manual Processes** | Delays, errors, paper-based documentation | Automated processes via smart contracts |
| **Involvement of Multiple Intermediaries** | High transaction costs and delays | Peer-to-peer transactions, reducing intermediaries |

*Figure 1. Traditional pain points vs blockchain levers in oil and gas.*

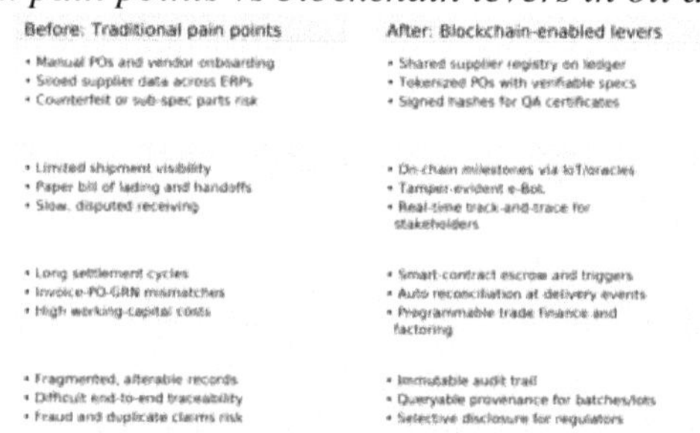


## 1.3 Why Blockchain Matters for This Industry

Blockchain technology has the potential to address many of the challenges faced by the oil and gas industry by providing a decentralized, transparent, and immutable ledger for recording transactions and tracking assets across the supply chain (Ahmad et al., 2022a). By using blockchain, companies can create a single, unified platform where all stakeholders' suppliers, logistics providers, regulators, and financial institutions can access real-time data and track the movement of goods and payments (Abdullahi et al., n.d.). This eliminates the need for manual record-keeping, reduces the risk of errors, and enhances the traceability of assets, ensuring greater transparency and accountability throughout the entire process (Hussain et al., 2024).

Moreover, the use of smart contracts on the blockchain enables the automation of agreements, reducing reliance on intermediaries and speeding up transaction cycles (Qabasiyu et al., 2023). These self-executing contracts automatically execute terms and conditions when predefined criteria are met, facilitating faster payments, reducing transaction costs, and enhancing liquidity. Blockchain also provides robust security features, as its decentralized nature makes it nearly impossible for any single party to alter or tamper with the data. This, combined with its ability to facilitate real-time data sharing, offers a powerful solution for enhancing the efficiency, security, and transparency of trade finance and supply chain management in the oil and gas industry.

## 2. FOUNDATIONS OF BLOCKCHAIN TECHNOLOGY

Blockchain technology is built upon the principles of decentralized data management, where multiple participants share a single, immutable ledger that records all transactions(De Filippi, 2016). At its core, blockchain utilizes Distributed Ledger Technology (DLT), which allows for the secure and transparent sharing of data across a network without a central authority. It relies on key components like smart contracts self-executing contracts that automatically enforce and execute terms and consensus mechanisms, which ensure that all participants in the network agree on the validity of transactions. This decentralized, transparent, and secure approach offers significant advantages over traditional centralized systems, particularly in industries where trust, traceability, and data integrity are critical. Blockchain's ability to eliminate intermediaries, reduce fraud, and automate processes is transforming the way transactions and data are handled across various sectors, including supply chain management, finance, and beyond (Aipoh et al., 2022).

### 2.1 Core Concepts: DLT, Smart Contracts, Consensus Mechanisms

At its core, blockchain technology relies on Distributed Ledger Technology (DLT), which is a decentralized network of nodes that collectively maintain a synchronized, secure, and transparent record of transactions (Antal et al., 2021). Unlike traditional centralized databases, DLT operates without a central authority, ensuring that all participants within the network have access to the same data in real time (Garzali Qabasiyu et al., 2023). This decentralized nature makes blockchain resistant to tampering and fraud, as no single party has control over the data. Smart contracts, another key feature of blockchain, are self-executing agreements with predefined rules encoded into the blockchain. These contracts automatically execute actions or transfer assets when certain conditions are met, minimizing the need for intermediaries and reducing the potential for human error (Egelund-Müller et al., 2017).

Consensus mechanisms are a critical component of blockchain networks, as they ensure that all transactions are validated and added to the blockchain in a secure and efficient manner (Lashkari & Musilek, 2021). There are various consensus mechanisms, such as Proof of Work (PoW), Proof of Stake (PoS), and Delegated Proof of Stake (DPoS), each offering different advantages in terms of scalability, security, and energy efficiency. These mechanisms help maintain the integrity of the blockchain, ensuring that all participants agree on the validity of the data being recorded, while preventing malicious actors from manipulating the system. The combination of DLT, smart contracts, and consensus mechanisms creates a robust and secure infrastructure for conducting transactions and managing data across a wide range of industries, including oil and gas (Ahmad et al., 2022a). Table 2 provides an overview of the core blockchain concepts, including Distributed Ledger Technology (DLT), smart contracts, and consensus mechanisms, and their relevance to the oil and gas industry.

*Table 2. Core Concepts of Blockchain*

| Concept | Definition | Relevance to Oil & Gas Industry |
|---|---|---|
| **Distributed Ledger Technology (DLT)** | A decentralized network of nodes that maintain synchronized records of transactions | Reduces fraud, ensures real-time data sharing, and improves transparency |
| **Smart Contracts** | Self-executing contracts with predefined conditions enclosed in the blockchain | Automates agreements, reducing manual intervention and errors |
| **Consensus Mechanisms** | Methods used to validate transactions in a blockchain network | Ensures secure and efficient validation of transactions across stakeholders |
| **Immutability** | The inability to alter or delete blockchain data once recorded | Enhances data security and accountability, preventing fraud |

## 2.2 Benefits of Decentralization, Immutability, and Transparency

One of the fundamental advantages of blockchain technology is decentralization, which removes the need for intermediaries and central authorities (De Filippi, 2016). In a traditional system, a central entity, such as a bank or a clearinghouse, controls and verifies transactions. This introduces the risk of fraud, errors, and inefficiencies. With blockchain, however, each participant in the network has access to the same version of the truth, ensuring that no single party can alter or manipulate the data. Decentralization also reduces the risk of system failures or data breaches, as the network is distributed across multiple nodes, making it more resilient to attacks or failures(Liu et al., 2022).

Immutability is another key benefit of blockchain, referring to the inability to alter or delete data once it has been recorded (Politou et al., 2021). Each transaction added to the blockchain is cryptographically linked to the previous one, creating a permanent and unchangeable record. This feature provides a high level of security and integrity, as it guarantees that historical records cannot be tampered with, even by malicious actors. Transparency is closely tied to immutability, as all participants can view the transaction history on the blockchain. This level of transparency fosters trust among stakeholders and reduces the potential for fraud, as it is easy to trace the provenance of assets or verify the accuracy of data (Nura & Abdullahi, 2022). Together, decentralization, immutability, and transparency make blockchain a powerful tool for enhancing accountability and security in industries that rely on complex, multi-party transactions (Chowdhury & Islam, 1 C.E.).

## 2.3 Blockchain vs. Traditional Systems

When comparing blockchain to traditional systems, the key difference lies in the structure and control mechanisms. Traditional systems typically rely on centralized databases, where a single authority, such as a bank or a government, is responsible for verifying and controlling transactions (Labonno & Chowdhury, 1 C.E.). While these systems are widely used and understood, they are prone to issues such as fraud, data manipulation, and system failures (Abdullahi et al., 2021). Moreover, the reliance on intermediaries in traditional systems introduces delays and additional costs, as each party must trust the central authority to validate and process transactions. This creates inefficiencies and makes it difficult to achieve real-time data sharing or traceability (Hader et al., 2022).

In contrast, blockchain operates on a decentralized network where all participants have access to the same information, ensuring that no single party can control or manipulate the data (Zyskind et al., 2015). The use of consensus mechanisms for transaction validation, coupled with the inherent immutability of blockchain, eliminates the need for intermediaries and ensures the integrity and security of the data. This decentralized, peer-to-peer model significantly reduces the risk of fraud, improves transaction speed, and enhances transparency across all stakeholders. While traditional systems have their place in many industries, blockchain offers a more secure, transparent, and efficient alternative, especially in sectors where trust, traceability, and real-time data sharing are critical (Ko et al., 2018).

# 3. BLOCKCHAIN IN OIL AND GAS SUPPLY CHAIN MANAGEMENT

The oil and gas industry are characterized by a complex, global supply chain that involves multiple stakeholders, including suppliers, contractors, logistics providers, and regulatory bodies (Gardas et al., 2019). Blockchain technology can significantly enhance the efficiency and transparency of this supply chain by providing a secure, decentralized platform for managing data and transactions. By enabling real-time tracking of assets, automating procurement processes, and improving vendor management, blockchain helps streamline operations, reduce costs, and minimize fraud. The application of blockchain in supply chain management not only enhances the traceability of goods from their point of origin to their destination but also ensures that all parties in the supply chain have access to the same up-to-date and immutable information (Zakari et al., 2021). This section explores how blockchain can transform various stages of the oil and gas supply chain, from procurement and logistics to asset management and fraud prevention.

## 3.1 Procurement and Vendor Management

In the oil and gas industry, procurement processes often involve numerous intermediaries, lengthy approval procedures, and a lack of transparency, which can lead to inefficiencies and errors (Olsen et al., 2005). Blockchain technology can streamline procurement by automating the approval workflow and enabling secure, real-time tracking of orders, invoices, and payments. Smart contracts, for example, can automatically execute agreements between buyers and vendors once predefined conditions are met, reducing the need for manual intervention and minimizing delays. Additionally, blockchain's transparency ensures that all parties involved in procurement have access to the same information, fostering trust and reducing the risk of fraud. Vendor management is also enhanced by blockchain, as companies can maintain a decentralized and immutable record of supplier performance, certifications, and compliance history, helping ensure the reliability and integrity of the supply chain (Omar et al., 2020). Table 3 demonstrates how blockchain applications can improve various stages of the oil and gas supply chain, from procurement to asset management.

*Table 3. Blockchain Applications in Different Stages of the Oil & Gas Supply Chain*

| Supply Chain Stage | Traditional Challenges | Blockchain Solution |
|---|---|---|
| **Procurement** | Multiple intermediaries, slow approval processes | Streamlined approval workflows, real-time tracking |
| **Logistics Tracking** | Limited visibility, risk of fraud | Real-time shipment tracking, transparent records |
| **Asset Management** | Poor record-keeping, difficulty in maintenance scheduling | Immutable asset history, easier tracking of maintenance/repairs |
| **Fraud Prevention** | Risk of tampering with documents or goods | Tamper-proof records, verification of goods authenticity |

## 3.2 Logistics and Shipment Tracking

Tracking shipments in the oil and gas industry involves managing vast amounts of data related to the movement of goods across multiple stages and geographies(Brennan & Schafer, n.d.). Blockchain offers a more efficient and secure solution for logistics by providing real-time visibility into the status and location of shipments. By recording every transaction along the supply chain on a shared ledger, blockchain ensures that all parties involved suppliers, transporters, and customers have access to the same accurate data. This enhances the ability to monitor shipments, reduce the risk of delays, and ensure that goods are delivered in a timely manner. Furthermore, the transparency and traceability of blockchain make it easier to verify the authenticity and origin of shipments, reducing the likelihood of fraud and counterfeiting, which are significant concerns in the global oil and gas trade (Afrin & Pathak, 2023).

## 3.3 Asset Lifecycle Management

Asset management in oil and gas is a critical component of maintaining operational efficiency and ensuring the longevity of expensive equipment and infrastructure (Adebisi et al., n.d.). Blockchain can improve asset lifecycle management by providing a secure, transparent record of an asset's entire journey from procurement to deployment, maintenance, and decommissioning. By leveraging blockchain to record every action taken on an asset, including maintenance schedules, repairs, and operational performance, companies can create a more comprehensive and accurate view of an asset's history (Abdullahi Hassan Usman ct al., 2020). This not only helps optimize asset utilization but also enables better decision-making regarding upgrades, replacements, and compliance with safety standards. Blockchain's immutable ledger ensures that the asset's history cannot be altered or falsified, providing a trustworthy record for stakeholders involved in the asset's management(Omar et al., 2020).

## 3.4 Traceability and Anti-Fraud Measures

One of the most significant challenges in the oil and gas supply chain is the risk of fraud, such as the misrepresentation of goods, tampering with invoices, or falsifying certifications (Burger et al., n.d.). Blockchain's inherent transparency and immutability make it an ideal solution for addressing these issues. By recording all transactions and asset movements on a tamper-proof ledger, blockchain provides an auditable trail that ensures the authenticity of goods and transactions (Zakari et al., 2020). This traceability allows companies to verify the source and journey of materials, ensuring that they comply with regulatory standards and are free from counterfeit or fraudulent activity. Additionally, the decentralized nature of blockchain makes it difficult for malicious actors to manipulate data, as all participants in the network have access to the same version of the ledger. As a result, blockchain significantly enhances the integrity of the supply chain and reduces the risk of fraud, ultimately contributing to a more secure and trustworthy oil and gas industry(Ahmad et al., 2022b).

# 4. BLOCKCHAIN IN AUTOMATED TRADE FINANCE

The oil and gas industry's trade finance system involves complex financial transactions, often across multiple jurisdictions, with various intermediaries and stakeholders. This traditional system relies heavily on paper-based documentation, third-party verification, and multiple banking institutions, which can result in inefficiencies, delays, and increased risks (*Conducting Search (Download All Papers for Each Database) Identification of Research Questions Selection of Search Databases Data Extraction Stop Start Screening of Papers Identification of Review Scope Developing Review Protocol Result and Discussion*, n.d.). Blockchain technology has the potential to significantly enhance trade finance by automating key processes, reducing the reliance on intermediaries, and improving the transparency and security of transactions. With its decentralized, tamper-proof ledger, blockchain can streamline the flow of payments, guarantee the authenticity of financial agreements, and provide real-time visibility into financial settlements. The integration of smart contracts and tokenization further contributes to automating processes, reducing manual intervention, and speeding up trade cycles, ultimately improving liquidity and cash flow management.

## 4.1 Current Challenges in Oil and Gas Trade Finance

Oil and gas trade finance faces significant challenges, primarily due to its complex, multi-party nature, with participants spread across various countries and legal jurisdictions (Taiwo, 2020). One of the main issues is the reliance on traditional banking systems, which can be slow, costly, and prone to errors. For example, the use of letters of credit, which are often required to secure payments, can involve multiple intermediaries and lengthy processing times, creating bottlenecks in financial transactions. Additionally, the industry's heavy reliance on paper documentation, such as contracts, invoices, and shipping documents, introduces the risk of fraud, miscommunication, and delays. This fragmentation and manual handling of documents make it difficult to achieve real-time tracking of payments and the status of trade transactions, hindering efficiency and increasing the likelihood of disputes (Bello et al., 2025).

Moreover, the oil and gas trade finance sector are exposed to geopolitical risks, currency fluctuations, and regulatory challenges that add further complexity (Gamso et al., 2024). These factors can complicate international transactions, making it challenging for companies to access capital and secure funding in a timely manner. The inability to get a clear and transparent view of cash flows across the supply chain also exacerbates liquidity management problems, making it harder for companies to make informed financial decisions. Blockchain offers a potential solution by providing a more secure, transparent, and efficient means of handling trade finance, thereby addressing these challenges and facilitating faster, more reliable financial transactions (Chang et al., 2020). Table 4 compares the traditional trade finance processes with blockchain-enhanced processes, highlighting improvements in transaction speed, costs, transparency, and intermediary roles.

*Table 4. Traditional vs Blockchain-Enhanced Trade Finance*

| Trade Finance Process | Traditional System | Blockchain-Enhanced System |
|---|---|---|
| **Transaction Time** | Slow, paper-based processes with multiple intermediaries | Instant settlements via smart contracts |
| **Transaction Costs** | High, due to multiple intermediaries | Reduced, eliminating intermediary fees |
| **Transparency** | Limited visibility, susceptible to fraud | Transparent, auditable ledger accessible to all stakeholders |
| **Settlement Process** | Delays due to manual verification | Automated via smart contracts, reducing human error |

## 4.2 Smart Contracts for Automated Payments and Settlements

Smart contracts, a key feature of blockchain technology, are self-executing contracts with the terms of the agreement directly written into code (Dutta, 2020). In the context of trade finance, smart contracts can be used to automate payment and settlement processes, reducing the reliance on manual verification and intermediaries. Once predefined conditions such as the delivery of goods or the completion of contractual obligations are met, the smart contract automatically triggers the payment or settlement process without requiring human intervention. This automation not only speeds up transactions but also reduces the risk of errors and fraud, as the contract is executed based on verifiable, tamper-proof data recorded on the blockchain. Furthermore, smart contracts ensure that all parties involved in the transaction have access to the same information, enhancing transparency and reducing disputes over payments or settlement terms (Nanayakkara et al., 2021).

For oil and gas companies, implementing smart contracts in trade finance can result in faster, more efficient transactions (Lu et al., 2019a). The automation of payment processes minimizes the delays that typically occur when waiting for approval or confirmation from intermediaries such as banks, which is particularly beneficial in a sector where time-sensitive operations are critical. In addition, smart contracts can enhance the overall trust between trading parties, as the blockchain's immutability ensures that the terms cannot be altered once they have been agreed upon. This level of transparency and security can foster stronger business relationships and more streamlined trade finance operations, ultimately improving the financial efficiency of the oil and gas sector (Nwankwo & Emmanuel, 2025). Figure 2 shows Automated Payment and Settlement vis Smart Contract.

*Figure 2. Automated Payment and Settlement vis Smart Contract*

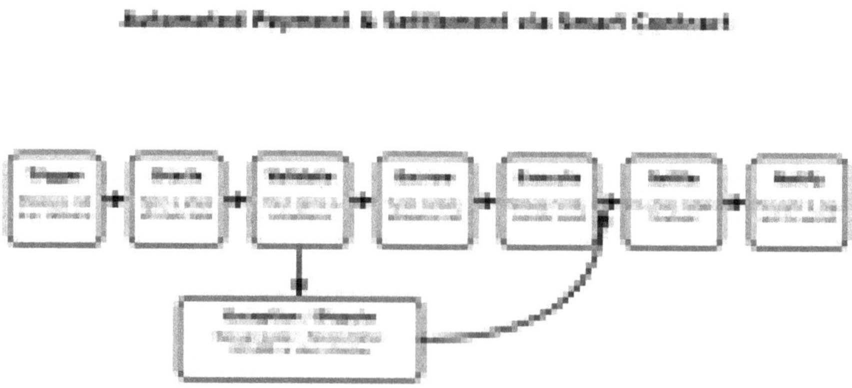

## 4.3 Reducing the Role of Intermediaries

One of the main advantages of blockchain technology in trade finance is its ability to reduce or eliminate the role of intermediaries, such as banks, clearinghouses, and insurance companies (Saka, 2024). In traditional trade finance, these intermediaries are responsible for verifying the authenticity of transactions, processing payments, and ensuring that both parties fulfill their obligations. However, each intermediary introduces additional costs, delays, and potential points of failure, making the trade process less efficient. Blockchain, with its decentralized and immutable ledger, allows for direct peer-to-peer transactions between parties, without the need for intermediaries to validate or process payments (Klems et al., 2017). This can significantly reduce transaction costs and accelerate the entire process, leading to faster, more efficient financial settlements.

For the oil and gas industry, reducing the role of intermediaries offers several key benefits (Ghoddusi et al., 2022). It lowers the cost of doing business by cutting out the fees associated with traditional banking systems and third-party verification. Additionally, it speeds up payment cycles, as transactions can be settled directly between buyers and sellers through smart contracts, without waiting for approval from banks or other intermediaries. This streamlining of processes enhances overall efficiency and makes it easier for oil and gas companies to manage their working capital, especially in a sector where large-scale transactions and cross-border payments are common (Kelvin Chima et al., 2020). Furthermore, by reducing reliance on intermediaries, blockchain also reduces the risk of errors and fraud, contributing to a more secure and trustworthy trade finance ecosystem.

## 4.4 Enhancing Liquidity and Cash Flow Visibility

Blockchain technology can significantly improve liquidity and cash flow management in the oil and gas sector by providing real-time visibility into financial transactions and payment statuses (Ahmad et al., 2022a). The transparency of blockchain allows all parties involved in a transaction to access the same up-to-date information, providing a clearer view of the flow of funds across the supply chain. This real-time access to payment data enables companies to make more informed decisions regarding working capital and cash flow management, helping them to better plan and allocate resources. By having a more accurate and transparent view of their financial transactions, oil and gas companies can optimize their liquidity and reduce the risk of cash flow problems (Barnabas & Oloyede, 2024).

Additionally, blockchain's ability to automate payments and settlements through smart contracts enhances liquidity by speeding up transaction cycles and reducing delays in payments (HASSOUNI & OUCHEKKIR, 2024). With the removal of intermediaries and the automation of payment processes, funds can be transferred faster, ensuring that suppliers, contractors, and other stakeholders receive timely payments. This not only improves cash flow visibility but also helps oil and gas companies avoid liquidity shortages and reduce the need for costly short-term financing options (Weijermars, 2011). By enhancing liquidity management, blockchain enables more efficient financial operations, reducing financial risks and improving the overall financial health of oil and gas companies.

## 5. INTEGRATION WITH EMERGING TECHNOLOGIES

The integration of blockchain with emerging technologies such as the Internet of Things (IoT), tokenization, and digital identity management is transforming the oil and gas industry by enabling more efficient, transparent, and secure operations. These technologies provide the necessary tools to collect, process, and share real-time data, manage physical assets, and ensure secure access control, all within a decentralized blockchain framework. By combining the strengths of IoT's real-time monitoring, blockchain's immutable ledger, and the power of tokenization and digital identity systems, the oil and gas sector can achieve new levels of automation, efficiency, and security. This chapter explores how these technologies are being integrated into the oil and gas supply chain and trade finance systems to streamline operations and enhance overall business performance.

### 5.1 IoT and Blockchain for Real-Time Monitoring

The Internet of Things (IoT) has revolutionized the way data is collected in industries, and when integrated with blockchain technology, it provides a robust framework for real-time monitoring of assets and operations in the oil and gas sector (Zuo & Qi, 2022). IoT devices, such as sensors, actuators, and GPS trackers, are deployed across critical infrastructure such as drilling rigs, pipelines, and storage facilities, gathering data on parameters like temperature, pressure, flow rates, and health equipment(Ur et al., 2024). By connecting these devices to a blockchain network, the data collected is automatically recorded on an immutable ledger, ensuring that all participants in the supply chain or trade finance ecosystem have access to the same real-time information. This not only enhances operational visibility but also enables proactive maintenance and decision-making, as blockchain guarantees that the data cannot be altered or tampered with, providing an accurate, trustworthy record (Shehu Yalli et al., n.d.).

Integrating IoT and blockchain allows oil and gas companies to monitor assets in real time, providing insights that can prevent costly downtime and improve resource allocation(Ghoddusi et al., 2022). For example, predictive maintenance algorithms can be deployed to analyze sensor data stored on the blockchain, identifying potential issues with equipment before they lead to failure(Tavakoli et al., 2024). This can significantly reduce maintenance costs and increase the lifespan of critical assets. Furthermore, real-time data on the status and location of shipments, production levels, and operational efficiency can be shared across the entire supply chain, ensuring that all stakeholders are up to date on the performance of key assets and operations (Sathio et al., 2021). The combination of IoT and blockchain creates a seamless, transparent, and highly secure environment for managing complex operations in the oil and gas sector.

## 5.2 Tokenization of Physical Commodities

Tokenization is a transformative application of blockchain technology that involves converting physical assets, such as oil, gas, and other commodities, into digital tokens that can be traded, sold, or stored on a blockchain network(Boggio Viola, 2024). This process allows oil and gas companies to represent ownership or a share of ownership in physical commodities as digital tokens, which can be easily transferred and traded on blockchain platforms. Tokenizing physical commodities not only enhances liquidity by allowing assets to be traded in smaller fractions, but it also simplifies the process of managing large-scale transactions, as ownership records are automatically updated and secured on the blockchain. These tokens can be used to streamline settlement processes, reduce administrative overhead, and increase the speed and security of transactions(Deshpande, 2025).

The tokenization of commodities also provides enhanced transparency, as the blockchain ensures a secure and auditable record of every transaction and asset transfer (Benedetti & Rodriguez-Garnica, 2023). This is particularly valuable in the oil and gas industry, where ownership and provenance of commodities are crucial to ensuring regulatory compliance and reducing fraud. Blockchain-based tokenization also opens new avenues for investment, as smaller investors can now participate in commodity markets without the need to deal with traditional intermediaries or large minimum investments (Anwar et al., 2021). Additionally, tokenized commodities can be integrated with smart contracts, enabling automated settlement and real-time tracking of asset ownership, further enhancing the efficiency and security of the oil and gas trade (Nkeonadi et al., 2025).

## 5.3 Digital Identity and Access Control

In the oil and gas industry, ensuring secure access to critical systems and facilities is essential for maintaining operational integrity and protecting sensitive data(Mohammed et al., 2022). Digital identity management, integrated with blockchain technology, provides a decentralized and secure solution for verifying the identity of individuals and controlling access to various resources (Ali Sathio Benazir Bhutto Shaheed University Lyari Karachi et al., 2021). With blockchain, digital identities can be securely stored and managed in a decentralized manner, where each participant's identity is cryptographically protected, ensuring that only authorized individuals have access to specific assets or information. This eliminates the need for centralized authority systems, which can be prone to data breaches and unauthorized access(Cheng et al., 2017).

Blockchain-enabled digital identity systems also allow for more granular control over access permissions, as companies can issue smart contracts that define access levels and automatically enforce them (Ghadge, 2024). For example, only authorized personnel might be allowed to approve procurement contracts, access sensitive financial data, or manage critical infrastructure (Ullah & Chowdhury, 1 C.E.). This approach not only improves security but also enhances compliance with regulatory standards by ensuring that access control records are immutable and traceable. Moreover, the use of blockchain for digital identity helps streamline onboarding and credentialing processes, as identities can be verified in real time, reducing administrative delays and ensuring that all workers and contractors meet the required standards. By integrating digital identity with blockchain, the oil and gas industry can enhance security, ensure regulatory compliance, and improve operational efficiency(Lu et al., 2019b).

## 6. CASE STUDIES AND INDUSTRY APPLICATIONS

This chapter explores how blockchain technology can revolutionize the oil and gas industry by enhancing transparency, efficiency, and trust, particularly in the supply chain management and trade finance processes (Rehman et al., 2024). The complexities of this industry, including fragmented systems, manual processes, and vulnerability to fraud, create significant challenges. By leveraging blockchain's decentralized and secure infrastructure, these challenges can be addressed, resulting in more streamlined operations. The chapter highlights real-world examples, potential barriers, and strategic frameworks for blockchain adoption in the oil and gas value chain, demonstrating its role in the broader context of Industry 4.0(Ali Sathio Anwar et al., 2021).

## 6.1 Pilot Projects in Upstream and Downstream Operations

In the oil and gas industry, blockchain pilot projects have been successfully initiated in both upstream and downstream sectors, focusing on optimizing operations through decentralized technologies. These projects aim to tackle challenges such as delayed transactions, fragmented data sharing, and inefficient asset tracking, especially in complex supply chains (Yalli et al., 2025). For instance, pilot projects in upstream operations, including exploration and production, have demonstrated how blockchain can facilitate real-time data sharing, allowing for better collaboration among stakeholders. This technology has also been tested in downstream operations like refining and distribution, where it ensures the accuracy of inventory tracking, payment settlements, and compliance with regulatory standards. By providing a transparent, immutable ledger, these pilots not only enhance operational efficiency but also improve the reliability of data and transactions across the value chain.

Additionally, blockchain pilots in upstream operations focus on automating and streamlining the reporting processes, providing faster access to accurate data for decision-making (Chandio et al., 2017). In downstream, the emphasis is on logistics, particularly through shipment tracking and ensuring product quality. These trials highlight blockchain's potential to address the logistical bottlenecks that commonly occur in supply chain management (ur Rehman et al., 2024). For example, smart contracts can automate payment triggers based on predefined milestones, further reducing manual interventions and delays in the supply chain. As these pilots progress, the industry is witnessing the potential of blockchain to make operations more agile, secure, and cost-effective (ur Rehman Shaikh et al., 2024).

## 6.2 Consortium-led Blockchain Platforms (e.g., VAKT, Komgo)

Blockchain consortiums like VAKT and Komgo have played a pivotal role in bringing together key industry players to collectively explore the transformative potential of blockchain technology (Rehman et al., 2025). These consortium-led platforms are designed to enhance the efficiency of trading, procurement, and financial transactions within the oil and gas industry. VAKT, for instance, focuses on the post-trade process and is designed to streamline operations, reduce the administrative burden, and ensure accurate record-keeping (Mhlanga, 2025). By offering a shared ledger, VAKT allows for real-time collaboration among traders, shippers, and insurers, making trade finance more transparent and secure. Similarly, Komgo, a platform built on blockchain for commodity trade finance, enhances transparency and reduces the risk of fraud by providing a digitalized and automated way of processing transactions and documents related to trade finance.

These platforms represent significant advancements in blockchain's application for cross-company collaboration in the oil and gas sector. By using blockchain's decentralized structure, these consortiums reduce the need for intermediaries, which traditionally slow down processes and increase costs. Furthermore, the integration of smart contracts into these platforms enables automation of key processes such as payment and shipment confirmations, reducing manual errors and ensuring timely settlements. These consortium-led platforms have not only brought together industry leaders to foster innovation but also created a more secure and efficient environment for trading and finance, setting a strong foundation for broader blockchain adoption across the industry.

## 6.3 Lessons Learned and Measurable Benefits

From the implementation of blockchain in various pilot projects and consortium platforms, the oil and gas industry has gathered valuable lessons about the practical challenges and measurable benefits of this technology. One key lesson is the importance of stakeholder collaboration and the need for clear governance structures. Successful blockchain adoption hinges on buy-in from all relevant parties, including suppliers, traders, regulators, and financial institutions. Additionally, the integration of blockchain with existing IT infrastructure poses significant challenges that require careful planning and investment in interoperability. These lessons emphasize the need for a phased, collaborative approach to blockchain adoption to ensure that all parties are aligned on goals and expectations.

On the benefits side, measurable improvements have been observed in transparency, operational efficiency, and cost reduction. By eliminating the need for multiple intermediaries and offering a secure, immutable ledger, blockchain has significantly reduced the time and costs associated with traditional trade finance and supply chain processes. This includes faster payment cycles, reduced fraud, and improved data integrity. Moreover, blockchain's ability to provide real-time tracking and transparent reporting has enhanced compliance and auditability, further driving operational efficiencies. As industry continues to embrace these technologies, the lessons learned from initial implementations provide a roadmap for scaling up blockchain adoption across the oil and gas supply chain.

# 7. STRATEGIC FRAMEWORK FOR IMPLEMENTATION

Implementing blockchain technology in the oil and gas industry requires a well-thought-out strategic framework to ensure successful adoption and integration across various operations. This framework includes a step-by-step roadmap to guide the transition, starting from feasibility studies and pilot projects to full-scale deployment. Key elements like governance, compliance, and stakeholder engagement play a critical role in ensuring that blockchain solutions meet legal requirements, remain secure, and align with industry standards. Additionally, effective change management strategies are necessary to support the workforce through the technological shift, ensuring smooth implementation and adoption across all levels of the organization. This holistic approach lays the foundation for long-term success in leveraging blockchain to enhance efficiency, transparency, and security in the oil and gas value chain.

## 7.1 Step-by-Step Blockchain Adoption Roadmap

The successful implementation of blockchain technology in the oil and gas industry requires a well-structured, step-by-step roadmap to guide the transition from traditional systems to blockchain-based solutions(Chourasiya & Malviya, 2025). The first step is to conduct a thorough feasibility study, assessing the current challenges and the potential impact of blockchain on specific operations within the supply chain and trade finance. This includes identifying key areas where blockchain can add value, such as procurement, logistics tracking, and financial settlements. Once the value propositions are clear, the next step is to design and prototype the blockchain solution. This involves selecting the appropriate blockchain platform (private or public), deciding on consensus mechanisms, and defining the scope of the blockchain network, including the number of stakeholders involved (Farshidi et al., 2020).

After the design phase, the implementation begins with setting up the blockchain infrastructure, followed by integration with existing systems, such as Enterprise Resource Planning (ERP) and Customer Relationship Management (CRM) systems(-Faccia & Petratos, 2021). A pilot project should be launched to test the blockchain solution on a smaller scale before full-scale deployment. During this phase, feedback from stakeholders is crucial for refining the technology and ensuring that the solution meets operational needs. The final steps of the roadmap involve scaling up the solution across the entire organization, continuously monitoring performance, and ensuring that the system evolves in line with technological advancements. It's important that this roadmap is adaptable, as blockchain technology is still evolving, and ongoing innovation will be necessary for long-term success (Wang et al., 2024). Figure 3 shows Step-by-Step Blockchain Adoption Roadmap.

*Figure 3. Step-by-Step Blockchain Adoption Roadmap.*

## 7.2 Governance and Compliance Considerations

When implementing blockchain in the oil and gas industry, governance and compliance are paramount to ensuring that the system operates securely and meets legal requirements(Lu et al., 2019c). A robust governance framework is necessary to define roles, responsibilities, and decision-making processes within the blockchain ecosystem. This includes identifying which parties have access to the blockchain, how data is managed, and the processes for handling disputes or conflicts. Compliance considerations involve ensuring that blockchain solutions align with industry-specific regulations, such as anti-money laundering (AML), know your customer (KYC), and data privacy laws. Given the highly regulated nature of the oil and gas industry, integrating blockchain into business operations requires careful attention to legal frameworks governing cross-border transactions, environmental standards, and reporting requirements.

Moreover, maintaining transparency and accountability within the blockchain system is essential (Ahmed, 2025). This can be achieved by establishing clear protocols for data storage, access rights, and audit trails, which are critical for ensuring compliance with industry standards. Smart contracts, which automate transactions, must be designed to comply with existing legal frameworks to avoid disputes. Additionally, regular audits should be conducted to monitor the system's compliance and ensure that it is functioning as intended. As regulatory environments evolve, the governance model for blockchain should be flexible enough to adapt to new legal requirements and industry standards, providing a clear path to long-term compliance(Sulkowski, 2018).

## 7.3 Stakeholder Engagement and Change Management

For successful blockchain adoption in the oil and gas industry, stakeholder engagement and effective management strategies are crucial(Hassani et al., 2020). Stakeholders include suppliers, customers, regulators, internal teams, and technology providers, all of whom must be on board with the shift to blockchain. The first step in stakeholder engagement is to identify the key players and understand their concerns, expectations, and readiness for change. Early engagement through workshops, presentations, and consultation ensures that stakeholders are informed about the benefits and potential risks of blockchain technology. Clear communication about how blockchain will address specific pain points, such as fraud reduction or supply chain inefficiencies, can build confidence and support across the board (Al-Farsi et al., 2021).

Change management, on the other hand, involves preparing the organization for the cultural and operational shifts that blockchain implementation brings (Varriale et al., 2021). It requires addressing employee concerns, redefining job roles, and ensuring that the workforce is adequately trained to handle new systems and processes. A well-crafted training program should be established to teach stakeholders how to interact with the new blockchain system, including how to use smart contracts and perform transactions on a decentralized network. Furthermore, a feedback loop should be implemented to gather insights from stakeholders during the initial phases of blockchain deployment. This will help in refining the system and adapting it to the real-world needs of users. By combining stakeholder engagement with structured change management, organizations can ensure smooth blockchain adoption and long-term success (Blockis, 2025).Top of Form

# 8. BARRIERS, RISKS, AND MITIGATION STRATEGIES

The adoption of blockchain in the oil and gas industry, while promising significant improvements in transparency and efficiency, faces several barriers and risks that need to be addressed(Babaei et al., 2024). Scalability and interoperability issues are critical challenges that can hinder the smooth integration of blockchain across the supply chain and trade finance operations. Additionally, regulatory and legal uncertainties can create roadblocks, as blockchain's decentralized nature complicates compliance with existing laws and industry standards. Security and data privacy concerns also pose significant risks, especially given the sensitive nature of data in the oil and gas sector. This section outlines these barriers in detail, explores the associated risks, and proposes strategies to mitigate them, ensuring a more secure and effective implementation of blockchain technology (Malhotra et al., 2022).

## 8.1 Scalability and Interoperability Issues

One of the most significant barriers to the widespread adoption of blockchain in the oil and gas industry is scalability(Lyu et al., 2020). Blockchain networks, especially public ones, often struggle to handle the large volume of transactions generated by global supply chains and trade finance operations. The slow processing times and high transaction costs associated with some blockchain solutions can limit their efficiency and applicability in industries that require real-time data exchange. Additionally, the lack of interoperability between different blockchain platforms presents a challenge. Oil and gas companies operate in a global environment where multiple stakeholders use different technologies, and the inability of these blockchain systems to communicate effectively can create fragmentation and inefficiency.

To address scalability, organizations can explore layer-2 scaling solutions or adopt private or consortium blockchains designed to handle higher transaction volumes more efficiently. These platforms can offer faster processing times and lower transaction fees. As for interoperability, industry consortia like VAKT and Komgo are already working on creating standards that can allow different blockchain networks to communicate with each other. Developing universal protocols or adopting cross-chain technologies can help bridge the gaps between systems and enable seamless data sharing across multiple stakeholders. These solutions, when implemented correctly, can reduce the friction caused by scalability and interoperability issues, ensuring that blockchain technology delivers its full potential to the oil and gas industry(Rane & Narvel, 2021).

## 8.2 Regulatory and Legal Uncertainty

Blockchain's decentralized nature presents challenges in adhering to existing regulatory and legal frameworks. In the oil and gas industry, where compliance with a wide range of international regulations is essential, integrating blockchain can create uncertainties regarding legal accountability and data governance (Zarrin et al., 2021). For example, smart contracts, while efficient and automated, may not always align with the current legal systems, particularly in jurisdictions where traditional contract law does not account for blockchain-based transactions. Furthermore, the lack of a unified regulatory approach to blockchain technology across countries can create complications for global operations, as different regions may impose different standards for blockchain use (Karisma & Moslemzadeh Tehrani, 2023).

To mitigate regulatory risks, it is essential for oil and gas companies to engage in proactive dialogue with regulatory bodies to help shape policy frameworks that accommodate blockchain technology (Lu et al., 2019d). Implementing legal oversight mechanisms, such as ensuring smart contracts are reviewed by legal teams before execution, can also help ensure compliance. Additionally, organizations should prioritize creating blockchain solutions that are flexible enough to adapt to changes in regulatory requirements. Collaborating with industry consortia to develop common standards can ensure that the legal uncertainties surrounding blockchain are addressed and help create a clearer regulatory landscape for its adoption in the oil and gas sector (Lu et al., 2019e).

## 8.3 Security and Data Privacy Concerns

Security and data privacy concerns are central to the adoption of blockchain in any industry, but they are particularly significant in the oil and gas sector, where sensitive operational, financial, and regulatory data is involved (Nguyen et al., 2020). While blockchain provides enhanced security through its decentralized nature and cryptographic techniques, it is not immune to threats such as cyberattacks, hacking, or insider threats. For instance, if the private keys required to access the blockchain network are compromised, it could lead to unauthorized transactions or data breaches. Additionally, the transparency of blockchain systems can sometimes conflict with privacy regulations, such as the General Data Protection Regulation (GDPR) in Europe, which imposes strict rules on data handling and erasure.

To mitigate these risks, oil and gas companies must implement robust cybersecurity protocols, including secure key management and access controls, to prevent unauthorized access to the blockchain network. Regular security audits and vulnerability assessments should be conducted to identify and address potential weaknesses in the system. Moreover, privacy concerns can be alleviated by using techniques such as zero-knowledge proofs or selective disclosure, which allow data to be shared without revealing sensitive information. By combining blockchain's inherent security with additional privacy-enhancing measures, companies can ensure that the technology is both secure and compliant with data protection laws (Javed et al., 2021).

# 9. FUTURE OUTLOOK AND INDUSTRY 5.0 ALIGNMENT

The future of blockchain technology in the oil and gas industry is closely aligned with the evolving landscape of Industry 5.0, where human intelligence and advanced technologies collaborate to create more sustainable, efficient, and transparent systems. As blockchain technology continues to mature, its integration into industry operations will play a pivotal role in reshaping the energy sector. Industry 5.0 focuses on human-centric technology, aiming to create systems that enhance human capabilities while ensuring environmental sustainability and economic growth. Blockchain's potential to transform energy systems, streamline operations, and contribute to sustainable practices aligns well with this vision. This section explores how blockchain is set to evolve through global collaborations, its role in decarbonization, and its alignment with the goals of Industry 5.0, particularly in creating a decentralized, transparent, and sustainable energy ecosystem.

## 9.1 Evolving Standards and Global Collaborations

As blockchain technology continues to gain traction across industries, the establishment of evolving standards and the fostering of global collaborations will be critical in ensuring its scalability and widespread adoption. In the oil and gas sector, industry-specific standards and protocols are essential to ensure that blockchain applications can operate seamlessly across different regions, technologies, and stakeholders. Organizations like the International Blockchain Oil and Gas Consortium (IBOGC) and various consortia platforms, such as VAKT and Komgo, are working toward establishing a unified set of standards for blockchain use in energy transactions. These standards aim to address interoperability issues, ensure legal compliance, and provide a framework for secure data sharing between diverse platforms. As blockchain adoption grows, these collaborations will ensure a more cohesive global blockchain ecosystem in the oil and gas industry.

Furthermore, evolving standards will drive innovation in blockchain technology by enabling cross-industry integration. The ability to integrate blockchain with other emerging technologies such as artificial intelligence (AI), machine learning (ML), and the Internet of Things (IoT) will allow the oil and gas sector to unlock new efficiencies and capabilities. Through global collaborations between technology providers, regulatory bodies, and industry leaders, blockchain will evolve from a niche technology to a foundational tool for managing and optimizing complex energy systems. These partnerships will create a robust framework that supports not only technological growth but also enhances the legal, regulatory, and ethical considerations surrounding blockchain applications, making them more viable for long-term adoption across the industry.

## 9.2 Blockchain's Role in Decarbonization and ESG Reporting

Blockchain technology is poised to play a significant role in the decarbonization efforts of the oil and gas industry, particularly through its integration with Environmental, Social, and Governance (ESG) reporting. As governments and regulatory bodies worldwide intensify their focus on sustainability and carbon reduction, blockchain's ability to provide transparent, immutable, and auditable records can support the industry's transition to more sustainable practices. By ensuring that environmental data, such as carbon emissions, energy consumption, and waste management, is accurately tracked and reported in real-time, blockchain can help oil and gas companies meet sustainability goals and regulatory requirements. Moreover, technology's inherent transparency allows for independent verification of ESG claims, which helps reduce greenwashing and enhances trust among stakeholders, including investors, regulators, and consumers.

Blockchain also facilitates the creation of tokenized carbon credits and renewable energy certificates, which can be traded on a secure and transparent platform, providing an efficient market for carbon offsetting. This tokenization of environmental assets could encourage greater participation in carbon reduction programs by creating financial incentives for businesses to adopt cleaner technologies. By offering a transparent, secure method for recording carbon credits, blockchain can ensure that credits are not double-counted and that they represent actual environmental benefits. As part of the broader push for decarbonization, blockchain's role in ESG reporting will ensure that oil and gas companies are held accountable for their environmental impact, supporting a global transition toward a low-carbon economy.

## 9.3 Vision for a Decentralized, Transparent Energy Ecosystem

The ultimate vision for blockchain technology in the oil and gas industry is the creation of a decentralized, transparent energy ecosystem where all stakeholders, from producers and consumers to regulators and financers, can interact within a secure and trustworthy environment. In this vision, blockchain serves as the foundational infrastructure that facilitates peer-to-peer transactions, data sharing, and decision-making processes. By eliminating intermediaries and providing a transparent, immutable record of all transactions, blockchain can reduce inefficiencies, fraud, and corruption within the industry, leading to a more efficient and equitable distribution of resources.

In this decentralized ecosystem, the energy supply chain becomes more agile and responsive to market changes, with real-time data enabling more efficient resource allocation. This could lead to a more distributed model of energy production and consumption, where decentralized renewable energy sources, such as solar and wind, are more easily integrated into the global energy mix. Blockchain's ability to provide secure, real-time monitoring and verification of energy generation, consumption, and emissions data would allow for a more accurate reflection of energy usage, making it easier to track progress toward sustainability targets. As Industry 5.0 continues to unfold, this vision of a decentralized, transparent energy ecosystem will not only align with the goals of technological innovation but also support broader societal goals of environmental sustainability, economic inclusivity, and improved governance within the global energy sector.

## 10. CONCLUSION

In conclusion, the integration of blockchain technology into the oil and gas industry offers transformative potential that can reshape the way supply chains, trade finance, and operations are managed. By addressing longstanding issues such as inefficiency, opacity, and fraud, blockchain provides a decentralized, transparent, and secure infrastructure that streamlines processes and fosters greater trust among stakeholders. The adoption of smart contracts and real-time data sharing enhances operational efficiency, accelerates transaction cycles, and reduces the reliance on intermediaries. Furthermore, the strategic implementation of blockchain in areas like procurement, logistics, and asset management offers measurable benefits, including cost reduction, enhanced traceability, and improved liquidity. As blockchain continues to evolve, its alignment with the goals of Industry 5.0 focused on human-centric, sustainable technology will drive future innovations in energy management, decarbonization efforts, and ESG reporting. While challenges such as scalability, interoperability, regulatory uncertainty, and data privacy need to be addressed, the ongoing collaboration among industry leaders, regulators, and technology providers will lay the groundwork for overcoming these barriers. Blockchain's role in creating a decentralized, transparent energy ecosystem promises to usher in a new era of more efficient, secure, and sustainable global energy markets. As these technological advancements unfold, they will not only enhance the operational dynamics of the oil and gas sector but also contribute to broader environmental and societal goals, fostering a more equitable and sustainable energy future.

## 11. REFERENCES


Abdullahi, S., Calem Ambi, Y., & Hali, I. A. Lawal, & Bagiwa, I. (n.d.). *A Radar System For Object And People Detection In Security-Challenged Areas of Katsina State*. Retrieved August 16, 2025, from www.seahipaj.org

Abdullahi, S., Qabasiyu, M. G., Danyaro, K. U., Zakari, A., Maitama, J. Z., & Imam, A. A. (2025). A Systematic Review of Metaheuristic Approaches to the Deployment Problem in Wireless Sensor Networks. [JTEC]. *Journal of Telecommunication, Electronic and Computer Engineering*, *17*(2), 1–14. DOI: 10.54554/jtec.2025.17.02.001

Abdullahi, S., Usman Danyaro, K., Zakari, A., Abdul Aziz, I., Amila Wan Abdullah Zawawi, N., & Adamu, S. (2025). Time-Series Large Language Models: A Systematic Review of State-of-the-Art. *IEEE Access : Practical Innovations, Open Solutions*, *13*, 30235–30261. DOI: 10.1109/ACCESS.2025.3535782

Abdullahi, S., Zayyad, M. A., Yusuf, N., Bagiwa, L. I., Nura, A., Zakari, A., & Dansambo, B. (2021). Software Requirements Negotiation: A Review on Challenges. *International Journal of Innovative Computing*, *11*(1), 1–6. DOI: 10.11113/ijic.v11n1.264

Abdullahi Hassan Usman, S., Abdullahi, S., Zakari, A., Abdu, H., Nura, A., Ahmed Zayyad, M., Suleiman, S., Adamu, A., & Samaila Mashasha, A. (2020). Software testing: review on tools, techniques and challenges Software Testing: Review on Tools, Techniques and Challenges. *International Journal of Advanced Research in Technology and Innovation*, *2*(2), 11–18. http://myjms.moe.gov.my/index.php/ijarti

Adamu, S., Alhussian, H., Abdulkadir, S. J., Alwadin, A., Khairy, S. O. F., Mamman, H., Abdullahi, S., Yahaya, S., Garba, A., Aliyu, D. A., Yakubu, M. M., & Oyefidein, D. T. (2025). Adaptive hybrid hyperparameter optimization with MRFO and Lévy flight for accurate melanoma classification. *Journal of King Saud University. Computer and Information Sciences*, *37*(4), 1–21. DOI: 10.1007/s44443-025-00078-3

Adebisi, B., Aigbedion, E., Ayorinde, O. B., & Onukwulu, C. (n.d.). *A Conceptual Model for Predictive Asset Integrity Management Using Data Analytics to Enhance Maintenance and Reliability in Oil & Gas Operations*. DOI: 10.54660/.IJMRGE.2021.2.1.534-541

Afrin, N., & Pathak, A. (2023). Blockchain-Powered Security and Transparency in Supply Chain: Exploring Traceability and Authenticity through Smart Contracts. *International Journal of Computer Applications*, *185*(49), 975–8887. DOI: 10.5120/ijca2023923318

Ahmad, R. W., Salah, K., Jayaraman, R., Yaqoob, I., & Omar, M. (2022a). Blockchain in oil and gas industry: Applications, challenges, and future trends. *Technology in Society*, *68*, 101941. DOI: 10.1016/j.techsoc.2022.101941

Ahmad, R. W., Salah, K., Jayaraman, R., Yaqoob, I., & Omar, M. (2022b). Blockchain in oil and gas industry: Applications, challenges, and future trends. *Technology in Society*, *68*, 101941. DOI: 10.1016/j.techsoc.2022.101941

Ahmed, S. (2025). Enhancing Data Security and Transparency: The Role of Blockchain in Decentralized Systems. *International Journal of Advanced Engineering, Management and Science (IJAEMS). Peer-Reviewed Journal*, *11*(1), 2454–1311. DOI: 10.22161/ijaems.111.12

Aipoh, G., Egbemhenghe, J., Ogunyankinnu, T., Francis Onotole, E., Osunkanmibi, A. A., & Adeoye, Y. (2022). Blockchain and AI synergies for effective supply chain management. *Article in International Journal of Multidisciplinary Research and Growth Evaluation*. DOI: 10.54660/.IJMRGE.2021.2.4-873-876

Al-Farsi, S., Rathore, M. M., & Bakiras, S. (2021). Security of Blockchain-Based Supply Chain Management Systems: Challenges and Opportunities. *Applied Sciences 2021, Vol. 11, Page 5585, 11*(12), 5585. DOI: 10.3390/app11125585

Ali Sathio Anwar, A. Mujeeb ur Rehman Shaikh, P., & Javeria Shah, P. (2021). Implementation of ETL Tool for Data Warehousing for Non-Hodgkin Lymphoma (NHL) Cancer in Public Sector, Pakistan. *LC International Journal of STEM (ISSN: 2708-7123), 2*(3), 98–102. DOI: 10.5281/ZENODO.5759519

Ali Sathio Benazir Bhutto Shaheed University Lyari Karachi. (2021). Dynamic Content Enabled Microservice for Business Applications in Distributed Cloudlet Cloud Network. *International Journal of Emerging Trends in Engineering Research*, *9*(7), 1035–1039. DOI: 10.30534/ijeter/2021/32972021

Antal, C., Cioara, T., Anghel, I., Antal, M., & Salomie, I. (2021). Distributed Ledger Technology Review and Decentralized Applications Development Guidelines. *Future Internet 2021, Vol. 13, Page 62, 13*(3), 62. DOI: 10.3390/fi13030062

Anwar, A., Ali, A., Benazir, S., Shaheed, B., Lyari, U., Bbsul, (, & Karachi,). (2021). *A Review on State of the Art in Flipped Classroom Technology A Blended E-Learning*. DOI: 10.30534/ijeter/2021/22972021

Babaei, A., Tirkolaee, E. B., & Anka, F. (2024). Efficiency-sustainability models to assess blockchain adoption strategies with uncertainty in the oil and gas sector. *Environment, Development and Sustainability*, •••, 1–27. DOI: 10.1007/s10668-024-05604-3

Barnabas, B., & Oloyede, J. (2024). *Cash Flow Optimization: Strategies for Enhancing Short-Term Liquidity*. DOI: 10.2139/ssrn.5004465

Bello, A. D., Adeoye, Y., Osunkanmibi, A. A., Onotole, E. F., Ogunyankinnu, T., Ederhion, J., & Abubakar, A. (2025). Blockchain and Global Trade: Streamlining Cross Border Transactions with Blockchain. *Article in International Journal of Multidisciplinary Research and Growth Evaluation*. DOI: 10.54660/.IJMRGE.2025.6.2.253-265

Benedetti, H., & Rodriguez-Garnica, G. (2023). Tokenized Assets and Securities. *The Emerald Handbook on Cryptoassets: Investment Opportunities and Challenges*, 107–121. DOI: 10.1108/978-1-80455-320-620221008

Blockis, M. (2025). *The role of stakeholder engagement in business process performance*.

Boggio Viola, A. (2024). *The Tokenization of Assets: Analysing the Emergence of a New Market Trend.*

Brennan, B., & Schafer, L. (n.d.). *Harness Oil and Gas Big Data with Analytics Wiley & SAS Business Series*. Retrieved August 15, 2025, from https://books.google.com/books/about/Harness_Oil_and_Gas_Big_Data_with_Analyt.html?id=imdiAwAAQBAJ

Burger, M., Taken, K., Smith, S. L. M., & Wood, J. (n.d.). An Examination of Fraud Risk at Oil and Gas Companies. *Journal of Forensic & Investigative Accounting*, *14*(1).

Campanella, F., Serino, L., Battisti, E., Giakoumelou, A., & Karasamani, I. (2023). FinTech in the financial system: Towards a capital-intensive and high competence human capital reality? *Journal of Business Research*, *155*, 113376. DOI: 10.1016/j.jbusres.2022.113376

Chandio, S. A., Mahar, J. A., & Shaikh, M. U. R. (2017). Gadget improved security alert monitoring, management and mitigation system to control the crowded occasions. *ICIEECT 2017 - International Conference on Innovations in Electrical Engineering and Computational Technologies 2017, Proceedings*. DOI: 10.1109/ICIEECT.2017.7916557

Chang, V., Baudier, P., Zhang, H., Xu, Q., Zhang, J., & Arami, M. (2020). How Blockchain can impact financial services – The overview, challenges and recommendations from expert interviewees. *Technological Forecasting and Social Change*, *158*, 120166. DOI: 10.1016/j.techfore.2020.120166

Cheng, L., Liu, F., & Yao, D. D. (2017). Enterprise data breach: Causes, challenges, prevention, and future directions. *Wiley Interdisciplinary Reviews. Data Mining and Knowledge Discovery*, *7*(5), e1211. DOI: 10.1002/widm.1211

Chourasiya, R., & Malviya, R. K. (2025). Unlocking Circular Potential and Empowering Circularity: Paving the Path for Circular Supply Chain Enablement in Indian Textile Industries. *Business Strategy and the Environment*, *34*(7), 9441–9462. Advance online publication. DOI: 10.1002/bse.70081

Chowdhury, M. T. A., & Islam, M. A. (1 C.E.). Blockchain Synergies With the Internet of Everything (IoE). Https://Services.Igi-Global.Com/Resolvedoi/Resolve.Aspx?Doi=10.4018/979-8-3373-1424-2.Ch001, 1–38. DOI: 10.4018/979-8-3373-1424-2.ch001

Cordes, E. E., Jones, D. O. B., Schlacher, T. A., Amon, D. J., Bernardino, A. F., Brooke, S., Carney, R., DeLeo, D. M., Dunlop, K. M., Escobar-Briones, E. G., Gates, A. R., Génio, L., Gobin, J., Henry, L. A., Herrera, S., Hoyt, S., Joye, M., Kark, S., Mestre, N. C., & Witte, U. (2016). Environmental impacts of the deep-water oil and gas industry: A review to guide management strategies. *Frontiers in Environmental Science*, *4*(SEP), 207190. DOI: 10.3389/fenvs.2016.00058

Cynthia Onukwulu, E., Efekpogua Fiemotongha, J., Ngochindo Igwe, A., Paul-Mikki Ewim, C., & Author, C. (2025). The Role of Blockchain and AI in the Future of Energy Trading: A Technological Perspective on Transforming the Oil & Gas Industry by 2025. *Int. j. Adv. Multidisc. Res. Stud*, *5*(2), 48–65. DOI: 10.62225/2583049X.2025.5.2.3809

De Filippi, P. (2016). The interplay between decentralization and privacy: the case of blockchain technologies. *Technologies. Journal of Peer Production*. https://hal.science/hal-01382006v1

Deshpande, A. V. (2025). *Enhancing Cross-Border Payment Efficiency with Stablecoins: Reducing Costs and Settlement Delays*. DOI: 10.2139/ssrn.5337435

Dutta, S. K. (2020). Smart Contracts. *The Definitive Guide to Blockchain for Accounting and Business: Understanding the Revolutionary Technology*, 61–78. DOI: 10.1108/978-1-78973-865-020201005

Ebrahimi, S. M., Koh, S. C. L., Genovese, A., & Kumar, N. (2018). Structure-integration relationships in oil and gas supply chains. *International Journal of Operations & Production Management*, *38*(2), 424–445. DOI: 10.1108/IJOPM-02-2016-0089

Egelund-Müller, B., Elsman, M., Henglein, F., & Ross, O. (2017). Automated Execution of Financial Contracts on Blockchains. *Business & Information Systems Engineering*, *59*(6), 457–467. DOI: 10.1007/s12599-017-0507-z

Faccia, A., & Petratos, P. (2021). Blockchain, Enterprise Resource Planning (ERP) and Accounting Information Systems (AIS): Research on e-Procurement and System Integration. *Applied Sciences 2021, Vol. 11, Page 6792, 11*(15), 6792. DOI: 10.3390/app11156792

Farshidi, S., Jansen, S., Espana, S., & Verkleij, J. (2020). Decision Support for Blockchain Platform Selection: Three Industry Case Studies. *IEEE Transactions on Engineering Management*, *67*(4), 1109–1128. DOI: 10.1109/TEM.2019.2956897

Gamso, J., Inkpen, A., & Ramaswamy, K. (2024). Managing geopolitical risks: The global oil and gas industry plays a winning game. *The Journal of Business Strategy*, *45*(3), 190–198. DOI: 10.1108/JBS-04-2023-0081

Gardas, B. B., Raut, R. D., & Narkhede, B. (2019). Determinants of sustainable supply chain management: A case study from the oil and gas supply chain. *Sustainable Production and Consumption*, *17*, 241–253. DOI: 10.1016/j.spc.2018.11.005

Garzali Qabasiyu, M., Ahmed Zayyad, M., & Abdullahi, S. (2023). Systematic Literature Review on Sentence Level Sentiment Analysis. [IJMRAP]. *International Journal of Multidisciplinary Research and Publications*, *6*(5), 1–8. http://scholars .google.com/

Ghadge, N. (2024). Analyzing the Role of Blockchain in Identity and Access Management Systems. SSRN *Electronic Journal*. https://doi.org/DOI: 10.2139/ SSRN.4872028

Ghoddusi, H., Moghaddam, H., & Wirl, F. (2022). Going downstream – An economical option for oil and gas exporting countries? *Energy Policy*, *161*, 112487. DOI: 10.1016/j.enpol.2021.112487

Hader, M., Tchoffa, D., El Mhamedi, A., Ghodous, P., Dolgui, A., & Abouabdellah, A. (2022). Applying integrated Blockchain and Big Data technologies to improve supply chain traceability and information sharing in the textile sector. *Journal of Industrial Information Integration*, *28*, 100345. DOI: 10.1016/j.jii.2022.100345

Hassani, M., Bazaeeand, G., & Shahmansouri, A. (2020). Identifying Blockchain Technology Maturity's Levels in the Oil and Gas Industry. *Petroleum Business Review*, *4*(3), 43–61. DOI: 10.22050/PBR.2020.256181.1138

Hassija, V., Chamola, V., Gupta, V., Jain, S., & Guizani, N. (2021). A Survey on Supply Chain Security: Application Areas, Security Threats, and Solution Architectures. *IEEE Internet of Things Journal*, *8*(8), 6222–6246. DOI: 10.1109/JIOT.2020.3025775

HASSOUNI, L. EL, & OUCHEKKIR, A. (2024). Revolutionizing Financial Markets: The Role of Distributed Ledger Technology in Payments, Clearing, and Settlements. *International Journal of Accounting Finance Auditing Management and Economics*, *5*(10), 198–226. DOI: 10.5281/zenodo.13907838

Hussain, M. I., Bhuiyan, M. K. I., Sumon, S. A., Akter, S., Hossain, M. I., & Akther, A. (2024). Enhancing Data Integrity and Traceability in Industry Cyber Physical Systems (ICPS) through Blockchain Technology: A Comprehensive Approach. *Advances in Artificial Intelligence and Machine Learning*, *4*(4), 2883–2907. DOI: 10.54364/AAIML.2024.44168

Ibrahim Shelash, S., & Ibrahim Al-Daoud, K. (2025). Impact of crude oil price volatility on procurement and inventory strategies in the Middle East International Journal of Energy Economics and Policy Impact of Crude Oil Price Volatility on Procurement and Inventory Strategies in the Middle East. *International Journal of Energy Economics and Policy*, *15*(2), 715–727. DOI: 10.32479/ijeep.18950

Ioannou, I., & Demirel, G. (2022). *Blockchain and supply chain finance: a critical literature review at the intersection of operations, finance and law*. *6*, 83–107. DOI: 10.1007/s42786-022-00040-1

Javed, I. T., Alharbi, F., Margaria, T., Crespi, N., & Qureshi, K. N. (2021). PETchain: A Blockchain-Based Privacy Enhancing Technology. *IEEE Access : Practical Innovations, Open Solutions*, *9*, 41129–41143. DOI: 10.1109/ACCESS.2021.3064896

Kaluvakuri, S., & Amin, R. (2018). From Paper Trails to Digital Success: The Evolution of E-Accounting. *Asian Accounting and Auditing Advancement, 9*(1).

Karisma, K., & Moslemzadeh Tehrani, P. (2023). Blockchain: Legal and Regulatory Issues. *Lecture Notes in Energy*, *98*, 75–118. DOI: 10.1007/978-3-031-30697-6_4

Kelvin Chima, O., Orobosa Ikponmwoba, S., Jacqueline Ezeilo, O., Monday Ojonugwa, B., Olumuyiwa Adesuyi, M., & Author, C. (2020). Advances in Cash Liquidity Optimization and Cross-Border Treasury Strategy in Sub-Saharan Energy Firms. *Journal of Frontiers in Multidisciplinary Research*. DOI: 10.54660/.IJFMR.2020.1.1.44-56

Klems, M., Eberhardt, J., Tai, S., Härtlein, S., Buchholz, S., & Tidjani, A. (2017). Trustless intermediation in blockchain-based decentralized service marketplaces. *Lecture Notes in Computer Science (Including Subseries Lecture Notes in Artificial Intelligence and Lecture Notes in Bioinformatics), 10601 LNCS*, 731–739. https://doi.org/DOI: 10.1007/978-3-319-69035-3_53/FIGURES/2

Ko, T., Lee, J., & Ryu, D. (2018). Blockchain Technology and Manufacturing Industry: Real-Time Transparency and Cost Savings. *Sustainability 2018, Vol. 10, Page 4274, 10*(11), 4274. DOI: 10.3390/su10114274

Labonno, S. I., & Chowdhury, M. T. A. (1 C.E.). Blockchain and IoE Transforming Industry Applications. Https://Services.Igi-Global.Com/Resolvedoi/Resolve.Aspx?Doi=10.4018/979-8-3373-1424-2.Ch007, 177–208. DOI: 10.4018/979-8-3373-1424-2.ch007

Lashkari, B., & Musilek, P. (2021). A Comprehensive Review of Blockchain Consensus Mechanisms. *IEEE Access : Practical Innovations, Open Solutions, 9*, 43620–43652. DOI: 10.1109/ACCESS.2021.3065880

Liu, W., Wang, Y., Shi, Q., Wan, H., & Fu, M. (2022). Optimization of decentralized control strategies of distributed resources under cyber failures in flexible distribution network. *International Journal of Electrical Power & Energy Systems, 142*, 108320. DOI: 10.1016/j.ijepes.2022.108320

Lu, H., Huang, K., Azimi, M., & Guo, L. (2019a). Blockchain technology in the oil and gas industry: A review of applications, opportunities, challenges, and risks. *IEEE Access : Practical Innovations, Open Solutions, 7*, 41426–41444. DOI: 10.1109/ACCESS.2019.2907695

Lu, H., Huang, K., Azimi, M., & Guo, L. (2019b). Blockchain technology in the oil and gas industry: A review of applications, opportunities, challenges, and risks. *IEEE Access : Practical Innovations, Open Solutions, 7*, 41426–41444. DOI: 10.1109/ACCESS.2019.2907695

Lu, H., Huang, K., Azimi, M., & Guo, L. (2019c). Blockchain technology in the oil and gas industry: A review of applications, opportunities, challenges, and risks. *IEEE Access : Practical Innovations, Open Solutions, 7*, 41426–41444. DOI: 10.1109/ACCESS.2019.2907695

Lu, H., Huang, K., Azimi, M., & Guo, L. (2019d). Blockchain technology in the oil and gas industry: A review of applications, opportunities, challenges, and risks. *IEEE Access : Practical Innovations, Open Solutions, 7*, 41426–41444. DOI: 10.1109/ACCESS.2019.2907695

Lu, H., Huang, K., Azimi, M., & Guo, L. (2019e). Blockchain technology in the oil and gas industry: A review of applications, opportunities, challenges, and risks. *IEEE Access : Practical Innovations, Open Solutions, 7*, 41426–41444. DOI: 10.1109/ACCESS.2019.2907695

Lyu, J., Qiu, M., Yang, H., Zhou, D., & Liu, J. (2020). Blockchain Applications in Midstream Oil and Gas Industry. *Society of Petroleum Engineers - Abu Dhabi International Petroleum Exhibition and Conference 2020, ADIP 2020*. DOI: 10.2523/IPTC-19937-Abstract

Malhotra, A., O'Neill, H., & Stowell, P. (2022). Thinking strategically about blockchain adoption and risk mitigation. *Business Horizons, 65*(2), 159–171. DOI: 10.1016/j.bushor.2021.02.033

Mhlanga, D. (2025). Leveraging Blockchain for Sustainable Finance: Insights, Challenges, and Opportunities for Africa. *Financial Inclusion and Sustainable Development in Sub-Saharan Africa*, 52–73. https://doi.org/DOI: 10.4324/9781003515715-4/LEVERAGING-BLOCKCHAIN-SUSTAINABLE-FINANCE-DAVID-MHLANGA

Mohammed, A. S., Reinecke, P., Burnap, P., Rana, O., & Anthi, E. (2022). Cybersecurity Challenges in the Offshore Oil and Gas Industry: An Industrial Cyber-Physical Systems (ICPS) Perspective. *ACM Transactions on Cyber-Physical Systems, 6*(3), 1–27. Advance online publication. DOI: 10.1145/3548691

Nanayakkara, S., Perera, S., Senaratne, S., Weerasuriya, G. T., & Bandara, H. M. N. D. (2021). Blockchain and Smart Contracts: A Solution for Payment Issues in Construction Supply Chains. *Informatics 2021, Vol. 8, Page 36, 8*(2), 36. DOI: 10.3390/informatics8020036

Nguyen, T., Gosine, R. G., & Warrian, P. (2020). A Systematic Review of Big Data Analytics for Oil and Gas Industry 4.0. *IEEE Access : Practical Innovations, Open Solutions, 8*, 61183–61201. DOI: 10.1109/ACCESS.2020.2979678

Nkeonadi, O. P., Kingsley Egbuna, I., Adjei, K. Y., Chukwuma, E. O., Davison Dirisu, C., & Ekechi, C. C.Obinna Paschal NkeonadiIfeanyi Kingsley EgbunaKofi Yeboah AdjeiEmmanuel Onyemeachi ChukwumaChristian Davison DirisuChijioke Cyriacus Ekechi. (2025). Corresponding author: Obinna Paschal Nkeonadi Blockchain technology for secure and transparent oil and gas supply chains. *World Journal of Advanced Research and Reviews, 2025*(03), 1818–1830. DOI: 10.30574/wjarr.2025.26.3.2308

Nura, A., & Abdullahi, S. (2022). A systematic review of multi-depot vehicle routing problems. *Systematic Literature Review and Meta-Analysis Journal*, *3*(2), 51–60. DOI: 10.54480/slrm.v3i2.37

Nwankwo, C. B., & Emmanuel, O. K. (2025). The Role of Blockchain Technology in Enhancing Tax Transparency and Revenue Collection in Nigeria's Oil and Gas Sector. *Journal of Customary and Religious Law*, *2*(2), 97–110. https://journals.unizik.edu.ng/jocarl/article/view/6494

Okah Elumah, L., & Sopelola, T. A. (2025). Exploring Financing Strategies in Oil and Gas Industry: Lessons from Nigeria. *Oil and Gas Economics and Management Research Article Petroleum Business Review*, *9*(1), 1–12. DOI: 10.22050/pbr.2025.502211.1380

Okoh, C. I., & Odorikpe, V. O. (2025). Smart Contracts and Secure Chains: Optimizing Oil and Gas Logistics in a Digital Age. *SPE Nigeria Annual International Conference and Exhibition*. DOI: 10.2118/228706-MS

Olsen, B. E., Haugland, S. A., Karlsen, E., & Husøy, G. J. (2005). Governance of complex procurements in the oil and gas industry. *Journal of Purchasing and Supply Management*, *11*(1), 1–13. DOI: 10.1016/j.pursup.2005.03.003

Omar, I. A., Jayaraman, R., Salah, K., Debe, M., & Omar, M. (2020). Enhancing vendor managed inventory supply chain operations using blockchain smart contracts. *IEEE Access : Practical Innovations, Open Solutions*, *8*, 182704–182719. DOI: 10.1109/ACCESS.2020.3028031

Politou, E., Casino, F., Alepis, E., & Patsakis, C. (2021). Blockchain Mutability: Challenges and Proposed Solutions. *IEEE Transactions on Emerging Topics in Computing*, *9*(4), 1972–1986. DOI: 10.1109/TETC.2019.2949510

Qabasiyu, M. G., Zayyad, M. A., & Abdullahi, S. (2023). An Ensembled Based Machine Learning Technique of Sentiment Analysis. [JTEC]. *Journal of Telecommunication, Electronic and Computer Engineering*, *15*(1), 23–28. DOI: 10.54554/jtec.2023.15.01.004

Rane, S. B., & Narvel, Y. A. M. (2021). Re-designing the business organization using disruptive innovations based on blockchain-IoT integrated architecture for improving agility in future Industry 4.0. *Benchmarking*, *28*(5), 1883–1908. DOI: 10.1108/BIJ-12-2018-0445

Rauniyar, K., Wu, X., Gupta, S., Modgil, S., & Lopes De Sousa Jabbour, A. B. (n.d.). *Risk management of supply chains in the digital transformation era: contribution and challenges of blockchain technology*. DOI: 10.1108/IMDS-04-2021-0235

Rehman, M. ur, Akbar, R., Omar, M., & Gilal, A. R. (2024). A Systematic Literature Review of Ransomware Detection Methods and Tools for Mitigating Potential Attacks. *Communications in Computer and Information Science, 2001 CCIS*, 80–95. DOI: 10.1007/978-981-99-9589-9_7

Rehman, M. ur, Hassan, M. F., Akbar, R., Al-rimy, B. A. S., Savita, K. S., Ullah, R., & Zafar, Z. (2025). *Analyzing Early Indicators of Ransomware: Pre-encryption Behavior Patterns*. 566–578. DOI: 10.1007/978-981-96-5848-0_46

Saka, B. (2024). *Trade Finance and Blockchain Technology: Opportunities to Scale for Big, Small and Medium Enterprises*. https://papers.ssrn.com/abstract=4878957

Sathio, A. A., Ali Dootio, M., Lakhan, A., Rehman, M. U., Orangzeb Pnhwar, A., & Sahito, M. A. (2021). Pervasive Futuristic Healthcare and Blockchain enabled Digital Identities-Challenges and Future Intensions. *Proceedings - 2021 International Conference on Computing, Electronics and Communications Engineering, ICCECE 2021*, 30–35. DOI: 10.1109/iCCECE52344.2021.9534846

Shehu Yalli, J., Hilmi Hasan, M., Samiha Haron, N., Ur Rehman Shaikh, M., Yousuf Murad, N., & Lawal Bako, A. (n.d.). Quality of Data (QoD) in Internet of Things (IOT): An Overview, State-of-the-Art, Taxonomy and Future Directions. *IJACSA) International Journal of Advanced Computer Science and Applications, 14*(12), 2023. Retrieved August 16, 2025, from www.ijacsa.thesai.org

Sulkowski, A. (2018). Blockchain, Business Supply Chains, Sustainability, and Law: The Future of Governance, Legal Frameworks, and Lawyers. *Delaware Journal of Corporate Law, 43*. https://heinonline.org/HOL/Page?handle=hein.journals/decor43&id=311&div=&collection=

Taiwo, T. O. (2020). *An evaluation of contractual clauses used to mitigate risks in long term oil and gas agreements*.

Tavakoli, P., Yitmen, I., Sadri, H., & Taheri, A. (2024). Blockchain-based digital twin data provenance for predictive asset management in building facilities. *Smart and Sustainable Built Environment, 13*(1), 4–21. DOI: 10.1108/SASBE-07-2023-0169

Ullah, F., & Chowdhury, M. T. A. (1 C.E.). Leveraging Smart Contracts for Enhanced IoE Security. Https://Services.Igi-Global.Com/Resolvedoi/Resolve.Aspx?Doi=10.4018/979-8-3373-1424-2.Ch005, 115–154. DOI: 10.4018/979-8-3373-1424-2.ch005

Ur, M., Shaikh, R., Ullah, R., Akbar, R., Savita, K. S., & Mandala, S. (2024). Fortifying Against Ransomware. *International Journal of Academic Research in Business & Social Sciences*, *14*(1). Advance online publication. DOI: 10.6007/IJARBSS/v14-i1/20566

ur Rehman, M., Akbar, R., Mujeeb, S., & Janisar, A. A. (2024). Deep-learning enabled early detection of COVID-19 infection in IoMT fog-cloud healthcare in LPWAN. *Low-Power Wide Area Network for Large Scale Internet of Things: Architectures, Communication Protocols and Recent Trends*, 235–257. https://doi.org/DOI: 10.1201/9781003426974-13/DEEP-LEARNING-ENABLED-EARLY-DETECTION-COVID-19-INFECTION-IOMT-FOG-CLOUD-HEALTHCARE-LPWAN-MUJEEB-UR-REHMAN-REHAN-AKBAR-SHAGUFTA-MUJEEB-AFTAB-ALAM-JANISAR

ur Rehman Shaikh, M., Fadzil Hassan, M., Akbar, R., Ullah, R., Savita, K., Rehman, U., & Shehu Yalli, J. (2024). Pre-Encryption Ransomware Detection (PERD) Taxonomy, and Research Directions: Systematic Literature Review. *IJACSA) International Journal of Advanced Computer Science and Applications, 15*(9). www.ijacsa.thesai.org

Varriale, V., Cammarano, A., Michelino, F., & Caputo, M. (2021). New organizational changes with blockchain: A focus on the supply chain. *Journal of Organizational Change Management*, *34*(2), 420–438. DOI: 10.1108/JOCM-08-2020-0249

Wang, Z., Yu, L., & Zhou, L. (2024). Navigating the Blockchain-Driven Transformation in Industry 4.0: Opportunities and Challenges for Economic and Management Innovations. *Journal of the Knowledge Economy*, *16*(1), 3507–3549. DOI: 10.1007/s13132-024-02007-7

Weijermars, R. (2011). Credit Ratings and Cash-Flow Analysis of Oil and Gas Companies: Competitive Disadvantage in Financing Costs for Smaller Companies in Tight Capital Markets. *SPE Economics & Management*, *3*(02), 54–67. DOI: 10.2118/144489-PA

Yalli, J. S., Hilmi Hasan, M., Tang Jung, L., Ibrahim Yerima, A., Adamu Aliyu, D., Danjuma Maiwada, U., Mahmood Al-Selwi, S., & Ur Rehman Shaikh, M. (2025). A Systematic Review for Evaluating IoT Security: A Focus on Authentication, Protocols and Enabling Technologies. *IEEE Internet of Things Journal*, *12*(12), 18908–18928. DOI: 10.1109/JIOT.2025.3545737

Zakari, A., Abdullahi, S., Shagari, N., Bello Tambawal, A., Musa Shanono, N., Zubairu Maitama, J., Abubakar Rasheed, R., Adamu, A., Mamman Abdulrahman, S., & Abubakar Zakari, B., Zakari α, A., Abdullahi σ, S., Shagari ρ, N., Bello Tambawal , A., Abubakar Rasheed χ Alhassan Adamu ν, R., & Mamman Abdulrahman Θ, S. (2020). Spectrum-based Fault Localization Techniques Application on Multiple-Fault Programs. *RE:view*.

Zakari, A., Modi Shagari, N., & Sofian, H. (2021). *Systematic Literature Review in Software Testing*. https://www.researchgate.net/publication/354632499

Zarrin, J., Wen Phang, H., Babu Saheer, L., & Zarrin, B. (2021). Blockchain for decentralization of internet: Prospects, trends, and challenges. *Cluster Computing*, *24*(4), 2841–2866. DOI: 10.1007/s10586-021-03301-8

Zuo, Y., & Qi, Z. (2022). A Blockchain-Based IoT Framework for Oil Field Remote Monitoring and Control. *IEEE Access : Practical Innovations, Open Solutions*, *10*, 2497–2514. DOI: 10.1109/ACCESS.2021.3139582

Zyskind, G., Nathan, O., & Pentland, A. S. (2015). Decentralizing privacy: Using blockchain to protect personal data. *Proceedings - 2015 IEEE Security and Privacy Workshops. SPW*, *180–184*, 180–184. Advance online publication. DOI: 10.1109/SPW.2015.27

# Chapter 4
# Harnessing the Synergy of AI and Blockchain in Energy Toward Hybrid Intelligent Systems

**Anita Shukla**
https://orcid.org/0009-0008-1906-3016
*Poornima University, Jaipur, India*

**Nikhil Kumar Goyal**
https://orcid.org/0009-0007-4532-8033
*Poornima University, Jaipur, India*

## ABSTRACT

*In this chapter, the transformative power behind AI-blockchain convergence in energy systems is explored. It investigates the use of AI-enhanced technologies to assist with load forecasting, predictive maintenance as well as energy efficiency, how blockchain can be used to enable verifying transactions, participating in a decentralized market and having tamper-proof records in areas like peer-to-peer energy trading or managing a micro-grid. The combination of the two technologies leads to a paradigm, in which energy systems may become both intelligent and trustless, both decentralised and coordinated.*

DOI: 10.4018/979-8-3373-5457-6.ch004

# 1. INTRODUCTION

## 1.1 Digital Transformation of the Energy Sector

One enormous change that the energy industry is going through is digitalization. In the past, energy systems were one-directional, moving the power towards customers under central power plants. Nevertheless, the landscape has changed due to several factors, including the rising penetration of distributed energy resources e.g., solar photovoltaics and wind turbines, the rise of energy needs and environmental regulations thereof. Energy networks are changing to become more complex, decentralized and data-rich systems that need to be responsive in real-time and intelligent decision making.

Such a transformation has led to the emergence of smart grids, microgrids, and distributed generation systems in which data are the core in monitoring, control, and optimization. The prevalence of sensors, Internet of Things (IoT), and smart meters has made it possible to produce floods of operation data on a continuous basis. It is also ineffective to handle this information manually, and in this regard, advanced digital technologies are being introduced to render value, grid stability and achieve sustainability objectives (Andoni et al., 2019).

Digitalization does not only increase the efficiency of operations it also makes energy systems more reliable and resilient. As the weather gets more extreme, renewable sources and cyber threats become more prevalent, and the renewable sources are dynamic to some degree, the use of conventional control measures is found wanting. Real-time analytics, intelligent automation, and decentralized decision-making is more crucial than ever before, establishing the environment of adopting advanced technologies such as Artificial Intelligence (AI) and blockchain.

The progress of digital technologies is not simply a convenience, it is becoming a matter of necessity in the view of providing energy systems with guarantees of sustainability, flexibility, and security in the future. With energy shifting to a consumer-based and renewable-friendly paradigm shift, digital transformation is shaping the foundation of innovation and modernization.

## 1.2 Emerging Technologies in Smart Energy

New technologies, especially Artificial Intelligence and blockchain are seeing the light of the day to become key facilitators of smart energy systems. AI equips energy infrastructures with AI-powered intelligent forecasting, optimization and automation. It is able to forecast electricity demand, diagnose bulbs failures beforehand, optimise the flow of power in real-time uses and predict the consumer behavior to improve energy efficiency. An example is that machine learning algorithms can combine consumption trends and weather patterns and predict renewable generation or grid load (Mengelkamp et al., 2018).

At the same time, blockchain technologies add a reliable, untamperable, and clear layer to energy systems. Blockchain has the potential to make peer-to-peer (P2P) energy trading secure and its contracts automated through smart contracts, as well as keep verifiable energy records by avoiding the need of intermediaries to provide a decentralized form of consensus. This makes it immutable and thus auditability of each and every transaction, which is very paramount in energy market, which aims at building trust and regulation.

A combination of such technologies can impact the energy industry, handling major difficulties that exist within it. AI would be able to make decisions, and blockchain would be able to store them securely and validate them. As an example, AI can be used to tell when the surplus solar energy must be sold and the blockchain can program the transaction to happen automatically and safely by means of a smart contract. This combination of intelligence and trust gives energy systems a better autonomy, transparency, and resilience (Stoll et al., 2019).

The combination of AI, blockchain will result in yet another category of energy solution: a discretionary, smart block, and also energy solutions that are foresighted as well as adaptive. These hybrid systems are a dramatic change towards the old forms of practice and they give the base of the intelligent energy infrastructures of the future.

## 1.3 Rationale for Synergizing AI and Blockchain in Energy Systems

The alignment of AI and blockchain in energy is driven by a desire to address the drawbacks of isolated application of any of the two technologies. Whereas AI is smart and adaptable, it is normally used as a central decision engine, and this therefore needs vast amount of data and reliable sources of data. On the other hand, blockchain is decentralised and has trust but it does not make decisions or draw conclusions based on complicated data. The two when combined provide a more balanced and competent solution (Khan et al., 2026).

Some of the decisions in energy systems have to be made on-site, in a secure, and timely manner. To provide just one example, both real-time intelligence and trusted execution environment will be needed to decide how to route electricity when there are high demand, how to absorb a surge capacity of local renewable generation sources, or how to automatically initiate a window to bring maintenance tasks on-line. AI gives us the decision model and blockchain makes sure that such decisions are verified, documented and implemented without anyone touching it or requiring a centralized system.

Decentralization offered by blockchain also increases the scalability and robustness of energy-based AI applications. Old-school AI models usually bring the problem of centralized data storage and processing that creates data security, privacy, and single point of failure concerns. With the help of blockchain, the integrity of the data present in a distributed set of nodes can be maintained and through smart contracts, decisions can be collectively made in a manner that is not dependent on trust (Goyal et al., 2025).

These technologies are combined by the need to develop another generation of user-centric intelligent autonomous energy systems. The systems are able to adjust to dynamic environments, minimise the cost of operation, empower the consumer and help realise sustainable energy objectives. The AI and blockchain synergy have the potential of more than just optimizing energy efficiency but also democratizing access and control which is a big step towards the global energy transition.

## 2. ARTIFICIAL INTELLIGENCE IN ENERGY SYSTEMS

### 2.1 AI Techniques for Energy Forecasting and Load Balancing

Artificial Intelligence (AI) is quickly changing the manner in which the modern energy systems are designed, run and optimized. One of the most important fields of its use is the sphere of energy forecasting and load balancing. The subduing of power grids demands proper forecasting, and in the phase where renewable energy sources, such as solar and wind, are becoming more prevalent. Such sources are highly unstable and sensitive to the weather conditions, so the classical methods of forecasting are not efficient.

Machine learning (ML) and deep learning models of AI are particularly good at working with non-linear, high-dimension, and complex data sets. In forecasting the future of energy, any past consumption data as well as meteorological patterns, time-of-use variables, and even consumer behavioral data can then be used as input into AI algorithms to produce an energy demand forecast. Such methods are typically artificial neural networks (ANN), long short-term memory (LSTM) nets and support vector machines (SVM). Since these models are abile to acquire prior patterns and regularly adjust to modifications in input variable, they are more likely to acquire accuracy with the progression of time (IEA, 2021).

Load balancing alternatively is the unsteady process of energy load-shedding over the multifaceted circuitry of the energy grid. The AI systems can help to monitor the real-time data provided by the smart meters and sensors installed anywhere in the grid and make decisions autonomously on how to redistribute loads to prevent the congestion, losses, and uninterrupted supply. The current version of AI (reinforcement learning, or RL) is especially applicable in this case, because it enables the system to simply test and figure out optimal strategies during the simulated environment and then execute them in real-time running.

The reality of AI-powered load balancing programs can be observed at the pilot of the smart grid in developed countries where the real-time analysis of the grid with the use of AI algorithms and the decision to share loads in several milliseconds are already implemented. Such real-time flexibility is vital in averting black-outs and enhancing the general performance of the energy distribution. Excessive renewable, through these AI systems, aligns generation capacity to demand and insures that there is little curtailment of renewable and efficient use of energy in areas that have had high penetration of renewables (Power Ledger, 2022).

Both the forecasting and load balance achieved through AI can save costs in addition to improving the operational efficiency and being environmentally friendly. Wait-offs Utilities that predict peak loads can avoid overuse of fossil-fuel based peaking plants by shifting loads off-peak through the use of demand response mechanisms. This intelligent balancing between supply and demand makes the energy system stronger, less environmentally harmful and customer focused.

## 2.2 Predictive Maintenance and Fault Detection

The second crucial AI use in the energy industry can be referred to as predictive maintenance and fault detection. Time or reactive strategies are the traditional models of maintaining energy systems, a process that is slowly being used out in favor of more modern condition based and predictive methods of maintenance. In such older models there can be a lot of inefficiency as it may result in maintenance where the equipment may be in good health whereas there can be no maintenance which may disrupt the business and lead to expensive repair works. AI can help resolve it since it allows conducting data-driven maintenance that prevents critical problems that cannot be predicted.

Predictive maintenance is based on information managed by sensors installed on transformer, turbine, circuit breaker, and switch-gear. This information consists of temperature, vibration, current, voltage, humidity, and other operation counts. AI algorithms read this data to predict trends, trends, and predict remaining useful life (RUL) of every component. Anomaly detection models, decision trees, and recurrent neural networks (RNNs) tools are used to constantly examine and analyze these signals (Bellagarda & Abu-Mahfouz, 2022).

As an example, it is possible to imagine a wind turbine having a system of several sensors control its gear assembly and rotor blade. A system AI works with this data and detects changes in the frequency of vibrations that might point at misalignment or wear. The system alerts the maintenance personnel about the problem and identifies the problem before the fault condition degenerates into a major shutdown and hence the maintenance team can attend to the problem during a planned shutdown with minimal interference.

In addition, to monitoring individual components, AI-based fault-detection systems can be applied globally to the entire energy network. In a substation and distribution lines, the AI eases in fault-locating, isolation of affected parts and restoration of service within a short interval of time. Remote inspection of transmission infrastructure (e.g., power lines and substations) is also being performed through computer vision systems which are built using AI. Drones with AI cameras can be used to scan areas to check on crack or corrosion or excessive growth of vegetation, this removes to large deals the need for inspection by technicians (Google, 2019).

Once predictive maintenance using AI is adopted, it increases safety, reliability, and efficiency through the execution of operations. It also results in significant cost savings, extending asset life and reducing the costs used in emergency repairs. Due to the higher degree of distribution and complexity in the energy systems, the need of AI in the maintenance of uninterrupted functioning systems becomes more vital.

## 2.3 Intelligent Energy Optimization and Demand Response

Energy optimization has taken on a new impetus, owing to the world that is slowly becoming dominated with the need to achieve sustainability, and changing energy requirements. AI allows such optimization in that large data is analyzed to regulate control and tune the energy production, distribution, and usage. The objectives are to minimize energy waste, cut operating expenses and ensure the high quality of services all without considering the need to incorporate renewable resources.

At the generation level, AI is able to tell the best time to reap energy source. In a solar, wind, and battery storage hybrid energy system, AI algorithms can çombine different real-time considerations, including weather forecasts, market prices, grid constraint, etc., to choose the most economically and efficiently priced energy mix. As an example, when the solar production is low, AI can decide to use battery-stored energy or withdraw power at wind plants and maintain the stable operation without surpassing carbon limits (Siano, 2014).

Demand-side On the demand side, AI maximises use of demand response programs in intelligent load management. The programs manipulate or adjust the electric consumption at peak hours according to the supply conditions. The AI models are able to examine the usage patterns of the past, occupancy, weather predictions, and appliance usages in order to suggest or even automatically perform energy saving measures. In commercial buildings, this may include temporarily turning down the HVAC or turning down non-essential lights during peak pricing hours, all in a coordinated fashion so as not to have the effect of affecting occupant comfort.

In the case of residential users, AI can be implemented into smart thermostats and home energy control systems and energy charging of electric vehicles (EVs) as a way of optimizing consumption. With time, AI may be able to learn user preferences and adjust itself autonomously to a middle ground in between comfort and efficiency. In such regions where there would be a dynamic pricing mechanism, such an optimization is also associated with huge savings on the part of the consumer.

Moreover, AI is critical in the optimization of grid-edge, where a real-time interaction of individual objects/buildings with the grid occurs. AI will allow prosumers (consumers who also produce energy) to decide when it is advantageous to sell energy to the market or when it is beneficial to store energy according to market conditions and their personal consumption needs. This non-central optimisation will help to the total stability of a grid and encourage active involvement of consumers to energy ecosystems (Lin et al., 2026).

In short, energy optimization on AI improves all tiers of the energy value chain. It promotes smarter decisions and allocation of resources; it provides more sustainable energy consumption patterns. The next generation of intelligent energy systems will be to increase the level of sophistication of AI in demand-side management and grid operations as it continues to develop.

## 3. BLOCKCHAIN TECHNOLOGY IN THE ENERGY SECTOR

### 3.1 Decentralization and Transparency in Energy Transactions

The Blockchain paradigm is essentially transforming the way transactions are being made and verified and more so in the sectors whose cartels are traditionally centered on a centralized authority to that of decentralized control and trust. Energy is another industry where the possibility of disintermediation is offered by blockchain as it can help in decentralizing the process of energy exchange by doing away with the role of utility companies and regulations by the government. Such a change of the concept of central authority system to a distributed ledger system is one of the innovations in energy markets design.

Decentralization allows all the participants of the energy network, including homeowners with solar panels and industrial power generators, to connect with others without involving a third party in such an interaction. Blockchain is able to do this because it has a distributed tamperproofed ledger in which all players are in agreement on the history of transactions with their agreement facilitated by consensus protocols. Such peer-to-peer (P2P) framework minimizes administrative overhead, and also increases operational efficiency and reductions in costs such as clearing, settlement and auditing (Bukhari et al., 2025).

The other core advantage is transparency. All of the transaction on the blockchain is broadcasted to all the authorized nodes making it fully traceable and accountable. This transparency plays a very significant role in energy market in terms of price fairness as well as regulatory compliance and prevention of fraud. In another example, a consumer feeding on electric energy supplied by a green energy supplier may use blockchain to verify the place of generation, assuring they are feeding on electric energy supplied by renewable energy sources. Such verifiability is significant as sustainability reporting and carbon credit schemes.

Additionally, the indelible quality of blockchain records ensure that transactions recorded in the ledger cannot be changed. The result of respective data integrity is the development of trust between the market participants, regulators and consumers. Blockchain provides a clean, secure, and transparent infrastructure around which the energy systems of the future can be developed as energy systems get more digitized and decentralized.

## 3.2 Peer-to-Peer (P2P) Energy Trading Systems

The use of blockchain in energy to enable peer-to-peer (P2P) energy trading may be one of the most promising applications of blockchain to the energy sector. The traditional energy markets are vertically integrated and big utilities dominate generation, transmission and distribution. Consumers are mere spectators who are unable to place their own controls on the rates at which energy is to be purchased. Blockchain is changing this paradigm by allowing consumers to be active prosumers producer and consumer of energy and be able to trade energy with those around them in a decentralized market place (Zhang et al., 2018).

The use of blockchain in P2P energy trading platforms consists in matching energy supply and demand on a local scale. As an example, households with rooftop solar panels in a residential neighborhood can be generating electricity surplus to usage in the daytime. Rather than selling this excess energy back to the grid at wholesale rates, they will be able to sell it in person to the people around them through smart contracts. Such contracts automate a transaction and change the owner of the energy and transfer the payment securely and in a moment.

Decentralized markets of this nature do not only promote use of renewable energy but also enhance the level of grid resilience. The rendering and utilization of the energy at the local level means reduction of transmission cuts, and makes the grid less dependent on the centralized infrastructure. Blockchain makes each trade transparent, traceable, and permanent, and the occurrence of fraud or disagreement becomes less likely (Khan & Salah, 2018).

Some practical applications prove the feasibility of this model. Efforts such as Brooklyn Microgrid in the United States and Power Ledger in Australia have created block chain platforms to encourage P2P trading amongst community members and generate revenue for community based owners. Through these platforms, energy independence will be advanced, dependence on fossil-energy sources will be minimized, and new economic potential will be received by small-scale energy generators.

## 3.3 Blockchain for Grid Security and Data Integrity

Modern energy systems require plenty of security and integrity of data. Since a variety of millions of IoT devices, sensors, and digital controllers come to be integrated into smart grids, the latter is getting more open to cyberattacks or data manipulation. The provision of a distributed and tamper-proof ledger through the use of blockchain is a viable defense mechanism capable of protecting the data on any level of the energy infrastructure.

A block in the blockchain includes a cryptographic hash of earlier block, a timestamp and a record of transactions. This block-chaining will make it extremely hard to tamper with any record without tampering with all following blocks in chained order, i.e., it makes it computationally infeasible to alter unless one has got the majority of the network. This makes blockchain suitable in obscuring sensitive information like the energy usage history, device records, transactional histories (Di Silvestre et al., 2020).

It is possible to apply blockchain to the control command sent to devices within the grid. (As an example, disconnection orders of a part of the grid, which may receive during the maintenance or the emergency, it is possible to validate on the blockchain, and only those orders that administrators allow to be fulfilled can be fulfilled). This does not allow rogue computers to gain unlawful control and access of the system by using unauthorized commands or sending spoofed messages.

Furthermore, blockchain-powered identity administration can confirm as well as validate equipment and users. With issuing digital identities through blockchain we can help energy systems regulate access rights and restrict irrelevant players or actors in potentially critical processes. The strategy will boost the system-wide cyber-resilience of the energy infrastructure.

Increasing the intelligence and the interconnectedness of the energy grid, it is necessary to focus on the integrity, confidentiality, and availability of data. A blockchain offers a stable bottom under which tampering is not possible and, additionally, auditability and compliance can be achieved in even more complicated virtual circumstances (IBM, 2020).

# 4. AI AND BLOCKCHAIN IN SMART ENERGY

## 4.1 Hybrid Intelligent Energy Systems

The technology of Artificial Intelligence (AI) and blockchain in the energy environment is not just a technological fashion, but the need to address difficult issues of energy systems. The conventional energy systems are fumbling against the increased demands, unforeseeable generation of renewable energy and the requirement of decentralization. These issues can be resolved in more of an all-in-one approach using a new kind of hybrid intelligent system combining the advantages of the AI decision making with the secure transaction network structure of blockchain.

Artificial intelligence provides the ultimate computational brainpower to ensure optimization, prediction, and automatization of grid operations are available in real-time. It will be able to dynamically respond to any changes in demand and detect outliers, and consequently, alter generation and distribution. But the structure of AI systems is usually central, and it is based on trusted sources of data, which contributes to single points of failure and data integrity problems (Shieh et al., 2026).

The weaknesses are complemented by blockchain through its distributed control of data and the rule of tamper-proof event loggings. It declares that the decisions making of the AI is on justified data that has been proven true, and its performance is safely logged. Such convergence can lead to the production of energy systems which are not only adaptive and smart but also transparent, self-regulating and secure.

Such systems are particularly needed where high reliability and low latency requirement is necessary and that includes industrial facilities, hospitals and emergency response centers. In this case, the capability of making independent decisions and implementing the decisions without human interference safely could be a difference between business sustainability and failure to operational maintenance.

*Figure 1. AI–Blockchain integration enabling trustable, decentralized, and intelligent energy applications.*

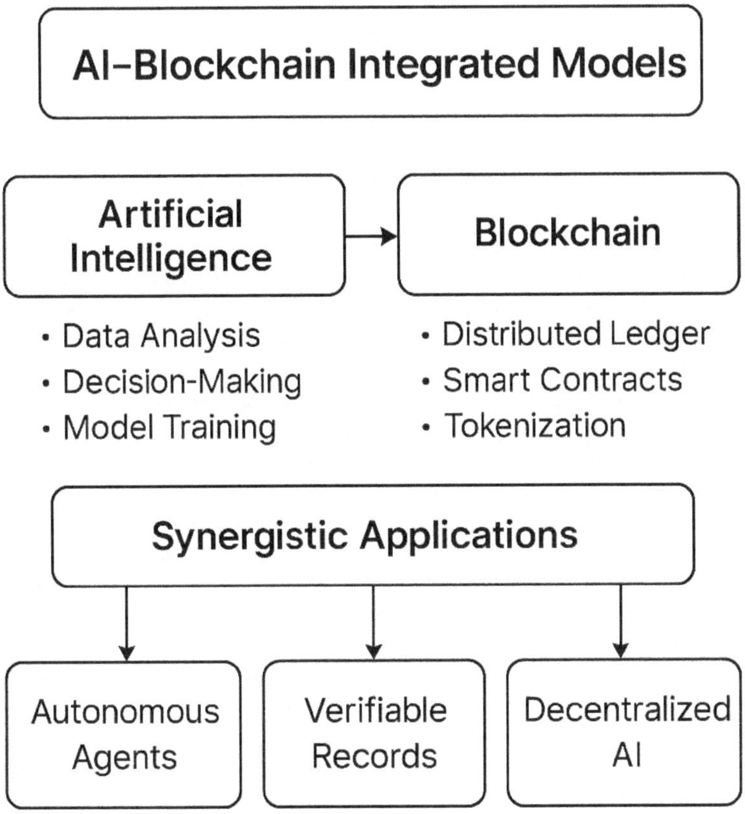


The hybrid intelligent systems play a key role in facilitating participation by the prosumers, decentralized energy transactions, and local energy controls. The integration of intelligence and trust to the communities enables the communities to look after their energy requirements, and this can allow the energy transition to become more inclusive and sustainable (Silic et al., 2025).

## 4.2 Architecture of AI–Blockchain-Integrated Models

The successful development of an integrated system based on the combination of AI and blockchain means the use of multi-level architecture where each layer is designed to meet certain tasks but make the entire system capable of interacting with each other. The system normally has a data acquisition layer, an AI processing layer, a blockchain consensus and execution layer and an application interface layer.

*Figure 2. Hybrid energy system using AI for decisions and blockchain for secure execution*

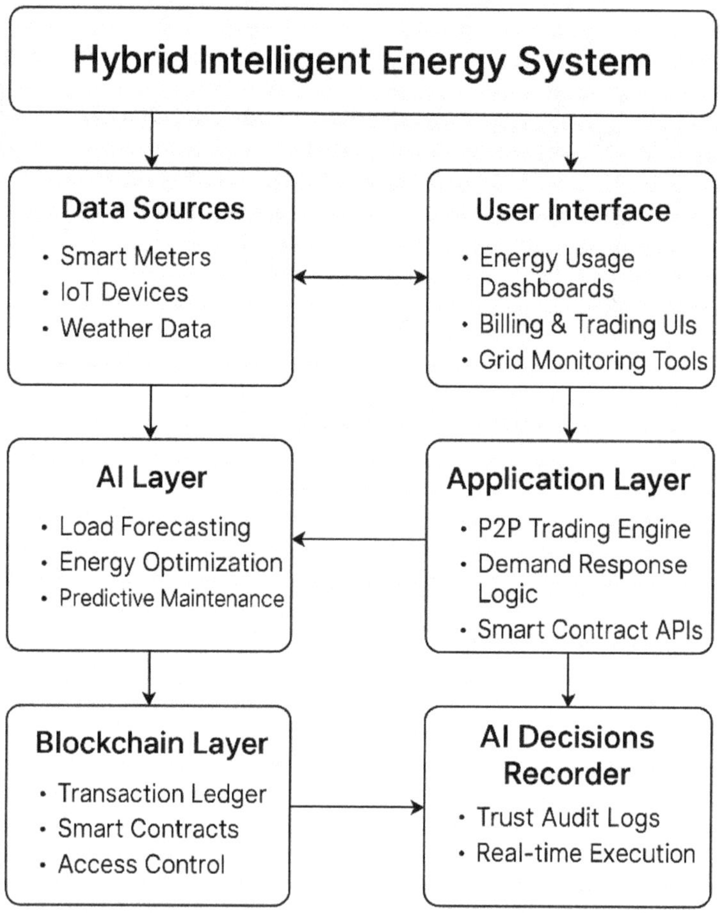


The lowest layer is data acquisition layer where the real-time data is gathered based on energy meters, IoT devices, weather stations, and user interface. It is raw data which is pre-processed and sent to the AI processing layer where machine learning model analyzes patterns, predicts outcomes and generates control actions. Such outputs are then relayed to a blockchain level where the logic is authenticated by smart contracts, and the transaction is registered and response is initiated (Kumari et al., 2020).

As an example, when an AI model forecasts a peak demand in a residential micro grid it can propose to obtain the power out of a nearby battery storage device. The smart contract approves of the decision and checks availability of energy and performs the transaction by updating the digital record and sending the control signals to the battery. The whole process which incorporates collection of data, to making the transaction settlement is automatic, secure and audit-able.

Intermediary entities secure these layers so that there is effective communication between them without any reduction in performance and security. They as well promote the interoperability with the already existing grid management systems allowing them to be integrated gradually without the necessity of a total overhauling of infrastructures. The application interface layer includes identity and access management, encryption services and monitoring dashboards to allow the user and operators to have real-time views and control (Osman et al., 2018).

This architecture guarantees its scalability, modularity and strength, which makes it usable in a variety of situations whether that be a national smart grid, an industrial microgrid or peer to peer energy community.

## 4.3 Use Cases: Energy Market Automation and Microgrid Management

Cartesian products of AI and blockchain have become already actively implemented in numerous practical cases all over the world. Automating the energy market is one of the most effective applications. The current conventional energy markets entail elaborate price discovery mechanism, demand matching, billing and settlements which are tedious and inefficient. Artificial intelligence is able to predict the trends of the market and the level of demand and blockchain makes it possible to auto and exchange all in real time with its involvement of smart contracts.

The model comes in handy in real-time wholesale market where fast decisions have to be made. AI makes decisions on the bid and supply at optimal levels in historical data and the prevailing grid conditions. It guarantees that trades are undertaken and statistics are kept in time, avoiding administrative delays and leading to efficiency in the market, through blockchain. This automaticity will improve liquidity and entry thresholds to minor competitors (Bendiab et al., 2023).

Another area that AI and blockchain implementation is useful is microgrid management. Microgrids refer to nearby power frameworks, which have some capacity to work freely or in combination with the general grid. AI can be useful in controlling generation, storage, and usage in the micro grid and the blockchain allows exchanging energy between users and documenting all the operations in a transparent way.

Take the example of a university campus whereby solar panels that produce extra energy during the day can be in a microgrid. This energy surplus is predicted by AI and then planned that it can share between other buildings on campus. Blockchain carries out the trade and makes sure the departmental bills are billed accurately. This is automated and a real-time system that promotes energy-efficiency, accountability, and cost-saving (Stolakis et al., 2026).

All these applications explain that the intersection of AI and blockchain is not a hypothetical structure but a functional platform to creates energy systems of the future, systems that are more intelligent, safer, and fairer.

## 5. BENEFITS OF AI–BLOCKCHAIN SYNERGY IN ENERGY

*Figure 3. Key benefits of combining AI and blockchain in the energy sector*

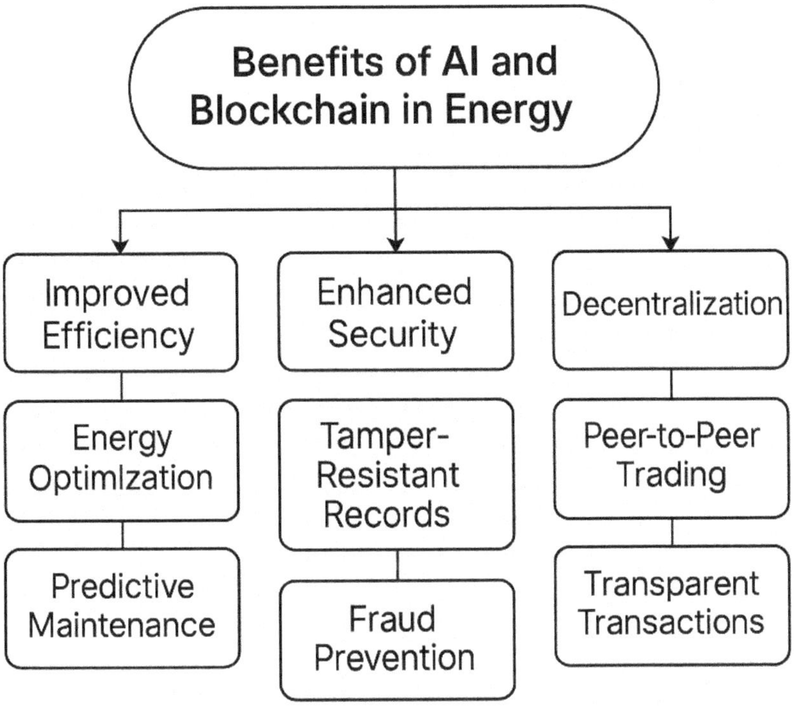


### 5.1 Enhanced Security, Efficiency, and Automation

With the development of Artificial Intelligence and blockchain technologies, an upgrade is achieved with several space dimensions in the classical energy infrastructure. Among the core advantages, there is the improvement of the system security. Security flaws including directing or manipulating information and illegal entry as well as cyber-physical assaults are a grave risk to continuity and reliability in digital energy networks. The power of AI to detect network and device intrusions and anomalies in real time conveys the ability to sift through large quantities of data. Machine learning algorithms built on past performance can identify fine variations that could be an alarm signal of breakage or system error.

Blockchain enhances this layer of security by providing the integrity and verifiability of the press data. All the actions, including a demand forecast, power transactions, and grid responses, are permanently written on the distributed ledger. This averts retroactive tampering and helps in audit trail on faith. Smart contracts also automate operations ensuring that there is no human custody over security policies. As an example, blockchain may be applied to ensure that the command sent by AI agents is authentic and only a command that is with certain criterion can be automatically completed (Swan, 2015).

Regarding operational efficiency, AI streamlines energy flows happening on the supply-side, as well as, the demand-side. It constantly tunes parameters such as load patterns, generation expenses and grid conditions to dynamically define the energy flow. These optimizations are validated and automated in blockchain, making the overhead of a traditional energy settlement process lower. The AI blockchain synergy brings down the cost of transactions, lowers latency or time delay, and makes the markets more receptive and responsive because no third parties are involved.

A logical result of this integration is automation. AI leads to autonomous decisions and blockchain makes sure they have been carried and recorded without an objection. Such a degree of closed-loop control will be important in the future energy networks with minimal human interaction where a system should be self-adjusted to changes caused by real-time initiations.

## 5.2 Empowering Decentralized Renewable Energy Networks

With the decarbonization process that the world is undergoing, decentralized renewable energy systems are on the rise. These entail roof-top solar, neighborhood wind parks, micro-hydro, and energy storage. Nevertheless, decentralized network management comes with fresh complications. Systems dumbed down In the absence of a centralized control organ, the systems must be flanked by smart, trust-based structures in order to function independently and equally.

Artificial intelligence and blockchain have synergy that enables such systems to be powerful by ensuring that they have the tools that they require to be intelligent and coordinated. Using the information on weather and past usage and device behaviour, AI models can predict energy generation and consumption patterns. This is critical to leveling local grids that are dependent on the intermittent sources such as solar and wind. As an example, AI can forecast a solar production that exceeds the needs of the next few hours and propose to deliver that excess to the neighborhood houses or pack it in batteries (Hassan et al., 2019).

Blockchain makes sure that distribution of this energy is provided securely and transparently. It is able to take note of the amounts of energy contributed by whom, consumed by whom and how much money was paid or charged. Within community microgrids, tokens that are blockchain-based may represent energy units, allowing a local energy economy, where prosumers may transact with each other without any references to utilities.

In this decentralization, inclusivity and resilience are encouraged. Underserved or Rural communities can leverage to be energy self-sustaining and can save in the money spent on the power business, making profits and reap economic benefits by selling extra energy. Blockchain makes such transactions tamper proof, and AI is making them economically and technically optimized. Collectively, the technologies are advantageous in terms of democratized energy environment where users are in charge, see, and are motivated to actively engage in the development of sustainable energy.

## 5.3 Trust Architecture and Consumer-Centric Design in Hybrid Energy Systems

Trust has been a major blockade in the use of digitalization of energy systems, especially over consumer concerns of price and fidelity, information security and resilience of the grid. The combination of AI and the blockchain will respond to them directly by introducing the assurance into the system design.

Blockchain brings transparency in its nature. Each transaction is time-stamped, verifiable and publicly auditable (in permissioned cases) in the form of payment, a control signal, or a record of consumption. Customers may check their bills, know their carbon footprint, and ascertain that the energy they buy is renewable. This openness creates trust in the system and it tempers quarrelling (Ouaissa et al., 2025).

Transparency is supplemented with individuality and smartness that is offered by AI. This can be used to provide consumers with actionable information depending on the usage of their energy. As an example, AI may indicate when to run high-power appliance equipment in order to save money, or it may inform about the economic value of rooftop solar. Such individualized recommendations enhance the engagement level and volume of behavioral changes that can favor efficiency and sustainability.

Moreover, blockchain gives the management of data ownership and consents. The user has the ability to manage what possibilities they have with relation to sharing their energy usage data, and is able to make it monetizable within data marketplaces given the option. One can utilize smart contracts to implement user-preferred privacy policies that facilitate a complete control of personal identities in the energy network (Hassani et al., 2018).

Combined, AI and blockchain do not only enhance the technical operation of the energy systems, but also the user experience, loyalty, and involvement. Such a comprehensive change is inevitably critical to the wide adoption of the next-generation energy solutions and worldwide meeting the sustainability goals.

## 6. TECHNICAL CHALLENGES AND FUTURE RESEARCH DIRECTIONS

### 6.1 Scalability and Interoperability Issues

AI-blockchain synergy has obvious potential, but there are a few technical hindrances that affect its scalability, and one of the most noticeable ones details the factors that affect the scalability. AI systems and particularly deep learning based systems need a lot of data and computing power. It is typically infeasible to run such systems at the edge, where bandwidth is scarce and processing and storage are limited (e.g. next to energy devices such as smart meters, or inverters).

Likewise, blockchain networks especially the publicly available networks such as Ethereum or Bitcoin, suffer limitations in terms of scalability because of its consensus process. Such systems are able to deal with only a finite amount of transactions per second, which results in lag and imminent delays. Such delays may not be tolerated in a high-frequency energy trading setup or in a real-time grid control system. Single layers, currently under experimentation are layer-2 solutions, sharding and newer models of consensus like Proof of Stake, Energy adoption of these solutions is at early stages.

There is another layer of complexity in interoperability. The energy ecosystems are based on different systems and devices produced by different manufacturers each of which has communication protocols and data formations. To run AI and blockchain in such a heterogeneous environment, one will have to standardize, and this is not in place yet. As an example, the smart contracts created to operate on a particular blockchain platform might not work on a different one, and the AI models created with the use of certain data sets might not generalize on further grids arrangements (De Mauro et al., 2016).

This is due to the fact that the issues leave silos and restrict the free flow of data and actions down the energy value chain. That means that the topic of scalability and interoperability is a significant research priority involving cooperation between the academic progress, the industry, and standards bodies.

## 6.2 Energy Consumption of Blockchain Protocols

Bizarrely, the use of blockchain in energy systems gives thoughts to energy consumption. The most recognized and at the same time the most infamous consensus mechanism is Proof of Work (PoW) that consumes a lot of energy. The energy cost involved in cracking cryptographic puzzles contributes to high carbon emission that goes against the objective of setting up sustainable energy plants.

Other consensus mechanisms that have more energy efficient solutions like Proof of Stake (PoS), Delegated Proof of Stake (DPoS) and Proof of Authority (PoA) usage are still in progress especially when it comes to utility-centric applications. In addition, the use of such mechanisms on permissioned blockchain networks that are more enterprise-friendly needs proper identity and access control models.

Besides, storage requirements using blockchain are extensive. Every node within the network has to maintain either a copy or partial copy of the ledger that keeps increasing. This presents a problem to the edge device and microgrid with a low bandwidth and memory characteristics. Such technologies as pruning, off-chain storage, and federated consensus can be used to balance such concerns, but researchers need to advance in order to optimize blockchain to be used in energy-limited settings (Abdulrahman et al., 2023).

In order to implement blockchain in the energy sector successfully, it is necessary to make it greener and avail more efficiently. That means not only technology innovations but also policy support, monetary incentives and strict performance comparison to the traditional systems.

## 6.3 Data Privacy, Governance, and Standardization

The other huge impediment is the issue of data privacy and governance within the realm of AI-blockchain-banished systems. AI lives off data, but the granularer (fine-grained), the better the predictions. Nevertheless, energy consumption records may be used to disclose confidential data such as user preferences, the way people use their appliances, including occupancy patterns. That is a fair warning concerning surveillance, profiling and data abuse.

By its nature, blockchain retains information in unchangeable records, available to several parties. Unless privacy controls are utilised sufficiently, such openness might result in problems with privacy. Proposed solutions Zero-knowledge proofs, homomorphic encryption, and differential privacy are emerging cryptographic techniques that could be candidates, but remain computationally demanding and hard to scale (Mamodiya et al., 2025).

The situation with governance is no less complicated. In the decentralized networks, there are the inquiries of who owns the infrastructure, who is going to update information, and how should the conflict be settled. Although many activities can be automated with smart contracts, it is not possible to cover all cases, particularly in dynamic and so high-stake environments, such as energy grids. A potential model of governance is Decentralized Autonomous Organizations (DAOs), however, they are not mature and are not recognized by regulators.

The last aspect of the puzzle is standardization. Absence of standard rules regarding the communication between the devices, data formats, AI models trading, and smart contract building programs, makes the idea of interoperability nothing more but a dream. The case needs international collaboration on establishing structures that maintain a balance between innovation, security, privacy and regulatory compliance.

## 7. APPLIED USE CASES OF AI–BLOCKCHAIN IN ENERGY SYSTEMS

### 7.1 AI–Blockchain in European Smart Grids

Europe is the world leader in the use of the latest advances in the energy sector: AI and blockchain are successfully tested in strip projects and put into implementation in a number of areas. There are a number of European Union (EU) projects that have looked at the possibilities of such technologies in aiding a smarter, greener, and more decentralized electrical systems. Among these, Enerchain project and ELNEDRA (Electricity Network Digital Revolution Alliance) initiative can be listed as one of the pioneers.

Energy Enerchain is a blockchain-powered network to trade energy peer-to-peer between utilities, large industrial consumers. It enables the market players to directly trade electricity with no central intermediaries. The components of AI are incorporated into the trading platform to predict prices fluctuations, optimize the bidding strategy, and track abnormalities or suspicious activity. The system increases the efficiency of the market due to the automaticness of real-time transactions and through transparency distributed ledger (Lee et al., 2015).

Separately, Germany and Netherlands have been experimenting with smart grid projects and combining AI to predict demands with blockchain to ensure reliable recording of transactions. As an example, a pilot network between the project TenneT, Sonnen and IBM was built with residential battery storage systems controlled through AI algorithms to achieve grid balancing. The Hyperledger blockchain validated and recorded all the interactions such as power power withdrawals and injections. This model did not just make the grid more stable, it also compensated users with tokens on their willingness to provide flexibility to the grid.

They are good European examples about scalability, interoperability, and regulation. They also prove that hybrid systems can not only be possible but beneficial to the grid operators, prosumers, and the environments. But, it needs powerful infrastructure, policy endorsement and the faith of the people in the digital technologies.

## 7.2 Decentralized Renewable Energy Exchanges in Developing Regions

Transmission losses, intermittent supply and low distribution grids are some of the challenges being experienced in many developing regions as compared to centralized and highly regulated energy markets in developed countries. These limitations render decentralized renewable energy system as the perfect solution. Nevertheless, to be efficient, these systems need platforms capable to handle transactions, enable confidence, and maximize performance, which AI and blockchain excell at.

Examples of pilot programs which demonstrate the energy access gap closure using these technologies appear in Africa and even in South Asia. As an example, in rural Kenya microgrids, solar panels are operational and governed by AI algorithms to predict generation and consumption patterns relying on past and environmental data. Smart meters are installed on local homes, and they are hooked up to a block-based platform that enables bills to be settled and energy to be sold between the local residents in real-time (Sheikh et al., 2026).

An exemplary one involves India partnering with Power Ledger, an Australian outfit that has implemented blockchain-based P2P trading platforms at the neighborhoods of some cities and in industrial areas. In such environments owner of solar panels installed on the rooftops may sell their surplus energy using smart contracts directly to geographically close consumers. Dynamic pricing can be done with the help of AI and consider such factors as the demand, the supply and time of the day.

## 7.3 AI-Driven Grid Resilience and Emergency Response

One of the most important priorities of grid resilience is in areas vulnerable to such occurrences as natural catastrophes, cyber-attacks or deteriorating infrastructure. Blockchain and AI are becoming a significant factor in the creation of resilient energy networks that can recover and heal themselves in the real-time. Such abilities are required in critical services where failure can be easily disastrous like in the case of hospitals, data centers and emergency response centers where outage of power can be disastrous.

This is well demonstrated by the use of AI-powered predictive analysis where utilities in California have been implementing it to limit wildfire threats. The machine learning models perform an analysis of the data about the weather stations, satellite images and grid sensors to predict fire-prone areas. In carrying out this process, the system is able to isolate selected areas within the grid in the case that threats are detected to ensure that the ignition of live wires is avoided. Blockchain will be employed to record such activities in a transparent manner, which produces a permanent record of decision-making that may be utilized to review what happened after the incident and meet the regulatory requirements.

AI and blockchain intelligence was used in tsunami-affected areas in Japan to distribute energy resources. When there is failure in the central grid, it is possible to continue with autonomous operations powered by solar microgrids that are also outfitted with battery storage as well as AI control. The blockchain will support coordination of various microgrids and make sure that energy sharing will be carried out equally and has no security vulnerabilities in emergencies (European Commission, 2020).

It is possible to notice the practical usefulness of the combination of AI and blockchain in these applications not only to improve performance in the normal functioning but also to secure continuity and safety in case of a crisis. With the rise in the number of climate-related risks all over the world, the use of such technologies in developing resilient and adaptive infrastructure will grow in importance.

## 8. FUTURE DIRECTIONS AND EMERGING TRENDS

### 8.1 Green Blockchain and Sustainable AI

Due to the increased implementation of AI and blockchain technologies in energy industry, there is an increasing problem of how the technologies can affect the environment. Most blockchain protocols like Proof of work are very computation-heavy, and therefore have significant carbon emission. Equally, the high-energy consumption of large AI models poses a challenge to the sustainability positives that those models are intended to yield.

The sector is investigating the green alternatives of blockchain to deal with these problems. More efficient consensus mechanisms such as Proof of Stake (PoS), Proof of Authority (PoA) and Directed Acyclic Graphs (DAG) are gaining adoption in the context of energy uses as their energy consumption is lower by several orders of magnitude. The protocols also allow accelerating, scaling, and energy-efficient operations without losing security or decentralization (Kumar & Mallick, 2018).

On the AI side to minimise the energy impact of machine learning, there are federated learning, model pruning, and quantisation techniques to explore. An example is federated learning, where data can be used to train models decentralized without centralizing data, leading to enhanced privacy and decreased requirements of high-bandwidth data transmission.

Sustainability will become a condition under which no digital technology in energy can be operated. The development of AIAI-blockchain that is smart, safe, and sustainable to the environment is going to be the research and innovation topic in future. The idea is to make sure that such technologies enhance, as opposed to undercut, the climate ambitions of energy transitions all over the world.

## 8.2 Federated Learning and Edge Intelligence in Energy Analytics

The classical process which included delivering of all data to a central server to process these data is less productive and dangerous as energy systems become more decentralized. A fresh solution that fits the needs of future energy systems very well is the federated learning and edge computing. In federated learning, AI models will be trained locally in smart meters, solar inverters, or EV chargers and the model updates rather than raw data are sent to a central coordinator.

The approach maintains privacy of data, saves on overhead communication and provides quicker decision making capabilities. Federated learning can be additionally secured and organized when used with blockchain. As an example, one might utilize blockchain to monitor the origin of every single model update: only venerable devices would be allowed to participate in the training. Model aggregation and validation can be automated using smart contracts and reduce the process to a transparent and immutable collaborative learning system (Sathio et al., 2025).

To complement this approach, edge intelligence comes into place, allowing real-time analytics and control on energy devices. Seeking an example, an edge AI system installed in a smart appliance will be able to figure out the most efficient operating schedule, and implement it automatically, with no requirement to contact a distant server. The decisions are recorded, verifiable and must conform to local regulations of energy in blockchain.

These technologies describe the next wave of intelligent energy systems, namely: from the centralized intelligence to distributed, collaborative, context-aware, privacy-sensitive, responsive intelligent power.

## 8.3 Policy, Regulation, and Ethical Frameworks for Hybrid Systems

Since AI and blockchain technologies are gaining more control over the development of energy systems, their governance has become an important issue. The policymakers will have to make decisions on the complicated inquiries regarding the possession and responsibility of data creation, the visibility of the algorithms used, and moral application of automation. The uncertainty brought about by the absence of standardized regulatory frameworks may impede the rate of innovation and adoption.

Explainability and transparency are becoming fundamental, in the area of AI. Energy companies have to demonstrate the ability to explain the automated decision-making processes, especially those touching on billing, access or safety. Black-box AI models are neither easy to audit nor control even though they can be technically correct. Therefore, future systems might require the preference to interpretable AI models that provide high performance and are understandable by people.

In case of blockchain, what is required by the regulators is clarity with respect to digital assets, smart contracts, and energy trade with respect to cross borders. Jurisdictions need to specify the legal treatment of energy tokens in a financial law and method of resolving disagreements in decentralized markets and protection of consumers. These standards can be set by such international organizations as International Energy Agency (IEA) and International Telecommunication Union (ITU) (Nayak et al., 2026).

Questions of ethics also come first. As AI becomes more autonomous, the problem of bias, discrimination, and accountability have to be addressed proactively. Blockchain as a transparent technology causes some concerns regarding surveillance in the case of being implemented wrongly. The existence of a prudent regulatory policy should not only protect the rights of the individuals but also encourage innovation (Boston Consulting Group, 2021).

In the future, technology developers with energy companies, regulators, and civil society must collaborate in order to influence the development of policies that realize trusted, inclusive, and sustainable hybrid intelligent energy systems.

## 9. CONCLUSION

Artificial Intelligence and blockchain technology are starting to meet and remake the world energy, providing an unprecedented direction toward finally viable, autonomous, smart energy networks. With the add-on requirements of the cleaner energy solutions, due to the need of reliable and user driven energy solutions, the traditional centralized models are failing to meet demands presenting the complexities of current energy generation, distribution and consumption. Synergistic combination of AI and blockchain represents an alternative emerging prospect-through

## REFERENCES


Abdulrahman, Y., Arnautović, E., Parezanović, V., & Svetinovic, D. (2023). AI and blockchain synergy in aerospace engineering: An impact survey on operational efficiency and technological challenges. *IEEE Access : Practical Innovations, Open Solutions*, *11*, 87790–87804. DOI: 10.1109/ACCESS.2023.3305325

Andoni, M., Robu, V., Flynn, D., Abram, S., Geach, D., Jenkins, D., McCallum, P., & Peacock, A. (2019). Blockchain technology in the energy sector: A systematic review of challenges and opportunities. *Renewable & Sustainable Energy Reviews*, *100*, 143–174. DOI: 10.1016/j.rser.2018.10.014

Bellagarda, J. S., & Abu-Mahfouz, A. M. (2022). An updated survey on the coverage of distributed ledger technology and artificial intelligence: Current state, major challenges and future direction. *IEEE Access : Practical Innovations, Open Solutions*, *10*, 50774–50793. DOI: 10.1109/ACCESS.2022.3173297

Bendiab, G., Hameurlaine, A., Germanos, G., Kolokotronis, N., & Shiaeles, S. (2023, April). Autonomous vehicles security: Challenges and solutions using blockchain and artificial intelligence. *IEEE Transactions on Intelligent Transportation Systems*, *24*(4), 3614–3637. DOI: 10.1109/TITS.2023.3236274

Boston Consulting Group. (2021). *How Digital Technologies Can Drive a Faster Energy Transition*. https://www.bcg.com

De Mauro, A., Greco, M., & Grimaldi, M. (2016). A formal definition of Big Data based on its essential features. *Library Review*, *65*(3), 122–135. DOI: 10.1108/LR-06-2015-0061

Di Silvestre, M. L., Gallo, P., Luna, A. C., Sanseverino, E. R., & Zobaa, A. F. (2020). Blockchain for power systems: Current trends and future applications. *Renewable & Sustainable Energy Reviews*, *119*, 109585. DOI: 10.1016/j.rser.2019.109585

European Commission. (2020). *Clean Energy for All Europeans Package*. https://energy.ec.europa.eu

Farooqi, A., Das, D., Tripathi, M., Dutta, R., Goyal, N. K., & Sheikh, M. F. (2026). Navigating Ethical Frontiers in AI-Driven Geriatric Care. In Stolakis, K., & Efthymiou, I. (Eds.), *AI for Geriatric Care in an Aging Society: Ethical, Clinical, and Policy Challenges* (pp. 243–266). IGI Global Scientific Publishing., DOI: 10.4018/979-8-3373-5462-0.ch009

Google, A. I. (2019). *Federated Learning: Collaborative Machine Learning without Centralized Training Data*. https://ai.googleblog.com/2017/04/federated-learning-collaborative.html

Goyal, N. K. (2025). Weaponizing Misinformation and Cyberattacks on Supply Chains. In Bukhari, S., & Zafar, I. (Eds.), *Mass Media and Impact of Fake News on Supply Chains* (pp. 177–210). IGI Global Scientific Publishing., DOI: 10.4018/979-8-3373-2175-2.ch007

Goyal, N. K. (2025). Security and Privacy in IoT, Fog, and Blockchain Networks. In Sathio, A., Rind, M., Awan, S., & Junejo, A. (Eds.), *Energy-Efficient Deep Learning Approaches in IoT, Fog, and Green Blockchain Revolution* (pp. 371–398). IGI Global Scientific Publishing., DOI: 10.4018/979-8-3373-0300-0.ch015

Goyal, N. K., Dandotiya, M., Kumari, M., Kaloria, S., & Anushya, A. (2025). AI-Powered Haptic Devices for Patient Rehabilitation. In Mamodiya, U., Kalam, A., Bossoufi, B., Awad, M., & Somwanshi, D. (Eds.), *Integrating AI With Haptic Systems for Smarter Healthcare Solutions* (pp. 143–170). IGI Global Scientific Publishing., DOI: 10.4018/979-8-3373-2307-7.ch007

Goyal, N. K., Dandotiya, M., Kumari, M., Sheikh, M. F., & Sharma, S. (2025). Emerging Job Roles in the Tourism Sector Leveraging Artificial Intelligence. In Silic, M., Luthia, M., Ahmad, F., & Chakraborty, P. (Eds.), *Empowering Sustainable Performance and Competitive Advantage in Tourism* (pp. 89–126). IGI Global Scientific Publishing., DOI: 10.4018/979-8-3373-4546-8.ch004

Goyal, N. K., Dandotiya, M., Qurashi, J. A., Kumari, M., & Sharma, S. (2025). AI-Driven Predictive Analytics for Disease Management. In Ouaissa, M., Ouaissa, M., Imad, M., Qurashi, J., & Farooq, M. (Eds.), *Utilizing AI of Medical Things for Healthcare Security and Sustainability* (pp. 231–276). IGI Global Scientific Publishing., DOI: 10.4018/979-8-3373-0690-2.ch008

Goyal, N. K., Kumari, M., Kushwah, V., Dandotiya, M., & Vijay, A. (2025). Evaluating blockchain security: Trade-offs in consensus mechanisms. *IET Conference Proceedings*, 2024(38), 80–88. DOI: 10.1049/icp.2025.0775

Hassan, M. U., Rehmani, M. H., & Chen, J. (2019). Privacy preservation in blockchain-based IoT systems: Integration issues, prospects, challenges, and future research directions. *Future Generation Computer Systems*, *97*, 512–529. DOI: 10.1016/j.future.2019.02.060

Hassani, H., Huang, X., & Silva, E. (2018). Big-crypto: Big data, blockchain and cryptocurrency. *Big Data and Cognitive Computing*, *2*(4), 34. DOI: 10.3390/bdcc2040034

IBM. (2020). *TenneT and IBM Use Blockchain to Balance the Power Grid*. Retrieved from https://www.ibm.com

IEA. (2021). *Digitalization and Energy*. International Energy Agency. https://www.iea.org/reports/digitalisation-and-energy

Khan, M., & Salah, K. (2018). IoT security: Review, blockchain solutions, and open challenges. *Future Generation Computer Systems*, *82*, 395–411. DOI: 10.1016/j.future.2017.11.022

Kumar, N., & Mallick, P. K. (2018). Blockchain technology for security issues and challenges in IoT. *Procedia Computer Science*, *132*, 1815–1823. DOI: 10.1016/j.procs.2018.05.140

Kumari, A., Gupta, R., Tanwar, S., & Kumar, N. (2020, September). Blockchain and AI amalgamation for energy cloud management: Challenges, solutions, and future directions. *Journal of Parallel and Distributed Computing*, *143*, 148–166. DOI: 10.1016/j.jpdc.2020.05.004

Kumari, M., & Goyal, N. K. (2026). Artificial Intelligence in the Cryptocurrency Ecosystem: Crime Mechanisms, Detection Strategies, and Legal Perspectives. In Lin, L. (Ed.), *Innovations in Cryptocrime and Financial Fraud* (pp. 245–282). IGI Global Scientific Publishing., DOI: 10.4018/979-8-3373-0675-9.ch007

Kumari, M., Kumawat, R., Tripathi, M., Suganthi, K., Goyal, N. K., & Sheikh, M. F. (2026). Blockchain for Transparency and Traceability in Supply Chains. In Khan, M., Mehmood, T., & Rao, M. (Eds.), *Maximizing Operational Efficiency at the Intersection of Supply Chain Management and Marketing* (pp. 35–64). IGI Global Scientific Publishing., DOI: 10.4018/979-8-3373-3109-6.ch002

Lee, J., Bagheri, B., & Kao, H. A. (2015). A cyber-physical systems architecture for industry 4.0-based manufacturing systems. *Manufacturing Letters*, *3*, 18–23. DOI: 10.1016/j.mfglet.2014.12.001

Mengelkamp, E., Gärttner, J., Rock, K., Kessler, S., Orsini, L., & Weinhardt, C. (2018). Designing microgrid energy markets: A case study: The Brooklyn Microgrid. *Applied Energy*, *210*, 870–880. DOI: 10.1016/j.apenergy.2017.06.054

Osman, Y. I. A., Li, J. P., Zhen, X. F., & Yang, A. R. (2018). Experimental Study of the Cloud Influence on PV Grid Connected System. *Smart Grid and Renewable Energy*, *9*(1), 1–15. DOI: 10.4236/sgre.2018.91001

Power Ledger. (2022). *Powering the Future of Energy*. Retrieved from https://www.powerledger.io

Sharma, P., Kumawat, R., Jain, G., Keswani, G., Goyal, N. K., & Sheikh, M. F. (2026). Machine Learning-Based Intrusion Detection Systems for Healthcare Internet of Things (HIoT). In Shieh, C., Goel, P., Horng, M., & Pandey, H. (Eds.), *Resilient Healthcare Internet of Things Systems: Architectures, Security, and Trust* (pp. 185–214). IGI Global Scientific Publishing., DOI: 10.4018/979-8-3373-7610-3.ch007

Sharma, S., Goyal, N. K., Dandotiya, M., & Sharma, V. P. (2026). An Intelligent Data Encryption Approach with the Entangled Mermin-Based Qkd Protocol for Secure Quantum Communications. In Nayak, R., Mittal, N., Khunteta, A., & Kumar, M. (Eds.), *Recent Advancements in Artificial Intelligence. ICRAAI 2025. Lecture Notes in Networks and Systems* (Vol. 1468). Springer., DOI: 10.1007/978-981-96-7760-3_9

Sheikh, M. F. A., Kapoor, S. K., Goyal, N. K., & Tuba, E. rao, A. (2026). Enhancing Healthcare Security with Fog Computing and Blockchain Technology. In: Nayak, R., Mittal, N., Khunteta, A., Kumar, M. (eds) Recent Advancements in Artificial Intelligence. ICRAAI 2025. Lecture Notes in Networks and Systems, vol 1468. Springer, Singapore. DOI: 10.1007/978-981-96-7760-3_38

Siano, P. (2014). Demand response and smart grids—A survey. *Renewable & Sustainable Energy Reviews*, *30*, 461–478. DOI: 10.1016/j.rser.2013.10.022

Stoll, C., Klaaßen, L., & Gallersdörfer, U. (2019). The carbon footprint of bitcoin. *Joule*, *3*(7), 1647–1661. DOI: 10.1016/j.joule.2019.05.012

Swan, M. (2015). *Blockchain: Blueprint for a new economy*. O'Reilly Media.

Zhang, C., Wu, J., Zhou, Y., Cheng, M., & Long, C. (2018). Peer-to-peer energy trading in a microgrid. *Applied Energy*, *220*, 1–12. DOI: 10.1016/j.apenergy.2018.03.010

# Chapter 5
# Integrating AI and Blockchain for Predictive Maintenance and Supply Chain Transparency in Upstream Oil Operations

**Muhammad Usman Tariq**
https://orcid.org/0000-0002-7605-3040
*Abu Dhabi University, UAE & University College Cork, Ireland*

## ABSTRACT

*The upstream oil and gas industry is being significantly revolutionized by new digital technology. Merging Artificial Intelligence (AI) with blockchain is an empowering way to improve the industry, especially in predicting when equipment will break down and making the supply chain transparent. AI helps track equipment in real time and feeds data to predict when something is likely to break, thereby minimizing the chances of sudden shutdowns and optimizing equipment performance. Blockchain ensures integrity by logging how equipment is used, when it is serviced, and what happens in the supply chain; these logs cannot be altered. The combination of Blockchain and AI results in a smart and sound system that enhances business, making it easier, cheaper, and more compliant with regulations. The AI models performed better when they operated on data that were secure and verified by the blockchain. Smart contracts can also be used to automate maintenance and supply purchases.*

DOI: 10.4018/979-8-3373-5457-6.ch005

## INTRODUCTION

The importance of efficiency, safety, and sustainability in upstream oil and gas has never been more pronounced than this time around. With the world energy demand growing, oil and gas prices changing, and carbon emissions being minimized even further, the idea of digital transformation is front and center in the minds of leaders. It can no longer be optional; it becomes a part of their plan. These types of technologies can be used to optimize operations, reduce downtimes, and maintain equipment in good working conditions. Artificial intelligence and blockchain are promising technologies that can transform the functionality of the industry. Not only do they make operations more efficient, but they also fundamentally change the way companies deal with predictive maintenance and supply chain reliability, two of the most vulnerable to problems and delays. The upstream oil and gas industry is experiencing a massive revolution in terms of predictive maintenance. Equipment failure can lead to serious issues regarding safety, the environment, and costs. Conventional maintenance methods, such as adhering to a calendar or only fixing things when they break down, are ineffective in locations where unexpected problems may result in significant losses. AI is changing this by allowing companies to predict problems before they occur. By analyzing extensive sensor data, past performance, and real-time operations, AI can identify patterns and trends that may lead to failure. This enables the maintenance team to act before a problem develops into an outright failure, which keeps machines operational for a longer period, optimizes resource utilization, and avoids production downtime (Peng, 2025). Having AI perform predictive maintenance also makes workplaces safer. Maintenance in several remote and dangerous environments, including offshore platforms and drilling sites, can be risky. AI helps reduce the frequency of unplanned physical inspections and uses only the effort when required. This decreases the risk to workers. In addition, AI systems that use machine learning can observe subtle changes in equipment behavior. These small changes can cause significant problems, and their early detection can prevent major failures. The more the system knows, the better it anticipates problems, and the more precise it is in the long term.

At the other end of the spectrum, supply chain integrity is crucial. The upstream supply chain is complex and involves many different people and organizations. Every element of this network must perform well to avoid costly delays and issues with compliance with the regulations. However, traditional supply chain practices rely on paper-based documentation and are not transparent; therefore, they are likely to become inefficient, corrupt, or non-compliant (Adisetya & Gunawan, 2024). Blockchain provides a strong solution by providing a secure, unalterable, and open record of everything that occurs in the supply chain. For upstream companies, this means that they can have more confidence in their material sources, quality, and regulatory compliance. Smart contracts, as well as contracts in the blockchain, can automate tasks such as payments, approvals, and checks, making things easier and requiring less paperwork. The implementation of both AI and blockchain in the upstream oil and gas industry improves not only some aspects, such as maintenance and supply chains, but also the overall resilience of operations. Resilience is the ability to manage unexpected problems within an organization while sustaining mission-critical operations and its performance. In oil fields, where weather, politics, and equipment failure are all part of the business as usual, resilience is the key. AI helps create insights that allow for better decision-making, smoother operations, and enhanced preparedness for unexpected events. Blockchain technology delivers transparency and trust in secure supply chains and stakeholder trust-building.

The pairing of AI and blockchain is particularly potent when examining the entire upstream supply chain. Suppose that an AI identifies the initial signs of wear on a key component of a drilling rig. This information is automatically fed into the blockchain, which triggers a smart contract to notify the supplier and initiate the part replacement process (Peng, 2025). The blockchain also monitors the new component from manufacturing to delivery to ensure that it meets the appropriate standards and regulations. The upstream sector has normally had fragmented teams working separately and on standalone systems; hence, collaborative sharing of information and problem solving become difficult. AI and blockchain change this because they turn data into a mutual source rather than something held as a secret. Organizations can better collaborate with suppliers, contractors, and regulators by exchanging real-time insights while keeping data safe and private using an encrypted blockchain protocol. Such a cooperative environment helps speed up innovation and leads to better practices, which is paramount in a high-exposure risk industry with considerable heterogeneity.

## AI IN UPSTREAM OPERATIONS: PREDICTIVE MAINTENANCE

Predictive maintenance can avoid unnecessary shutdowns, reduce maintenance costs, and ensure safety of the equipment. Machine learning and deep learning, two types of AI, have been extremely helpful in this context. These technologies enable predictive models to learn from massive collections of data that have been sampled from all over, enabling operators to identify patterns that are difficult to notice. In upstream oil and gas production, AI is using AI not only to fix problems as they arise but also to detect them well ahead of time, sustaining production and preserving equipment at peak condition. The center of predictive maintenance in such environments is the gathering and analysis of real-time data from key items, such as drilling rigs, wellheads, blowout preventers, and submerged pumps. These parts are usually found in hard-to-access places, such as offshore platforms or deep wells, where physically examining them can be dangerous, expensive, and time-consuming. Figure 1 illustrates the cycle of data collection for AI-enabled predictive maintenance.

*Figure 1. AI-Enabled Predictive Maintenance in Upstream Oil & Gas*

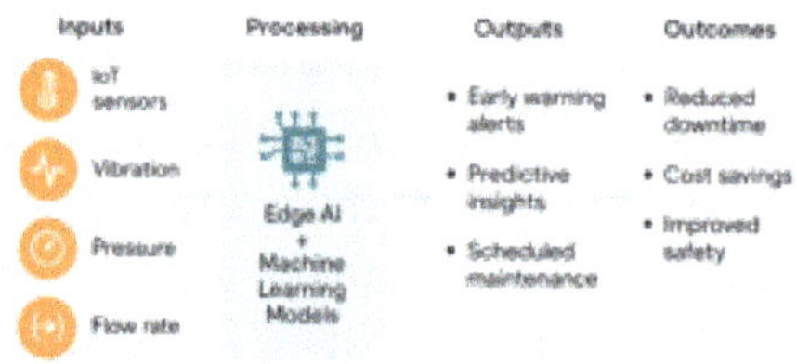


However, with the Internet of Things (IoT), all these parts are now equipped with sensors that track parameters such as temperature, pressure, vibration, fluid levels, and other critical parameters. With Edge AI, or without the AI processing power from the core portion and shifting it close to where data are being created, a lot of initial data processing occurs on premises. It minimizes delays and helps make faster decisions. Edge AI is especially beneficial when there is slow or limited connectivity because it allows operators to detect issues quickly and in real time. Training is achieved using historical data, such as the history of previous equipment faults, operational status, maintenance history, and weather. Through the observation of these sets of data, AI models can discern between normal operations and the early signs of something being amiss. These pumps are integral to the manufacturing process and experience a lot of stress due to varying pressures, corrosive chemicals, and rough weather. Maintenance on such pumps was previously carried out mostly after an issue had occurred, leading to untimely stoppages and heavy losses in the business. Despite regular maintenance schedules, it is difficult to determine when parts must be replaced, often leading to unnecessary replacements and wasted time (Adisetya & Gunawan, 2024). With AI on board, this is not the case with AI. Pumps carry sensors that continuously gather data on factors such as noise, vibration, motor current, and flow rate of the pump. Edge AI processes this data in real time and detects any abnormalities. For instance, a minor fluctuation in the noise and a minor increase in vibration could trigger the AI system to understand that there could be an impending cavitation issue within the pump. Instead of waiting for the pump to break or having a technician check it, the AI system utilizes failure history to predict that the pump might have a critical problem within the next 48 h if something is not done.

According to this prediction, maintenance units can arrange interventions at a moment of least disruption to production, organize the required parts, and shut down the pump for a brief period for maintenance without stopping the entire operation. Not only does it lower unplanned downtime, but it also makes equipment last longer and improves safety by reducing the likelihood of surprise failures. Over time, the AI system on the platform continues to learn from each failure, improving its models to detect problems such as cavitation more quickly and precisely (Peng, 2025). . This creates a cycle in which the capability of AI to predict problems improves with each use, leading to better maintenance planning. Another significant advantage of using AI in oil and gas predictive maintenance is the ability to aggregate and analyze data from multiple sites. Offshore platforms, onshore wells, and pipeline networks can all send data to a central system, where machine learning models can study performance trends across the entire operation. This helps ensure that maintenance is performed in the same manner throughout and enables companies to compare equipment performance within areas, identify issues that might be common, and apply the best practices across the entire company. For example, if the AI system finds that a certain type of pump tends to fail prematurely in a certain set of conditions, the procurement and engineering teams can include this insight when purchasing future equipment Predictive maintenance based on AI renders the working environment safer. By reducing the need for manual inspections and last-minute repairs in risky areas, businesses can lower the risk to employees. Instead of sending technicians to physically inspect parts, most tests can now be performed remotely using AI guidance. This is also an opportunity for further automation because AI machines work together with robots and remote vehicles to inspect gears and carry out minor maintenance on their own, especially in offshore and underwater settings. Although there are numerous benefits, predictive maintenance using AI requires robust data and infrastructure. The functioning of machine learning models depends on the data employed, which should be accurate, consistent, and sufficiently large in volume. Dirty, incomplete, or inconsistent data may lead to erroneous alerts or undetected issues. Therefore, companies must spend money not only on AI software but also on IoT and data solutions that support them. Moreover, there is a need for educated employees who can analyze AI results, fine-tune models, and ensure that the conclusions benefit the business. This typically involves a change in business practices and increased data-based decision-making and communication between the engineering, IT, and operations departments.

In the broader context of upstream oil and gas production, AI-enabled predictive maintenance is a key building block for digital transformation. It changes the management of maintenance from reactive and preventive to predictive maintenance. This implies that decisions are made based on real-time information and data-driven forecasts. This reduces risks, optimizes equipment performance, and minimizes maintenance expenses, which is critical in a thin-profit-margin industry where reliable equipment is key to success. It also allows companies to react faster to changes in the market, regulations, and the environment. In summary, predictive maintenance is being revolutionized through AI, machine learning, and deep learning in upstream oil and gas operations. From obtaining real-time information through IoT devices to deploying AI models at the edge and in the cloud, the entire system is becoming intelligent, responsive and robust. In-use applications, such as the detection of premature failure in offshore pumps, describe clear benefits, such as cost reduction, efficiency, and improved safety and equipment long-term health (Adisetya & Gunawan, 2024). With advancing technology, it will be the standard of the industry and welcome a new age of smart preventive maintenance and open doors for more digital advancements in the coming years.

## BLOCKCHAIN IN UPSTREAM SUPPLY CHAINS

The upstream oil and gas industry, where the risk is high and the costs of error could be huge, requires a slimmed-down and open supply chain. Oil and gas exploration and extraction activities are typically complex, incorporating several suppliers, logistical firms, and regulations by government agencies. Equipment and supplies must be monitored over long distances, sometimes from a factory to an offshore platform many miles away or a distant drilling field, and must be done on short notice. Old systems with isolated databases, paper records, and disguised processes fail to comply with these demands. Blockchain technology is becoming an important change, offering a shared, safe, and open record system that can solve many of the age-old challenges in supply chain tracing, purchasing goods, following regulations, and keeping equipment over its entire life (Kasych et al., 2019). One of the biggest uses of blockchain is in drilling tools and real-time location tracking of materials. From drill bits to metal pipes, chemical additives, or safety components, all have a life cycle of buying and then getting pulled. In traditional systems, all of these are followed by different systems, emails, spreadsheets, or isolated software. This kind of disconnect can result in delays, loss of equipment, and trouble confirming the actual state or authenticity of a thing once received. Blockchain accomplishes this through a shared digital ledger in which all activity, movement, and use of a unit are captured in real time and exposed to anyone who is authorized to see it.

Using blockchain platforms, oil and gas firms can track the location of each unit, its possession, its status, and where it has been along the supply chain. For example, a drill bit manufactured from a plant in Houston and sent to an offshore facility in the North Sea can have each step of its life cycle, from packaging through customs, shipping, warehousing, and final application, recorded onto the blockchain. Every step is marked with the date and signed with cryptography, which cannot be changed (Egbumokei et al., 2024). In addition to asset tracking, blockchain helps with more intelligent and safe ways of managing purchases, maintaining equipment operation, and maintaining warranties with smart contracts. They are similar to automated agreements written into software that automatically runs when conditions are met. Upstream oil and gas companies utilize this to incorporate buying contracts, maintenance cycles, and warranty details into the blockchain. After satisfying the required conditions, such as delivery confirmation, compliance checks, or the completion of a service, the contract will automatically remunerate the vendor, update reports, or arrange subsequent steps without requiring someone to do them manual intervention. This abolishes the extra work and delays of traditional buying processes and reduces the risk of conflict, deception, and errors.

For instance, a recurring high-pressure valve maintenance contract between an oil corporation and supplier. A maintenance schedule can be built into a smart contract through a blockchain platform. Upon satisfactory completion and verification by sensors, reports, or digital signatures, the contract pays the vendor and documents the history of maintenance on record. If the equipment is damaged during the warranty period, the blockchain has an immutable record of all the usage, maintenance, and extraneous factors and, therefore, makes it simpler to handle the claim under warranty. Such automation and transparent tracking not only improve the efficiency of the procedure but also boost the trust between the company and its suppliers, as all the conditions are clear and followed without bias. Another area in which blockchain adds real value is in helping companies become environmentally, socially, and governance (ESG)-compliant. As an increasing number of investors, regulators, and other stakeholders focus on ESG performance, oil and gas companies are being forced to prove that they are responsibly sourcing, minimizing environmental footprints, and maintaining ethical practices throughout their supply chains. Standard reporting practices typically cannot provide the level of transparent and open information needed to meet these needs. Blockchain offers a solid solution through the capacity to establish records that cannot be changed on the source, environmental impact, and compliance status of materials drilled with (Lodhi & Zeb, 2025). For instance, consider a firm that is buying steel pipes from various suppliers. With blockchain, they can trace where the raw material came from, how it was made, what energy was used, and how much pollution was emitted during its production and transportation. All of this can be authenticated by third-party auditors and safely stored on the blockchain, providing an open book of environmental responsibility. This will enable operators to be sure that they are accurately reporting on ESG goals, such as the share of materials from low-emission processes or the number of suppliers adopting sustainable processes. Blockchain can also validate that work conditions and safety measures are followed in the supply chain, especially where these verifications might not be legally obligated. This kind of transparency is becoming a great benefit, as more people want tangible proof of sustainability and ethical business leadership. A great example of the robustness of blockchain is the maintenance of the complete life cycle of major equipment in hard-to-reach offshore operations. Offshore rigs are far off and difficult to reach; therefore, it is challenging to obtain equipment and materials in time and in adequate quantities. In one case, a deep-water field operator used a blockchain platform to monitor the life of important subsea equipment. The moment an item is produced, data such as its serial number, build dimensions, test data, and proof of compliance documents are lodged in the blockchain. As the equipment traveled along the supply chain, from factory to port, through customs, onto a vessel, and finally installed on the seafloor, each phase was recorded and authenticated by different parties in the network, such as logistics staff, customs, and offshore workers.

Once the equipment is in place, data captured, such as pressure readings, temperature changes, and inspection findings, are continuously logged on the blockchain using sensors and edge computing devices. An accurate and unchangeable record helps engineers track the status of equipment, schedule regular maintenance, and predict potential failures more effectively. Once it is time to retire or dispose of the equipment, all the vital information is available at hand; therefore, it is easier to meet environmental standards and make better decisions regarding retiring the life of the equipment. Transparency within the blockchain system allows for improved performance of how secure the machinery is, lowers maintenance costs, and creates a common sense of responsibility among persons involved, including regulators and insurance companies, who can see performance and risk levels in real time. The use of blockchain in upstream supply chains also allows various stakeholders to cooperate more harmoniously. This will lead to duplicated efforts, confusion and delays. Blockchain solves this by creating a reliable source of information that everyone can access. Access can be controlled to protect data but facilitate effective collaboration. This leads to shorter project periods, easier compliance, and fewer disputes (Peng, 2025). However, developing blockchain technology for upstream supply chains is not without challenges. The technology itself is still emerging, and industry standards are only now being established. Applying blockchain to established systems such as ERP, logistics, and asset management can be difficult and expensive, involving high investments in technology and change management. In addition, the way blockchain works with no control point raises issues of who owns the data, who authenticates the transactions, and how to resolve problems when smart contracts go wrong. To effectively manage the mitigation of the threats encountered by the upstream oil and gas supply chain, new types of technologies must be implemented, and collaboration among companies, technology suppliers, and governments should be organized to create best practices and harmonized standards. Despite these challenges, upstream supply chains using blockchain technology have significant advantages (Peng, 2025). The capability to track equipment and materials in real time, robotize contractual arrangements with smart contracts, and provide proof of ESG compliance with inimitable records is altering industrial practices. Wider adoption is gaining pace as more companies run pilot projects and see definite results. The blockchain ceases to be the subject of theoretical thought; it is a practical way of addressing tangible issues in one of the most complex industries on the globe.

## CONVERGING AI AND BLOCKCHAIN: A HYBRID MODEL

With the upstream oil and gas sector facing more difficulties and changes, the use of innovative digital tools is a crucial strategy. AI and blockchain are two technologies, each with strong strengths individually, but they complement each other. AI helps make predictions from data, whereas blockchain offers a secure, open way of logging transactions and events. However, the best results are obtained when both these technologies are used together. By synergizing AI's analytical abilities of AI and the secure data storage of blockchain, the industry can make operations smarter, predictable, and trustworthy. Together, these two technologies enable real-time decision-making, ensuring that data are accurate and dependable end-to-end (Tariq, 2025). The collaboration between AI and blockchain depends on enabling free data flow between the two. Information on oil and gas is retrieved from various sources, including drilling equipment, sensors, supply chains, and maintenance records. Such information is typically captured using IoT devices and processed using AI to obtain useful insights. In hybrid systems intended to operate at the highest efficiency, the data utilized in the training of artificial intelligence should be accessible and verifiable by applying blockchain technology. This need prompts the creation of data channels that will simultaneously provide information to artificial intelligence systems and blockchain infrastructures. As the AI system finds patterns and predictions, a cryptographic hash of the information, or, in certain systems, the entire data, is stored on the blockchain, thus allowing a safe, time-stamped log of the data read and the time-stamps of the events. Storing information in the blockchain can perform a few fundamental roles in the AI development lifecycle (Kumar et al., 2023). This ensures that the information sent to develop AI models is genuine and has not been tampered with, which is particularly important in high-stakes settings where inaccurate data may cause the development of harmful judgments. In turn, this strategy would encourage openness and responsibility so that stakeholders can correctly monitor AI choices regarding input data. The audit trail obtained is priceless in regulatory situations and in disputes, where it is of primary importance to prove exactly which data have been used and how such data have been processed.

Blockchain storage provides more reliable and verifiable AI results because of the assurance of data integrity over time. The application of blockchain technology in real-time operational situations is becoming increasingly critical. This type of artificial intelligence is used to identify anomalies when they occur, such as a change in pressure or irregular vibration of equipment, which ensures quick intervention that reduces risk, increases productivity, and improves safety. Nevertheless, unless there is a secure way to store both the alerts and the underlying information that caused the alert, concerns about their timeliness or accuracy may arise, especially during post-hoc analysis. Blockchain makes this issue less worrisome by storing all AI-generated alerts and the circumstances that led to each alert in a non-editable registry. The factuality of such records provides a true account of what has transpired that can be called upon many years after an event. As shown in Figure 2, the insights and predictions that AI produces are correlated with the secure and traceable records stored on the blockchain, thus creating a closed circle of verifiable decisions.

*Figure 2. Hybrid AI + Blockchain Model for Upstream Supply Chains*

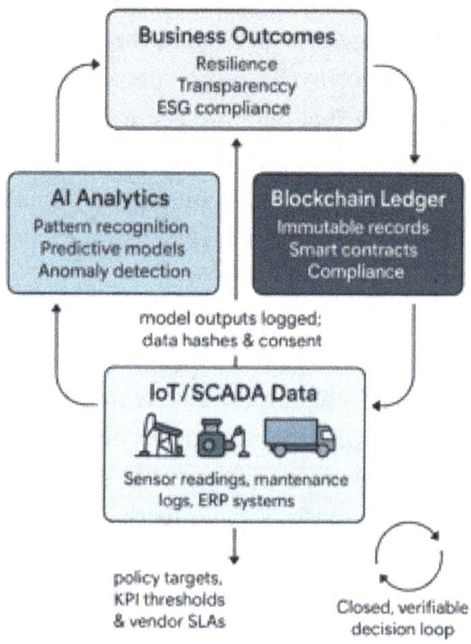


The second powerful advantage of an AI-blockchain approach is the way in which it integrates predictive analytics and guaranteed records. Artificial intelligence devices can effectively forecast outcomes using a pattern, whereas blockchain technology provides a secure, unalterable, and immutable record of activities. They do this through collaborative and smarter operations. An example is predictive maintenance, where AI is used to predict equipment failure based on past and present events. This prediction, sensor data, and recommended activities are stored on the blockchain. Once maintenance is conducted, the work done, materials used, and verification information are stored in the blockchain. This makes it a complete, traceable account of the life of the equipment and can make predictions of actual actions and results.

This concerted action transforms digital wisdom into reality. Traditional models tend to keep AI-driven predictions in a vacuum, not connected with real-world activities. Through the AI-blockchain hybrid solution, everything that is forecasted, acted upon, and results is tied together in an impermeable and traceable platform. This increases operational harmony and yields a satisfactory loop. With increasing predictions and actions being recorded, the AI system can learn from them and become more accurate with its predictions as time goes on. Meanwhile, blockchain ensures that this learning is based on firm, auditable data (Lahami and Chaabane, 2023). The hybrid model also improves the way different groups working on upstream projects interact with each other. Oil and gas ventures often involve a multitude of stakeholders, such as equipment suppliers, operators, service firms, government agencies, and insurance companies. All these groups may use their own systems and data formats and have varying goals (Peng, 2025). This could result in problems such as inefficiencies, communication, and a lack of proper exchange of information. With blockchain as a shared bookkeeping system, all these groups can share the same reliable data. The benefits are compounded when AI is used. For example, if AI identifies a defect in a certain type of machinery used on multiple rigs, it can alert all users on the blockchain network. This alerts all involved and enables a collective response. Designs can be changed by equipment makers, maintenance crews can change maintenance schedules, and regulators can examine industry impact, all based on reliable information.

Although this AI-blockchain solution offers many benefits, it requires strategic planning to function optimally. One of the biggest challenges is dealing with data in the right way, ensuring that the data are correct, individual, and respect the rules. It is also necessary to switch smoothly between AI systems and blockchain networks so that they can interact with one another securely. There are speed and space issues as well. AI demands fast processing of data, but blockchain slows it down because of the way it operates to agree on data changes. Techniques such as processing some data off the blockchain, using sidechains, or plugging in cloud systems can be beneficial. Such approaches make it possible to process AI quickly while keeping important records safely on the blockchain (Kishnani et al., 2023). A very important factor is having people from different disciplines work together on the same projects. It takes more than just plugging technology to establish an AI-blockchain system; it requires input from data analysts, blockchain specialists, security engineers, operations engineers, and industry experts. It will only work if the entire team speaks the same language about business goals, how the system enables operations, and each component's technical capability. People must also be trained and supported to understand the new system to use it well, understand its results, and apply the insights to make data-driven decisions. In the overall context of digital transformation, the combination of AI and blockchain is a strategic move towards more intelligent, open, and secure operations in the upstream oil and gas industry. It is a shift from reacting after things happen and working in siloed teams to proactive and integrated. Whether forecasting equipment failures, running supply chains, or showing ESG compliance, this hybrid method provides a steady way of performing better operations while building trust with stakeholders.

## IMPLEMENTATION STRATEGY

The upstream oil and gas industry requires a clever strategy for using AI and blockchain, which involves mapping technology to industry operations. There is much legacy, heavy infrastructure, and stringent safety standards in the industry, and any new digital solution needs to be robust and agile in integration (Peng, 2025). The point of departure is the creation of a unified and structured technology system that integrates SCADA systems, IoT sensors, AI implementations, and blockchain nodes. This framework must assist in data collection, real-time analysis, secure data storage, and automatic decision-making in both remote and distributed operations.

In upstream areas, SCADA systems are concentrated, which is the main control center for equipment and processes. Pumps, valves, compressors, wellheads, and drilling rigs already provide them with a large amount of data. To update this, SCADA may be related to IoT devices that receive more exact and detailed information, such as vibration, temperature, pressure, and chemical levels. These are the IoT sensors that the AI system uses as the eyes and ears and transmits data at a high speed in near real-time. Raw IoT and SCADA data are then input into AI programs that execute predictive maintenance, problem identification, and optimization of operations. In parallel or in combination with this structure, blockchain nodes incessantly document significant events and data inputs, such as equipment work, notifications, maintenance, and quality inspections. This hierarchical design enables every system to perform its tasks and create a smart, secure digital ecosystem (Durán et al., 2024). To determine how to configure this tech stack, companies must strike the right balance between the merits and demerits of edge and cloud computing. Scaling, central analysis, and updating of AI models are areas in which cloud computing excels. In the cloud solution, field data are transmitted to central servers, where sophisticated models can be developed and optimized with abundant historical and real-time data. It is also possible to make comparisons across sites using the cloud, which is ideal for running a business and strategic planning. However, certain unique issues in the oil and gas industry can make the utilization of the cloud problematic. Field operations are often in remote or offshore areas where there is no internet, the internet is slow, or the internet is highly limited. In these locations, waiting for data to be transmitted to the cloud and back can be too slow for real-time decisions (Tariq, 2025).

This is where edge computing comes into play. By placing AI capabilities closer to the data collection point, right at the network edge, in field devices, or local systems, key decisions can be made locally in real time. Edge AI facilitates real-time issue detection, safety responses, and operational changes based on localized analyses. For instance, if an edge AI algorithm detects cavitation in a subsea pump, it can instantly trigger alerts and safety responses without waiting for a response from the cloud. Edge setups also minimize bandwidth usage and enhance data security by filtering or masking the data before transmission. However, edge computing is low-powered and not suited for training massive AI models or storing large datasets. A hybrid of edge and cloud computing is what works best, running time-sensitive tasks on the edge and using the cloud for data-intensive workloads and long-term storage (Chen et al., 2024). Along with architecture choices, cybersecurity, delays, and connectivity are also important issues in the digital transformation of the upstream oil and gas sector. Cybersecurity is especially important because of the growing threat of attacks on industrial systems, which can lead to serious repercussions, such as safety incidents, environmental disasters, and financial losses. The convergence of SCADA, IoT, AI, and blockchain adds new points of potential attack; therefore, these need to be strongly secured. Every device, node, and communication path represents a potential entry point for the attackers. Security must be ingrained in every part of the configuration, from encrypted sensor communications and secure login procedures to blockchain consensus and artificial intelligence-powered threat detection. Blockchain delivers security benefits by making data immutable and leveraging distributed consensus to prevent tampering, thus ensuring the integrity of operational records. However, these systems must be properly configured to avoid such vulnerabilities. Private blockchains are typically preferred in industrial settings because they allow only approved participants, unlike public blockchains, where anyone can join. Secure APIs and data policies must be implemented to control the flow of data between AI systems, blockchain ledgers, and user interfaces. Regular security scans, penetration testing, and threat modeling must also be part of maintenance to keep up with new threats (Lodhi & Zeb, 2025). Connectivity is another serious challenge, especially in areas such as offshore rigs, desert fields, or Arctic installations, where network infrastructure can be sparse. In these areas, it is necessary to employ technologies such as satellite communication, private LTE networks, or local mesh networks to keep the system online. AI applications need to be constructed to work in disconnected or partly connected environments, be able to run autonomously at the edge, and sync with the central system once connectivity is resumed. Similarly, blockchain nodes can cache data locally and then sync the distributed ledger when there is Internet connectivity, ensuring that everything agrees across the system. These design choices are not merely technical details but are essential for delivering a strong and reliable digital spine in the industry.

Such design decisions are not merely technical aspects but are critical to developing a robust and stable digital spine to run the entire industry. The successful adoption of AI and blockchain in the upstream oil and gas business goes beyond a workforce with good technical capacity. Companies collaborating with AI and blockchain startups, innovation laboratories, and investigation centers have the opportunity to accelerate the implementation of these methods and decrease the risk involved. Innovation is frequently in the first-mover phase in startups, with solutions that are lighter, more nimble, focused, and open to experimentation than internal teams. Such partnerships help oil and gas enterprises to pioneer new technologies, experiment with various applications, and react to market trends swiftly without bearing the entire cost of research and development on their own. For example, collaborating with a start-up developing edge AI to work with industrial machines might accelerate the implementation of predictive maintenance systems on offshore drilling equipment. Digital solutions are tested in controlled test beds in innovation labs and accelerators, which are usually established by major oil industries or industry associations. These labs enable cross-functional teams to test AI models, blockchain networks, digital twins, and industrial IoT solutions in a real-world environment. They also encourage cross-industry cooperation, including energy companies, technology vendors, universities, and regulatory authorities, to develop common standards and shared data practices. This collaborative framework is precisely what is needed to solve issues such as the isolation of data, regulatory ambiguity, and system compatibility, which predominantly inhibit the process of digital transformation in more traditional sectors (Naveena et al., 2024). In addition, cooperation with external partners fills the human resource gap.

AI and blockchain often demand specialist knowledge that is not found in traditional oil and gas firms. Experts such as data scientists, machine learning engineers, blockchain developers, and cybersecurity specialists must work together with petroleum engineers and field personnel to create feasible solutions. Working with partners allows companies to access a larger talent pool and gain access to new capabilities faster than they would be able to develop everything in-house, for example. This partnership could eventually evolve into a strategic alliance, powering joint innovation and allowing companies to remain competitive in the digital energy ecosystem. Despite the difficulty in integrating AI and blockchain across upstream operations, the long-term benefits outweigh the effort. Companies that take a planned approach, starting with pilot projects, developing modular systems, prioritizing cybersecurity, and working with innovative partners, can achieve new levels of efficiency, safety, and sustainability. For example, a system that uses AI to predict drill string failure and blockchain to securely record each inspection and maintenance event can minimize non-productive time, improve compliance, and provide a clear asset history, which are important considerations in capital-intensive sectors. Finally, the implementation plan must be based on real operating needs. Robust governance structures are required to manage data ownership, system reliability, and coordination between departments (Adisetya & Gunawan, 2024). By prioritizing these real-world considerations in the adoption of new technology, upstream operators can transition from traditional ways of working to a more digitally empowered future.

## BUSINESS VALUE AND KPIS

Applying AI and blockchain to the upstream oil and gas sector is not about adding layers of new technology; it is a strategy shift with real business value. This change affects every aspect of the business, from how operations are performed to how risks are managed, compliance is maintained, and profits are realized. When used appropriately, these technologies allow companies to make quicker and smarter decisions, monitor things in real time, and keep data safe and unobtrusive. With any big spend, it makes sense to prove that these enhancements serve the business. Key performance indicators (KPIs) are required. By looking at actual results, such as lower unplanned stoppages, improved supply chain performance, improved safety, and improved compliance, companies can measure how much they are saving and prove that it is worth continuing to innovate. One of the fastest methods by which AI helps in upstream activities is by lowering unplanned downtime. If the equipment fails in oil fields, be it on the well, drilling facility, or on platforms offshore, it will cost tens of millions in lost production, emergency repair, and logistics headaches (Aziz et al., 2024). Maintenance can be better scheduled, reducing overtime spending and avoiding the need for express parts or expensive service teams. In the long term, AI insights will also be used to aid in design and procurement decisions, for example, recognizing recurring problems with specific equipment or problems with specific suppliers. Some of the KPIs tracking this value are the mean time between failures, fewer emergency maintenance events, planned over-reactive maintenance ratio, and overall equipment effectiveness. A notable decrease in unexpected downtime, typically 20% to 30% when totally adopted, can produce millions of additional revenue and boost the bottom line of the company.

Another area where AI and blockchain are providing substantial returns is by delivering improved supply chain transparency. Upstream oil and gas supply chains are often international, complex, and multilayered. Materials and equipment pass through many hands multiple times before reaching remote or inaccessible regions of the world. Delays, deception, or communication breakdowns at any point can bring operations to a standstill or lead to noncompliance. Blockchain technology creates a shared, unchangeable record of every movement and transaction. Every shipment, transfer, compliance check, and utilization is recorded and can be viewed in real time by approved users. AI adds another dimension by being capable of making the supply chain intelligent. It can identify patterns such as late shipments, vendor problems, or quality issues, and notify teams to investigate or act. For instance, if a supplier is consistently late, the AI can prompt procurement adjustments or audits. Blockchain stores all these occurrences indefinitely, providing a clear and trustworthy history of supply chain performance. The KPIs within this category include on-time delivery percentages, faster procurement cycles, fewer fraud cases, supplier compliance rates, and inventory turnover rates. Companies can see delivery accuracy improve by 15% or more and a considerable decrease in loss due to fraud when everything is documented on the blockchain (Tariq, 2025). Reducing operational risks and improving safety are some of the most significant benefits of using AI and blockchain. Oil and gas production is a hazardous business owing to high-pressure systems, flammable materials, and rough terrain. Mistakes, equipment malfunctions, or weather patterns may quickly become safety risks or environmental infractions. AI helps by constantly monitoring operating data to detect abnormal patterns or hazardous conditions, such as temperature swings, vibration issues, or gas leaks. It may then send early warning signals or shut down on its own. By using predictive models of historical safety data and real-time data, AI can identify potential high-risk situations and suggest mitigation steps before harm occurs.

Blockchain introduces security by maintaining a safe and unalterable record of all safety events, from near misses to accidents, and how they were handled. This record increases internal accountability and enables regulatory reporting and insurance claim filing. In security audits or investigations, being able to trace what occurred, when, and how the company responded allows for a certain level of trust that can never be achieved with paper records or split databases (Naveena et al., 2024). In this case, the KPIs vary from the frequency of occurrence of events, speed of detection, time to remediate, compliance percentages, and risk levels. Companies that implement AI and blockchain in safety-critical use cases have reportedly lowered safety incidents by 20–40% in two years after starting the program. Digital asset management and compliance are also areas where the value of digital technology is evident. Every piece of equipment in the upstream business, from small valves to large rigs, moves through the life cycle of buying, using, maintaining, certifying, and eventually retiring. Manual or isolated systems have difficulty keeping track of all these assets, leading to inefficiency, lost papers, and compliance problems. AI helps track asset performance, predict when maintenance is needed, and maximize utilization. Blockchain provides a secure record of all life cycle events, including certification logs, inspection reports, warranty data, and disposal records (Tariq, 2025). This complete transparency enhances operational efficiency and prepares companies for audits. Regulators, joint venture partners, and insurers are now requesting proof of well-maintained assets and compliant operations. With blockchain records, companies can provide instant formal documentation of when inspections have been conducted, maintenance records, suppliers' names, and how they conduct safety and environmental compliance. AI insights will even show that risks are being managed in advance and that things are getting better. Among the most significant measures of return on investment here are asset utilization quality, time saved in audit preparation, the number of compliance incidents that arise, maintenance cost per asset, and how much is saved on warranties. Most firms can recover up to 10% of their maintenance budget simply by implementing warranties more effectively, and they can reduce audit times by more than half because of the automatic and consistent records they store.

The cost savings from employing these computer tools can be quantified using a complete return on investment calculation. Although the cost of installing AI and blockchain systems, such as sensors, computers, software, integration fees, and training, is high, the returns are also significant (Adisetya & Gunawan, 2024). The avoided losses based on reduced downtime, lower maintenance expenses, improved supply chain function, better safety results, and fewer fines paid to regulators all make it a good investment. The systems also have the capacity to keep getting better even after they have been installed, so their value keeps increasing. A well-run predictive maintenance plan with blockchain for compliance can return dividends in 18–24 months, with subsequent returns accruing.

In addition to cost savings, there are substantial strategic advantages that make long-term businesses competitive. The sophistication of a business in data usage is now a major factor for investors, business partners, and even employees. Companies that show they are capable of exploiting data correctly and generating innovation have a better opportunity to bring in investment and talent. ESG reports benefit from the clear and verifiable information that blockchain and AI offer. Stakeholders do not need promises; users need concrete proof of sustainability, security, and ethical sourcing. Quick and secure access to these data is now a condition of doing business in the energy industry (Attah et al., 2024). Another non-material benefit is the cultural change and the way the organization functions when these technologies are used.

Groups become more proficient in using data, decisions become more fact-based, and different departments start working together more because they can share and use the same data. The purchasing, operations, safety, and compliance departments all gain a broader view of the firm, aided by AI analysis and backed by blockchain data. By working together, they can lead to better planning, less conflict, and a stronger capability to absorb unexpected events, such as supply chain interruption, new regulation, or political change (Tariq, 2025).

## CHALLENGES AND RISK FACTORS

Data silos and interoperability between different systems are among the biggest and most long-standing issues. In most oil and gas companies, useful data are tied up in separate systems, such as SCADA, asset management tools, procurement systems, or even older paper records that were never meant to be shared. AI technologies require vast quantities of high-quality data from multiple areas to make precise forecasts and draw insightful conclusions. Blockchain also requires standardized and frequent data to function properly (Tariq, 2025). It is difficult to get such systems to "talk" to each other, both from a technical standpoint and from the viewpoint of company operations. Legacy systems may not have the proper tools or data export features to be integrated with newer digital solutions, involving expensive and time-consuming workarounds, such as custom connections.

Another issue is that different teams and departments operate in silos because of the company culture, data ownership, or lack of incentive to share. Not only does it limit what is possible with AI and blockchain, but it also makes data less trustworthy. To fix this, a mix of technical solutions, such as data lakes, integration tools, and API platforms, need to be applied, along with organizational changes in how the company is structured and how it prioritizes data sharing and transparency. Until these data silos are dismantled, the full promise of AI and blockchain cannot be realized, and digital investments can deliver only partial results. The cost and ability to scale blockchain networks to remote locations in the oil and gas industry is another serious challenge. Blockchain networks, especially those used for industrial use cases, require computer power, the Internet, and electricity, which may not be available in remote areas such as offshore platforms, drilling rigs, or deserts. Although permission blockchains are more efficient than public blockchains, they still require hardware, secure storage, and systems that can operate optimally in difficult and disconnected environments. Here, ensuring that the blockchain operates at its best without using too much energy and experiencing latency is a major concern (Kumar et al., 2023). Scaling is also more difficult with an increase in the number of transactions. A blockchain system that tracks every asset movement, sensor reading, maintenance record, and AI alert must handle a large volume of data without introducing delays or making the data unavailable. It is not practical to put all such data on the blockchain itself; therefore, a strategy of storing large data off-chain and hashes or pointers on-chain must be used. However, it is challenging to maintain these pieces in sync across far-flung areas with poor Internet and requires smart system design and extensive testing. These limitations may lead to decisions regarding which data are important enough to be tracked by blockchain and which can be managed by traditional databases, perhaps making the full promise of transparency harder to fulfill (Alazab & Alhyari, 2024). Beyond the technical aspects, human factors are vitally important. Training and change management are typically overlooked in digital transformation programmes. Dealing with AI and blockchain technologies requires a workforce that understands how the industry functions and how these emerging systems function and their limitations. Most employees in the oil and gas sector have been dealing with legacy systems for decades and may not be accustomed to data science, machine learning, or blockchain technology. The gap between computer know-how and traditional knowledge can be vast, requiring extensive training, learning, and on-the-ground experience to fill the gap. These regulatory challenges are exacerbated by the political realities around the world. Therefore, organizations must be both proactive and well-informed about regulations, working closely with lawyers, government agencies, and international standards bodies to ensure that their digital systems comply with local and international laws without affecting their performance.

In addition to these challenges, it is difficult to demonstrate the effectiveness of the return on investment for digital initiatives. While digital transformation may yield substantial long-term benefits, the initial price tag, both in terms of dollars and in changing how a company works, can be hefty. Executives may struggle to argue for spending, especially in an industry where oil prices are unpredictable and companies habitually retrench (Dev et al., 2020). To make a strong business case, hard numbers illustrating how digital investments improve things such as fewer breakdowns, lower repair costs, better safety, and compliance with legislation are necessary. However, such benefits do not occur overnight, and early projects might not deliver profits earlier, which can lead to projects being abandoned midway or garnering less support from top management.

Another challenge is the development of digital systems. When companies dabble in new ideas in small, disconnected pockets and do not connect them to the whole firm, they end up with many disconnected systems that cannot grow. Companies need a long-term plan and to move step-by-step, using early victories to build credibility for further investments (Peng, 2025). . They must also create guidelines so that digital projects fall in line with the primary goals of the company, so that each trial not only works on its own but also adds value to larger operations. Sometimes, even companies providing digital services or tools can be dangerous. If they do not have expertise in the oil and gas industry or do not deliver as committed, it can lead to problems. Because AI and blockchain are so new, startups and software providers are still testing their products, and the solutions might not be stable or proven in real-life use. Due diligence must be performed carefully, piloting the new tools in real-world settings, and having strong agreements on what will be delivered by the provider. Overdependence on one company for a key element of the digital system is also risky, especially if the company fails or changes its strategy.

## OUTLOOK AND INNOVATION PATHWAYS

The upstream oil and gas digital future is being shaped by a mix of new technologies that were, not so long ago, considered nothing more than ideas or for other industries. Now, with AI and blockchain showing real value across areas ranging from predictive maintenance to supply chain visibility to asset integrity, people are expecting the next big changes that will drive the industry's digital future. Some of the most thrilling transitions are digital twins, blockchain tokenization of assets, quantum-resistant protocols, and autonomous decentralized organizations (DAOs) to automate equipment maintenance and increase vendor responsibility (Borade et al., 2025). Although these technologies differ in maturity, they have started to pave the way for a more autonomous, efficient, and trustworthy oilfield environment. Digital twins are one of the most significant breakthroughs in upstream automation. A digital twin is a simulation in the virtual space of an actual-world asset, process, or system that is updated in real time based on sensor and operational system real-time data. Upstream oil and gas could mean anything from an isolated wellhead or drilling rig to an entire field. When integrated with AI algorithms, these twins evolve into intelligent entities capable of implementing what-if scenarios, verifying operation strategies, and optimizing performance without risking actual equipment.

The impact of digital twins on oilfield automation is significant. Operators can operate advanced assets remotely from one location, test new configurations in a simulated setting before implementing them in the field, and train AI models on the twin in simulation. This minimizes downtime and maximizes the accuracy of the operation. Digital twins are also essential for monitoring and diagnosing offshore or remote sites where access is limited. For example, if a subsea pump digital twin warns of imminent wear from real-time sensor data, maintenance can be planned prior to failure and without incurring costly delays. In the long run, these models not only forecast issues but also prescribe solutions. As digital twins become increasingly common and advanced, they will be at the forefront of upstream automation plans, especially when used with blockchain technology to track and verify all actions and changes (Islam et al., 2024). Another cutting-edge idea that is gaining prominence is the blockchain-based tokenization of assets, especially for predictive maintenance. Tokenization refers to the creation of a virtual representation of an actual asset or service right. Herein, it can be used to denote a maintenance contract, a service-level agreement, or even an asset. Each token contains data regarding the asset, such as its ID, maintenance records, usage permissions, warranty details, and AI-based health forecasts. Such tokens can be transferred, shared, or traded in blockchain marketplaces, thus facilitating more open and flexible service environments (Hossain et al., 2025).

Imagine that an offshore pump is predicted to fail after 90 days. Asset tokens with AI-generated prognoses and blockchain-validated maintenance records can be displayed in a decentralized marketplace. Service providers can bid on it with access to the blockchain for maintenance work with prices, availability, and performance assurance, all managed by smart contracts. When a provider is selected, the contract comes to life when the required conditions are fulfilled, for example, when the technician completes the work or the post-maintenance AI test of the asset. This develops a more dynamic, open maintenance system that leaves scheduled or reactionary maintenance to a marketplace-based and dynamic approach. It also boosts transparency, as the history and performance of the assets of the service provider are clearly documented and readily available (Cui et al., 2022). As blockchain is embedding itself into such places, the question of future exposure is becoming notable, particularly due to up-and-coming technologies such as quantum computing. Cryptography is safe in legacy blockchain protocols but may be broken by the quantum computers of tomorrow. This is a serious threat in oil and gas, where the history of the asset, compliance data, and contracts must be reliable and safe over decades. Therefore, the industry is currently investigating quantum-resistant blockchain protocols based on lattice-based, hash-based, and multivariate cryptography. These measures are not just a precaution that you are taking, but it goes to show a desire to implement long-term data integrity and security. Upstream operations have high capital requirements, and the asset life is extensive; thus, digital records should be reliable for a minimum of 30 years. In future planning, quantum resilience will be considered an important aspect of the choice of blockchain platforms. Enterprise security policies and government regulations also fall under this project, some of which are already undergoing changes to require post-quantum readiness in critical infrastructure (Islam et al., 2025). The most radical innovation frontier of upstream operations is potentially yielded by autonomous decentralized autonomous organizations (DAOs) that operate equipment and make suppliers liable. DAOs are blockchain-based entities that use smart contracts, which are automatically operated to make decisions and implement policies according to rules and real-time information. In oil and gas, a DAO can be used to manage the maintenance of critical assets in various locations, from booking repairs and tracking service performance to paying bills and making compliance checks.

For instance, a DAO can be designed to track digital twins and AI alerts to detect when maintenance is required. When a certain threshold is achieved, such as a critical pump running at destructive vibration levels, the DAO can automatically request an approved vendor to send a service request. These suppliers would be selected based on their past performance, which is maintained on the blockchain, for example, how responsive they are, how costly they are, and whether they have complied with rules in the past. The job would be completed and authenticated by sensor data and AI authentication, and payment would then be sent automatically via a smart contract. In such a system, human intervention is minimal, everything is transparent and obvious, and the entire process is simplified. With such self-regulation comes a factor of responsibility: vendors cannot fake records, skip steps, or delay reports without the DAO catching up on them and penalizing them (Adisetya & Gunawan, 2024). The impact of DAOs goes beyond making things easier for people. DAOs change the nature of how business relationships are formed and maintained. In an industry once reliant on long contracts, lawyers, and reams of paperwork, DAOs offer a smoother, real-time solution based on data-driven decision-making. They also enable smaller specialty firms to be involved in service work and compete on a level playing field based on history of performance and openness instead of who they know or the size of a contract. This would bring additional ideas and competition into the oilfield services sector, lowering costs and raising quality. These innovative changes are not singular; they are interconnected. Digital twins provide real-time data and detailed insights to enable the management of smart DAOs. Blockchain tokens for assets and services allow rights, responsibilities, and results to be tracked with precision. Quantum-resistant security systems guarantee the security of the entire system in the long term (Lahami & Chaabane, 2023).

## CONCLUSION

The prospective upstream oil and gas industry finds itself floating in an uncertain, environmentally aware, and tech-filled future, whereas doing business as usual will no longer do the trick. To remain competitive, resilient, and sustainable, organizations must embrace smart systems that enable them to see better, predict more accurately, and have a stronger assurance of their operations. This is not merely a technical upgrade; artificial intelligence and blockchain reconstruction amalgamate the decision-making process, the ways assets are handled, and the distributed authority. AI offers profound insights based on real-time data, whereas blockchain ensures data security, transparency, and dissemination. They combine to generate a digital customer-focused environment that supports the sophisticated requirements of upstream oil and gas. However, it is not just about software installation. It should have a clear plan, one that brings business objectives, technical requirements, and capabilities of the individuals involved into line. The first is to clearly define business goals. Digital transformation does not work when technology is seen as an end in itself and not as a means to an end. The most effective use of AI and blockchain requires leaders to identify the significant issues that they intend to address, including untenable equipment malfunctions, unseen supply chains, safety and security risks, and regulatory obstacles. With these goals in mind, organizations can decide which data are most useful, which processes can most easily be automated or shared, and which assets yield the best return on predictive maintenance and monitoring over time. Then, one needs to look at the existing systems in place, such as SCADA, IoT sensors, maintenance software, and procurement systems, and determine how well they communicate with each other. AI requires strong data pipelines, and blockchain must be integrated with legacy databases and processes. This inevitably uncovers problems such as aging systems, siloed data, and process gaps that must be resolved before any intelligent system can operate.

With the foundation in place, pilot projects are needed to experiment with how AI and blockchain work in real-world situations and what value they can provide. They should be aimed at distinct, high-value tasks, such as forecasting when pumps on offshore platforms may fail or tracing high-value drilling equipment through blockchain. These initial projects enhance algorithms, experiment with how data are handled, and develop user confidence. Such projects should be planned so that they can expand, utilizing adaptable frameworks, API interfaces, and standard data formats that can be applied in various sites and regions. Along with technical installation, companies must prepare their employees for a new digital reality (Ktari et al., 2024). For developers, the challenge is to develop tools that are powerful, reliable, and easy to use for oilfield users. It is not enough for AI to make good predictions or for blockchain to secure records; these technologies must be usable by engineers, procurement teams, safety officers, and executives. User interfaces must be intuitive and simple to learn, and the systems beneath them must be able to handle extreme environments and low Internet connectivity in the field (Tamtam & Tourabi, 2025). Firms should also become members of associations engaged in creating standards for data formats, blockchain protocols, and AI governance. Industry-wide knowledge sharing eliminates duplication of effort, speeds up development, and creates trust in the use of digital technologies. Partnerships with universities, research organizations, and startups can bring fresh ideas, new research, and faster development that might be unobtainable in mature companies. Finally, the path to the convergence of AI and blockchain in the upstream oil and gas industry is arduous but exciting. The technologies are available, use cases are evident, and early successes are already showing promise. What is needed now is the determination to act with a decisive vision, steady effort, and alignment of priorities. By focusing on concrete business value, investing in core capabilities, building integrated platforms, and creating cross-discipline collaboration, the industry can bring responsible innovation with concrete results in operations, finance, and the environment. The future of upstream oil and gas is not just digital; it is smart, decentralized, and closely networked. It is time to build the future.

## REFERENCES


Adisetya, E., & Gunawan, S. (2024, July). The conceptual model of Indonesian palm oil supply chain based on blockchain. [). IOP Publishing.]. *IOP Conference Series. Earth and Environmental Science, 1377*(1), 012007. DOI: 10.1088/1755-1315/1377/1/012007

Alazab, M., & Alhyari, S. (2024). Industry 4.0 innovation: A systematic literature review on the role of blockchain technology in creating smart and sustainable manufacturing facilities. *Information (Basel), 15*(2), 78. DOI: 10.3390/info15020078

Attah, R.U., Matthew, B., Garba, P., Gil-Ozoudeh, I., & Iwuanyanwu, O. (2024). Strategic frameworks for digital transformation across logistics and energy sectors: Bridging technology with business strategy. *Open Access Research Journal of Science and Technology*.12(02), 070-80.

Aziz, S., Ahmed, I., Khan, K., & Khalid, M. (2024). Emerging trends and approaches for designing net-zero low-carbon integrated energy networks: A review of current practices. *Arabian Journal for Science and Engineering, 49*(5), 6163–6185. DOI: 10.1007/s13369-023-08336-0

Borade, S. A., Bansod, S., Hati, A. J., & Singh, S. K. (2025, May). AI Edge Processor Using RISC-V Instruction Set Architecture Design. In *2025 Global Conference in Emerging Technology (GINOTECH)* (pp. 1-8). IEEE. DOI: 10.1109/GINOTECH63460.2025.11076631

Chen, W., Men, Y., Fuster, N., Osorio, C., & Juan, A. A. (2024). Artificial intelligence in logistics optimization with sustainable criteria: A review. *Sustainability (Basel), 16*(21), 9145. DOI: 10.3390/su16219145

Cui, L., Gao, M., Dai, J., & Mou, J. (2022). Improving supply chain collaboration through operational excellence approaches: An IoT perspective. *Industrial Management & Data Systems, 122*(3), 565–591. DOI: 10.1108/IMDS-01-2020-0016

Dev, N. K., Shankar, R., & Qaiser, F. H. (2020). Industry 4.0 and circular economy: Operational excellence for sustainable reverse supply chain performance. *Resources, Conservation and Recycling, 153*, 104583. DOI: 10.1016/j.resconrec.2019.104583

Durán, C., Yazdi, A. K., Derpich, I., & Tan, Y. (2024). Leveraging blockchain for maritime port supply chain management through multicriteria decision making. *Mathematics, 12*(10), 1511. DOI: 10.3390/math12101511

Egbumokei, P. I., Dienagha, I. N., Digitemie, W. N., Onukwulu, E. C., & Oladipo, O. T. (2024). The role of digital transformation in enhancing sustainability in oil and gas business operations. *International Journal of Multidisciplinary Research and Growth Evaluation*, *5*(5), 2582–7138. DOI: 10.54660/.IJMRGE.2024.5.5.1029-1041

Hossain, M. D., Faruk, M. I., Plabon, F. W., & Jyoti, J. S.Mohammad Didar Hossain-Md Imtiaz FarukFatin Wahab PlabonJeba Sadia Jyoti. (2025). Sustainable Supply Chain Project Management: Strategies for Reducing Carbon Footprints. *Journal of Business and Management Studies*, *7*(2), 78–90. DOI: 10.32996/jbms.2025.7.2.7

Islam, M. J., Pathan, M. N., Rahman, A., Islam, S., Sultana, A., & Das, S. C. "Priority-based Traceability in Crude Oil Refined Products Supply Chain Through Blockchain." In *2024 6th International Conference on Sustainable Technologies for Industry 5.0 (STI)*, pp. 1-6. IEEE, 2024. DOI: 10.1109/STI64222.2024.10951058

Kasych, A., Yakovenko, Y., & Tarasenko, I. (2019, September). *Optimization of business processes with the use of industrial digitalization. In 2019 ieee international conference on modern electrical and energy systems (mees).* IEEE.

Kishnani, U., Madabhushi, S., & Das, S. (2023, July). Blockchain in oil and gas supply chain: a literature review from user security and privacy perspective. In *International Symposium on Human Aspects of Information Security and Assurance* (pp. 296-309). Cham: Springer Nature Switzerland. DOI: 10.1007/978-3-031-38530-8_24

Ktari, J., Frikha, T., Hsairi, M. M., Lakhal, I. B., Naifar, F., & Bouaziz, A. (2024, May). Development of a Decentralized Application for Managing Food Supply Chain Based on Blockchain. In *2024 IEEE 4th International Maghreb Meeting of the Conference on Sciences and Techniques of Automatic Control and Computer Engineering (MI-STA)* (pp. 36-40). IEEE. DOI: 10.1109/MI-STA61267.2024.10599659

Kumar, S., Lim, W. M., Sivarajah, U., & Kaur, J. (2023). Artificial intelligence and blockchain integration in business: Trends from a bibliometric-content analysis. *Information Systems Frontiers*, *25*(2), 871–896. PMID: 35431617

Lahami, M., & Chaabane, F. (2023, November). Improving the supply chain management via Blockchain: an olive oil case study. In *TACC* (pp. 182-193).

Lodhi, S. K., & Zeb, S. (2025). The Role of AI in Circular Manufacturing: Towards a Zero-Waste Economy Provides its Headings. *Enrichment: Journal of Multidisciplinary Research and Development*, *3*(1), 124–134. DOI: 10.55324/enrichment.v3i1.339

Naveena, M., Ellaturu, N., Kumari, T. L., Bambuwala, S., & Rajalakshmi, M. (2024). Ai-Driven Solutions for Supply Chain Management. *Journal of Informatics Education and Research*, *4*, 861–868.

Peng, Z. (2025). Transforming Energy Resilience through Supply Chain Digitization: Risk Management as a Mediator. *International Review of Economics & Finance*, *102*, 104293. DOI: 10.1016/j.iref.2025.104293

Tamtam, F., & Tourabi, A. (2025). Advancing Digital Supply Chains through Generative AI: A Strategic Framework with the ELECTRE III Method. *Complex Systems Informatics and Modeling. Quarterly*, *43*, 17–33.

Tariq, M. (Ed.). (2025). *Merging Artificial Intelligence With the Internet of Things*. IGI Global., DOI: 10.4018/979-8-3693-8547-0

Tariq, M. (Ed.). (2025). *Emerging Multisector Applications of AI and IoT*. IGI Global., DOI: 10.4018/979-8-3373-4332-7

Tariq, M. U. (2025). *AI-Driven Learning and Engagement in Higher Education*. IGI Global., DOI: 10.4018/979-8-3693-4074-5

Tariq, M. U. (2025). The Role of AI-Powered Learning Analytics in Enhancing Student Engagement and Performance. In J. Moore, S. Gupta, M. Sharma, A. Garg, & H. Josephine V. L. (Eds.), *Transforming Education With Data Science in the AI Era* (pp. 123-148). IGI Global Scientific Publishing. DOI: 10.4018/979-8-3373-2185-1.ch005

Tariq, M. U. (2025). Integration of Artificial Intelligence and Machine Learning in Business Intelligence: Enhancing Decision Making and Operational Efficiency. In Ishtaiwi, A., Al-Qerem, A., Al Khaldy, M., & Alauthman, M. (Eds.), *Driving Modern Business Intelligence Architecture for Operational Efficiency* (pp. 279–306). IGI Global Scientific Publishing., DOI: 10.4018/979-8-3373-2125-7.ch009

## KEY TERMS AND DEFINITIONS

**Blockchain Ledger:** Immutable digital record for transactional verification.
**Predictive Maintenance:** AI-driven predicting equipment failure timing.
**Smart Contracts:** Automated rules implementing blockchain-based agreements.

# Chapter 6
# Integrating Large Language Models and Blockchain Technology for Digital Transformation in the Oil and Gas Industry:
## Enhancing Efficiency and Transparency in Operations

**Shamsu Abdullahi**
https://orcid.org/0009-0003-2498-5078
*Department of Computing, Faculty of Science, Management and Computing, Universiti Teknologi Petronas, Malaysia*

**Fasee Ullah**
https://orcid.org/0000-0001-6167-5253
*Department of Computing, Faculty of Science, Management and Computing, Universiti Teknologi Petronas, Malaysia*

**Tahmid Chowdhury Ashraf**
*Department of Computing, Faculty of Science, Management and Computing, Universiti Teknologi Petronas, Malaysia*

**Muhammad Sabo Yahaya**
https://orcid.org/0000-0002-7993-9269
*Department of Computing, Faculty of Science, Management and Computing, Universiti Teknologi Petronas, Malaysia*

**Kamaluddeen Usman Danyaro**
https://orcid.org/0000-0003-1022-4983
*Department of Computing, Faculty of Science, Management and Computing, Universiti Teknologi Petronas, Malaysia*

**Musa Ahmed Zayyad**
*Umaru Musa Yaradua University, Katsina, Nigeria*

DOI: 10.4018/979-8-3373-5457-6.ch006

**Mujeeb Ur Rehman Shaikh**
*Department of Computing, Faculty of Science, Management and Computing, Universiti Teknologi Petronas, Malaysia*

## ABSTRACT

*Growing operational complexity, ageing infrastructure, and rising demands for efficiency and sustainability are all contributing factors to the oil and gas industry's current dramatic transformation. To improve operations in offshore facilities, this chapter investigates the combination of two innovative digital technologies: blockchain and large language models (LLMs). LLMs offer sophisticated features for handling unstructured technical data, automating documentation, enhancing decision-making, and assisting with predictive maintenance. Blockchain guarantees trust, transparency, and safe, decentralised data management throughout the value chain. Applications like smart contract automation, secure data exchange, real-time compliance, and intelligent asset monitoring are made possible by these technologies working together. The chapter also discusses issues with workforce development, data quality assurance, integration, and compatibility with legacy systems.*

## INTRODUCTION

Oil and gas (O&G) industry has long been regarded as the cornerstone of the global economy, but is under deep transformation. Despite its legacy of the adoption of advanced operational technologies, the sector has been cautious in its adoption of digital innovation in its entirety (Zakizadeh & Zand, 2024). It is facing increasing pressure to tackle operational complexity, strict environmental standards, and increasing efficiency, safety and transparency demands. Two disruptive technologies, the Large Language Models (LLMs) and the Blockchain, appear to be powerful catalysts for digital transformation. The LLMs, supported by an advanced transformer architecture, provides the ability to understand, produce and reason for large quantities of text and sequence data. Their strength lies in the processing of unstructured information such as maintenance logs, drilling reports, sensor feeds and regulatory documents (Mahal, 2024), making them especially suitable for O&G's data-intensive nature. Unlike traditional intelligent assistants, which are developed for narrow tasks, LLMs provide adaptive general intelligence that enhances the documentation, decision-making, preventive maintenance, and knowledge discovery throughout the value chain. In addition, Blockchain introduces a decentralised, confidential and transparent infrastructure to manage data, transactions and stakeholders' interactions. It provides a key "trust layer" for the safe sharing of data, tracking, compliance automated execution of intelligent contracts.

The convergence of LLM and blockchain technologies offers transformative opportunities. LLMs can extract real-time information from unstructured or time series data, and Blockchain ensures that data and information derived from it can be verified, variable and secure (Gong, Yan, Zhang, An, & Liu, 2024). They provide a synergistic framework to redefine the creation, validation, and application of knowledge in the O&G sector. However, the widespread adoption of these technologies is still in its infancy. Most of the research already carried out in the industry focuses on conventional mechanical learning and deep learning applications in areas such as seismic interpretation, reservoir modelling, and production optimisation (A. Ullah, Qi, Hussain, Ullah, & Ali, 2024). LLM's transformative potential to handle domain-specific unstructured data and the role of blockchain in providing secure digital infrastructure are still underexplored (Kanka, 2024). In addition, industry-specific challenges, such as fragmented data silos, outdated legacy systems, trust deficits and complex regulatory landscapes, are still obstructing large-scale deployment. This chapter aims to bridge this gap by providing a comprehensive study of how LLMs and Blockchain can contribute individually and together to the digital transformation of the O&G industry.

This discussion is particularly appropriate in the current state of digital transformation in the O&G sector. A recent survey revealed that more than 70% O&G companies still classified themselves as digital beginners, while only 7% percent of them reached the level of digital champions (Prestidge, 2022). The average digital maturity of the industry is 4.68 out of 10, highlighting significant opportunities for systemic progress. The economic crisis, such as the recent volatility of oil prices, emphasises the urgency of adopting resilient and data-driven approaches that not only improve operational productivity but also restore investor confidence. However, there is still a paradox: while the O&G industry is known for sophisticated operational technologies such as precision drilling, seismic imaging, and advanced refining systems, its adoption of business-wide digital platforms and intelligent software is still relatively underdeveloped. This gap indicates that the limitation is not technical capacity, but rather strategic uncertainty and cultural inertia. Technological progress in this sector is often driven more by external forces than by internal digital innovations. Therefore, the failure to pursue comprehensive digital integration remains the fundamental obstacle to maximising operational efficiency, reducing costs, and achieving long-term sustainability. In this regard, the integration of emerging technologies such as LLMs and blockchains offers transformational opportunities. These tools can enable real-time decision making, improve data transparency, and lead to continuous automation of value chains. However, achieving these benefits requires a clear strategic vision for digital transformation in the O&G industry, a visionary leadership, inter-departmental alignment and alignment.

## 1. LEVERAGING LARGE LANGUAGE MODELS IN O&G DIGITAL TRANSFORMATION

LLMs represent a significant advancement in artificial intelligence, serving as powerful deep learning architectures capable of understanding, generating, and manipulating human language with remarkable proficiency (Qabasiyu, Zayyad, & Abdullahi, 2023a). Their core capabilities include advanced text generation, nuanced sentiment analysis, and efficient code generation (Abdullahi, Danyaro, et al., 2025; Qabasiyu, Zayyad, & Abdullahi, 2023b). These capabilities are powered by vast corpora of diverse data and sophisticated algorithms rooted in Natural Language Processing (NLP). Despite their general proficiency, LLMs are not inherently tailored for specialised domains. In sectors such as the O&G industry, where domain-specific jargon, technical abbreviations, and unique linguistic patterns (e.g., in drilling reports or maintenance logs) are prevalent, fine-tuning or customisation becomes essential. Without domain adaptation, general-purpose LLMs may underperform or produce inaccurate and even misleading results.

The development of Small Language Models (SLMs), which are lightweight, optimised models trained on particular domain datasets, is a noteworthy breakthrough in this regard. These models address important issues with cloud-based LLMs, including latency, data security, and the high energy consumption of large-scale model inference, while providing industry-specific applicability. SLMs are frequently installed on-site, offering businesses managing sensitive operational data and meeting environmental standards a more sustainable and safe option. This paradigm change draws attention to an important factor: using generic, off-the-shelf LLMs may have limited advantages and present hazards in highly technical settings. By customising these models to domain-specific tasks, which necessitates a significant investment in data acquisition, cleaning, and training, LLMs have the potential to revolutionise the O&G industry. An increasing emphasis on effective, safe, and ecologically friendly AI solutions is reflected in the growing preference for SLMs. Additionally, it emphasises how O&G companies should develop their own AI capabilities and maintain control over proprietary data instead of depending solely on external, general-purpose models.

## 1.1 Transformer Architecture: The Backbone of LLMs

Transformer architectures were introduced in the groundbreaking work of Vaswani et al, which originally aimed to use GPU power to perform efficient parallel computations (Vaswani et al., 2017). The core of the transformer is the self-attention mechanism, which effectively captures long-term contextual information and surpasses the ability of the repetition and reversal mechanism. The architecture was initially applied to a mechanical translation and is structured as a novel encoder-decoder model, consisting of several blocks of self-attention. Figure 1 gives a high-level overview of the transformer. In the following sections, we explore the main elements and variations of this architecture.

i. **Encoder:** The encoder processes all the input sequences simultaneously, so that the attention layer can access all tokens at each step. These models are usually pre-trained for purposes such as masking language modelling, in which parts of the input are corrupted and the model is responsible for reconstructing the original sequence. This method allows models to learn bidirectional contextual representations, making encoder architectures particularly effective for tasks such as sentence classification, named entity recognition, questions and answers. In addition, residual connections and layer normalisation contribute to stabilising training and improving performance by ensuring effective gradient distribution.
ii. **Decoder:** Decoder follow an auto-regressive approach, where attention layers are restricted to attending only to preceding tokens within the sequence at each step. During pre-training, these models are trained using causal language modelling, predicting the next token in a sequence given prior context. This training paradigm makes decoder-only architectures highly suitable for text generation tasks, including machine translation, dialogue systems, and content summarization. To maintain proper autoregressive behaviour, decoder models employ masked self-attention, ensuring that predictions at any position I depend only on previously generated tokens and not future inputs.
iii. **Input Embedding:** The input of the transformer model consists of learning token inscriptions that represent words or sub-words in high-dimensional dense vectorised representations. In order to preserve the sequential order of the token, these embeddings are enhanced with positional encoding, an aspect that is not intrinsically captured by self-attention. These codes are usually derived from sinusoidal functions or learner position embeddings and provide essential information about the token position in the sequence. In addition, the same learning matrix is usually shared between the input layer and the final linear transformation before the softmax output layer, ensuring the efficiency of the parameters and improved generalization.

iv. **Positional Encoding:** Attention mechanisms don't naturally understand token order; instead, they process input sequences as unordered sets of embeddings. A Transformer model is unable to adequately capture the structure required for language comprehension if sequence positions are not represented. Positional encodings, which embed order-related information directly into the model's input, are introduced to address this. In order to guarantee that the model can differentiate token positions and generalise to longer sequences, the original Transformer accomplishes this by employing sinusoidal functions of different frequencies.

$$PE_{(pos,2i)} = \sin\left(\frac{pos}{10000^{\frac{2i}{d_{model}}}}\right), PE_{(pos,2i+1)} = \cos\left(\frac{pos}{10000^{\frac{2i}{d_{model}}}}\right)$$

where i is the embedding dimension index and pos is a token's position in the sequence. The model can learn both absolute and relative positional relationships thanks to these encodings' sinusoidal pattern for each dimension. Extrapolation to longer sequences than those observed during training is made easier by the selection of sinusoidal functions. Experimental results show that both approaches produce comparable performance, even though learnt positional embeddings have also been investigated. However, because they offer a continuous and structured representation of token positions, sinusoidal encodings are frequently chosen because they enhance generalisation to sequences of different lengths.

v. **Self-Attention:** Regardless of how far apart tokens are in the sequence, the attention mechanism captures their dependencies to create a rich representation of the input sequence. Each token can assess its relationship with every other token thanks to self-attention, which helps the model develop a global contextual understanding. Self-attention uses a mechanism called Scaled Dot-Product Attention at the heart of the Transformer architecture to dynamically assign tokens relative to other tokens. This works in three main steps:

- **Query (Q):** Represents the token making an attention request.
- **Key (K):** Represents the token being attended to.
- **Value (V):** Holds the actual content information.
- **Attention Scores:** The model calculates attention scores by taking the dot product of the query vector with all key vectors, then applies a softmax function to obtain a probability distribution.

$$\text{Attention}(Q, K, V) = \text{softmax}\left(\frac{QK^{\top}}{\sqrt{d_k}}\right)V$$

- **Weighted Sum:** The final representation of each token is computed as a weighted sum of the value vectors, where the attention scores determine the contribution of each value.

vi. **Multi-head attention**: By adding several parallel attention heads that each focus on a different aspect of the input, multi-head attention improves the self-attention mechanism. The model can learn different representations and capture different relationships between tokens by dividing the input into multiple heads. This enhances the transformer's comprehension of the sequence by enabling it to analyse multiple contextual dependencies at once. The outputs of the various attention heads are concatenated and linearly transformed after processing, guaranteeing that the model combines the disparate data into a single representation.

$$MultiHead(Q, K, V) = Concat(\text{head}_1, \ldots, \text{head}_h) W^O$$

where each head is computed as:

$$\text{head}_i = Attention(Q W_i^Q, K W_i^K, V W_i^V)$$

vii. **Feedforward:** Following the multi-head attention sub-layer, a fully connected feed-forward network (FFN) processes each position in the sequence. The model can capture intricate hierarchical representations thanks to this FFN, which consists of two linear transformations divided by a ReLU activation function. The parameters of the FFN differ between layers, even though it is applied in the same way at every position.

## 1.2 Applications of LLMs in O&G

The application of LLMs across the O&G value chain offers a wide array of benefits:

### 1.2.1 Operational Efficiency and Optimisation

The integration of LLMs into O&G operations marks significant progress in improving operational efficiency and process optimisation. LLMs can analyse large volumes of structured and unstructured real-time data and can identify complex patterns and trends that traditional analysis methods can overlook. These insights support predictive data-based decision-making that contributes directly to better performance in drilling, production, maintenance and supply chain functions. In upstream operations, LLMs are used to optimise decision-making by generating predictive data analytics that improve drilling data analysis. For example, a chatbot with a generative AI engine that was specifically designed for drilling and production analysis was introduced to interpret rig reports and provide operational recommendations. With cloud-based machine learning and LLMs, chatbot responds to user requests and offers data-based insights. The effectiveness of the system has been demonstrated in the use cases: automatic daily drilling reports analysis, Plunger Lifter performance diagnosis and intelligent queries over large document storage. These applications illustrate how generative AI simplifies the interpretation of complex data and improves awareness of the situation, leading to safer and more cost-effective operations. In addition to field operations, LLMs also plays an important role in back-office optimisation. A study proposed an LLM-based solution for automating invoice classification in the development of unconventional assets, including drilling, drilling completion and field maintenance. The model, fine-tuned in more than 1,500 cost categories, has achieved high accuracy, significantly improving cost management and supply chain efficiency compared to manual methods. This shows LLM's versatility in improving both operational and administrative efficiency. Predictive maintenance is another important area in which LLMs offer considerable value. This model can predict equipment failures by processing real-time sensor data and recommend a timely intervention. This minimises costly downtime and ensures continuous high-performance operation of key assets throughout the value chain of O&G. Commercial interest in LLMs and generative AIs is increasing, reflecting the potential for transformation. Within the O&G industry, the market for generative AI is expected to increase from approximately US$526.15 billion in 2024 to US$601.82 billion in 2025. This trend of upwards indicates the increase in industry adoption and investment in AI technologies that drive digital transformation. In summary, LLMs integration into O&G operations supports more accurate, efficient and reliable decision-making. From optimising drilling strategies to automating document analysis and improving predictive maintenance, LLMs redefines operational workflows and unlocks new productivity and cost-effectiveness.

### 1.2.2 Data Analysis and Knowledge Management

LLMs facilitate the data analysis and knowledge management in the O&G. These models enable the interaction of natural language with complex datasets, allowing engineers, geoscientists analysts to access data-based insights without deep technical knowledge of query languages or database structures. By generating natural language summaries from geological reports, well logs and maintenance records, LLMs significantly reduces the time to view. The O&G industry produces large quantities of structured and unstructured data, including seismic investigations, drilling reports, and production records. Traditional data retrieval methods often require knowledge of complex database schemas, thereby restricting accessibility. LLMs translates natural language requests into structured query languages (SQLs), extracts insights directly from unstructured documents, makes data more accessible, and improves operating efficiency. Several recent studies justify the LLMs' application in data analysis within oil and industry. Pacis et al. (2024) applied zero-shot in-context learning to enhance information management in drilling operations, reducing the need for domain-specific model training (Pacis, Alyaev, Pelfrene, & Wiktorski, 2024). Eckroth el. Al 2023 Introduced tools such as PetroQA and GraphQA, which provide verified and contextual answers to petroleum-related questions using structured knowledge graphs and selected sources using LLMs (Eckroth et al., 2023). Lokhande et al. (2023) developed a system using the T5 model for translating natural language queries into database commands, supported by context categorisation and data augmentation to improve performance (Lokhande, Pillai, & Mangsuli, 2023). Pillai et al. (2022) built an LLM-powered platform for semantic search, classification, and attribute extraction from unstructured oilfield documents, enhancing productivity (Pillai, Ryali, Maniar, Mangsuli, & Abubakar, 2022).

To support digital transformation through automated event tagging, Valliyatt et al. (2024) integrated BERT and BiLSTM for event classification in daily drilling reports (DDRs) (Valliyatt, Tharayil, Razhi, AlQarni, & AlThubaiti, 2024). As illustrated in PETRONAS case studies, Martin et al. (2024) suggested a searchable LLM-ontology hybrid system for unstructured data repositories (Martin, Zanuri, Sockalingam, & Andersen, 2024). To improve accuracy and relevance, Alsultan & Razak (2024) and Idris & Alsultan (2023) emphasised the necessity of tailoring LLMs with industry-specific vocabularies and training corpora (Alsultan & Razak, 2024; Idris & Alsultan, 2023). These developments highlight how LLMs have the potential to completely transform knowledge management, data discovery, and decision-making in the oil and gas sector. LLMs facilitate strategic innovation and operational excellence by providing easy access to insightful information.

### 1.2.3 Compliance and Regulatory Reporting

LLMs play an increasingly important role in improving compliance and regulatory reporting in O&G industry. These models support automated monitoring and interpretation of the evolution of regulatory requirements, streamline the generation of legal reports and ensure timely and accurate submissions across the jurisdictions. LLMs allows you to monitor legal and environmental standards in real time and help extract and analyse structured data from complex documents, such as those submitted EDGAR database. This capability is particularly important for corporate governance, environmental, social and governance (ESG) reports and compliance with global disclosure frameworks (Li & Maiti, 2025). By combining the ability of unstructured data from incident logs, audit trails, and safety reports, LLMs can extract important compliance-related information, detect errors, and automate the production of documents under industry regulations (OKEDELE, AZIZA,

ODURO, & ISHOLA, 2024). In financial reporting, LLM-powered tools improve the readiness for audits by identifying and recommending passages that comply with the requirements of legal disclosure (Berger et al., 2023). LLMs also contribute to data protection compliance. For example, models were used to ensure compliance with GDPR by categorising data from activity logs and supporting consent management practices (von Schwerin & Reichert, 2024). However, the dependence on LLMs brings legal and ethical concerns, particularly the validity of content generated by AI in legally binding documents. Recent studies have suggested that formal assurance frameworks should be introduced to verify the robustness of LLMs products against hostile warnings and compliance with emerging AI regulations such as the EU AI Act (2024). In addition to text analysis, LLMs can be integrated with other technologies such as drone-based methane detection systems.

Safety compliance is another area where LLMs provides significant value. LLMs analyse operational procedures and safety logs to detect deviations from protocols, which is one of the main causes of high-risk industry accidents (Bensonch, Argyropoulos, Dimopoulos, Mikellidou, & Boustras, 2022). In addition, compliance with national and international environmental tax policies is essential for reducing the impact of operations on the environment, and LLMs can support forecasts and accountability for environmental taxes (Mas' ud, Yusuf, Udin, & Al-Dhamari, 2020). In countries where data protection laws are strict, such as China and Brazil, the application of AI and LLMs also requires strict governance frameworks to manage legal risks associated with data location and privacy (Qothrunada & Handayani, 2023). At the organisational level, the integration of LLMs into sustainability accounting and GRI 300 environmental disclosures improves regulation performance and transparency (Aman, 2024). Overall, LLMs are automating reporting processes, improving regulatory data quality, ensuring compliance with global legal standards, and restructuring compliance practices in the O&G industry. However, their adoption must be accompanied by robust legal security and ethical surveillance mechanisms to mitigate risks and ensure trustworthiness.

### 1.2.4 Exploration and Drilling Optimization

LLMs are increasingly being used for O&G exploration and drilling optimisation to improve decision-making, operational efficiency, and cost reduction (Gamal, Omotunde, Duarte, Mohamed, & Elkatatny, 2024). These models can analyse large amounts of structured and unstructured data and provide actionable insight to optimise drilling parameters and improve performance (El Khatib, Al Hammadi, Oraby, & Al Hamar, 2023). LLMs supports the interpretation of seismic data, geological simulation, and well location by identifying subtle subsurface anomalies and forecasting the best drilling conditions. Artificial intelligence-enhanced machine learning algorithms can predict key drilling metrics such as bit weight (BOB), flow rate and movement per minute (RPM),thus maximising the penetration rate (ROP) by integrating real-time sensor data (Lakhanpal & Samuel, 2018). Logistic regression models are also used to estimate ROP and contribute to rational and efficient drilling design (Marlot, Srivastava, Wong, & Lee, 2023). Furthermore, LLMs uses NLP techniques to extract valuable information from historical well records (usually in structured, highly variable formats) to improve drilling decisions (Du, Huang, Jin, & Wan, 2024). They can also adapt drilling programs based on lithological variations observed during operations to improve both accuracy and efficiency. In addition to reducing routine tasks and manual labour, LLMs contribute to reducing operating costs and optimising workflows (Jung et al., 2022). They also showed the potential for the identification and use of low-permeability hydrocarbon resources, a field of increasing interest in international research (Nie et al., 2024).

### 1.2.5 Supply Chain and Logistics Optimisation

LLMs are transforming supply chains and logistics in the O&G industry. LLMs can identify demand forecasts, optimize inventory and improve production planning by using extensive historical data and current market trends. This reduces operational costs and increases profits (Odimarha, Ayodeji, & Abaku, 2024). Given the complexity of O&G logistics characterised by global operations, remote locations and strict safety standards, LLM is well suited for improving planning, coordination and implementation across the supply chain (Onukwulu, Fiemotongha, Igwe, & Ewim, 2023). LLMs support predictive analysis, route optimisation, and real-time decision making by processing large data sets from different sources, including IoT devices and market data (H. Wu, Li, & Zheng, 2024). These capabilities improve tracking, delivery timetables, and maintenance planning, while reducing risks and operating time (Badshah et al., 2024). Sustainability is another critical area where LLMs add value. They can identify emission reduction opportunities, promote the use of alternative fuels, and environmental practices, supporting green logistics. In addition, LLMs can automate administrative tasks such as generating shipping documents and customs forms, improve accuracy, and reduce the burden of paperwork. Despite their promises, challenges such as data quality, system integration, and the need for specific domain expertise persist. To maximise the benefits of LLMs in this sector, a strategic, phased implementation approach is essential.

## 1.3 Blockchain Technology in O&G

Blockchain technology is fundamentally a decentralized, distributed, and immutable ledger system. Its core principles decentralization, cryptographic security, consensus-based validation, and tamper-proof data storage offer a transformative solution to many of the O&G industry's inherent challenges, particularly those related to trust, transparency, and data integrity across multi-party operations (Abdullahi, Yusuf, et al., 2020; Labonno & Chowdhury, 2025). In a sector marked by complex supply chains, high-value transactions, and regulatory scrutiny, blockchain enables stakeholders including operators, contractors, regulators, and suppliers to access a shared, verifiable source of truth (Chowdhury & Islam, 2025). This ensures that every transaction or data record is transparently logged, time-stamped, and resistant to alteration, thereby reducing disputes, fraud, and audit complexity (Ahmad et al., 2022; Munim et al., 2022). Additionally, smart contracts self-executing agreements coded on the blockchain automate routine processes such as equipment procurement, shipment verification, and emissions reporting, improving efficiency and minimizing reliance on intermediaries (F. Ullah & Chowdhury, 2025)(Oleru, 2024). By embedding accountability and real-time traceability into digital workflows, blockchain supports not only operational excellence but also regulatory compliance and environmental responsibility, making it a strategic enabler of digital transformation across the O&G value chain.

### 1.3.1 Applications of Blockchain in O&G

Blockchain's unique attributes translate into several transformative applications and benefits for the O&G industry:

#### *1.3.1.1 Supply Chain Management*

Blockchain enables real-time data sharing, enhanced traceability, and simplified audit trails across complex supply chains. This leads to reduced disputes and improves overall efficiency in processes like inventory management and logistics. A notable example is VAKT, a blockchain-based post-trade platform adopted by industry giants like Shell and BP to streamline crude oil trading operations, reducing transaction times from weeks to hours. Beyond trading, blockchain enhances visibility and coordination across the entire O&G supply chain from upstream exploration to downstream distribution by creating a unified, tamper-proof record of transactions, asset movements, and compliance documentation (Aslam et al., 2022). Each stakeholder in the supply chain, including suppliers, contractors, transporters, and regulators, can securely access verified data in real time, which reduces duplication, prevents information asymmetry, and fosters trust. Smart contracts can further automate procurement, quality checks, and delivery confirmations, ensuring that payments and service-level obligations are executed seamlessly and transparently (Lu et al., n.d.). This level of automation not only reduces operational costs but also improves risk management and responsiveness to disruptions, which is critical in a volatile, globally distributed industry like O&G.

### *1.3.1.2 Smart Contracts and Automated Transactions*

Blockchain introduces smart contracts, which are self-executing agreements with terms directly written into code. These automate various procedures, reducing paperwork, streamlining processes, and accelerating settlements by eliminating intermediaries. Sensor-enabled invoicing, where IoT sensors feed operational data directly into smart contracts to automate billing, is a practical application (Chikov et al., 2023). Additionally, smart contracts have been increasingly adopted to improve business efficiency by automating invoicing, payment processes, and contract execution, reducing the reliance on traditional methods and ensuring faster transactions with fewer errors. Smart contracts also enable the automation of supply chain transactions by integrating data from IoT devices, ensuring that payments and goods deliveries are processed immediately when conditions are met. As businesses increasingly turn to blockchain solutions for streamlining operations, smart contracts offer a way to enhance data integrity, reduce fraud, and enable transparency in transaction workflows. Furthermore, the integration of blockchain technology with smart contracts in industries like supply chain management has shown significant promise in automating and securing complex multi-party agreements, improving coordination between stakeholders and ensuring compliance in real-time.

### *1.3.1.3 Data Security and Integrity*

Blockchain offers a fundamentally safer way to store data due to its decentralized nature, making it inherently more resilient against cyber threats compared to centralized systems. It ensures that critical data, such as geological surveys, drilling reports, and maintenance logs, are securely stored and tamper-proof. By distributing data across multiple nodes in the network, blockchain eliminates the risks associated with single points of failure, reducing the vulnerability to hacking or unauthorized access (Ahmad et al., 2022). Each piece of data is cryptographically linked to the previous one, forming an immutable chain that is resistant to alteration or deletion. This makes blockchain an ideal solution for industries like O&G, where the integrity of sensitive operational data is paramount for regulatory compliance, safety, and decision-making. Additionally, the transparent and auditable nature of blockchain allows stakeholders to trace the origin and history of any piece of data, further enhancing trust and accountability in environments where accurate and reliable information is critical (Rahman et al., 2022). Blockchain also enables secure data sharing across organizations, ensuring that only authorized parties have access to specific information, which strengthens collaboration while protecting intellectual property and confidential data.

#### 1.3.1.4 Land and Asset Management

For an industry with geographically dispersed assets and complex land rights, blockchain provides an incorruptible method to record land titles, transactions, and leases. It allows for real-time tagging and logging of assets, ensuring traceability, operational status, and security, which minimizes downtime and boosts safety (Haque et al., 2021). By offering a decentralized and transparent ledger, blockchain facilitates the efficient management of asset ownership and lease agreements, reducing the risk of disputes over land titles or contractual obligations. Furthermore, it enhances collaboration among stakeholders, such as landowners, operators, regulators, and service providers, by providing a single, verifiable record that can be accessed and updated in real time. This level of transparency also ensures compliance with regulatory frameworks, enabling swift verification of land use, environmental impact, and adherence to local laws (Kishnani et al., 2023). Blockchain's ability to store immutable, tamper-proof records ensures that critical data related to land and asset management is protected from fraud and unauthorized alterations, ultimately promoting long-term sustainability and operational efficiency in the O&G sector.

#### 1.3.1.5 Regulatory Compliance and ESG Reporting

Governments and regulators are increasingly emphasizing emissions tracking, sustainable sourcing, and transparent reporting as part of their commitment to achieving climate targets and promoting corporate social responsibility. Blockchain technology plays a crucial role in enhancing the accuracy and reliability of Environmental, Social, and Governance (ESG) reporting by providing a decentralized, immutable ledger for monitoring carbon output, equipment maintenance, and waste management across the entire supply chain. With blockchain, companies can record verifiable, timestamped data entries that are resistant to tampering, ensuring that all ESG-related activities are fully auditable and compliant with international regulations (Mulligan et al., 2024). This transparency not only helps businesses meet stringent regulatory standards but also fosters trust among investors, customers, and other stakeholders by demonstrating accountability in sustainability practices. Additionally, blockchain's ability to tokenize carbon credits opens new opportunities for firms to participate in carbon markets, incentivizing sustainable practices and providing an innovative way to trade verified carbon offsets (Vladucu et al., 2024). This integration of blockchain into ESG reporting systems is transforming the way companies manage and demonstrate their environmental and social impacts, ultimately contributing to the achievement of long-term sustainability goals.

#### *1.3.1.6 Energy Trading*

Blockchain can revolutionize O&G trading by creating transparent, real-time, and error-resistant transaction systems. It enables peer-to-peer energy trading, allowing direct transactions and potentially slashing consumer electricity bills by 40% (Din & Su, 2024). Companies utilizing blockchain for energy trading have reported significant cost reductions (30-40% savings) and settlement time reductions (from days to minutes), enhancing market liquidity and reducing fraud. By eliminating intermediaries, blockchain reduces the complexity and cost associated with traditional energy trading systems, allowing for faster and more efficient transactions. The decentralized nature of blockchain also ensures that all transactions are traceable and immutable, providing a higher level of security and transparency in energy markets. Additionally, blockchain's ability to automate processes through smart contracts facilitates real-time adjustments in energy pricing, grid management, and supply-demand balancing (Yang & Wang, 2020). This creates opportunities for dynamic pricing models, better resource allocation, and more accurate forecasting, which can further drive down operational costs and increase profitability. Moreover, the integration of blockchain in energy trading helps improve regulatory compliance by ensuring accurate, verifiable data for audits, while also encouraging sustainable energy practices by facilitating the trading of renewable energy credits and carbon offsets, thus supporting the transition to a low-carbon economy.

## 2. THE LLMs AND BLOCKCHAIN INTEGRATION FOR DIGITAL TRANSFORMATIONS

The integration of large-scale LLMs and blockchain technology marks a fundamental change in the digitalisation of the O&G industry. This convergence not only promises to maximise operational efficiency, but also reinforces data integrity, improves decision-making, and promotes greater transparency in complex industrial processes (Sousa, Ribeiro, Relvas, & Barbosa-Póvoa, 2019). LLMs excel in extracting insight from large volumes of structured and unstructured data and enable real-time analysis, predictive maintenance, and informed decision-making. Combined with the blockchain, it offers secure, decentralised data storage and verified data sources, and solves critical problems such as data piracy, security vulnerabilities, and fragmented data ecosystems (Gajjar, Parikh, & Shekokar, 2025).. This combination creates an internal reinforcement system: LLM generates intelligence from historical and real-time data, while blockchain ensures that underlying data is unchanging, auditable and trustworthy. Such a tamper-proof infrastructure improves the reliability of AI-driven insights and simplifies compliance with regulatory requirements (Abdullahi, Zakari, et al., 2020; Munim, Balasubramaniyan, Kouhizadeh, & Hossain, 2022).

In addition, blockchain plays an important role in recording data flow and use, solving one of the most pressing problems in artificial intelligence applications data transparency and traceability (Gajjar et al., 2025). This is especially important in the O&G industry, where data accuracy and origin have a direct impact on safety, efficiency and profitability. Integration also supports decentralised AI training, allowing multiple stakeholders - including operators, service providers and regulators to collaborate on the development of models without compromising privacy or ownership (Gumut et al., 2024). This democratized approach not only strengthens the robustness of the model but also accelerates the energy sector's innovation cycle. On a wider scale, the convergence of LLM and blockchain enabled the evolution of an intelligent trust network, a paradigm in which data was not only encrypted and shared, but also intelligently interpreted (Nura & Abdullahi). In this network, the blockchain is the verified basis, and LLM is the interpretive engine, enabling reliable, real-time decisions based on reliable data. Eventually, this fusion would lead to the creation of a new digital ecosystem in the value chain of O&G, characterized by greater operational agility, reduced risk of fraud, enhanced cooperation, and the security and data-driven foundations of sustainable growth and the transition to decentralised energy system.

## 2.1 Architectural Considerations for Integration

Implementing this powerful synergy requires careful architectural planning:

- **Hybrid Systems:** A practical approach involves designing hybrid systems that combine reactive workflows for predictable, high-volume tasks with deliberative agent-based systems for complex, ambiguous decisions.
- **Shared Data Layer:** Blockchain can serve as a shared data layer for transparent on-chain data aggregation, particularly for data that requires consistency and transparency across multiple systems or organizations. This can be achieved through event-driven pipelines, message queues, or middleware microservices, depending on the existing system design.
- **Integrated Frameworks:** Frameworks like LLM-Net propose integrating fine-tuned expert models with blockchain technology for transparent transaction and performance validation, establishing an immutable record of service delivery.
- **Decentralized AI:** The broader concept of decentralised AI involves distributing data provision and processing across a network of nodes, which enhances security, fairness, and transparency of AI models.

- **Layered Architecture:** A typical technical architecture for integration involves an AI layer (responsible for data ingestion, processing, and a continuous feedback loop) and a Blockchain layer (providing smart contracts, consensus mechanisms, and data integrity). This setup enhances security and accessibility through decentralized data storage.

Despite the immense potential, significant architectural challenges exist. These include interoperability issues arising from heterogeneous blockchain networks, complexities in cross-chain communication, divergences in consensus mechanisms, difficulties in data standardization across disparate systems, and the inherent security and trust considerations of bridging different blockchain environments. Addressing these challenges requires robust design patterns and potentially new protocols to ensure seamless and secure data exchange. Figure 2 describes the architectural considerations for LLMs and Blockchain Integrations.

## 3. INTEGRATED USE CASES ACROSS THE OIL & GAS VALUE CHAIN: LLMs AND BLOCKCHAIN

The convergence of LLMs and Blockchain unlocks a new generation of use cases across the upstream, midstream, and downstream segments of the O&G industry:

### 3.1 Intelligent Asset Management and Predictive Maintenance

The O&G industry is undergoing a technological transformation, with Intelligent Asset Management (IAM) and Predictive Maintenance (PdM) emerging as strategic pillars for operational excellence. These approaches are increasingly enhanced by the integration of LLMs and blockchain technology, offering advanced capabilities for data interpretation, operational insight, and secure information management across the value chain (Suhail et al., 2022). IAM leverages digital technologies and data analytics to manage the lifecycle of assets, optimising performance, minimising downtime, and informing investment decisions. PdM focuses on anticipating equipment failures through predictive modelling and real-time monitoring, allowing maintenance to be scheduled proactively (Raza, 2020). Together, they provide the foundation for a smarter, safer, and more efficient O&G infrastructure. LLMs bring new depth to this landscape. These models can analyse vast amounts of structured and unstructured data, such as sensor streams, operational reports, and technician notes to generate predictive insights with high precision. For example, LLMs can detect early indicators of mechanical degradation by recognising linguistic and numerical patterns in historical maintenance records, improving the foresight of PdM systems. In parallel, blockchain technology offers a decentralised and tamper-resistant framework for recording maintenance data and operational logs. This ensures data integrity, authenticity, and compliance, especially in regulated environments. When LLM-generated maintenance predictions are securely recorded on a blockchain ledger, the system creates a traceable and auditable record of decision-making, building trust among stakeholders and auditors (Chen, Baird, & Straub, 2022). Moreover, this integration significantly enhances digital twin capabilities. LLMs provide enriched behavioural insights into asset operation, while blockchain secures the input data feeding these virtual replicas. The result is a highly reliable simulation environment that supports real-time monitoring, scenario testing, and lifecycle optimisation.

## 3.2 Automated Compliance and Regulatory Reporting

LLMs and blockchain technologies are changing compliance and regulatory reporting throughout the O&G value chain as described in Figure 4. LLMs can analyse complex regulatory texts, extract key information from documents, and generate accurate compliance reports. This automation greatly reduces manual efforts and reduces the risk of human errors (Gumut et al., 2024). Blockchain complements LLMs by providing an immutable, time-discharged record of all compliance activities. This ensures data integrity, improves transparency and builds trust between operators, regulators and auditors (Arafat et al., 2024). LLMs reduced data extraction from non-structured sources (contracts, legal documents, and operational records) by identifying key performance indicators (KPIs), compliance gaps, and potential risks. They can also generate formatted compliance reports with trend analyses and effective recommendations. Blockchain ensures the security of these reports by protecting sensitive data, maintaining audit trails and preventing unauthorised changes (Hassan et al., 2024). This integrated approach improves efficiency, ensures compliance with regulations and fosters cooperation among stakeholders in the O&G sector.

## 3.3 Enhanced Supply Chain Transparency and Efficiency

Integration of LLMs and blockchain technology can revolutionize the O&G value chain by addressing the issues of inefficiency, data silos, and trust between stakeholders (Siddique et al., 2025). LLM excels in the processing of structured and unstructured data, generating insights that drive better decision-making, and blockchain ensures data integrity and transaction transparency through a decentralised, unchangeable ledger (Aghaei et al., 2025). LLM can optimise inventory levels, logistics, and demand forecasts by analysing historical trends, while blockchain is used to verify the origin of materials, detect fraud, and ensure traceability (Rajasekaran,

Azees, & Al-Turjman, 2022). Smart contracts triggered by LLM insights automate transactions such as payments, improve operating speed, and reduce human errors. In upstream operations, LLM analyses geological data and market signals to identify optimal exploration areas and improve resource allocation (N. Khan, Hossain, Khadka, & Sarkar, 2024). Blockchains ensure data sharing agreements, lease records, and exploration contracts and ensure transparency and trust.

In asset management, LLM predicts equipment failures and proposes preventive maintenance strategies to reduce short-term and long-term costs (Onukwulu, Agho, Eyo-Udo, Sule, & Azubuike, 2024). Blockchains track the complete lifecycle of devices, verify performance data, and prevent manipulation and abuse (Krishna, n.d.). LLMs also help to interpret complex contractual languages and compliance reports and make them available to all parties concerned. Blockchain ensures a single source of truth and minimises discrepancies and disputes in data (Rajasekaran et al., 2022). LLMs and blockchains combined enable seamless automation of administrative tasks, reduce documents, and accelerate decision-making (Siddique et al., 2025). Real-time prediction analysis improves resource allocation and reduces waste throughout the supply chain (Tiwari, Channakkalavara, Singh, & Sarella, 2024). From a security point of view, blockchains protect against data leakage and hacking using cryptographic protocols, and LLMs detect potential threats and vulnerabilities and strengthen overall cybersecurity.

## 3.4 Secure Energy Trading and Financial Reconciliation

The integration of LLMs and blockchain technology offers a transformative approach to secure energy trading and financial reconciliation in the O&G industry. LLMs bring powerful capabilities in NLP and data analytics, enabling real-time market forecasting, contract interpretation, and risk assessment by analysing vast volumes of structured and unstructured data (Rehman, Akbar, Omar, & Gilal, 2023) . Building on these insights, blockchain ensures transparency, trust, and automation through its decentralized and immutable ledger system (Chai et al., 2023). It addresses long-standing industry challenges such as manual documentation, process inefficiencies, and stakeholder mistrust (Sun, Zhao, & Wang, 2021). Together, these technologies streamline operations and enable secure, autonomous transactions in a highly dynamic environment. Smart contracts can be triggered automatically by LLM-generated outputs, enabling faster, more accurate trade settlements and reducing human error (Berkani, Moumen, Benharzallah, Kechadi, & Bounceur, 2025). This convergence significantly reduces counterparty risk and compresses settlement times from days to minutes (Nwulu, Elete, Erhueh, Akano, & Omomo, 2024). Blockchain provides a shared, tamper-proof ledger that enhances auditability and reduces information asymmetry (Nura & Abdullahi, 2022). LLMs extract legal obligations and financial terms from complex documents, while blockchain enforces them via smart contracts (Raza, 2020). LLMs analyse market conditions to support predictive and adaptive energy trading strategies, with blockchain securing all transactional records (Dhayal, Giri, Esposito, & Agrawal, 2023). LLMs identify irregularities in transactional data, while blockchain ensures full audit trails for regulatory compliance (Azieva, 2020). Despite these advantages, challenges remain, particularly in terms of data privacy, system interoperability, and scalability. Future directions point toward the development of privacy-preserving blockchain frameworks and improving LLM robustness, especially for high-stakes financial and regulatory contexts (Abdullahi, Qabasiyu, et al., 2025).

## 4. CHALLENGES AND STRATEGIC RECOMMENDATIONS FOR IMPLEMENTATION

Although the integration of LLMs and Blockchain offers transformative potential, its successful implementation in the O&G industry is not without significant challenges. These hurdles span technical, operational, cultural, and regulatory domains, requiring a comprehensive and strategic approach for effective mitigation.

### 4.1 Hallucinations

LLMs show remarkable abilities in understanding and generating of natural languages. However, they often suffer from a critical limitation called hallucination - the production of plausible but factually inaccurate or misleading outputs. This problem greatly undermines their reliability, especially in high-value industries such as O&G, where accuracy is paramount (Ji et al., 2023). LLM hallucinations often result from a combination of factors, including biases in training data, architectural constraints, and a lack of access to real-time data (Jin et al., 2025). In the O&G industry, this challenge is particularly consequential. Decisions in areas such as drilling, reservoir management, environmental impact assessment and risk analysis are based on accurate and trustworthy information (Choubey & Karmakar, 2021). Any factual error introduced by LLM can lead to costly mistakes and even safety hazards. In addition, the complexity of the data and operational tasks of this sector, such as the interpretation of seismic data, the optimization of pipeline logistics, or the analysis of equipment diagnosis, makes LLM hallucinations more difficult to detect and damaging (Bodensohn, Brackmann, Vogel, Sanghi, & Binnig, 2025). This highlights the need for a robust strategy to mitigate such risks.

To successfully integrate LLMs into the O&G sector, several strategic measures are essential. First, it is necessary to implement robust data verification protocols to ensure the accuracy, relevance and specificity of the domain. Blockchain technology can support this by providing in variable and susceptible data records (Shridhar Singh & Vorster, 2024). It is equally important that LLMs continue to be re-informed with industry-specific datasets to improve domain awareness and reduce hallucinations. Human supervision is also crucial: area experts should review LLM outputs to correct hallucinations, biases or errors in information (Kim et al., 2025). Bias mitigation should not be overlooked. Effective detection frameworks supported by blockchain log scans ensure fairness and transparency in model behaviour (Lin et al., 2025). Blockchain increases LLM reliability by ensuring data integrity through auditable source records for training and operational data (Shridhar Singh & Vorster, 2024). Smart contracts can automate model evaluation and report outputs that deviate from verified knowledge (Jin et al., 2025). In addition, blockchain allows transparent decision-making through the inference of the log model, thus supporting responsibility (Choubey & Karmakar, 2021). It also facilitates the sharing of secure data between stakeholders and improves cooperation with reliable and high-quality data sets (Zuo et al., 2024).

## 4.2 Interoperability Between Blockchains and LLMs

The integration of LLMs into the O&G industry's blockchain systems is a promising step but presents significant interoperability challenges. These technologies operate on fundamentally different principles: LLM depends on large-scale, unstructured data and machine learning pipelines, while blockchain depends on secure, structured and decentralised data records. The main obstacles are inconsistencies in data formats, communication protocols, and consensus mechanisms over the blockchain network, which complicate the seamless exchange of data with LLMs (Saurabh Singh et al., 2020). Middleware solutions are essential for standardised exchange and compatibility (Madine et al., 2021). Furthermore, LLMs require access to a large number of datasets for fine-tuning inference. However, the sensitive nature and property of the data stored on the blockchain raise privacy concerns. Furthermore, the computational demands of the blockchain consensus algorithm and LLM estimates could result in performance problems and scaling issues (Leng et al., 2023). Due to the high-volume data generated by real-time O&G operations, this integration must be optimised for speed and efficiency. Without robust interoperability solutions, in O&G applications, it is impossible to achieve the full advantages of combining the security of blockchain and LLM analytical power.

## 4.3 Data Quality and Standardization

High-quality standard data is crucial to the successful integration of LLM and blockchain in the O&G industry (Onukwulu, Fiemotongha, Igwe, & Paul-Mikki, 2023). However, industry data is often fragmented, unstructured, and it comes from a variety of sources, such as traditional systems, IoT sensors, manual records, and real-time streams. These discrepancies in data formats, measurement units and terminology pose significant challenges both in the field of LLM training and in the field of the integrity of the blockchain (Zakari et al., 2020). Poor data quality leads to bias, reduces the reliability of LLM, and hampers the immutability of the blockchain. Noise, missing values and outdated information further hinder the accuracy and decision-making of the model. Without unified data standards and cleaning protocols, the achievement of accurate, complete and consistent data remains a key obstacle to maximising the potential of LLM-blockchain integration in O&G operations.

## 4.4 Scalability Challenges of Blockchain Networks in LLM Integration

Traditional blockchain networks, such as Bitcoin and Ethereum, have strong scaling limits due to consensus mechanisms, especially Proof of Work (PoW) and Proof of stake (PoS) (Hasan, Sajid, Lapina, Shahid, & Kotecha, 2024). These mechanisms give priority to decentralisation and security, often at the expense of transaction throughput and latency. For example, Bitcoin handles only a limited number of transactions per second(TPS) and Ethereum continues to experience similar bottlenecks (D. Khan, Jung, & Hashmani, 2021). In the O&G sector, the integration of LLMs has introduced a heavy data-intensive applications such as real-time monitoring, predictive maintenance, and supply chain optimization (J. Wu, Yuan, Xie, & Dai, 2024). These tasks require high-speed data processing and storage efficiency, capabilities that are often lacking in traditional blockchains. Latency caused by lengthy consensus processes and constraints on block sizes can hamper the timely execution of LLM-driven analytics. Furthermore, energy consumption associated with blockchain technology poses environmental sustainability concerns, especially in the increasingly environmentally responsible industry. Although the latest consensus algorithm may be improved, scalability remains a key obstacle to the seamless adoption of the blockchain-LLM integration in enterprise-level O&G applications.

## 5. CONCLUSION

The integration of LLMs and blockchain technology provides a fundamental opportunity for digital transformation in the O&G industry. This chapter highlights that the O&G sector, while possessing advanced operational technologies, has historically lagged behind in comprehensive digital integration, causing a "maturity paradox" in which important efficiency and value potentials remain unexploited. The problems of data management, which is widespread and hinder the full implementation of digital initiatives, make this gap even more complicated. LLMs provide the ability to unlock and interpret large amounts of unstructured data, as an intelligent bridge to transform fragmented information into actionable knowledge. Their applications include predictive maintenance, operational optimisation, compliance reporting and improved safety. At the same time, Blockchain provides a key "trust layer" for this multi-stakeholder, complex industry by ensuring data integrity, transparency and automation through smart contracts. This convergence of technologies creates a "coherent trust network" that goes beyond the limits of individual capabilities and sets up a system that tracks and certifies AI-derived insights. This transformation of raw data into actionable and verifiable knowledge assets is the cornerstone of future operational excellence. Quantifiable benefits include significant cost reductions, improved operational efficiency, increased safety, improved transparency and solid support for sustainable development goals. However, the way to integration presents several challenges, from the complexities of legacy systems to ensuring data quality to address scaling issues, interoperability concerns and LLM's inherent computational requirements.

Despite these obstacles, the strategic benefits of this convergence cannot be ignored. To navigate the complex future of the O&G industry, the proactive and strategic adoption of integrated LLM and blockchain solutions is not only an option but an important pathway towards sustainable competitiveness, operational resilience, and environmental management. The success depends on a phase-by-phase approach to value-driven, strong commitment to data management, the promotion of a first-class digital culture, and collaboration in industry partnerships to shape the future of energy.

## REFERENCES


Abdullahi, S., Danyaro, K. U., Zakari, A., Aziz, I. A., Zawawi, N. A. W. A., & Adamu, S. (2025). Time-series large language models: A systematic review of state-of-the-art. *IEEE Access : Practical Innovations, Open Solutions, 13*, 30235–30261. DOI: 10.1109/ACCESS.2025.3535782

Abdullahi, S., Qabasiyu, M. G., Danyaro, K. U., Zakari, A., Maitama, J. Z., & Imam, A. A. (2025). A Systematic Review of Metaheuristic Approaches to the Deployment Problem in Wireless Sensor Networks. [JTEC]. *Journal of Telecommunication, Electronic and Computer Engineering, 17*(2), 1–14. DOI: 10.54554/jtec.2025.17.02.001

Abdullahi, S., Yusuf, N., Zayyad, M. A., Bagiwa, L. I., Zakari, A., Adamu, A., & Shehu, S. (2020). The Big Data Technology: Assessing the Impact in the Banking Industry. *Open Journal of Science and Technology, 3*(2), 71–77. DOI: 10.31580/ojst.v3i2.1464

Abdullahi, S., Zakari, A., Nura, A., Mashasha, A. S., Abdu, H., & Suleiman, S. (2020). Criteria for Accepting Software Requirements Negotiation Tools in the Software Industry. *Science Proceedings Series, 2*(1), 39–45. DOI: 10.31580/sps.v2i1.1241

Aghaei, R., Kiaei, A. A., Boush, M., Vahidi, J., Barzegar, Z., & Rofoosheh, M. (2025). The potential of large language models in supply chain management: advancing decision-making, efficiency, and innovation. *arXiv preprint arXiv:2501.15411*.

Alsultan, A., & Razak, F. A. (2024). *Limitations of Language Models in The Oil & Gas Upstream Operations*. Paper presented at the International Petroleum Technology Conference. DOI: 10.2523/IPTC-23649-EA

Aman, Q. (2024). Adoption of Artificial Intelligence in Accounting and its Impact on Business Performance: Oil and Gas Perspective. *Open Access Organization and Management Review, 3*(1), 66–73. DOI: 10.59644/oagmr.3(1).129

Arafat, M. S., Mirza, J. B., Jony, M. A. M., Islam, R., Rafi, S. S., Jalil, M. S., & Hossen, F. (2024). Blockchain and IoT Integration for Secure Supply Chain Operations: Unlocking Real-Time Transparency and Business Continuity. *AIJMR-Advanced International Journal of Multidisciplinary Research, 2*(6).

Azieva, R. (2020). Blockchain technology as a key element of the development of the oil and gas industry. *Internetjournal «Waste and resources*(2).

Badshah, A., Daud, A., Alharbey, R., Banjar, A., Bukhari, A., & Alshemaimri, B. (2024). Big data applications: Overview, challenges and future. *Artificial Intelligence Review, 57*(11), 290. DOI: 10.1007/s10462-024-10938-5

Bensonch, C., Argyropoulos, C. D., Dimopoulos, C., Mikellidou, C. V., & Boustras, G. (2022). Analysis of safety climate factors and safety compliance relationships in the oil and gas industry. *Safety Science, 151*, 105744. DOI: 10.1016/j.ssci.2022.105744

Berger, A., Hillebrand, L., Leonhard, D., Deußer, T., De Oliveira, T. B. F., Dilmaghani, T., . . . Bauckhage, C. (2023). *Towards automated regulatory compliance verification in financial auditing with large language models.* Paper presented at the 2023 IEEE International Conference on Big Data (BigData). DOI: 10.1109/BigData59044.2023.10386518

Berkani, A.-S., Moumen, H., Benharzallah, S., Kechadi, M. T., & Bounceur, A. (2025). PrGChain: A privacy-preserving blockchain-enabled energy trading system. *Computers & Electrical Engineering, 123*, 110289. DOI: 10.1016/j.compeleceng.2025.110289

Bodensohn, J.-M., Brackmann, U., Vogel, L., Sanghi, A., & Binnig, C. (2025). Unveiling challenges for llms in enterprise data engineering. *arXiv preprint arXiv:2504.10950.*

Chai, S., Zhang, X., Abedin, M. Z., Chen, H., Lucey, B., & Hajek, P. (2023). An optimized GRT model with blockchain digital smart contracts for power generation enterprises. *Energy Economics, 128*, 107153. DOI: 10.1016/j.eneco.2023.107153

Chen, L., Baird, A., & Straub, D. (2022). The impact of hierarchical privilege levels and non-hierarchical incentives on continued contribution in online Q&A communities: A motivational model of gamification goals. *Decision Support Systems, 153*, 113667. DOI: 10.1016/j.dss.2021.113667

Choubey, S., & Karmakar, G. (2021). Artificial intelligence techniques and their application in oil and gas industry. *Artificial Intelligence Review, 54*(5), 3665–3683. DOI: 10.1007/s10462-020-09935-1

Chowdhury, M. T. A., & Islam, M. A. (2025). Blockchain Synergies With the Internet of Everything (IoE). In *Convergence of Blockchain, Internet of Everything, and Federated Learning for Security* (pp. 1-38): IGI Global Scientific Publishing.

Dhayal, K. S., Giri, A. K., Esposito, L., & Agrawal, S. (2023). Mapping the significance of green venture capital for sustainable development: A systematic review and future research agenda. *Journal of Cleaner Production, 396*, 136489. DOI: 10.1016/j.jclepro.2023.136489

Du, S., Huang, Z., Jin, L., & Wan, X. (2024). Recent Progress in Data-Driven Intelligent Modeling and Optimization Algorithms for Industrial Processes. *Algorithms, 17*(12), 569. DOI: 10.3390/a17120569

Eckroth, J., Gipson, M., Boden, J., Hough, L., Elliott, J., & Quintana, J. (2023). Answering Natural Language Questions with OpenAI's GPT in the Petroleum Industry. Paper presented at the *SPE Annual Technical Conference and Exhibition.*

El Khatib, , MAl Hammadi, , AOraby, , KAl Hamar, , A. (2023). A Functional vs Projectized approach in Oil and Gas Industry: The added value of Projectized approach. [IJTOP]. *International Journal of Theory of Organization and Practice, 3*(2), 197–209.

Gajjar, T., Parikh, S., & Shekokar, K. (2025). *Integrating blockchain technology with AI to enhance security measure.* Paper presented at the IET Conference Proceedings CP920.

Gamal, H., Omotunde, O., Duarte, M., Mohamed, O., & Elkatatny, S. (2024). *How complex lithology schemes affect drilling rate prediction: machine learning study.* Paper presented at the International Petroleum Technology Conference. DOI: 10.2523/IPTC-23898-MS

Gong, J., Yan, P., Zhang, Y., An, H., & Liu, L. (2024). Blockchain Meets LLMs: A Living Survey on Bidirectional Integration. *arXiv preprint arXiv:2411.16809.*

Gumut, G., Umar, B. U., Abdullahi, I. M., Ajao, L. A., Olaniyi, O. M., & Adeniyi, S. (2024). *A Real-Time Secure-Based Oil and Gas Supply Chain Management using Blockchain.* Paper presented at the 2024 IEEE 5th International Conference on Electro-Computing Technologies for Humanity (NIGERCON). DOI: 10.1109/NIGERCON62786.2024.10927207

Hasan, K. M. B., Sajid, M., Lapina, M. A., Shahid, M., & Kotecha, K. (2024). Blockchain technology meets 6 G wireless networks: A systematic survey. *Alexandria Engineering Journal, 92*, 199–220. DOI: 10.1016/j.aej.2024.02.031

Hassan, M. F., Akbar, R., Ullah, R., Savita, K., Rehman, U., & Yalli, J. S. (2024). Pre-Encryption Ransomware Detection (PERD) Taxonomy, and Research Directions: Systematic Literature Review. *International Journal of Advanced Computer Science and Applications, 15*(9).

Idris, M. A., & Alsultan, H. (2023). *Smart knowledge submission system based on natural language processing (NLP) leveraging on language modelling approach.* Paper presented at the SPE Gas & Oil Technology Showcase and Conference.

Ji, Z., Yu, T., Xu, Y., Lee, N., Ishii, E., & Fung, P. (2023). *Towards mitigating LLM hallucination via self reflection.* Paper presented at the Findings of the Association for Computational Linguistics: EMNLP 2023. DOI: 10.18653/v1/2023.findings-emnlp.123

Jin, Y., Li, C., Fan, P., Liu, P., Li, X., Liu, C., & Qiu, W. (2025). LLM-BSCVM: An LLM-Based Blockchain Smart Contract Vulnerability Management Framework. *arXiv preprint arXiv:2505.17416.*

Jung, H., Subban, C. V., McTigue, J. D., Martinez, J. J., Copping, A. E., Osorio, J., Liu, J., & Deng, Z. D. (2022). Extracting energy from ocean thermal and salinity gradients to power unmanned underwater vehicles: State of the art, current limitations, and future outlook. *Renewable & Sustainable Energy Reviews, 160*, 112283. DOI: 10.1016/j.rser.2022.112283

Kanka, V. (2024). *Scaling Big Data: Leveraging LLMs for Enterprise Success.* Libertatem Media Private Limited.

Khan, D., Jung, L. T., & Hashmani, M. A. (2021). Systematic literature review of challenges in blockchain scalability. *Applied Sciences (Basel, Switzerland), 11*(20), 9372. DOI: 10.3390/app11209372

Khan, N., Hossain, S., Khadka, U., & Sarkar, S. (2024). Blockchain in Supply Chain Management: Enhancing Transparency, Efficiency, and Trust. *AIJMR-Advanced International Journal of Multidisciplinary Research, 2*(5).

Krishna, V. V. (n.d.) Economic development of Tamil Nadu (1956-2025): agricultural transformation, industrialization, rise of the service sector, infrastructure development, and the state's role in exports-an overview.

Labonno, S. I., & Chowdhury, M. T. A. (2025). Blockchain and IoE Transforming Industry Applications. In *Convergence of Blockchain, Internet of Everything, and Federated Learning for Security* (pp. 177–208). IGI Global Scientific Publishing. DOI: 10.4018/979-8-3373-1424-2.ch007

Lakhanpal, V., & Samuel, R. (2018). Implementing blockchain technology in oil and gas industry: A review. Paper presented at the *SPE Annual Technical Conference and Exhibition.*

Leng, , JZhu, , XHuang, , ZXu, , KLiu, , ZLiu, , QChen, , X. (2023). ManuChain II: Blockchained smart contract system as the digital twin of decentralized autonomous manufacturing toward resilience in industry 5.0. *IEEE Transactions on Systems, Man, and Cybernetics. Systems, 53*(8), 4715–4728.

Li, J., & Maiti, A. (2025). Applying Large Language Model Analysis and Backend Web Services in Regulatory Technologies for Continuous Compliance Checks. *Future Internet, 17*(3), 100. DOI: 10.3390/fi17030100

Lin, B., Jin, Y., Cao, Q., Meng, H., Pang, H., & Wei, S. (2025). Developing a large language model for oil-and gas-related rock mechanics: Progress and challenges. *Natural Gas Industry B, 12*(2), 110–122. DOI: 10.1016/j.ngib.2025.03.007

Lokhande, A., Pillai, P., & Mangsuli, P. (2023). *Enabling Contextual Natural Language Search on Oil and Gas Databases.* Paper presented at the Abu Dhabi International Petroleum Exhibition and Conference. DOI: 10.2118/216349-MS

Madine, M., Salah, K., Jayaraman, R., Al-Hammadi, Y., Arshad, J., & Yaqoob, I. (2021). appxchain: Application-level interoperability for blockchain networks. *IEEE Access : Practical Innovations, Open Solutions, 9*, 87777–87791. DOI: 10.1109/ACCESS.2021.3089603

Mahal, Z. (2024). Exploring the Impact of Attention Mechanisms in Big Data Analysis and Large Language Models. *American-Eurasian Journal of Scientific Research, 11*(06), 68–76.

Marlot, M., Srivastava, D. N., Wong, F. K., & Lee, M. X. (2023). *Unsupervised multitask learning for oil and gas language models with limited resources.* Paper presented at the Abu Dhabi International Petroleum Exhibition and Conference. DOI: 10.2118/216402-MS

Martin, J. L., Zanuri, M. N. A., Sockalingam, M. K., & Andersen, E. (2024). *LLMs, Embeddings and Indexing Pipelines to Enable Natural Language Searching on Upstream Datasets.* Paper presented at the International Petroleum Technology Conference. DOI: 10.2523/IPTC-23626-EA

Mas' ud, A., Yusuf, R., Udin, N. M., & Al-Dhamari, R. (2020). Enforce environmental tax compliance model for the oil and gas industry. *International Journal of Energy Sector Management, 14*(6), 1073-1088.

Munim, Z. H., Balasubramaniyan, S., Kouhizadeh, M., & Hossain, N. U. I. (2022). Assessing blockchain technology adoption in the Norwegian oil and gas industry using Bayesian Best Worst Method. *Journal of Industrial Information Integration, 28*, 100346. DOI: 10.1016/j.jii.2022.100346

Nie, A., Su, Y., Chang, B., Lee, J. N., Chi, E. H., Le, Q. V., & Chen, M. (2024). Evolve: Evaluating and optimizing llms for exploration. *arXiv preprint arXiv:2410.06238.*

Nura, A., & Abdullahi, S. (2022). A systematic review of multi-depot vehicle routing problems. *Systematic Literature Review and Meta-Analysis Journal, 3*(2), 51–60. DOI: 10.54480/slrm.v3i2.37

Nura, A., & Abdullahi, S. aa systematic Literature Review and Meta-E3E.

Nwulu, E. O., Elete, T. Y., Erhueh, O. V., Akano, O. A., & Omomo, K. O. (2024). Leveraging predictive modelling to enhance equipment reliability: A generic approach for the oil and gas industry. *International Journal of Engineering Research and Development*, *20*(11), 951–969.

Odimarha, A. C., Ayodeji, S. A., & Abaku, E. A.Agnes Clare OdimarhaSodrudeen Abolore AyodejiEmmanuel Adeyemi Abaku. (2024). Machine learning's influence on supply chain and logistics optimization in the oil and gas sector: A comprehensive analysis. *Computer Science & IT Research Journal*, *5*(3), 725–740. DOI: 10.51594/csitrj.v5i3.976

Okedele, P. O., Aziza, O. R., Oduro, P., & Ishola, A. O. (2024). Renewable Energy Policies and Global Socioeconomic Impacts: A Comparative Study of Policy Implementation and Outcomes.

Onukwulu, E. C., Agho, M. O., Eyo-Udo, N. L., Sule, A. K., & Azubuike, C. (2024). Advances in automation and AI for enhancing supply chain productivity in oil and gas. *International Journal of Research and Innovation in Applied Science*, *9*(12), 654–687.

Onukwulu, E. C., Fiemotongha, J. E., Igwe, A. N., & Ewim, C. P.-M. (2023). Transforming supply chain logistics in oil and gas: Best practices for optimizing efficiency and reducing operational costs. *Journal of Advance Multidisciplinary Research*, *2*(2), 59–76. DOI: 10.54660/.JAMR.2023.2.2.59-76

Onukwulu, E. C., Fiemotongha, J. E., Igwe, A. N., & Paul-Mikki, C. (2023). The role of blockchain and AI in the future of energy trading: A technological perspective on transforming the oil & gas industry by 2025. *Methodology: European Journal of Research Methods for the Behavioral and Social Sciences*, *173*, 1–15.

Pacis, F., Alyaev, S., Pelfrene, G., & Wiktorski, T. (2024). *Enhancing Information Retrieval in the Drilling Domain: Zero-Shot Learning with Large Language Models for Question-Answering*. Paper presented at the SPE/IADC Drilling Conference and Exhibition. DOI: 10.2118/217671-MS

Pillai, P., Ryali, S., Maniar, H., Mangsuli, P., & Abubakar, A. (2022). *NLP applications in the oil and natural gas industry*. Paper presented at the SEG/AAPG International Meeting for Applied Geoscience & Energy. DOI: 10.1190/image2022-3739659.1

Prestidge, K. L. (2022). *Digital Transformation in the Oil and gas industry: Challenges and potential solutions*. Massachusetts Institute of Technology.

Qabasiyu, , M. GZayyad, , M. AAbdullahi, , S. (2023a). An ensembled based machine learning technique of sentiment analysis. [JTEC]. *Journal of Telecommunication, Electronic and Computer Engineering, 15*(1), 23–28.

Qabasiyu, M. G., Zayyad, M. A., & Abdullahi, S. (2023b). Systematic Literature Review on Sentence Level Sentiment Analysis. [IJMRAP]. *International Journal of Multidisciplinary Research and Publications, 6*(5), 1–8.

Qothrunada, N., & Handayani, W. (2023). Does Environmental Disclosure of the Oil and Gas Industry Comply with the GRI? Evidence from Indonesia. *Journal of Business Management and Accounting, 13*(2), 153–180. DOI: 10.32890/jbma2023.13.2.1

Rajasekaran, A. S., Azees, M., & Al-Turjman, F. (2022). A comprehensive survey on blockchain technology. *Sustainable Energy Technologies and Assessments, 52*, 102039. DOI: 10.1016/j.seta.2022.102039

Raza, J. (2020). *From Prevent to "Predict & Prevent (PnP)": Optimizing Oil and Gas Asset Integrity Decisions.* Paper presented at the Engineering Assets and Public Infrastructures in the Age of Digitalization: Proceedings of the 13th World Congress on Engineering Asset Management. DOI: 10.1007/978-3-030-48021-9_57

Rehman, M. u., Akbar, R., Omar, M., & Gilal, A. R. (2023). *A Systematic Literature Review of Ransomware Detection Methods and Tools for Mitigating Potential Attacks.* Paper presented at the International Conference on Computing and Informatics.

Siddique, M. T., Jamee, S. S., Sajal, A., Mou, S. N., Mahin, M. R. H., Obaid, M. O., & Hasan, M. (2025). Enhancing Automated Trading with Sentiment Analysis: Leveraging Large Language Models for Stock Market Predictions. *The American Journal of Engineering and Technology, 7*(03), 185–195. DOI: 10.37547/tajet/Volume07Issue03-16

Singh, S., Sharma, P. K., Yoon, B., Shojafar, M., Cho, G. H., & Ra, I.-H. (2020). Convergence of blockchain and artificial intelligence in IoT network for the sustainable smart city. *Sustainable Cities and Society, 63*, 102364. DOI: 10.1016/j.scs.2020.102364

Singh, S., & Vorster, L. (2024). *LLM Supply Chain Provenance: A Blockchain-Based Approach.* Paper presented at the Proceedings of the International Conference on AI Research. DOI: 10.34190/icair.4.1.3128

Sousa, A. L., Ribeiro, T. P., Relvas, S., & Barbosa-Póvoa, A. (2019). Using machine learning for enhancing the understanding of bullwhip effect in the oil and gas industry. *Machine Learning and Knowledge Extraction, 1*(3), 57. DOI: 10.3390/make1030057

Suhail, S., Malik, S. U. R., Jurdak, R., Hussain, R., Matulevičius, R., & Svetinovic, D. (2022). Towards situational aware cyber-physical systems: A security-enhancing use case of blockchain-based digital twins. *Computers in Industry, 141*, 103699. DOI: 10.1016/j.compind.2022.103699

Sun, J., Zhao, G., & Wang, R. (2021). *Application of Blockchain Technology in Oil and Gas Industry.* Paper presented at the Proceedings of the 2021 3rd International Conference on Blockchain Technology. DOI: 10.1145/3460537.3460538

Tiwari, G., Channakkalavara, P., Singh, G., & Sarella, P. N. K. (2024). Enhancing Security, Transparency, and Efficiency of Blockchain Technology in Pharmaceutical Supply Chain. *Int. J. Pharm. Qual. Assur, 15*(02), 1009–1016. DOI: 10.25258/ijpqa.15.2.71

Ullah, A., Qi, G., Hussain, S., Ullah, I., & Ali, Z. (2024). The role of llms in sustainable smart cities: Applications, challenges, and future directions. *arXiv preprint arXiv:2402.14596.*

Ullah, F., & Chowdhury, M. T. A. (2025). Leveraging Smart Contracts for Enhanced IoE Security. In *Convergence of Blockchain, Internet of Everything, and Federated Learning for Security* (pp. 115–154). IGI Global Scientific Publishing. DOI: 10.4018/979-8-3373-1424-2.ch005

Valliyatt, M. P., Tharayil, S. M., Razhi, A. A., AlQarni, S., & AlThubaiti, L. (2024). AI-Driven Optimization of Refinery Configurations: A Novel Approach to Predicting Production Outputs and Capacities. Paper presented at the *SPE Annual Technical Conference and Exhibition.* DOI: 10.2118/220241-MS

Vaswani, A., Shazeer, N., Parmar, N., Uszkoreit, J., Jones, L., Gomez, A. N., . . . Polosukhin, I. (2017). Attention is all you need. *Advances in Neural Information Processing Systems, 30.*

von Schwerin, M., & Reichert, M. (2024). A systematic comparison between open- and closed-source large language models in the context of generating gdpr-compliant data categories for processing activity records. *Future Internet, 16*(12), 459. DOI: 10.3390/fi16120459

Wu, H., Li, G., & Zheng, H. (2024). How does digital intelligence technology enhance supply chain resilience? Sustainable framework and agenda. *Annals of Operations Research,* •••, 1–23.

Wu, J., Yuan, L., Xie, T., & Dai, H. (2024). A sharding blockchain protocol for enhanced scalability and performance optimization through account transaction reconfiguration. *Journal of King Saud University. Computer and Information Sciences*, *36*(8), 102184. DOI: 10.1016/j.jksuci.2024.102184

Zakari, A., Abdullahi, S., Shagari, N., Tambawal, A. B., Shanono, N. M., Maitama, J. Z., Rasheed, R. A., Adamu, A., & Abdulrahman, S. M. (2020). Spectrum-based fault localization techniques application on multiple-fault programs: A review. *Global Journal of Computer Science and Technology*, *20*, 41–48. DOI: 10.34257/GJCSTGVOL20IS2PG41

Zakizadeh, M., & Zand, M. (2024). *Revolutionizing Oil & Gas: A Comprehensive Review of Smartening Technologies in the oil & Gas Industry*. Paper presented at the Proceedings of the International Conference of New Technologies in Oil, Gas and Petrochemical Engineering in Iran, Tehran, Iran.

Chapter 7

# Integration of Artificial Intelligence and Blockchain for Hybrid Intelligent Systems With Innovations, Applications, and Future Directions

**Ashutosh Verma**
https://orcid.org/0000-0003-0926-2747
*Parul University, Vadodara, India*

## ABSTRACT

*This chapter aims to bring out the integration between Artificial Intelligence and blockchain. While AI helps systems learn from data and produce insights, Blockchain ensures that the data remains clear, secure and traceable. The integration of these technologies results in hybrid intelligent systems. Such systems are leveraged to deliver secure and accountable outputs. This chapter covers integration models, technical foundations, and real-world applications in multidisciplinary areas. The chapter further addresses the substantial challenges in terms of scalability, data privacy, ethical responsibility and allied issues. The chapter concludes by addressing policy issues and research pathways related to the adoption of these hybrid systems. The chapter would offer great insights to researchers, policymakers, and practitioners. The aim of the chapter is to present the information in a manner that helps provide clarity and practical understanding regarding the integration of Artificial Intelligence and blockchain technologies and how they combine to create intelligent hybrid systems.*

DOI: 10.4018/979-8-3373-5457-6.ch007

## 1. INTRODUCTION

Artificial intelligence is the ability of machines to do things that usually need human thinking. It helps systems spot patterns, learn from data, and make choices based on what they've seen before. It is widely applied in sectors such as banking, healthcare, transportation, and education. The prime purpose of using AI is to improve efficiency, reduce errors, and enhance decision-making. In contrast, blockchain technology offers a transparent and safe way to record and store data over dispersed networks. Blockchain utilizes smart contracts which ensures that data cannot be altered without consensus once it has been entered into the system. Blockchain is a revolutionary technology that has enhanced accountability and trust among users across domains. Although these technologies have proven their value independently, their integration presents even greater opportunities. When used together, AI can analyze data that has already been verified through blockchain, leading to more accurate predictions and better decision-making. Blockchain technology can be utilized to track the results produced by AI systems. This offers an advantage over conventional systems by providing a higher level of transparency. Blockchain has further revolutionized fields where automation and trust are of prime importance. These hybrid intelligent systems have started to show genuine results across a gamut of industries. When we look at finance industry, these systems have facilitated in terms of high security and automated contract execution. The healthcare industry, on the other hand, has gained tremendously by increasing diagnostic precision while ensuring patient privacy is protected at all times. The supply chain sector has also greatly benefited from these hybrid systems, enabling product traceability and fraud detection. Public governance is yet another area that has made advancements owing to these technologies. Accountability and transparency have increased, and administrative procedures have been streamlined. Despite the fact that the hybrid intelligent systems are promising in nature, they still are in an early phase of development. There are many challenges to overcome and questions to answer. Pressing issues such as system design, data governance, and regulation need to be addressed. At the same time, the interest of the academic fraternity, who recognize the potential of these systems to address real-world issues, cannot be undermined.

This chapter presents a structured overview of how Artificial Intelligence and blockchain can collectively enhance the design of more intelligent and reliable systems. It outlines the foundational concepts behind both technologies, examines practical use cases, and discusses the technical and ethical considerations involved. The chapter also highlights future directions in this rapidly evolving space. Whether the reader is a researcher, practitioner, or policymaker, it offers valuable insights into the dynamic intersection of these transformative technologies.

## 2. TECHNICAL FOUNDATIONS AND HYBRID ARCHITECTURES

Before exploring the integration of Artificial Intelligence and blockchain, it is essential to understand the core principles of each technology. Artificial Intelligence, a branch of computer science, enables machines to learn from data, adapt to new inputs, and make autonomous decisions that would typically require human reasoning. This field includes subdomains such as machine learning, deep learning, natural language processing, and computer vision. These techniques allow systems to identify patterns in complex data and produce predictive or prescriptive insights (Russell & Norvig, 2021). Blockchain, on the other hand, is a distributed ledger secured through cryptographic techniques and designed to maintain a sequential record of data entries. It enables participants to achieve consensus on shared information without relying on a central authority. Each block is linked to the previous one, forming a transparent and immutable chain of transactions that supports trust and data integrity (Nakamoto, 2008; Tapscott & Tapscott, 2016). When these technologies are integrated, they reinforce each other's capabilities. Blockchain provides a trustworthy, tamper-proof data foundation for AI systems, while AI contributes advanced reasoning and anomaly detection to blockchain processes. For instance, AI can detect suspicious transaction patterns, and blockchain ensures those decisions are auditable and transparent (Zhang & Lee, 2020).

Multiple architectural models have been developed to support this convergence. In the AI-on-Blockchain model, AI computations are directly deployed on data stored or verified through blockchain networks, ensuring verifiable inputs and reproducible outcomes. Alternatively, the Blockchain-for-AI model uses blockchain to manage the AI lifecycle, such as storing model versions, validating data inputs, and tracing the origins of algorithmic updates (Casino, Dasaklis, & Patsakis, 2019). Recent developments include combining federated learning with blockchain. Federated learning enables models to be trained across decentralized devices without aggregating raw data in a central location. Blockchain helps coordinate training, verify updates, and incentivize participation using smart contracts (Li, Sahu, Talwalkar, & Smith, 2020). This approach facilitates collaborative AI development while maintaining privacy. Middleware platforms and edge computing have also been adopted to support hybrid system performance. Middleware ensures smooth communication between AI modules and blockchain infrastructure, while edge computing reduces latency by processing data locally (Nguyen, Ding, Pathirana, & Seneviratne, 2021). Although promising, these integrations present technical challenges. Developers must address consensus algorithms, model validation methods, cross-platform compatibility, and hardware limitations. However, continued research and pilot programs are rapidly advancing this field.

In addition to integration, the focus has shifted toward enhancing the security and governance of hybrid intelligent systems. These architectures are being designed to monitor and verify every phase of the AI lifecycle — from data sourcing and training to deployment and adaptation. Blockchain supports lifecycle management by documenting each stage in a tamper-proof manner. Training datasets can be hashed and stored on-chain, and model updates can be logged through smart contracts. This improves traceability and reduces the risk of unauthorized changes (Lu et al., 2020). In high-risk fields such as healthcare diagnostics, financial fraud prevention, or autonomous driving, blockchain ensures that only validated models are used. This verification process is vital for ensuring the safety and trustworthiness of AI outputs. AI systems are also exposed to threats such as adversarial attacks and data poisoning. Blockchain can mitigate these risks by validating inputs, securing model histories, and enabling consensus-based verification (Zhao et al., 2021).

Decentralized AI systems benefit from blockchain's resilience. In federated learning or swarm-based robotics, blockchain can govern interactions, track reputations, and isolate compromised nodes to protect system integrity. A crucial component of this setup is the use of oracles — agents that connect off-chain data with blockchain networks. Oracles ensure that real-world data, such as financial feeds or sensor outputs, are validated before being recorded on-chain. Their design affects system reliability, and ongoing research is focused on their fault tolerance and governance mechanisms (Xu, X., et al. 2021). As AI systems become more distributed, trust between autonomous agents becomes essential. Blockchain can provide a shared infrastructure for verifying agent behavior, storing immutable histories, and ensuring coordination without central oversight. These trust models are critical in environments like logistics, traffic control, or decentralized finance. Mechanisms such as token-based incentives, digital identities, and reputation scores can be used to encourage reliable cooperation between agents. Together, AI and blockchain are transitioning from theoretical constructs to applied technologies. Their integration enhances automation, security, and transparency across sectors.

In finance, this convergence supports real-time fraud detection, where AI flags suspicious activity and blockchain logs the alerts through smart contracts (Aldweesh et al., 2021). This improves accountability and enables automated responses. In healthcare, blockchain secures patient data while AI enables intelligent diagnostics and personalized treatment plans. These systems help build decentralized, privacy-preserving health networks that improve clinical outcomes and operational efficiency, where data is shared across institutions without a central authority while maintaining verifiability. Projects such as MedRec and IBM Watson Health demonstrate how this synergy can increase trust and improve outcomes in patient care (Dubovitskaya et al., 2018).

## 3. APPLICATIONS ACROSS SECTORS

This section explores how hybrid intelligent systems, formed by combining AI and blockchain, are being adopted in important areas. From supply chains and agriculture to education and public governance, these real-world deployments highlight the transformative potential and challenges of this convergence.

### 3.1 Supply Chain and Logistics

Transparency and traceability are essential features of modern global supply chains. Organizations increasingly rely on blockchain to log each step a product takes and to verify its provenance, a practice particularly common in the food, pharmaceutical, and luxury-goods sectors. When paired with artificial intelligence, however, these systems shift from reaction to prediction. AI analyses trends in market data, weather, and delivery times, enabling forecasts of demand, the early detection of route inefficiencies, and the quick identification of supply risks. Because blockchain maintains an immutable record, the insights generated are based on verified information rather than estimates that could later be manipulated. Initiatives such as IBM Food Trust and Ve Chain already deploy this integrated approach to strengthen food safety and combat counterfeiting (Wang, Y., et al., 2019).

### 3.2 Smart Cities and Urban Governance

Urban leaders must coordinate infrastructure maintenance, public safety, utility distribution, and citizen-facing services. Artificial intelligence parses traffic patterns, energy loads, and environmental indicators, revealing opportunities to streamline operations across multiple domains. When blockchain technology is layered on top, it secures those data streams and preserves an auditable trail, a feature especially valuable for citizen identities, voting registers, and records of public spending. For example, AI-powered facial recognition verified against a blockchain-based identity ledger grants clear, tamper-proof access to municipal services. In energy markets, AI adjusts demand forecasts and price signals, while blockchain tracks each transaction, ensuring equitable billing and transparent accountability for all users (Zhou et al., 2020).

### 3.3 Education and Credential Verification

Verification of academic qualifications and transcripts remains predominantly manual, often yielding inconsistencies and delays. By issuing digital credentials recorded on a blockchain, institutions create immutable certificates that any third party can validate without intermediary effort. Complementarily, artificial intelligence can map learner competencies to job openings, track study habits, and tailor course material, thus fostering a tighter linkage between education and employment. A growing number of universities and vocational platforms are piloting blockchain-based credentials alongside AI-driven adaptive systems in hopes of enhancing both retention and labour-market alignment (Chen, G., et al., 2018).

## 3.4 Legal and Intellectual Property

Artificial intelligence is now routine in legal research, contract review, and predictive analytics within courts and firms. When paired with blockchain, these functions benefit from a tamper-proof, timestamped ledger that preserves provenance for agreements, intellectual property assertions, and precedential materials. The dual infrastructure establishes an auditable chain of custody for digital files and enables partial automation of enforcement mechanisms such as smart contracts, royalty distributions, and provenance proofs.

## 3.5 Cybersecurity and Threat Intelligence

As cyberattacks become larger and more sophisticated, organizations increasingly rely on systems that can spot threats instantly and even act on their own. Artificial Intelligence is now widely employed to scan network traffic, flag unusual activity, and forecast possible breaches. When these AI tools are paired with blockchain, the whole process gains an extra layer of trustworthiness and protection against tampering. Blockchain can safely log every system event, access attempt, and configuration change, giving investigators a clear trail to follow after an incident. AI then sifts through those tamper-proof logs to identify repeat patterns of harmful action. In critical infrastructure fields such as energy and defense, threat-intelligence systems built on both technologies deliver speed without sacrificing reliability (Conti et al., 2018).

## 3.6 Insurance and Risk Management

The insurance industry is also going digital, and Artificial Intelligence is playing an ever-larger part in underwriting, fraud checks, and claims handling. By adding blockchain, companies give those processes a new level of transparency and auditability. For instance, AI can analyze satellite images and sensor data to judge crop damage, while blockchain confirms that the claims rest on data anyone can verify.

Smart contracts are advancing the speed and accuracy of insurance schemes. Under parametric designs, payouts occur as soon as measured indicators—such as excess rainfall or extended flight delays—exceed defined thresholds. By replacing manual verification with recorded data, the process trims administrative cost and solidifies confidence between insurer and policyholder. Pilot programmes run by several insurtech firms now test this hybrid approach, especially in developing regions where access to conventional cover remains sporadic.

## 3.7 Agriculture and Food Traceability

In agriculture, the joint application of artificial intelligence and blockchain is lifting yields, curbing waste, and bolstering safety along the supply chain. Machine-learning models ingest weather readings, soil profiles, and pest sweeps to recommend precise planting, feeding, and harvesting schedules. Simultaneously, blockchain nodes chronicle every transaction-from field gate to consumer checkout-confirming that each product is genuine and uncontaminated.The combined system proves invaluable during foodborne incidents: distributed ledgers pinpoint the source in minutes, while predictive algorithms flag downstream batches at risk. Enterprises such as TE-FOOD, SAP, and IBM Food Trust now deploy these tools to monitor livestock and produce across Asia, Europe, and North America.

## 3.8 Environmental Monitoring and Climate Resilience

Climate change has created an urgent need for systems that can monitor environmental conditions and inform responsive action. AI is being used to model climate scenarios, analyse satellite imagery for biodiversity accounting, and optimise water and energy flows in real time. By cryptographically sealing the provenance of each data point, blockchain provides a reliable auditory trail that policymakers and stakeholders alike can consult.When linked to AI-driven insights, blockchain-based carbon credits help guard against greenwashing by anchoring each offset to measurable outcomes. Streaming sensor readings from IoT networks—temperature, humidity, pollution—can be hashed and timestamped on the ledger, certifying a projects environmental impact with far greater granularity than earlier methods allowed (Bamakan et al., 2021).

## 3.9 Digital Identity and Humanitarian Aid

In settings where legal identity is scarce, conflicting, or simply unavailable—think refugee camps or earthquake-stricken towns—AI and blockchain now work in tandem to deliver aid with traceability and trust. Machine-learning models that read faces or fingerprints enable biometric verification, performing reliably on entry-level hardware and even under challenging lighting. Once validated, an individual's digital credential is recorded on an immutable chain, making it portable, secure, and independent of any single registry. This model proves particularly valuable in contexts such as distributing humanitarian aid, managing health-related records, and authenticating educational credentials for people forced to relocate. Initiatives by ID2020 and the World Food Programme demonstrate early-stage integrations of these systems. By pairing artificial intelligence with blockchain, agencies can process assistance efficiently while upholding individual dignity and safeguarding privacy.

## 3.10 Summary of Sectoral Applications

This concluding subsection consolidates the practical use of cases explored so far. It emphasizes that hybrid intelligent systems are no longer restricted to theoretical research or limited pilots. AI and blockchain are being jointly deployed to deliver measurable outcomes across sectors ranging from logistics, education to climate monitoring and humanitarian relief.

Their adoption continues to grow as public and private institutions pursue intelligent automation, secure traceability, and user-centered innovation. These real-world applications highlight both the versatility and complexity of hybrid architectures, setting the stage for a deeper exploration of the integration challenges that must be addressed for broader adoption.

# 4. INTEGRATION CHALLENGES

Despite the promise of merging artificial intelligence and blockchain, achieving broad deployment remains a complex, gradual undertaking. The two technologies rest on contrasting architectures and guiding assumptions, and their reconciliation confronts a tangle of technical, operational, and ethical hurdles. The following section outlines the key challenges that must be addressed for hybrid intelligent systems to achieve scalable and responsible adoption.

## 4.1 Technical Challenges

One major technical hurdle is the limited scale and slow processing speed of current blockchain networks. Public ledgers such as Ethereum and Bitcoin can handle only a few dozen transactions per second and the confirmation times may stretch from seconds to minutes. Those latencies clash with artificial-intelligence models that expect immediate, high-bandwidth reads and writes to keep training or inference moving (Zhang & Lee, 2020). In short, blockchains are built for tamper-proof record-keeping, not for the lightning-fast number crunching AI demands, and the mismatch can strangle joint applications. A second obstacle is the fragmented landscape of tools and protocols. Most AI frameworks and blockchain stacks are developed independently, with little thought given to out-of-the-box compatibility. When teams try to join them, they end up writing ad hoc layers of middleware that seem to work until an update breaks them or a new attack vector appears (Nguyen et al., 2021). Because there are no agreed-upon standards or reference architectures, every integration project low-speed developer down, limits innovation, and tally adds potential weak points in the overall system. Data storage presents a critical challenge when integrating artificial intelligence with distributed ledgers. Blockchains were never intended to accommodate voluminous datasets because of the expense associated with adding each transaction and the permanence of every entry. Conversely, contemporary machine-learning models depend on large, high-quality corpora for both training and real-time inference. The resulting incompatibility forces practitioners to confine sensitive or frequently updated records to the chain while off-loading bulk information to external databases; this partitioning, however, invites urgent inquiries regarding data synchronization, authenticity, and the overall reliability of the unified system (Casino et al., 2019).

## 4.2 Resource Intensity

Artificial Intelligence and blockchain are both remarkably resource-demanding technologies. Deep-learning algorithms, to produce accurate results, demand high-throughput processing units and copious memory bandwidth. Likewise, proof-of-work blockchains draw large quantities of electrical power because nodes repeatedly solve cryptographic puzzles to validate transactions. When these domains are united, infrastructure demands multiply as compute, network, and storage loads converge, raising both operational costs and environmental concerns (Li et al., 2020). Researchers are investigating mitigation strategies—edge computing, energy-conscious consensus protocols, parameter-efficient model compression—but most remain prototypes rather than production-ready solutions.

## 4.3 Operational and Deployment Barriers

Real-world integration transcends mere circuitry. It demands orchestrating varied professional disciplines. A fully functional hybrid system typically calls for data scientists, cryptographers, software engineers, compliance experts, and specialists fluent in the application domain. Few enterprises, especially government agencies, possess the fiscal bandwidth or organizational patience to recruit, equip, and retain such a cross-functional squad on an enduring basis. Deployment is further complicated by the high cost of failure. Blockchain transactions are permanent records, and erroneous smart contracts can lock funds or erroneously execute commands; conversely, AI models sometimes produce opaque, biased, or unsafe outputs that mislead end users or regulators. Reliable roll-out therefore hinges on expanded test suites that marry unit and integration testing of smart contracts with adversarial robustness checks, biased auditing routines, and transparent model verification pipelines. Those charters have yet to achieve wide consensus within the engineering community.

## 4.4 Ethical and Legal Complexities

One of the most critical issues lies at the intersection of ethics and compliance. Artificial Intelligence systems are often viewed as black boxes, meaning that their decision-making processes are not easily explainable to non-technical users. When these decisions impact real-world outcomes—such as loan approvals, medical diagnoses, or legal interpretations—lack of transparency becomes a serious concern. Adding blockchain does provide traceability, but it does not necessarily make AI models more interpretable (Zhou et al., 2020). Moreover, there is tension between blockchain's immutability and data privacy laws. Regulations such as the General Data Protection Regulation (GDPR) grant individuals the right to be forgotten. Blockchain, by design, prevents deletion or alteration of records. Balancing these conflicting principles requires creative legal and technical solutions, such as storing only hashed data or using permissioned blockchains that allow selective redaction (Chen, G, et al., 2018). Questions also arise about liability. If a blockchain-based AI system makes a harmful decision—who is accountable? The developers? The data providers? The network validators? These are still open legal questions that need to be addressed before these systems can be widely trusted or regulated.

## 4.5 AI Model Drift and Blockchain Synchronization

Over time, artificial intelligence models may exhibit a gradual decline in predictive accuracy because the statistical properties of incoming data no longer match those on which the model was originally trained. This phenomenon, known as model drift, can be corrected through retraining or fine-tuning. In conventional IT architectures, the update process can be executed rapidly, often with a single operator validating the new model. However, when AI components are embedded within a blockchain framework, every alteration must be immutably logged, distributed to every participant, and authenticated according to the network's consensus rules. When these conditions are not met, nodes may adopt divergent interpretations of "the current" model, raising both performance shortfalls and governance questions about which artifact constitutes an authoritative reference. Accordingly, future infrastructures should embed timestamped, cryptographically verifiable version registries that permit synchronized model refreshes without undermining the core principles of transparency and immutability that underpin blockchains.

## 4.6 Latency and Real-Time Responsiveness

A second important obstacle is network latency. Most blockchain paradigms—whether proof-of-work, practical Byzantine fault tolerance, or similar mechanisms—sacrifice time efficiency to maintain security and consistency across distributed ledgers. Those delays accumulate as propagation, verification, and block-finalization phases sequentially consume milliseconds that a high-frequency application cannot afford. In use cases such as collision-averse autonomous driving, rapid intrusion detection in smart cameras, or coordinated emergency dispatching, decision cycles frequently demand latencies measured in microseconds, not seconds. The tension between the determinism expected by real-time agents and the probabilistic timing guarantees typical in permissionless or permissioned ledgers constitutes a critical design bottleneck that must be addressed before blockchain-derived AI applications can operate at the level of safety and trust required by regulators and the public.

In scenarios that demand rapid consensus, even a brief delay from blockchain validation can compromise throughput and introduce safety hazards. Researchers and engineers are therefore investigating Layer 2 railroads, the orchestration of off-chain computations, and frameworks for pre-validated smart contracts as interim remedies; yet every acceleration strategy appears to chip away at the decentralized ideal that motivates the entire architecture.

## 4.7 Human Factors and Cognitive Load

Technical treaties, regulatory guidance, and performance benchmarks invariably command centre stage, leaving the human dimensions as an afterthought. Hybrid infrastructures add abstraction layers that many non-specialists find opaque and hard to trust. When a smart contract reverts or an AI-driven recommendation falters, tracing causality, assigning accountability, and prescribing remediation can quickly outpace the domain knowledge of even seasoned operators. Cognitive demand climbs sharply at the intersection of blockchain and machine learning, amplifying the risks of error. Addressing this challenge will require adaptive user interfaces, interactive audit trails, and real-time interpretability dashboards that translate algorithmic logic into actionable insight for human overseers.

## 4.8 Resource Inequality and Access Barriers

Hybrid systems demand robust computing resources, reliable data pipelines, and specialized talent. Unfortunately, those assets are seldom distributed evenly among regions or organizations, and the gap is widening. Unless deliberate countermeasures are taken, the advantages of combining artificial intelligence with blockchain will remain locked within wealthier countries and their largest firms, leaving smaller enterprises and low-income locales at an enduring disadvantage.

The situation could deteriorate further if open-source software, modular hardware, and low-cost deployment templates are not continuously improved and documented. To avert this outcome, research universities, philanthropic agencies, and responsible technology consortia must pool expertise and funding, facilitating wider, shared access. Only then can the transformative potential of hybrid systems benefit a broader array of users rather than a privileged few.

## 4.9 Governance in Dynamic and Multi-Stakeholder Environments

Decentralized hybrid systems will inevitably operate across multiple, overlapping stakeholders, meaning no single authority can command the entire infrastructure. That shift complicates governance: who mediates disputes, sets upgrade schedules, or enforces compliance when interests diverge? Answers cannot rely solely on technical specifications; they must also address legitimacy, accountability, and shifting power relations among participants. Future architectures therefore require adaptive governance frameworks that preserve transparency while permitting timely adjustment. Possible features include on-chain referenda, quadratic voter-curbing mechanisms, and predefined arbitration modules coded directly into smart contracts. Frame by frame, those instruments can help users balance flexibility against collective trust, ensuring that networks evolve without sacrificing the rule of law or shared responsibility.

This section stresses that merging Artificial Intelligence with blockchain can yield striking benefits, yet achieving those gains calls for careful awareness of each technology's boundaries. Addressing these weaknesses will be essential for realizing the true promise of joined, intelligent systems.

## 5. BRIDGING TECHNICAL GOVERNANCE AND ETHICAL OVERSIGHT

Technical and institutional governance mechanisms are essential but they don't suffice on their own. The integration of AI and blockchain into public systems and individual lives introduces ethical challenges which are beyond code and protocols. There are multiple issues concerning ethics and governance, accountability and explainability, data ownership and other allied issues that require their own focused examination. The following section outlines these concerns along-with foundational principles that must guide the responsible evolution of hybrid intelligent systems.

### 5.1 Ethical and Governance Dimensions

As A.I. and blockchain advance and become more entwined, their ethical and governance fallout demands close attention. These blended systems do not operate in a vacuum; they touch people, institutions, and fundamental rights. Developers, firms, and public authorities therefore must act early and deliberately to ensure that real-world use follows shared values, legal norms, and democratic ideals. Users may see that data passed through an immutable chain, yet they still cannot tell how hundreds of hidden parameters changed the outcome. Without meaningful explanations, transparent ledgers become little more than secure notebooks that do not help an applicant, defendant, or job candidate understand why they were turned down. Accountability therefore demands not only an immutable log but also interpretability; regulators and affected individuals must be able to trace a decision back to clear rules and weighty features, not to black-box heuristics obscured behind layers of code. Combining AI and blockchain therefore calls for parallel efforts: guarding against immutable bias while still allowing genuine users to comprehend why a system behaved as it did. Only then can the hoped-for synergy between the two technologies deliver results without fostering either blind trust or endless uncertainty. Users may have access to the records, but they may still not understand why a decision was made or who was responsible for it.

### 5.2 Accountability and Explainability

Accountability becomes a critical concern when automated decisions have real-world consequences. Whether a loan application is denied or a medical condition is misclassified, affected individuals and regulators must be able to trace the logic behind such outcomes. Meeting this standard underscores the ongoing need for explainable AI, ethical modeling practices, and comprehensive documentation of decision pipelines (Doshi-Velez & Kim, 2017).

## 5.3 Data Ownership and Consent

Questions around data ownership raise equally pressing ethical challenges. Who controls the data used to train AI? Who governs the blockchain infrastructure that stores or references that data? Current legal frameworks often provide individuals with limited control over how their information is collected, stored, or sold. The decentralized nature of blockchain only amplifies this uncertainty, especially when nodes operate across different jurisdictions (Zuboff, 2019). Consent, too, is evolving. Traditional one-time agreements are inadequate in dynamic data environments. Instead, real-time, adaptive consent models are emerging as more appropriate for AI and blockchain systems. Concepts such as self-sovereign identity and user-controlled data wallets aim to shift control back to individuals, ensuring transparency and informed participation in data governance.

## 5.4 Governance Models

Hybrid intelligent systems require governance structures that span technical, regulatory, and societal domains. No single entity can—or should—retain full authority over systems that affect public infrastructure or essential services. Developers, policymakers, civil society, and users must share responsibility through participatory governance models. Blockchain itself complicates governance. Decentralized networks are difficult to coordinate, especially when updates or patches must propagate across all nodes. Solutions such as on-chain voting, protocol councils, and consensus-driven upgrades offer promise but are not universally applicable. The introduction of AI further complicates oversight. Governance boards must regularly assess performance metrics, fairness indicators, and compliance with ethical standards (De Filippi & Wright, 2018) .A multi-stakeholder governance approach appears most viable. It allows diverse voices—technical, institutional, and public—to shape the deployment, monitoring, and accountability of hybrid systems.

## 5.5 Manipulated Media and Deepfakes

The rise of AI-generated manipulated media—deepfakes—poses a growing risk, especially when blockchain is used to anchor or circulate such content. Blockchain's immutability may unintentionally reinforce the credibility of harmful or misleading material. Once inscribed, even proven falsehoods are difficult to retract or amend.

To address this, hybrid systems must incorporate tools for media authentication, such as persistent watermarks, content provenance tracking, and verified source attribution. These measures should be integrated well before manipulated media becomes permanent on-chain—particularly in domains like journalism, law, and digital identity.

## 5.6 Global Value Conflicts in Hybrid Systems

Hybrid intelligent systems often embed implicit value frameworks. A governance model developed in Europe may prioritize privacy and individual rights, while one from East Asia may emphasize efficiency and collective interest. As these systems interact through international trade, migration, and digital exchange, underlying value conflicts can emerge (Floridi, 2019). In this context, ethical governance demands a flexible pluralism—respecting cultural variation while maintaining non-negotiable principles such as transparency, consent, and human dignity. Regulatory models must be adaptable yet grounded in shared ethical guardrails.

## 5.7 Autonomy Versus Surveillance

AI-blockchain systems in smart cities and welfare services offer efficiency and traceability—but they also risk deepening surveillance. Technologies like biometric identification, real-time facial recognition, and behavioral scoring, when combined with immutable records, may create continuous monitoring environments with limited escape. The core ethical challenge is safeguarding individual autonomy while ensuring system integrity. Developers must anticipate and mitigate the unintended consequences of overly traceable systems, especially in regions lacking strong legal protections.

## 5.8 The Need for Standardized Ethical Frameworks

Currently, ethical oversight in hybrid intelligent systems is fragmented. Standards are often voluntary and regionally defined. Organizations like IEEE, ISO, and OECD are drafting global frameworks that prioritize fairness, transparency, inclusivity, and technical robustness. However, many of these remain aspirational. Institutionalizing ethical certification for large-scale or sensitive systems would be a logical next step. This could include third-party audits, embedded user rights, and clear compliance modules. Just as physical infrastructure is subject to regulation, digital infrastructures should also be evaluated for ethical soundness.

# 6. POLICY AND REGULATORY FRAMEWORKS FOR HYBRID SYSTEMS

The convergence of AI and blockchain creates novel challenges for regulators. Both technologies are evolving rapidly, and their combination introduces layered technical and ethical complexities. While many countries have started regulating AI and blockchain independently, few have developed frameworks that account for their combined use. Without cohesive policies, hybrid systems may face gaps in oversight, security, and legal accountability.

## 6.1 Legal Ambiguity and Fragmentation

The lack of standard definitions remains a major barrier. Legal interpretations of "Artificial Intelligence" vary by jurisdiction, sector, and policy document. The same applies to blockchain terminology. This definitional inconsistency complicates the drafting of clear rules and hinders international alignment (Cath et al., 2018). Fragmentation further disrupts regulatory cohesion. For example, the European Union has advanced detailed policies like the GDPR and the proposed AI Act, but many other regions remain in early development phases. Where policies do exist, they often treat AI and blockchain in isolation—leaving blind spots at the intersection of both technologies (Veale & Borgesius, 2021).

## 6.2 Data Privacy and Sovereignty

Data protection remains central to regulatory debates. Frameworks such as the GDPR and California Consumer Privacy Act (CCPA) emphasize individual control over personal data. However, blockchain's design—anchored in immutability—conflicts with the right to erasure, correction, or modification (Finck, 2019). To resolve this, hybrid systems must adopt privacy-preserving measures such as data minimization, selective encryption, off-chain storage, and hashed representations. These approaches can balance regulatory obligations with technical constraints.

Permissioned blockchains, which restrict participation to pre-approved entities, are increasingly favored by enterprises and government agencies seeking regulatory compliance. By limiting access to a defined group, these systems aim to reconcile the tension between operational transparency and the equally critical need for data confidentiality.

## 6.3 Cross-Border Jurisdictions

Many blockchain networks function across national lines, and datasets used to train artificial intelligence models are typically drawn from multiple jurisdictions. This borderless composition complicates the identification of the applicable legal framework should a breach or disagreement arise. At present, international reciprocal enforcement remains patchy, leaving questions of liability, taxation, intellectual-property protection, and contract validity largely unsettled in decentralized contexts (Wright & De Filippi, 2015). In response, multiple multilateral organizations—among them the OECD, the World Economic Forum, and the United Nations— urge member states to adopt harmonized governance principles for both technologies. The proposed standards emphasize transparency, accountability, and ethical design, though their non-binding nature means that real progress still depends on concrete political agreement and adequate institutional capability.

## 6.4 Standardization and Compliance

The current lack of widely accepted technical and ethical standards generates considerable uncertainty for developers and organizations working with hybrid systems. In the absence of shared benchmarks, assessing the safety, fairness, and trustworthiness of those systems becomes a challenging and subjective task. The International Organization for Standardization and the Institute of Electrical and Electronics Engineers have both started to outline separate frameworks for artificial intelligence and blockchain. Nevertheless, a comprehensive set of integration standards remains unfinished and its rapid development is essential (ISO, 2023; IEEE, 2022).One promising approach to reconciling innovation with compliance is the regulatory sandbox, a controlled setting in which firms can experiment under temporary governmental oversight. Such environments allow policymakers to observe real-world impacts, test enforcement mechanisms, and refine safety criteria before wider deployment. Pilot schemes have run successfully in jurisdictions including the United Kingdom, Singapore, and Canada, generating insights that have subsequently informed more precise regulations.

## 6.5 Public Sector Adoption and Regulation

Public administrations, too, are beginning to experiment with hybrid technologies in areas such as digital identity, voting, benefits distribution, and land registries. While these projects can enhance efficiency and transparency, they also intensify risks related to surveillance, algorithmic bias, and data concentration in a small number of platforms. To safeguard citizens' rights and ensure that system enhancements translate into genuine public-value improvements, regulations must be explicit, open to review, and tailored to the distinctive risks that each application presents (UNDP, 2021).

Regulatory systems must promote long-term sustainability. To this end, they should require ethical impact assessments, mandate the disclosure of algorithmic decisions in public services, and establish citizen oversight committees. Legal innovations therefore need to support industrial growth while simultaneously safeguarding public trust and upholding democratic accountability.

## 6.6 Ethical Policy Instruments for Hybrid Systems

Most regulatory initiatives today treat artificial intelligence and blockchain as separate domains. Yet the convergence of these technologies demands policy instruments that account for their blended capabilities and shared risks. One promising method is the ethical policy sandbox, in which government agencies and developers engage together to design governance models that operate under real-world conditions but within controlled boundaries.

Such sandboxes test not only legal compliance but also the ethical behavior of systems in public and semi-public contexts. For instance, a decentralized health-care application can be examined for its handling of consent, transparency, and error correction over an extended period. Increasingly, policymakers regard these environments not as temporary loopholes but as forward-looking laboratories capable of generating insights that scale to comprehensive legislation (Ziegeldorf et al., 2022).

## 6.7 Anticipatory Governance and Adaptive Regulation

Rapidly evolving technologies frequently outpace conventional rule-making, leaving regulators scrambling once a problem has surfaced. In response, anticipatory governance has emerged as a forward-looking discipline that emphasises systematic foresight, speculative scenario-building, and early-risk mitigation. Under this approach, regulatory agencies collaborate with engineers, social scientists, and local communities to map possible technological trajectories and judge their prospective societal effects before they materialise. Adaptive regulation complements that vision by permitting policy instruments to be recalibrated on the fly, drawing on hard evidence from bias audits, model drift measurements, and privacy breaches. Smart contracts can convert some of those evidence thresholds into self-executing constraints, enabling what proponents' term "algorithmic compliance."

## 6.8 Open Government and Public Procurement Standards

As public authorities deploy AI and blockchain for digital identity, benefit delivery, and tax administration, many jurisdictions are seeking to embed these initiatives within broader open-government norms. That ambition translates into procurement specifications calling for transparent processes, meaningful public participation, and demonstrable accountability at every project stage. Examples now under discussion include mandatory release of open-source code, independent participatory impact assessments, and third-party verification milestones in contracts governing digital public infrastructure.

The stated policies seek to curtail vendor lock-in, deepen technical oversight, and direct information systems toward the public good as opposed to private profit.

## 6.9 Policy Gaps in Emerging Domains

New application domains-such as decentralized autonomous organizations (DAOs), algorithmic token economies, and sovereign digital-identity networks-are testing the edges of existing legal categories. Because many of these systems cross borders, lack identifiable ownership, and elude conventional enforcement, regulators struggle to fit them into customary frameworks. There is no shared international view on the classification of DAOs, for instance. Should a particular DAO be treated as a corporation, a cooperative, or something novel? Analogously, must an AI model that executes smart contracts in multiple jurisdictions be seen as a legal agent subject to law? Questions of that sort compel a reassessment of foundational legal notions such as responsibility, intent, and compliance within digital ecosystems.

## 6.10 Inclusive Policymaking and Global Cooperation

Regulatory design needs to be inclusive, embracing not only the priorities of large economies and dominant technology firms, but also the concerns of smaller states, Indigenous communities, and historically marginalized groups. Coordinated international action will therefore be essential to close jurisdictional gaps and deter arbitrage, whereby companies move capital-or simply relocate-to evade meaningful accountability under any one regime.

Initiatives such as the UNs Digital Public Infrastructure agenda and the World Banks GovTech programme are beginning to tackle these issues. Yet, more concerted effort is required to build equitable governance frameworks that translate global standards into local contexts and uphold rights-based principles.

This section stresses that regulation should not trail innovation. A forward-looking, collaborative policy process-rooted in transparency, inclusiveness and accountability-is vital for the responsible roll-out of hybrid intelligent systems.

## 7. FUTURE RESEARCH DIRECTIONS

The pairing of artificial intelligence and blockchain presents an encouraging but still developing area of research. As the two technologies advance, they pose fresh challenges around scalability, ethical oversight, technical practicality and social consequences. Early prototypes and deployed use cases show the potential landscape, yet architects, engineers and analysts must keep working to sharpen designs, boost performance and set responsible norms. This section identifies priority topics where continued scholarship can support the enduring growth and ethical operation of hybrid intelligent systems.

### 7.1 Scalable and Sustainable System Design

Future digital infrastructure must accommodate growth without sacrificing performance or increasing energy demand. Contemporary artificial-intelligence models, particularly those driven by deep learning, draw heavily on compute cycles; blockchain networks that employ proof-of-work exhibit similar cavalier consumption of electricity. Merging both families of workloads amplifies the aggregate burden, raising serious questions about the feasibility of à-la-carte sustainability targets (Stoll, Klaaßen, & Gallersdörfer, 2019).

To mitigate this trend, scholars are trialling lightweight consensus alternatives, notably proof-of-stake and delegated proof-of-stake, that curtail the baseline energy expense of ledger maintenance. Parallel advances in model compression, quantisation, and edge orchestrators allow deep-learning inference to operate within modest hardware envelopes. Moving forward, multidisciplinary research should emphasise joint specification of AI and blockchain pipelines, embedding efficiency and ecological stewardship into their architectural DNA from the outset.

### 7.2 Federated Learning and Privacy-Preserving Models

Federated learning enables the training of artificial-intelligence models across distributed devices without the need to centralize raw data, making it an attractive option for protecting user privacy. When blockchain technology is paired with federated learning, the system gains secure coordination, verifiable model updates, and incentive mechanisms governed by smart contracts (Li et al., 2020). Despite these advantages, practical implementations still wrestle with high communication costs, variations in model accuracy, and vulnerabilities to malicious attacks.

To move the field forward, researchers must design blockchain architectures that scale with federated-learning networks, particularly in data-sensitive sectors like healthcare and finance. Concurrent innovations in homomorphic encryption, differential privacy, and secure multiparty computation will be crucial for ensuring the integrity of shared gradients and for upholding user confidentiality during every training round.

## 7.3 Explainable and Auditable Artificial Intelligence

As artificial-intelligence systems increasingly influence critical decisions, the ability to understand their inner workings becomes a regulatory as well as an ethical necessity. Unfortunately, many powerful machine-learning models, especially deep neural networks, operate as opaque black boxes, offering little explanation of how inputs are translated into predictions. In jurisdictions where accountability is mandatory, such opacity raises serious compliance and fairness concerns.

Blockchain provides immutable logs that capture every operation in the AI decision pipeline, yet such auditing does not clarify the reasoning behind specific choices. Future investigations should integrate blockchain record-keeping with interpretable-AI methods so that systems are both verifiable and cognitively accessible (Doshi-Velez & Kim, 2017). A central part of this effort will be the development of concrete standards for model documentation, versioning, and provenance tracking.

Interoperability will critically shape the enduring viability of hybrid blockchain-AI architectures. In real-world settings, distinct organizations select different distributed ledgers and tooling stacks. Current bridges between these environments are sparse and usually depend on bespoke middleware or translation nodes, which amplify attack surfaces and introduce single points of failure (Zhang & Jacobsen, 2018).

Subsequent research should therefore devise resilient protocols for cross-chain messaging and cross-model invocation. Essential components include standardized data schemas, shared ontologies, and open application programming interfaces that empower AI services to converse across heterogeneous blockchains. Widespread adoption of such interoperable frameworks will in turn lower barriers to collaboration and accelerate experimental advances.

## 7.4 Human-Centered and Participatory Design

Designing hybrid AI-blockchain systems cannot rest solely on technical benchmarks. Such systems touch on deeply human concerns, including privacy, personal agency, social equity, and general societal trust. Consequently, forthcoming investigations must foreground human-centered strategies that meaningfully engage users, affected communities, and public regulators throughout both system creation and retrospective appraisal.Doing so requires assembling a broad constellation of perspectives during coding, user testing, and policy drafting. Equally important are methods that enable people to see, question, and govern the ways AI and blockchain reshape their daily choices. For that reason, participatory design practices, prospective impact assessments, and broadly inclusive governance architectures stand out as high-priority fields for sustained research and engineering effort (Crawford & Calo, 2016).

## 7.5 Ethical AI-by-Design in Decentralized Environments

At present, most responsible-AI scholarship concentrates on external audits following system launch. Yet when AI-blockchain arrangements grow more autonomous and widely shared, opportunities to amend policy or code post-deployment shrink rapidly. That trend heightens the urgency of coding ethical intentions directly into systems from the outset. Meeting this challenge demands a fresh research orientation that treats ethical AI-by-design as an essential pillar in decentralized contexts. Such an orientation would center ethics during architecture decisions and algorithm selection, rather than relegating it to retrospective review boards. Recent advances in programming languages and associated toolkits now permit developers to encode ethical principles—fairness, transparency, non-discrimination—directly within smart contracts and neural network architectures. At the same time, investigators must examine how these encoded constraints coexist with blockchain's foundational immutability and whether amendments can be applied without undermining the underlying trust assumptions.

## 7.6 Multi-Disciplinary Co-Design Methodologies

Designing hybrid socio-technical systems therefore demands sustained collaboration among computer scientists, lawyers, sociologists, economists and ethicists. Yet the bulk of contemporary investigation remains locked within disciplinary silos, impairing mutual learning and the joint articulation of pertinent questions. A coordinated co-design practice is urgently needed, one in which scholars from divergent domains jointly frame problems, prototype remedies and assess societal impact.

Participatory simulation environments offer one viable pathway toward such integrated work. In these virtual labs, developers, regulators, user representatives and other stakeholders manipulate evolving prototypes backwards and forwards, supplying immediate, observational feedback that can be factored into the code on the fly. By placing alternative governance arrangements alongside quantitative performance metrics, the simulations reveal unintended consequences much earlier in the project lifecycle.

## 7.7 Long-Term Social Impact Assessment

Research on the convergence of artificial intelligence and blockchain has tended to focus on immediate technical advantages, yet the compound effects of these hybrid architectures are likely to unfold over decades. Questions arise about durable shifts in employment patterns, citizen participation, and the reliance on encoded solutions for social trust. Longitudinal investigations that gather qualitative and quantitative indicators from multiple stakeholder groups—including users, engineers, regulators, and marginalized populations—are therefore essential for distinguishing transient trends from structural transformation.

## 7.8 AI Governance in Post-Nation-State Contexts

The global and often stateless nature of distributed-ledger platforms challenges existing frameworks of legal and political authority. Scholars must examine how obligations, incentives, and remedial pathways are negotiated when no central government is universally accepted as legitimate. Promising avenues include hybrids of smart contracts, reputation registries, and multilateral treaties that can adapt to regional variations and technical innovation. Critical to success will be community-driven oversight mechanisms that remain agile in the face of emergent security threats while upholding principles of fairness, accountability, and shared prosperity.

## 7.9 Narratives, Values, and Cultural Contexts

Finally, scholars and practitioners should attend systematically to the narratives, norms, and values that each technology carries within its code, interfaces, and standard-setting processes. Both artificial intelligence and blockchain systems embed tacit models of trust, autonomy, control, and fairness that, while often presented as neutral, reflect particular socio-economic preferences. Those embedded assumptions are by no means universal, and they may come into conflict with communal values in regions where decentralized governance, collective risk-sharing, or procedural equity hold greater normative sway. Rigorous empirical research is therefore needed to document how specific local constituencies interpret, adapt, and sometimes re-engineer these systems so that design standards can accommodate cultural pluralism rather than erase it. Researchers should pair quantitative modelling with ethnographic analysis, narrative archiving, and participatory prototyping, using those approaches to expose hidden heuristics and to open pathways for genuinely inclusive forms of innovation. The sustainability of "hybrid intelligent" ecosystems will hinge less on the technical feasibility of each component than on the manners in which they are constructed, used, and governed in socially situated environments. Accordingly, academic centres, industrial consortia, civil-society groups, and public authorities must collaborate in crafting governance regimes that prioritise fairness, transparency, and ecological resilience. The future-oriented research avenues sketched here point, collectively, toward a more responsible integration of artificial intelligence and blockchain in diverse social settings.

## 8. CONCLUSION

The convergence of artificial intelligence and blockchain is fundamentally changing the design of digital systems, enabling solutions that are at once intelligent and verifiable. Each technology, when examined in isolation, demonstrates distinct strengths: artificial intelligence translates data into adaptive insights, while blockchain anchors transactions in transparency, immutability, and decentralized assurance. Their integration produces hybrid intelligent systems capable of reshaping sectors such as finance, healthcare, supply chains, governance, and education, and reinforces the underlying architectures of public trust.

In this chapter the author has surveyed the technical underpinnings of these converged systems, sketched emerging architectural models, and highlighted a growing catalogue of real-world deployments. Nevertheless, their union is not problem-free. Scalability, interoperability, and governance remain formidable hurdles, while ethical questions about data sovereignty, fairness, and accountability demand ongoing scrutiny. Tackling these issues will call for coordinated advances in cryptographic protocols, machine learning explicability, regulatory design, and public discourse.

Because contexts vary markedly, a universal solution template is unrealistic. Designers, policymakers, and researchers must therefore proceed case-by-case, grounding choices in the specific risks, performance criteria, and stakeholder values of each scenario. Moreover, meaningful progress depends on sustained interdisciplinary collaboration, in which engineers, lawyers, economists, and ethicists work side by side from the outset. Only through such concerted efforts can hybrid systems realize their promise in ways that respect both technological ambition and the broader public good. With the continuing maturation of hybrid intelligent systems, their impact is expanding well beyond stand-alone use cases. These tools are progressively evolving into the connective tissue of contemporary digital infrastructure. Whether the task at hand is managing health records, regulating carbon markets, or coordinating autonomous agents, the fusion of artificial intelligence and blockchain is poised to shape the future interplay of trust, intelligence, and automation in society. A successful hybrid-intelligent system therefore depends on far more than raw computing power or refined algorithms. It needs a sustained design ethic that matches technical possibility with social responsibility. When innovation races ahead of governance, unwanted forms of bias, exclusion or inequity can become baked into tools that society is later expected to trust. The consequences may include deepened disparities in economic opportunity, expanded surveillance capabilities concentrated in a few hands, and a persistent gap between those who generate data and those who endure its analysis. Conversely, doing little is not without expense. Vital sectors such as finance, supply chains and healthcare can drift along with obsolete practices while fraud, misallocation and systemic risk multiply. Escalating global pressures—climate breakdown, pandemic preparedness, cross-border cyber conflict—demand coordinated, data-driven responses that only hybrid systems operating at scale can deliver. Meeting that need will require collaboration at all levels. Engineers must partner with social scientists, ethicists, lawyers and affected communities to embed shared public values directly into architecture. Policymakers, in turn, should nurture flexible, adaptive regulatory regimes capable of keeping pace with rapid change. Researchers, finally, have the critical task of observing not just what these systems perform but how they reconfigure social norms, labour markets and the foundations of democratic governance. Perhaps most importantly, AI and blockchain should be deployed not simply for cost savings or faster transactions, but to advance human welfare, uplift marginalized communities, and protect shared public rights. Achieving this mission demands broader digital literacy, deeper civic engagement, and richer public discourse so that every affected group can help shape the systems that now steer daily life. The destiny of hybrid intelligent systems therefore rests on the choices we make in their design, governance, and application. The potential is vast, yet so too is the obligation that accompanies it. This chapter has clarified the stakes, sketched emerging possibilities, and pointed toward immediate needs. Our forthcoming actions must be infused with care, sustained courage, and deliberate collaboration.

Looking ahead, effective integration of AI and blockchain will hinge on joint research, aligned international policies, and an unwavering pledge to ethical design. Innovations that flow from this convergence can boost industry, fortify democratic institutions, and furnish fresh tools for hard problems. They must, however, be crafted with vigilance, mindful of beneficiaries, risk-bearers, and the way these technologies will remap our shared digital horizon.

# 9. AI AND BLOCKCHAIN FOR SUSTAINABLE DEVELOPMENT

The combination of artificial intelligence and blockchain moves beyond a merely technical advance; it represents a strategic asset for meeting pressing global-development priorities. When deployed consciously, the pair can accelerate progress toward the United Nations Sustainable Development Goals, addressing persistent challenges such as poverty, inequality, climate disruption, and uneven access to vital services. By deepening transparency, automating repeatable decisions, and refining how materials are allocated, these complementary technologies furnish new pathways for confronting multitiered problems in resource-constrained environments.

## 9.1 Improving Transparency in Humanitarian Aid and Governance

Across numerous contexts, aid initiatives encounter waste, corruption, and weak lines of accountability. Distributed-ledger platforms can generate tamper-resistant logs of budget transfers, procurement steps, and grant disbursements. Coupled with machine-learning surveillance tools, field offices can observe where funds travel, how goods are used, and whether objectives are met. For example, blockchain preserves an auditable trail in medical-stock networks while AI flags deviations in immunisation-rates across districts. Such synergies curtail misdirection and reinforce confidence among funding partners, local agencies, and the citizens they serve.

## 9.2 Enhancing Access to Education and Employment

Artificial Intelligence is increasingly deployed to tailor learning experiences, evaluate student progress, and align graduates with relevant job openings. These functions rely, however, on precise educational records and dependable identity verification. Blockchain technology can archive immutable credentials, allowing learners—including refugees and other displaced individuals—to transport their academic histories across national borders with confidence. Initiatives such as BitDegree and ODEM already blend AI-customized study routes with blockchain-validated diplomas, helping individuals in remote or under-resourced regions assemble credible skill portfolios. In turn, these portfolios widen access to international labour markets that might otherwise remain closed.

## 9.3 Sustainable Agriculture and Food Security

Smallholder producers routinely confront limited weather guidance, inadequate pest surveillance, and restricted credit, all of which constrain output. Artificial

Intelligence examines satellite images alongside environmental datasets to deliver timely advice on sowing windows, disease threats, and price forecasts. When coupled with blockchain, a secure ledger captures every step-production inputs, harvest volumes, sales-so that buyers, regulators, and financiers may independently verify the process. AgUnity, for instance, has tested such a framework in East Africa, letting farmers log transactions and share agronomic data through mobile applications linked to the blockchain. By fostering transparency in supply chains, these instruments also cultivate a financial identity for growers, opening pathways to microloans and insurance.

## 9.4 Clean Energy and Climate Resilience

Artificial intelligence and blockchain technology are advancing decentralized energy systems. AI analyses consumption patterns and predicts demand, while blockchain tracks peer-to-peer transactions, carbon credits, and grid loads. Such solutions are especially useful in regions where the central power grid remains unreliable or absent.

Initiatives like Power Ledger in Australia and Grid Singularity in Europe allow households to generate, share, and purchase solar electricity in a secure manner. By enabling community-led markets, these projects directly support Sustainable Development Goal 7—Affordable and Clean Energy—while enhancing transparency and local control over resources.

## 9.5 Challenges and Equity Considerations

Promising as they are, these tools remain out of reach for many low-income and rural populations. Limited internet speed, intermittent electricity, and scarce training opportunities often impede adoption; consequently, hybrid platforms risk deepening rather than closing the digital divide.

To counter this trend, implementers should emphasise open-source software, hands-on workshops, and governance managed by resident stakeholders. Evaluation frameworks need to embed consent processes, linguistic accessibility, and ongoing cultural dialogue so that AI and blockchain serve as vehicles of agency instead of new forms of dependency.

# 10. SECTOR SPOTLIGHTS: REAL-WORLD APPLICATIONS OF HYBRID SYSTEMS

While theoretical models highlight the potential of integrating artificial intelligence and blockchain, real-world deployments offer tangible insights into how these systems are being used, what benefits they deliver, and what limitations they still face. This section presents sector-specific case spotlights that illustrate the practical application of hybrid intelligent systems across industries.

## 10.1 Finance: JPMorgan's Contract Intelligence (COIN)

JPMorgan's COIN platform uses natural-language processing to interpret commercial loan agreements, a task that once occupied legal teams for more than 300,000 hours a year. With the algorithm running on dedicated hardware, that workload now completes in seconds. Blockchain complements the solution by storing contract metadata, transaction flows, and audit trails in a cryptographically verifiable ledger. The hybrid model thus boosts operational speed and safeguards records against fraud or data tampering. Adoption, however, remains cautious because many jurisdictions still rely on diverse legal codes and formatting standards that make cross-border interoperability difficult.

## 10.2 Healthcare: MedRec for Decentralized Patient Records

Developed at MIT Media Lab, MedRec employs blockchain to coordinate patient records across independent providers. The approach makes every entry tamper-proof, while embedded AI agents scan the history to suggest therapies, flag duplicate prescriptions, and alert clinicians to dosing conflicts.

This model enhances data portability and lets patients decide who can view their health records. Key hurdles are linking to legacy hospital platforms and staying within privacy rules such as HIPAA and GDPR.

## 10.3 Supply Chain: VeChain's Cold Chain Monitoring

VeChain has rolled out hybrid systems in food and drug chains, focusing on cold-chain routes. Blockchain timestamps sensor readings for temperature and humidity along the journey; meanwhile, A.I. uses past and live data to forecast spoilage or delay. Firms like Walmart China rely on this mix to meet safety rules and prove compliance. A major caveat is the trustworthiness of the sensors themselves—faulty readings can corrupt the process even if the blockchain stays untampered.

## 10.4 Insurance: Lemonade's AI-Driven Claim Processing

Lemonade, a peer-to-peer insurer, uses A.I. to settle claims, spot fraud, and tailor coverage quickly. Smart contracts on the blockchain log claims, premiums, and terms, cutting paper trails and the bottlenecks of manual checks.As a result, some small, low-risk claims are paid in under three minutes. Customers, however, still question how the A.I. reaches its calls, and regulators watch closely to ensure decisions can be audited and appealed.

## 10.5 Education: ODEM's Skill Credentialing Platform

At the intersection of distributed ledgers and artificial intelligence, ODEM operates a skill-credentialing platform that allows students to mint verifiable certificates directly onto blockchain. Using machine-readable, tamper-proof records, employers may validate qualifications in real-time, effectively sidestepping intermediaries and curtailing misrepresentation during recruitment.

The system's AI engine reviews learners' engagement data and performance metrics, subsequently curating adaptive study pathways that align with labour-market demand. Although adoption has accelerated in coding and vocational arenas, traditional universities remain cautious, often encumbered by legacy transcripts and regulatory inertia.

## 10.6 Logistics: IBM and Maersk's TradeLens

Developed jointly by IBM and Maersk, TradeLens digitises the flow of maritime bills, invoices and certificates via a shared blockchain ledger, thereby mitigating fraud, reducing paper handling and accelerating audit trails in global shipping. Complementary AI algorithms forecast transit disruptions, streamline customs actions and minimize vessel downtime at congested terminals.

With participation from more than ninety stakeholders, including port operators and national customs offices, the network illustrates how a hybrid architecture can achieve cross-organisational transparency. Nevertheless, inconsistent regulatory frameworks and limited digital capability among smaller players continue to hinder full interoperability.

Across these disparate sectors, ODEM and TradeLens exemplify the practical emergence of hybrid intelligent systems outside laboratory confines. Their experiences therefore inform ongoing discussions about scaling digital trust, while also underscoring the systemic barriers—technical, bureaucratic and cultural—that still complicate widespread deployment.

# 11 STRATEGIC ROADMAP FOR SCALABLE AND ETHICAL ADOPTION

The joint application of Artificial Intelligence and blockchain holds considerable promise catalyzing sectors ranging from finance to public services. To translate that promise into widespread, responsible use, stakeholders must guide technology from laboratory demonstrations to societal deployment. A coordinated strategy that aligns innovation with policy, and technical progress with human values, is therefore essential.

This section presents a phased roadmap for developers, regulators, researchers, and civil society, aimed at constructing hybrid systems that deliver measurable benefits while respecting public and individual interests.

## 11.1 Establishing Open, Interoperable Ecosystems

Technical scale rests on interoperability. Many prototypes today run on disconnected platforms, impeding cross-border data flows and repeated reuse. Self-describing, machine-readable data standards, modular application programming interfaces, and publicly documented protocols should become the default for new projects. Initiatives such as the Interledger protocol and the Web3 Foundation point in this direction, yet their adoption remains partial. National governments, regional regulators, and major industry consortia can accelerate progress by endorsing, testing, and collaborating around a small set of open specifications. Complementary open-source repositories will further lower entry barriers and strengthen public confidence through auditability and continuous community review.

## 11.2 Embedding Ethics from the Start

Ethical considerations should be integral to system development rather than added at the end. Developers and their organizations are better served by an ethics-by-design mindset, one that treats bias mitigation, informed data consent, and algorithmic transparency as architectural decisions, not operational ones. Engineering teams can, for example, code fairness goals into machine-learning training loops, employ smart contracts that encode opt-out and redress rights, and leave clear, machine-readable trails so users can audit, challenge, and understand decisions. Ethics review boards, prospective impact assessments, and participatory co-design with affected communities need to be woven into every sprint and milestone, not scheduled as separate, distant exercises.

## 11.3 Strengthening Legal and Regulatory Alignment

Lawyers, inventors, and investors often share the same headache: legal uncertainty slows down AI and blockchain projects that otherwise seem technically sound. To move forward, startups require clear answers on liability, intellectual property, privacy, data portability, and the complications of cross-border governance. Governments can help by harmonizing existing statutes and creating definitional gateways for new entities, such as decentralized autonomous organizations (DAOs) and algorithmic agents. In parallel, expanded regulatory sandboxes allow mixed architectures to operate under controlled, temporary exemptions while regulators observe real use and adjust future rules, turning a short-term testing space into long-term legal intelligence.

## 11.4 Building Talent and Capacity Across Sectors

The effective use of hybrid intelligent systems demands a diverse skill set: engineers who know the moral stakes, lawyers who tamper with lines of code, and policymakers who can shift between the two worlds. Universities, vocational programs, and professional bodies should revise their models to embed modules on hybrid systems, socio-technical design, and forward-looking regulation.

At the same time, capacity-building must reach underserved regions and groups, so that skills, infrastructure, and investment are spread more evenly rather than concentrated in wealthy hubs.

## 11.5 Encouraging Cross-Sector Collaboration and Public-Private Partnerships

To scale hybrid systems, public, private, non-profit, and academic actors must join forces through consortia, alliances, and shared testbeds. When public-private partnerships are transparent and driven by broad policy aims, they can quicken deployment in sectors such as energy, identity, and finance. Well-designed, multi-stakeholder governance keeps innovation on course by guarding against the capture or misdirection of any one player in the system.

## 11.6 Preparing for the Unknown

A forward-looking roadmap must candidly engage uncertainty. Hybrid systems unfold within layered, changing contexts, each introducing novel, interlocking hazards. Risks like unanticipated emergent behavior in autonomous models or governance fractures among distributed nodes will keep appearing. Structured practices—scenario-planning workshops, contrarian red-teaming, and disciplined horizon scanning—equip teams to confront high-impact, low-probability shocks. Layering those exercises with a culture of transparent decision-making, adaptive policy, and continuous performance review positions organizations to steer complex systems toward enduring public benefit.

Following this disciplined path lets stakeholders move from pilot projects to systemic use, placing intention above technical trend. As hybrid intelligence and blockchain mature, our managerial habits must also advance so that progress remains measured by social purpose, not by momentum alone.

## DISCLOSURE OF DELEGATION TO GENERATIVE AI

The authors declare the use of generative AI in the research and writing process. According to the GAIDeT taxonomy (2025), the following tasks were delegated to GAI tools under full human supervision:

- Writing the literature review
- Proofreading and editing
- Reformatting

The GAI tool used was: OpenAI ChatGPT (GPT-5.2).

Responsibility for the final manuscript lies entirely with the authors.

GAI tools are not listed as authors and do not bear responsibility for the final outcomes.

Declaration submitted by: The tasks were delegated by the author.

Additional note: Generative AI tools were used in a limited manner solely for language editing and formatting support, with full author oversight and responsibility.

## REFERENCES


Aldweesh, A., Alshamrani, M., Almuairfi, S., & Alabdulmohsin, I. (2021). AI-based fraud detection and blockchain-powered transactions in banking. *Computers, Materials & Continua*, *69*(2), 2023–2037. DOI: 10.32604/cmc.2021.016618

Bamakan, S. M. H., Motavali, A., & Bondori, A. (2021). A review of blockchain-based platforms for sustainable energy and environment. *Journal of Cleaner Production*, *280*, 124461. DOI: 10.1016/j.jclepro.2020.124461

Casino, F., Dasaklis, T. K., & Patsakis, C. (2019). A systematic literature review of blockchain-based applications: Current status, classification and open issues. *Telematics and Informatics*, *36*, 55–81. DOI: 10.1016/j.tele.2018.11.006

Cath, C., Wachter, S., Mittelstadt, B., Taddeo, M., & Floridi, L. (2018). Artificial intelligence and the 'good society': The US, EU, and UK approach. *Science and Engineering Ethics*, *24*(2), 505–528. DOI: 10.1007/s11948-017-9901-7 PMID: 28353045

Chen, G.. (2018). *Exploring blockchain technology and its potential applications for education*. Smart Learning Environments., DOI: 10.1186/s40561-017-0050-x

Conti, M., Dehghantanha, A., Franke, K., & Watson, S. (2018). Internet of Things security and forensics: Challenges and opportunities. *Future Generation Computer Systems*, *78*, 544–546. DOI: 10.1016/j.future.2017.07.060

Crawford, K., & Calo, R. (2016). There is a blind spot in AI research. *Nature*, *538*(7625), 311–313. DOI: 10.1038/538311a PMID: 27762391

De Filippi, P., & Wright, A. (2018). *Blockchain and the law: The rule of code*. Harvard University Press.

Doshi-Velez, F., & Kim, B. (2017). Towards a rigorous science of interpretable machine learning. arXiv preprint arXiv:1702.08608. https://arxiv.org/abs/1702.08608

Dubovitskaya, A., Xu, Z., Ryu, S., Schumacher, M., & Wang, F. (2018). Secure and trustable electronic medical records sharing using blockchain. *AMIA Annual Symposium Proceedings*, 650–659.

Finck, M. (2019). Blockchain and the General Data Protection Regulation: Can distributed ledgers be squared with European data protection law? European Parliamentary Research Service. https://www.europarl.europa.eu/thinktank

Floridi, L. (2019). *The logic of information: A theory of philosophy as conceptual design*. Oxford University Press. DOI: 10.1093/oso/9780198833635.001.0001

ISO. (2023). Information technology—Artificial Intelligence—Overview of trustworthiness in AI. International Organization for Standardization. https://www.iso.org

Li, T., Sahu, A. K., Talwalkar, A., & Smith, V. (2020). Federated learning: Challenges, methods, and future directions. *IEEE Signal Processing Magazine*, *37*(3), 50–60. DOI: 10.1109/MSP.2020.2975749

Lu, Y., Huang, X., Dai, Y., Maharjan, S., & Zhang, Y. (2020). Blockchain and federated learning for privacy-preserved data sharing in industrial IoT. *IEEE Transactions on Industrial Informatics*, *16*(6), 4177–4186. DOI: 10.1109/TII.2019.2942190

Nakamoto, S. (2008). Bitcoin: A peer-to-peer electronic cash system. https://bitcoin.org/bitcoin.pdf

Nguyen, D. C., Ding, M., Pathirana, P. N., & Seneviratne, A. (2021). Federated learning with blockchain for privacy-preserving and secure communications. *IEEE Communications Surveys and Tutorials*, *23*(2), 1336–1382. DOI: 10.1109/COMST.2021.3065060

Russell, S., & Norvig, P. (2021). *Artificial Intelligence: A modern approach* (4th ed.). Pearson.

Stoll, C., Klaaßen, L., & Gallersdörfer, U. (2019). The carbon footprint of bitcoin. *Joule*, *3*(7), 1647–1661. DOI: 10.1016/j.joule.2019.05.012

Tapscott, D., & Tapscott, A. (2016). *Blockchain revolution: How the technology behind Bitcoin is changing money, business, and the world*. Penguin.

Veale, M., & Borgesius, F. Z. (2021). Demystifying the draft EU Artificial Intelligence Act. *Computer Law Review International*, *22*(4), 97–112. DOI: 10.9785/cri-2021-220402

Wang, Y.. (2019). Blockchain for industrial manufacturing: Security and trust issues. *Computers in Industry*. Advance online publication. DOI: 10.1016/j.compind.2019.103120

Wright, A., & De Filippi, P. (2015). Decentralized blockchain technology and the rise of lex cryptographia. Social Science Research Network. DOI: 10.2139/ssrn.2580664

Xu, X.. (2021). *Blockchain-based decentralized data storage and access control for edge computing*. IEEE IoT Journal., DOI: 10.1109/JIOT.2021.3060894

Zhang, Y., & Jacobsen, H. A. (2018). Towards dependable, scalable, and pervasive distributed ledgers with Blockchains. *Proceedings of the VLDB Endowment International Conference on Very Large Data Bases*, *10*(4), 385–386. DOI: 10.14778/3159176.3159184

Zhang, Y., & Lee, J. (2020). Data security and trust in hybrid blockchain and machine learning systems: A review. *Future Generation Computer Systems*, *108*, 1106–1120. DOI: 10.1016/j.future.2019.11.014

Zhao, Z., Xie, X., Wu, Y., Liu, Y., & Yin, H. (2021). Federated learning with blockchain: A new architecture for industrial AI. *IEEE Transactions on Industrial Informatics*, *17*(11), 7778–7787. DOI: 10.1109/TII.2021.3060996

Zhou, Q., Huang, H., Zheng, Z., & Bian, J. (2020). Solutions to scalability of blockchain: A survey. *IEEE Access : Practical Innovations, Open Solutions*, *8*, 16440–16455. DOI: 10.1109/ACCESS.2020.2967218

Ziegeldorf, J. H., Grossmann, F., Roth, J., & Wehrle, K. (2022). Transparent experimentation with regulatory sandboxes for AI and blockchain: A framework for co-creation. *Technology in Society*, *69*, 101885. DOI: 10.1016/j.techsoc.2022.101885

Zuboff, S. (2019). *The age of surveillance capitalism: The fight for a human future at the new frontier of power, edn*. PublicAffairs.

# Chapter 8
# Monitoring Oil and Gas Using Edge Intelligence and IoT for Remote Field Operations

**Shoaib Ul Hassan**
https://orcid.org/0009-0000-1020-6561
*Universiti Teknologi Petronas, Malaysia*

**Noureen Talpur**
*Universiti Teknologi Petronas, Malaysia*

**Mohd Hilmi**
*Universiti Teknologi Petronas, Malaysia*

**Mohd Hafizul Afifi Abdullah**
https://orcid.org/0000-0002-1427-2571
*Universiti Tunku Abdul Rahman, Malaysia*

**Fasee Ullah**
https://orcid.org/0000-0001-6167-5253
*Universiti Teknologi Petronas, Malaysia*

**Md Tahmid Ashraf Chowdhury**
*Universiti Teknologi Petronas, Malaysia*

## ABSTRACT

*Distributed Acoustic Sensing (DAS) is a rapidly advancing technology in the oil and gas industry, enabling remote field operations monitoring in harsh and inaccessible environments. Utilizing laser-based optical fiber cables, DAS provides high-resolution, real-time spatiotemporal data over long distances. It generates massive volumes of data, necessitating advanced preprocessing methods. Integrating edge intelligence, including machine learning and AI, enables automated analysis, event detection (e.g., fluid leakage), and predictive capabilities such as $CO_2$ flux estimation. DAS supports applications like wellbore, caprock, reservoir, and pipeline monitoring, offering advantages over conventional sensors like geophones. Its use extends beyond oil and gas to marine, traffic, infrastructure, and seismic monitoring. Combining DAS*

DOI: 10.4018/979-8-3373-5457-6.ch008

*with Edge Intelligence and IoT technologies delivers a cost-effective, sustainable, and autonomous solution for continuous surveillance, marking a significant shift toward smarter and safer operations in various industries.*

# INTRODUCTION

## Overview

Over many decades, the oil and gas industry played an important role in the transformation of the world. Nowadays, this field is on the cusp of the new and modern era of digital world. This transformation of manuals to autonomous can offer and deliver more advanced and increased operational efficiency and workplace safety for stakeholders either in direct way or vice versa. The oil and gas industry are considered as a billion-dollar industry. Greater challenges and complexities in operation are common. Monitoring in harsh environments and on-site conditions is difficult for humans (Sircar et al., 2021). In such scenarios, remote sensing or remote monitoring devices and systems are utilized to timely monitor oil and gas fields. Remote sensing technology, such as distributed acoustic sensing (DAS) and geophones, is being used to monitor almost all tasks required in the oil and gas industry (Landrø et al., 2024). This remote sensing offers wide and long-range monitoring capabilities with robust techniques and methods. In remote areas monitoring oil and gas fields is a challenging task. Often, companies encounter difficulties in addressing problems, where timely and rapid actions are needed. To handle such issues, edge intelligence and IoT technologies are transforming. However, this transformation is beneficial for the industry, as it offers more efficient and real-time monitoring capabilities. And this utilization enables us to have more advanced and robust monitoring across various aspects of oil and gas operations. Such as micro seismic events detection, fluids flow, reservoir performance, well integrity e.g., detection of oil and gas leakage, monitoring wellbore activities, CO2 storage monitoring, CO2 plum migration etc. By providing early signs and warning on monitoring system (Yurikov et al., 2022).

DAS technology has a tremendous influence on oil and gas exploration. With the integration of Machine Learning (ML) and Deep Learning (DL) which play a significant role shaping and transforming era of digitization. Since its use is growing worldwide, it also offers diverse applications in oil and gas, starting from the exploration of reservoirs to environmental impact assessment. Reducing costs and improving safety are always prioritized in the oil and gas industry. For this reason, companies seek innovative solutions to enhance productivity by leveraging AI- and ML-based systems. Since DAS produces terabytes of data per day over extended periods, robust use of edge intelligence helps companies avoid wasting millions of dollars drilling into unproductive wells (Kozman et al., 2024). And it is capable of much more than just these cases, can be expand in forms. So, this chapter covers all monitoring applications of DAS along with its pros, limitations and advancements in the oil and gas industry using edge intelligence and IoT. Moreover, this chapter offers readers of this book how modern devices like DAS, with edge intelligence, and IoT are transforming the way to monitor and manage oil and gas industry. Furthermore, in chapter you will explore working principles of the latest devices used in oil and gas, key advantages. This chapter serves as a valuable resource for scholars, providing a comprehensive understanding of modern techniques and tools useful for remote monitoring in the oil and gas industry, especially Distributed Acoustic Sensing (DAS), through the integration of Edge Intelligence and IoT technologies. Additionally, this chapter acts as a worthy guide, which almost covers key topics that bridge theoretical concepts with practical applications in the oil and gas industry. By offering insights into advanced sensing methods and ML- and AI-based solutions with IoT.

*Figure 1. Idea of Edge Intelligence with IoT*

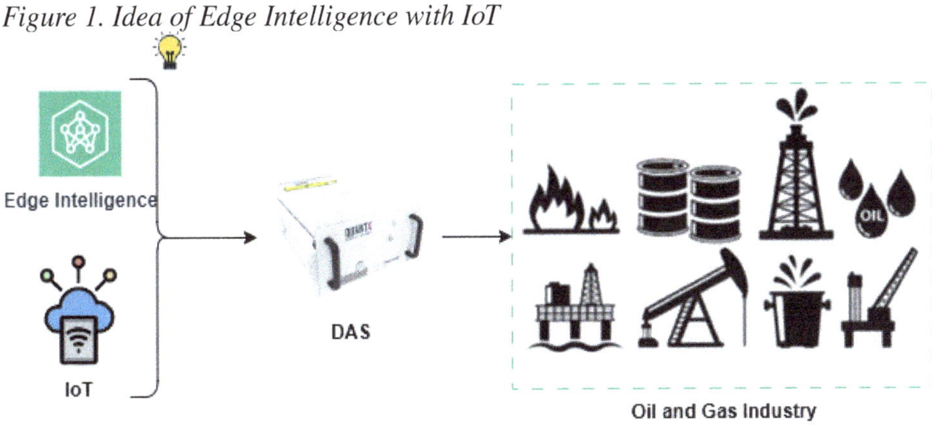


## Need for Smart and Autonomous Solutions

In the era of edge intelligence, we can't deny the usage of smart and autonomous systems in any field. It is quite simple; utilization of smart systems offers many advantages to humans. In the oil and gas growing usage and adoption of technologies like Distributed Acoustic Sensing (DAS), they are required to provide a smart and autonomous solution to address all challenges(Turov et al., 2023). And there are several reasons to make use of intelligent systems. In this chapter we will discuss most of the important topics related to monitoring applications. Alongside, pros, limitations or challenges in remote sensing. Where traditional techniques and methods struggle to address robustly(Butcher et al., 2022). DAS generates massive amount data, often hit terabytes per day and even petabyte over the lifetime of different projects. Such as Carbon Capture and Storage (CCS) (Vandeweijer et al., 2022). Now imagine with this much of immense amount of data definitely necessitates edge intelligence and sophisticated data management strategies. To filter, compress and analyze data efficiently at the source. And systems based on ML and DL are essential to process and analyze the data quickly and accurately (Alali, 2023; Anikiev et al., 2023). Additionally, optimizing the production operations, and extracting data insights that would be difficult for engineers to understand in that perspective. Alongside, it enables real-time insights and decision making. Where quick, near real-time analysis into critical processes is paramount for operational decisions, risk management, and timely intervention. This industry encounters various difficulties, that require the adaptation of smart and autonomous solutions. For instance, to increase operational efficiency and reduce costs, safety and risk management in remote areas e.g., in hazardous environments mitigating risk of human workers, by automation of hazardous task since machines can perform task repetitively and perform precision beyond human capability. These are important aspects, to reduce the risk and provide timely alerts to prevent accidents. Autonomous and smart solutions help engineers in reducing environmental impact. Furthermore, leveraging technologies: AI, ML, and IoT enable better management and optimization of operation in oil and gas industry (Ganesh et al., 2022).

Remote sensing has proven to be an integral tool for downstream and upstream oil and gas operations. So therefore, the integration of smart and autonomous systems like DAS powered by AI and ML is no longer optional for such industries but essential and important. These edge intelligence and IoT base technologies address critical challenges in data handling, noise reduction, remote operations, and real-time decision-making, enabling safer, more efficient, and more informed operations. As industry evolves, such intelligent systems will be at the core of driving innovation, sustainability, and operational excellence in increasingly complex environments. Therefore, in oil and gas industry autonomous and smart solutions are indispensable. To improve operational efficiency, safety, sustainability. Utilization of edge intelligence and IoT are crucial to address and resolve challenges. Additionally, challenges such as reducing expenses, risk management, environmental impact, and necessity for innovative solutions to manage declining company resources and complex operations (Vandeweijer et al., 2022).

*Figure 2. Edge Intelligence for Smart Monitoring*

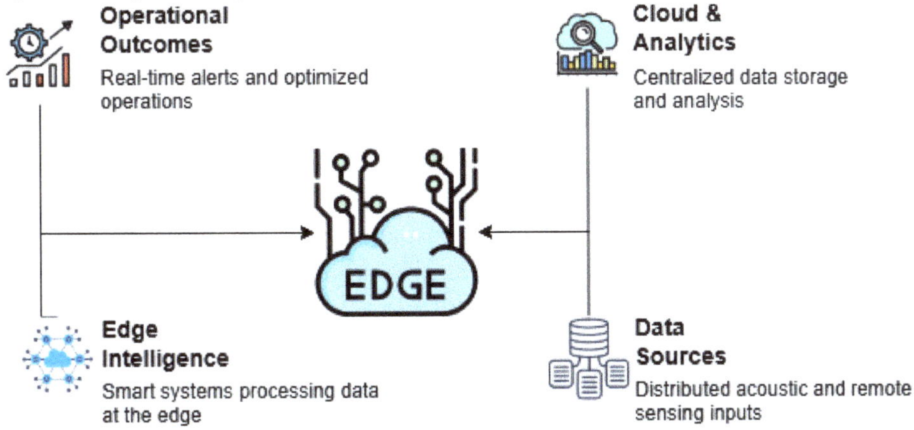


## Promising Technology in Monitoring

This marvelous technology using existing or propose fully laid infrastructure of optic cables started back in the 1990s (Li, 2021). However, the first application was monitoring earthquake seismology. But in recent decades, usage of DAS in various fields has increased. Since, the early form of DAS was known differently and referred to as Distributed Vibration Sensors (DVS). Later, the exact technologies based on the phase of Rayleigh backscattering (RBS) were developed. Which accurately restored vibration information such as amplitude, frequency, and phase. Today, these systems are known as DAS. In 2009, Shell Canada reportedly execute the use of this system to monitor downhole to assess the application of hydraulic fracture monitoring. Soon after, in April 2012 using the same technology SECARB site determine its robustness for monitoring of CO2 injection project. Despite challenges and complexities in the early version of DAS Interrogator Units (Trautz et al., n.d.). DAS versatility and the sense of providing high-resolution data make it a reliable solution for various applications, from hydraulic fracturing to pipeline safety and reservoir characterization (M. Chen et al., 2022).

## Edge Intelligence and IoT in Enhancing DAS Capabilities

Edge intelligence refers to the use of artificial intelligence and ML, power by IoT, significantly improves and enhances capabilities of DAS. Since, DAS generates massive data because of their high spatial and temporal resolution. According to (Al-okaily & Tbakhi, 2024; Carpentieri, 2025) produces terabytes per day for long term monitoring. This complex data is coupled with many challenges including SNR, data storage, and real-time insights. Which makes the Edge Intelligence and the Internet of Things (IoT). Integration is crucial for enhancing DAS capabilities. Additionally, timely decision-making, autonomous responses in different fields, ranging from marine to urban traffic monitoring, structural health monitoring, and Geologic CO2 sequestration (GCS) in the oil and gas industry. Therefore, the role of Edge Intelligence and IoT are essential for automation of tasks. Also, IoT frameworks for the interconnection of DAS channels enable the seamless transmission of the data (Yalli et al., 2023). This seamless transmission and real-time data flow enables DAS for frequent timely monitoring in a robust way. Which ultimately enables timely decision-making and automated operations in oil and gas fields. For instance, CO2 plume evolution and quantification, wellbore and caprock integrity monitoring, and leakage detection or early warnings gas leaking events (Landrø et al., 2024).

## MONITORING TECHNOLOGIES

## WORKING PRINCIPLE OF DAS

DAS technology is purely based on fiber optic cables; DAS uses entire cable as a sense of source (Butcher et al., 2020). It accurately senses and record strain rate and monitor vibration produced by different events, either anthropogenic or morphological. When disturbance occurs, IU analyzes and assesses this phase-change to determine the fiber strain via vibration induced along each segment cable. And record differences between these microscopic imperfections lead by vibration. This solution as an accurate is also a cost-effective monitoring system used in various fields. In the oil and gas industry there are numerous monitoring applications such as CO2 flow, leakage, fracture monitoring etc. To ensure the safety stored $CO_2$ in deep saline aquifers or in subsurface formations. When $CO_2$ is injected into deep geological formation (Kim et al., 2018; Wen et al., 2021). The fiber optic IU at the surface is connected to a permanently installed fiber cable infrastructure in either an injection well or a monitoring well. This utilization of DAS has only one purpose. To digitize the storage site making it more intelligent, safe and reliable storage site for oil and gas. Where it offers cost effective solutions for CO2 plume mapping and tracking through seismic imaging, earthquake risk assessment through induced seismicity monitoring (*Distributed Acoustic Sensing | EarthScope Consortium*, n.d.). and leak free wells through well integrity monitoring. By repeating this process continuously. This device is processed thousands of times per second. And DAS system measures very minimal and tiny fiber stretches. So, due to this the mechanism of interrogator or unit results in a huge volume of data which later becomes a major challenge in all scenarios.

*Figure 3. DAS working: (a) architecture; (b) RBS phenomena; (c) RBS microphysical model in DAS*

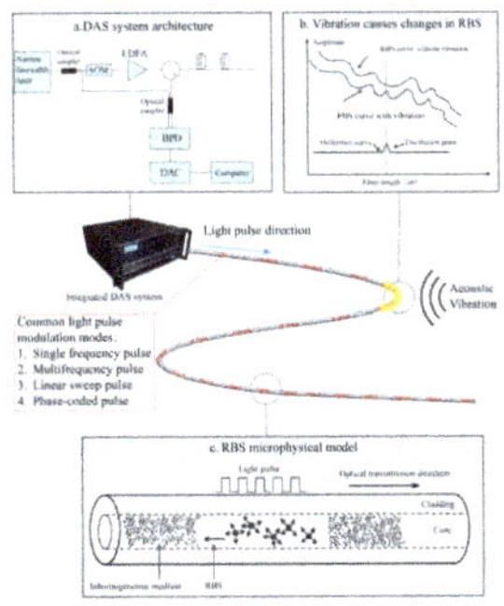


*(Zhang et al., 2024).*

## Working Principle of Geophones

A geophone is another traditional yet effective sensor system, often more efficient than other seismometers (Lellouch et al., 2020). This technology is primarily used for detecting high-frequency signals in surveys and is particularly helpful in the exploration of oil and gas. It converts ground movements into signals, enabling computer systems to map the structure of subsurface or underground reservoirs. Geophones use electromagnetic induction, where a copper coil within a magnetic field produces voltage and moves in response to ground movement caused by events such as gas and oil leaks, seismic waves, or anthropogenic activity. These waves are then recorded and interpreted to determine the properties of the surface or subsurface, including signs of natural resource presence. Geophones can be installed vertically (to detect vertical ground movements) or horizontally (to detect ground motion in one or two dimensions). They are widely used in natural resource surveys and for monitoring earthquakes, providing early detection and helping engineers understand faults (Dong et al., 2020).

*Figure 4. Geophone Data Processing for Reservoirs Mapping*

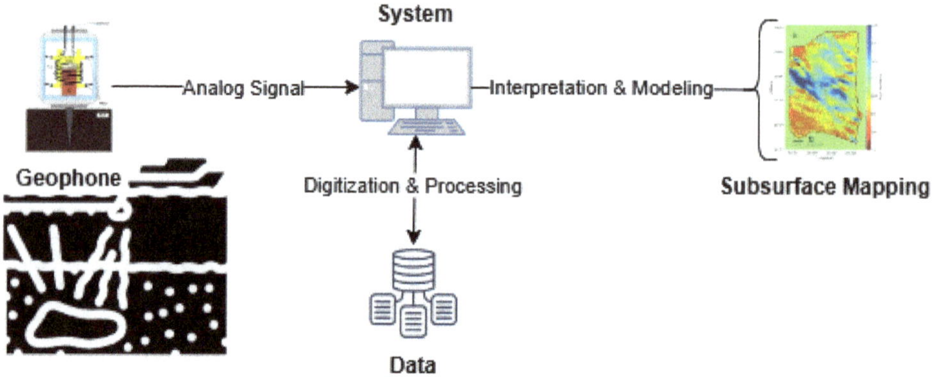


## Optical Fiber as a Sensing Medium in Remote Monitoring.

For sensing DAS uses optical fibers. The IU consistently send out laser pulses and listen echoes and calculate the difference between these echoes as vibrations and at the end map it precisely along the entire length of cable. This sensing power of DAS robustly extracts the signals from kilometers and is used in remote areas to autonomously monitor oil and gas fields using Edge Intelligence and IoT (Lapins et al., 2023). Throughout the length of optic cable virtual sensors are assumed. Which sense and tell IU about the occurrence of microscopic imperfections. These fiber cables are highly reliable sources in monitoring. Since, their sensitivity analyzing and detecting acoustic vibration along the overall length of fiber. Offering real-time and rapid monitoring with long-distance coverage(Panhwar et al., 2022). These cables are generally robust and can withstand in harsh and difficult-to-access environmental conditions. These fiber cables are designed to monitor and measure the various parameters, such as strain rate, temperature, vibration etc. And these are highly sensitive to vibrations and changes in the strain rate, with flexibility and durability.

## Noise Over Long Distance.

Many ML algorithms have immense potential and remarkable performance in many fields owing to their flexible modular architecture and strong representation capability. Such architectures include convolutional neural networks (CNNs) have a good performance on the spatial dataset (Zhong et al., 2019) by achieving excellent results in image recognition as multiple layers of filters have greater capability to recognize images. The weight factor in neural networks is used to remove complex noise and outperform than a feedforward network producing a balance between efficiency and performance of the denoised image. A network-based Blind Image Quality Assessment (BIQA) was applied to evaluate the quality of the output (Hu et al., 2020). Beyond general image denoising tasks, CNNs have extended their well-known abilities gaining exceptional output in broader, specialized, and challenging tasks such as blind denoising, in which characteristics of noisy data are unknown to us, and dealing with real-world noisy images, which often involve complex and diverse noise patterns in image processing (Ilesanmi & Ilesanmi, 2021). Recurrent neural networks (RNNs) (handle sequential data by using a memory element to capture temporal dependencies), Autoencoders (A variant of an artificial neural network (ANN) (Song et al., 2020) with input, hidden, and output layers), Boltzmann machines (symmetric connections between the input and hidden layers, and internal connections within the hidden layer), Generative adversarial networks (GANs) (Use a deconvolutional layer to generate data or images), Multilayer perceptron (MLP) (Also known as a classical neural network, this architecture can estimate continuous functions and solve non-linear separable problems), ResNet (A residual learning framework that improves training of deeper networks) are well known building blocks and frameworks used for seismic data preprocessing, analyzing and building early prediction systems.

Yet the above NN framework algorithms are being used because of having great capabilities to extract features from raw data later feeding into a ML algorithm for better predictions and decision in the future of geoscience application. Such applications and events include earthquakes, volcanic tremors, rock falls, monitoring of construction, landslide, mining activities, rock fracturing, fluid injection, leaks in pipelines, surface fluid flow, hydraulic fracturing, geothermal wells and health of reservoirs used for $CO_2$ storage etc. Many novel frameworks are even derived using NN family algorithms. On the other hand, the question remains on finding the effective methodologies and techniques for developing an automated data pre-processing pipeline that enhances the quality and usability of DAS data for $CO_2$ storage and fluid production monitoring. So that this clean and healthy data can be fed into the ML algorithm. However, before feeding data into model, there is a phase of pre-processing of data. It is the most important and first step of every ML model. Preprocessing involves techniques like filtering, which may include band-pass filtering tailored to the wavelengths of interest, F-K transformations, and wavelet analysis. Advanced methods may also be used, such as combining wavelet filtering, high-pass filtering, and autocorrelation, or employing machine learning for denoising, as seen in techniques like DAS-N2N and attention-guided denoising convolutional neural networks (ADNet) (Lapins et al., 2023; Zhan et al., 2024). In addition to noise reduction, data management and data reduction strategies are needed to handle the sheer volume of data produced by DAS systems. Authors of

[12] they stated parameterization can be used for 2D to reduce the dimension of spatio-temporal data.

## Conventional and Modern Sensors Based Systems.

Conventional sensors include geophones, accelerometers, and strain gauge sensors. However, the use of geophone is wider than other two. Geophones are traditional and considered reliable sensing techniques to detect ground movements and vibration along cable length. When compared to all three systems mentioned DAS is more powerful and robust in many cases. However, at some point geophone surpasses the DAS in noise profiling. Despite the DAS critical benefits mentioned earlier in the chapter. Thanks DAS to be very resistant in hot environment. Closely monitoring capability and deployment near the reservoir; active wells instead of monitoring well. The installed fiber can be used for years or even decades over the life of the project.

## Advantages and Limitations of Monitoring Devices in Harsh Environments.

In the earlier section of chapter, you observed DAS has always been promising in various fields and conditions. By offering various benefits and advantages for harsh environment or difficult to access remote sites because of robustness and long range of sensitivity (Piana Agostinetti et al., 2021). It can survive and operate in challenging environments and conditions such as high pressures, temperatures, extreme weather, and geo-hazard events monitoring and detection. Despite these factors, in certain conditions its capabilities can be downgraded and affected by factors such as optical cables type, noisy environment (Anikiev et al., 2023). These conditions are possible in wide-area applications like oil and gas pipeline monitoring, where safety and reliability of pipelines are ensured at certain distances. Since, the sites in the oil and gas fields are ideal for potentially explosive and hazardous like wells. High sensitivity of DAS can easily detect events that are far away. Since remote sensing base devices provide sophisticated and valuable tools for monitoring operation from a distance. As, remote sensing can operate in various conditions and environment, such as land, marine etc. utilizing broader range of virtual sensors and spectral wavelengths.

# EDGE INTELLIGENCE SYSTEMS

## Role of Edge Computing

Edge computing in DAS refers to utilization of intelligent techniques to compute, analyze data and finding statics to enhance the applicability of DAS in various fields. Since, it produces terabytes and petabytes over life of monitoring projects in oil and gas. Handling such massive data and transmission to a centralized storage areas for analysis requires robust techniques and methods using the edge intelligence. These petabytes of data can be deliberately processed with cutting edge solution (Al-okaily & Tbakhi, 2024). Edge computing enables real-time and near-real-time preprocessing and analysis at the field units in harsh and hazardous areas. This use significantly reduces data transmission loads, speeds up response in a timely manner, and allows for immediate detection of events such as leaks, caprock integrity etc. Edge computing offers a reliable solution, which alleviates the computational burden. DAS generates massive amounts of data. It is a better solution to address the challenge of managing large datasets. Furthermore, it offers rapid analysis which is a backbone for real-time monitoring and quick actions. This reduced the overall cost of projects (Ashry et al., 2022).

Furthermore, it offers intelligent filtering techniques, compression strategies, noise reduction frameworks, and feature extraction engineering (Carpentieri, 2025). It also improves resilience and autonomous behavior in remote and harsh environments. Where network connectivity may be limited and challenges. However, by utilization of ML models and frameworks at the edge, DAS systems can perform tasks like anomaly detection, signal classification, or event localization without human intervention, thus making DAS more adaptive and efficient in harsh environment.

## Need for Real-Time and Automated Data Analysis

Enhancing operational efficiency, improving decision-making, ensuring operational safety, and implementing reliable strategies and techniques across various scenarios particularly in harsh environments are key goals in industries such as oil and gas. Minimizing human intervention is a consistent priority, with the transition from manual processes to digital solutions being essential. DAS offers a wealth of data for monitoring subsurface activities. To extract insights and taking quick decisions require real-time preprocessing and assessment of data. Later, can be utilized in the oil and gas industry for real-time applications (Ravi Ganesh et al., 2022; Rehman Shaikh et al., 2024). Such as subsurface imaging, reservoir monitoring, $CO_2$ characterization and plume migration, $CO_2$ leakage detection, seismic event monitoring, oil and gas production oversight, and pipeline monitoring. In the above-mentioned application, timely alerts and warnings are crucial. For instance, if a $CO_2$ leakage occurred at a certain location and field officers didn't notice, it could be dangerous, as $CO_2$ is a greenhouse gas and hazardous. However, the use of edge intelligence for such harmful events requires a smart monitoring system that can raise timely alerts and prevent greater risk. Increasing adoption rate of real-time application and automated data analysis due various factors. For example, oil and gas reservoir nature is dynamic (Mehnert et al., 2014). Its complexity of monitoring day-to-day operation necessitates constant monitoring. To maximize the production of oil and gas. This real-time capability allows timely and accurate information of events and incidents. To take rapid and quick actions for more informed decisions. Moreover, this integration of existing technologies with automated systems enhances the operational environment.

## Integration of AI and ML

Over the century, this industry has been instrumental and game changer in shaping the world. Today, it stands at the threshold of a new digital era. The shift from manual to autonomous operations promises greater operational efficiency and improved workplace safety for stakeholders. AI and ML have wider scope and domain in various industries including the oil and gas industry. Since we are referring to edge intelligence as the utilization of AI and ML, let's delve deeper into this era of edge intelligence, where the use of AI and ML is growing across many sectors. In both domains, we utilize computer intelligence to train machines to perform tasks without human intervention. Specifically, if we discuss ML, it is categorized into supervised, unsupervised, semi-supervised, and reinforcement learning. In each category, models are trained using different techniques and methods (Asfha et al., 2024). For instance, in supervised learning, we require a labeled dataset to train a model, whereas in unsupervised learning, we train the model on unlabeled data to identify patterns. In DAS, this presents a significant challenge and gap, as it records strain rates and the data is not labeled. Meanwhile, the semi-supervised approach uses both labeled and unlabeled data, and reinforcement learning improves and enhances learning patterns and behaviors based on a reward system (Yan et al., 2021a). Since DAS generates high volumes of data, traditional methods often fail and encounter difficulties when handling such large datasets. It is also worth mentioning a subdomain of ML. Deep Learning, which significantly and deliberately addresses and resolves these issues. It has made a high and lasting impact in the realm of computer vision and is widely used in subsurface oil and gas exploration. Utilization of this edge intelligence with IoT is beneficial in many ways (Ravi Ganesh et al., 2022). In this integration DAS can be intelligent and smart in monitoring potential applications of this big industry. Multiple uses in oil and gas truly require and need autonomous smart remote monitoring solutions. However, this integration needed crucial and critically crafted solutions beneficial in many forms. As most of the smart systems used in oil and gas industry they generate voluminous amounts of data. Producing actionable and valuable insights from data requires robust and reliable techniques. For which, many traditional and ML algorithms are applied to DAS data for preprocessing ignoring data size and complexities. Many challenges are raised while handling such huge data that could not be processed on regular PC hardware. Such complex data contains many types of noise which makes the data more inefficient for feeding into ML for preprocessing (Arief et al., 2021). To automate this process there are certain AutoML libraries and baseline models e.g. RF. The authors of this study worked on DAS storage and analysis for subsurface event detection (Dong et al., 2022). They developed DasLib to perform analysis on large-scale DAS data. This integration will enhance data analysis capabilities, which eventually increase the production of oil and gas. By doing this companies can detect and monitor in real-time, optimize production, reduce damage to equipment, and ensure the safety of oil fields (Asfha et al., 2024).

## Sustainability and Cost Benefits

We know this advancement is beneficial in many ways. Companies track gas emissions during production and work to lower environmental impact. For instance, the notable reduction in flaring practices helps keep fuel consumption at low levels. Optimizing energy use and reducing carbon footprints during the exploration and production of oil and gas makes operations cleaner and more efficient, contributing to a more sustainable future (Sun et al., 2021). AI and ML can deliberately analyze data coming from DAS sensors to predict failures and faults (Lapins et al., 2023). Whereas the geophones might be impractical or costly to install and maintain, to predict failures and faults. This proactive and rapid action not only saves money but also improves the lifespan of critical assets, such as early fault detection of equipment before major losses occur. This applies across all sectors of the oil and gas industry: upstream, midstream, and downstream (Sircar et al., 2021). As AI and ML automation required less labor cost and allow scaling of potential monitoring applications robustly in the above-mentioned sectors. Furthermore, it minimizes human biases in estimation of production in enhanced oil and gas reservoirs. And offers extraction of more hydrocarbons and capturing of $CO_2$ produced by anthropogenic (Zhuang et al., 2024).

## USE CASES IN OIL AND GAS INDUSTRY

This section of chapter discusses the use cases and application of AI and ML. Where this Edge Intelligence can be totally applied to monitoring application are given below. These are a few potential applications in oil and gas industry. Furthermore, challenges encounter by modern devices in specific applications. Moreover, this section highlights how advanced technologies with integration of Edge Intelligence are being applied to oil and gas field operations that demand real-time or near real-time, precise, and autonomous monitoring solutions for potential applications.

### Wellbore and Caprock Monitoring

Wellbore and caprock monitoring are crucial and important areas for the smooth operation of subsurface applications in the oil and gas industry. In CCS, our primary goal is to avoid and prevent the unintended migration of gases and fluids. For example, $CO_2$ injection in saline aquifers, and its unintended flow, could pose a huge risk to the climate and humans, while also compromising CCS initiatives (Kim et al., 2018). For $CO_2$ leakage, caprock is the primary cause. If it occurs and is not handled or treated properly, it can eventually pose greater challenges to the Earth's crust and damage the climate. Often, ML and big data have emerged as potential tools for such monitoring in oil and gas reservoirs. In wellbores, standard optic cables are laid either cemented or uncemented to offer continuous and real-time monitoring of gas and fluids. As DAS is being widely used, it records changes in strain rates and temperature within wellbores. Furthermore, with edge intelligence, we can pinpoint leakage segments too small for traditional techniques, with high precision and accuracy (Ganesh et al., 2022).

### Reservoir and Fracture Monitoring

Among many other monitoring applications using smart and autonomous systems, the reservoir and fracture are potential monitoring areas. These are crucial in the oil and gas industry, mainly for enhanced oil recovery and understanding of subsurface changing behaviors, such as monitoring and tracking properties and characteristics. This helps to optimize production, identify risks, and improve well placement. Properties like pressure, temperature, and saturation are monitored over time (Molenaar et al., 2011). Furthermore, this monitoring provides information such as the location and movement of gas and fluid, along with the properties of rock formation (Molenaar et al., 2011; Otchere et al., 2024). In the long run, we can predict the future behavior of the reservoir for gas and fluid. Since this monitoring also produces vast amounts of data and traditional methods often fail to provide insights, ML and AI are essential to implement to understand reservoir dynamics. DAS provides high spatiotemporal data and can deliberately address and manage reservoirs. Additionally, it improves the accuracy and resolution of reservoir management and monitoring (Otchere et al., 2024). Edge intelligence algorithms offer various benefits and can autonomously monitor even in harsh conditions.

## $CO_2$ Storage Monitoring

CCS technology has emerged as a promising solution to mitigate climate change by reducing $CO_2$ (Yu et al., 2024). Among its components, $CO_2$ storage in geological formations such as saline aquifers and depleted oil reservoirs holds significant promise due to their high storage capacity and available infrastructure. Any site drilled for $CO_2$ storage is a potential candidate when a porous and permeable rock formation exists at depths approximately 1.0 kilometer (KM), which helps prevent the upward leakage and migration of $CO_2$ (S. Chen et al., 2024). The application of ML in $CO_2$ storage is gaining attention for its potential to enhance monitoring, leakage detection, and prediction of storage performance [30]. The existing studies highlights the current state of research on machine learning applications in $CO_2$ storage. Some of the applications are given below. In CCS projects, there are so many $CO_2$ storage applications which require advanced ML base models for better monitoring and control of this hazardous greenhouse gas. For example, reservoir characterization, optimization of $CO_2$ storage operations, $CO_2$ risk assessment, site integrity, and leakage detection etc. In $CO_2$ storage application, this gas is injected into deep saline aquifers. A few 1000 m, with temperature (T=31.1oC) and Pressure (P =7.38 MPa) maintained in supercritical state. In which $CO_2$ possesses liquid density which improves transmission into deep formation (Pavan et al., 2024).

*Figure 5. $CO_2$ Leak events in deep saline aquifers during migration*

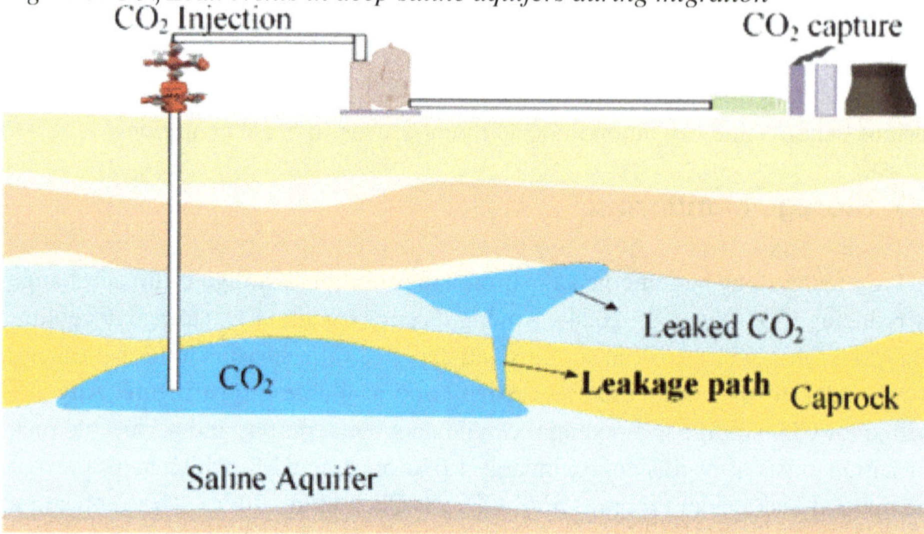


*(Pavan et al., 2024).*

## Pipeline Monitoring for Gas or Fluid Leak Detection

Pipeline monitoring is a critical aspect in oil and gas industry. Where detecting gas and fluid leakage from storage sites is essential to ensure the safety and effectiveness of the site (Otchere et al., 2024). However, this escape from gases and fluids not only cost economic losses. Furthermore, raise potential threats to humans, climate change and huge waste of natural resources. Factors often include corrosion in pipelines, welding defects when pipelines are not welded properly and gases escape and mix in the environment, or someone damaged the pipeline. ML techniques, such as Convolutional Neural Networks (CNNs) and Recurrent Neural Networks (RNNs), have been applied to interpret seismic and downhole monitoring data to identify leakage pathways (Otchere et al., 2024; Panhwar et al., 2022; Zhong et al., 2019). These models integrate pressure, temperature, seismic velocity, latitude and longitude data to improve the accuracy of leakage detection and location identification respectively (Yan et al., 2021b). Generally, injection of $CO_2$ has a direct influence on the pressure, in-situ stress and strain condition in the subsurface (Ravi Ganesh et al., 2022). Also, correlation between strain rates variations in response to injections is a potential way to track the movement of $CO_2$ and identify the $CO_2$ leakage into caprock (Ganesh et al., 2022). Whenever $CO_2$ leakage occurs temperature and pressure drop rapidly and then remain unchanged in first few seconds (Rehman et al., 2025; Xu et al., 2022). Moreover, the parameters like pressure and temperature and strain are critical to monitor $CO_2$ in subsurface. Deep aquifers also require an effective overlying caprock to ensure that the $CO_2$ does not escape into the shallow area subsurface and ultimately back into the atmosphere (English & English, 2022).

## Benefits and Limitations of the Integrated Approach

Addressing any issues in a timely manner is a good approach and demonstrates our priorities to the stakeholders involved. In the oil and gas industry, this aspect is very crucial. Ignoring critical areas to monitor can result in huge losses. Therefore, handling and addressing such issues requires robust and reliable solutions. However, edge intelligence and IoT are the only domains that can deliberately monitor. Integrating both approaches offers real-time monitoring; for example, combining DAS and edge intelligence enables the detection of events such as leakage, fractures, or intrusions, provides high spatial resolution data, reduces data transmission needs, is cost-effective e.g., using existing fiber cables reduces installation costs, and offers capabilities in harsh environments where day-to-day operations are difficult to execute.

Despite these pros, there are certain drawbacks and cons to these technologies. For instance, oil and gas fields require uniform connectivity, which can be limited by older infrastructures, lack of interoperability, and issues with data transmission and acquisition. Surface and subsurface monitoring heavily rely on data quality. However, these are sensitive devices when it comes to recording sensing data. Real-world data often contains noise and is rarely clean, leading to poor data quality for training ML models (Bilal et al., 2022). This can be due to sensor faults, drift, offset, degradation over time, etc. Additionally, these systems produce terabytes of data per day, and over the life of a project, the volume can reach petabytes (Lapins et al., 2023). Such a large amount of data creates challenges in preprocessing and analysis, requiring high computational power, which is not a cost-effective solution for companies (Turov et al., 2023).

# CONCLUSION

The integration of DAS, edge intelligence, and IoT marks a significant advancement in the oil and gas industry. Since, nowadays, every industry is evolving towards more computerized, autonomous, data driven workflows. This integration offers resilient, real-time and autonomous smart field monitoring systems. By transforming optic cables into high-resolution and offering long coverage sensing environment. Furthermore, all these domain collectively enables automated, real-time, remote monitoring over long distance across complex and dangerous situations in oil and gas industry. Such transformation reduces human intervention, reduces risk, and increases site productivity because of automation. Therefore, integrating the latest and modern devices with AI, ML, and IoT is not only shaping the future of this industry. But also enabling smarter and autonomous infrastructure across other industries. Moreover, advancement such as AI and ML further supporting accurate and actionable insights to optimize the field production and ensure more sustainable growth over years. Since, the fortune of this industry lies in more advanced analytics, and collaborative platforms, towards more smarter and sustainable operations.

## REFERENCES


Al-okaily, A., & Tbakhi, A. (2024). A novel lossless encoding algorithm for data compression–genomics data as an exemplar. *Frontiers in Bioinformatics*, *4*, 1489704. Advance online publication. DOI: 10.3389/fbinf.2024.1489704 PMID: 39917339

Alali, A. (2023). Modeling CO2 Geologic Storage Using Machine Learning. *SPE Middle East Oil and Gas Show and Conference, MEOS, Proceedings*. DOI: 10.2118/213565-MS

Anikiev, D., Birnie, C., Waheed, U., Alkhalifah, T., Gu, C., Verschuur, D. J., & Eisner, L. (2023). Machine learning in microseismic monitoring. *Earth-Science Reviews*, *239*, 104371. DOI: 10.1016/j.earscirev.2023.104371

Arief, H. A., Wiktorski, T., & Thomas, P. J. (2021). A Survey on Distributed Fibre Optic Sensor Data Modelling Techniques and Machine Learning Algorithms for Multiphase Fluid Flow Estimation. *Sensors 2021, Vol. 21, Page 2801*, *21*(8), 2801. DOI: 10.3390/s21082801

Asfha, D. T., Latiff, A. H. A., Otchere, D. A., Tackie-Otoo, B. N., Babikir, I., Rafi, M., Riyadi, Z. A., Putra, A. D., & Adeniyi, B. A. (2024). Mechanisms of sand production, prediction–a review and the potential for fiber optic technology and machine learning in monitoring. *Journal of Petroleum Exploration and Production Technology 2024 14:10*, *14*(10), 2577–2616. DOI: 10.1007/s13202-024-01860-1

Ashry, I., Mao, Y., Wang, B., Hveding, F., Bukhamsin, A., Ng, T. K., & Ooi, B. S. (2022). A Review of Distributed Fiber-Optic Sensing in the Oil and Gas Industry. *Journal of Lightwave Technology*, *40*(5), 1407–1431. DOI: 10.1109/JLT.2021.3135653

Bilal, M., Ali, G., Iqbal, M. W., Anwar, M., Malik, M. S. A., & Kadir, R. A. (2022). Auto-Prep: Efficient and Automated Data Preprocessing Pipeline. *IEEE Access : Practical Innovations, Open Solutions*, *10*, 107764–107784. DOI: 10.1109/ACCESS.2022.3198662

Butcher, A., Hudson, T., Baird, A., & Mellors, R. (2020). DAS Preprocessing Workflow. *18*. https://norceresearch.brage.unit.no/norceresearch-xmlui/handle/11250/3069183

Butcher, A., Zhou, W., Vandeweijer, V., Lapins, S., Kendall, J.-M., Boullenger, B., Paap, B., Broman, B., Stork, A., & Macquet, M. (2022). Monitoring CO2 injection at CAMI FRS using Distributed Acoustic Sensing networks. SSRN *Electronic Journal*. https://doi.org/DOI: 10.2139/SSRN.4286315

Carpentieri, B. (2025). Data Compression with a Time Limit. *Algorithms 2025, Vol. 18, Page 135, 18*(3), 135. DOI: 10.3390/a18030135

Chen, M., Tang, J., Zhu, D., & Hill, A. (2022). Classification and Localization of Fracture-Hit Events in Low-Frequency Distributed Acoustic Sensing Strain Rate with Convolutional Neural Networks. *SPE Journal, 27*(2), 1341–1353. DOI: 10.2118/205136-PA

Chen, S., You, H., Xu, J., Wei, M., Xu, T., & Wang, H. (2024). *Leakage monitoring of carbon dioxide injection well string using distributed optical fiber sensor*. Petroleum Research., DOI: 10.1016/j.ptlrs.2024.08.003

*Distributed Acoustic Sensing | EarthScope Consortium*. (n.d.). Retrieved July 17, 2025, from https://www.earthscope.org/what-is/das/

Dong, B., Popescu, A., Tribaldos, V. R., Byna, S., Ajo-Franklin, J., & Wu, K. (2022). Real-time and post-hoc compression for data from Distributed Acoustic Sensing. *Computers & Geosciences, 166*, 105181. DOI: 10.1016/j.cageo.2022.105181

Dong, B., Tribaldos, V. R., Xing, X., Byna, S., Ajo-Franklin, J., & Wu, K. (2020). DASSA: Parallel das Data Storage and Analysis for Subsurface Event Detection. *Proceedings - 2020 IEEE 34th International Parallel and Distributed Processing Symposium, IPDPS 2020*, 254–263. DOI: 10.1109/IPDPS47924.2020.00035

English, J. M., & English, K. L. (2022). An overview of carbon capture and storage and its potential role in the energy transition. *First Break, 40*(4), 35–40. DOI: 10.3997/1365-2397.fb2022028

Ganesh, P. R., Kelley, M., Tamrakar, S., Hill, B., Schuetter, J., Tribaldos, V. R., & Omosebi, O. (2022). *Machine Learning-Based, Near Real-time Leakage Detection for Caprock Integrity Monitoring using Distributed Acoustic Sensing (DAS) Data from Carbon Capture and Sequestration (CCS) Operations*. https://ssrn.com/abstract=4281129

Hu, J., Wang, X., Shao, F., & Jiang, Q. (2020). TSPR: Deep network-based blind image quality assessment using two-side pseudo reference images. *Digital Signal Processing, 106*, 102849. DOI: 10.1016/j.dsp.2020.102849

Ilesanmi, A. E., & Ilesanmi, T. O. (2021). Methods for image denoising using convolutional neural network: A review. *Complex & Intelligent Systems, 7*(5), 2179–2198. DOI: 10.1007/s40747-021-00428-4

Kim, G. W., Kim, T. H., Lee, J., & Lee, K. S. (2018). Coupled Geomechanical-Flow Assessment of CO2 Leakage through Heterogeneous Caprock during CCS. *Advances in Civil Engineering, 2018*(1), 1474320. Advance online publication. DOI: 10.1155/2018/1474320

Kozman, J., Lowery, S., & Lamb, J. (2024). End-to-End Workflow for Managing Large Volume Data from CCUS. *Society of Petroleum Engineers - SPE/AAPG/SEG Carbon, Capture, Utilization, and Storage Conference and Exhibition. CCUS, 2024*. Advance online publication. DOI: 10.15530/ccus-2024-4014747

Landrø, M., Ringrose, P., & Wienecke, S. (2024). Using DAS for CO2-Monitoring – Possibilities and Limitations. *Fifth EAGE Global Energy Transition Conference & Exhibition (GET 2024),* 2024(1), 1–5. DOI: 10.3997/2214-4609.202421042

Lapins, S., Butcher, A., Kendall, J. M., Hudson, T. S., Stork, A. L., Werner, M. J., Gunning, J., & Brisbourne, A. M. (2023). DAS-N2N: Machine learning distributed acoustic sensing (DAS) signal denoising without clean data. *Geophysical Journal International, 236*(2), 1026–1041. DOI: 10.1093/gji/ggad460

Lellouch, A., Lindsey, N. J., Ellsworth, W. L., & Biondi, B. L. (2020). Comparison between Distributed Acoustic Sensing and Geophones: Downhole Microseismic Monitoring of the FORGE Geothermal Experiment. *Seismological Research Letters, 91*(6), 3256–3268. DOI: 10.1785/0220200149

Li, Z. (2021). Recent advances in earthquake monitoring I: Ongoing revolution of seismic instrumentation. *Earth Science, 34*(2), 177–188. DOI: 10.29382/eqs-2021-0011

Mehnert, E., Damico, J., Frailey, S., Leetaru, H., Okwen, R., Storsved, B., & Valocchi, A. (2014). Basin-scale modeling for CO2 sequestration in the basal sandstone reservoir of the Illinois Basin—Improving the geologic model. *Energy Procedia, 63*, 2949–2960. DOI: 10.1016/j.egypro.2014.11.317

Molenaar, M. M., Hill, D. J., Webster, P., Fidan, E., & Birch, B. (2011). First downhole application of Distributed Acoustic Sensing (DAS) for hydraulic fracturing monitoring and diagnostics. *Society of Petroleum Engineers - SPE Hydraulic Fracturing Technology Conference 2011*, 751–759. DOI: 10.2118/140561-MS

Otchere, D. A., Latiff, A. H., & Tackie-Otoo, B. N. (2024). Distributed acoustic sensing in subsurface applications – Review and potential integration with artificial intelligence for an intelligent CO2 storage monitoring system. *Geoenergy Science and Engineering, 237*, 212818. DOI: 10.1016/j.geoen.2024.212818

Panhwar, A. O., Sathio, A. A., Shaikh, M. R., Lakhan, A., Umer, M., Mithiani, R. M., & Khan, S. (2022). Plant Health Detection Enabled CNN Scheme in IoT Network. *International Journal of Computing and Digital Systems*, *12*(1), 335–344. DOI: 10.12785/ijcds/120127

Pavan, T. N. V., Devarapu, S. R., & Govindarajan, S. K. (2024). Characterization of Leaky Deep Saline Aquifer for Storing sc-CO2. *Energy & Fuels*, *38*(12), 11051–11063. DOI: 10.1021/acs.energyfuels.4c01599

Piana Agostinetti, N., Villa, A., & Saccorotti, G. (2021). *Distributed acoustic sensing as a tool for exploration and monitoring: a proof-of-concept*. DOI: 10.5194/se-2021-37

Ravi Ganesh, P., Kelley, M., Tamrakar, S., Hill, B., Schuetter, J., Rodriguez Tribaldos, V., & Omosebi, O. (2022). Machine Learning-Based, Near Real-time Leakage Detection for Caprock Integrity Monitoring using Distributed Acoustic Sensing (DAS) Data from Carbon Capture and Sequestration (CCS) Operations. SSRN *Electronic Journal*. https://doi.org/DOI: 10.2139/SSRN.4281129

Rehman, M. ur, Hassan, M. F., Akbar, R., Al-rimy, B. A. S., Savita, K. S., Ullah, R., & Zafar, Z. (2025). *Analyzing Early Indicators of Ransomware: Pre-encryption Behavior Patterns*. 566–578. DOI: 10.1007/978-981-96-5848-0_46

Rehman Shaikh, M. U., Ullah, R., Akbar, R., Savita, K. S., & Mandala, S. (2024). Fortifying Against Ransomware: Navigating Cybersecurity Risk Management with a Focus on Ransomware Insurance Strategies. *International Journal of Academic Research in Business & Social Sciences*, *14*(1). Advance online publication. DOI: 10.6007/IJARBSS/v14-i1/20566

Sircar, A., Yadav, K., Rayavarapu, K., Bist, N., & Oza, H. (2021). Application of machine learning and artificial intelligence in oil and gas industry. *Petroleum Research*, *6*(4), 379–391. DOI: 10.1016/j.ptlrs.2021.05.009

Song, Y., Sung, W., Jang, Y., & Jung, W. (2020). Application of an artificial neural network in predicting the effectiveness of trapping mechanisms on CO2 sequestration in saline aquifers. *International Journal of Greenhouse Gas Control*, *98*, 103042. DOI: 10.1016/j.ijggc.2020.103042

Sun, Y., Liu, J., Xue, Z., Li, Q., Fan, C., & Zhang, X. (2021). A critical review of distributed fiber optic sensing for real-time monitoring geologic CO2 sequestration. *Journal of Natural Gas Science and Engineering*, *88*, 103751. DOI: 10.1016/j.jngse.2020.103751

Trautz, R., Daley, T., Miller, D., Robertson, M., & Koperna, G. (n.d.). *Geophysical Monitoring Using Active Seismic Techniques at the Citronelle Alabama CO2 Storage 1 Demonstration Site 2 3.*

Turov, A. T., Konstantinov, Y. A., Barkov, F. L., Korobko, D. A., Zolotovskii, I. O., Lopez-Mercado, C. A., & Fotiadi, A. A. (2023). Enhancing the Distributed Acoustic Sensors' (DAS) Performance by the Simple Noise Reduction Algorithms Sequential Application. *Algorithms 2023, Vol. 16, Page 217, 16*(5), 217. DOI: 10.3390/a16050217

Vandeweijer, V., Candela, T., Lien, M., Koedel, U., Fechner, T., Bond, T., Zhou, W., Butcher, A., Kendall, M., Stork, A., & Mellors, R. (2022). *A technology readiness assessment for CCS site monitoring systems.*

Wen, G., Hay, C., & Benson, S. M. (2021). CCSNet: A deep learning modeling suite for CO2 storage. *Advances in Water Resources, 155*, 104009. Advance online publication. DOI: 10.1016/j.advwatres.2021.104009

Xu, L., Li, Q., Tan, Y., & Li, X. (2022). Characterization of carbon dioxide leakage process along faults in the laboratory. *Journal of Rock Mechanics and Geotechnical Engineering, 14*(3), 674–688. DOI: 10.1016/j.jrmge.2021.12.019

Yalli, J. S., Hasan, M. H., Haron, N. S., Shaikh, M. U. R., Murad, N. Y., & Bako, A. L. (2023). Quality of Data (QoD) in Internet of Things (IOT): An Overview, State-of-the-Art, Taxonomy and Future Directions. *International Journal of Advanced Computer Science and Applications, 14*(12), 1075–1091. DOI: 10.14569/IJACSA.2023.01412110

Yan, Y., Borhani, T. N., Subraveti, S. G., Pai, K. N., Prasad, V., Rajendran, A., Nkulikiyinka, P., Asibor, J. O., Zhang, Z., Shao, D., Wang, L., Zhang, W., Yan, Y., Ampomah, W., You, J., Wang, M., Anthony, E. J., Manovic, V., & Clough, P. T. (2021a). Harnessing the power of machine learning for carbon capture, utilisation, and storage (CCUS) – a state-of-the-art review. *Energy & Environmental Science, 14*(12), 6122–6157. DOI: 10.1039/D1EE02395K

Yan, Y., Borhani, T. N., Subraveti, S. G., Pai, K. N., Prasad, V., Rajendran, A., Nkulikiyinka, P., Asibor, J. O., Zhang, Z., Shao, D., Wang, L., Zhang, W., Yan, Y., Ampomah, W., You, J., Wang, M., Anthony, E. J., Manovic, V., & Clough, P. T. (2021b). Harnessing the power of machine learning for carbon capture, utilisation, and storage (CCUS)-a state-of-the-art review. *Energy & Environmental Science, 14*(12), 6122–6157. DOI: 10.1039/D1EE02395K

Yu, P., Zhu, T., Marone, C., Elsworth, D., & Yu, M. (2024). DASEventNet: AI-Based Microseismic Detection on Distributed Acoustic Sensing Data From the Utah FORGE Well 16A (78)-32 Hydraulic Stimulation. *Journal of Geophysical Research: Solid Earth, 129*(9), e2024JB029102. DOI: 10.1029/2024JB029102

Yurikov, A., Tertyshnikov, K., Yavuz, S., Shashkin, P., Isaenkov, R., Sidenko, E., Glubokovskikh, S., Barraclough, P., & Pevzner, R. (2022). Seismic monitoring of CO2 geosequestration using multi-well 4D DAS VSP: Stage 3 of the CO2CRC Otway project. *International Journal of Greenhouse Gas Control, 119*, 103726. DOI: 10.1016/j.ijggc.2022.103726

Zhan, Y., Zhang, W., Wang, Z., Yang, J., Li, K., Liu, L., & Ye, Q. (2024). Fast earthquake recognition method based on DAS and one dimensional QRE-net. *Optics Communications*, *559*, 130382. DOI: 10.1016/j.optcom.2024.130382

Zhang, X., Qi, J., Liang, X., Guan, Z., Liu, Z., Zhang, C., Chen, D., Deng, W., Xu, C., Wang, X., & Liu, H. (2024). Fiber-Optic Distributed Acoustic Sensing for Smart Grid Application. *Photonics 2025, Vol. 12, Page 7, 12*(1), 7. DOI: 10.3390/photonics12010007

Zhong, Z., Sun, A. Y., Yang, Q., & Ouyang, Q. (2019). A deep learning approach to anomaly detection in geological carbon sequestration sites using pressure measurements. *Journal of Hydrology (Amsterdam), 573*, 885–894. DOI: 10.1016/j.jhydrol.2019.04.015

Zhuang, X., Wang, W., Su, Y., Li, Y., Dai, Z., & Yuan, B. (2024). Spatio-temporal sequence prediction of CO2 flooding and sequestration potential under geological and engineering uncertainties. *Applied Energy*, *359*, 122691. DOI: 10.1016/j.apenergy.2024.122691

# Chapter 9
# Self-Sovereign Identity in Energy: A New Era of Workforce

**Sonal H. Parmar**
https://orcid.org/0009-0009-9419-9199
*Ganpat University, India*

## ABSTRACT

*The petroleum sector is evolving through AI, blockchain, IoT, and edge computing—but identity management for energy workers remains outdated. This chapter proposes Self-Sovereign Identity (SSI) as a decentralized solution that empowers workers to control and share verified credentials like licenses and certifications via secure digital wallets. Using Verifiable Credentials (VCs) and Decentralized Identifiers (DIDs) anchored on blockchain, SSI streamlines onboarding, ensures compliance, and enhances global workforce mobility. It explores technical architecture, tools, governance, and real-world use cases—from blockchain-verified offshore worker onboarding to smart PPE access. The chapter also addresses privacy, interoperability, and regulatory challenges, offering strategies for phased implementation and scalable adoption. Ultimately, it argues that digital identity isn't just a tech upgrade—it's key to building a safer, faster, and more human-centered energy sector.*

## 1. INTRODUCTION

The digital transformation of the energy sector is ushering in sweeping changes that extend far beyond operational technologies and asset optimization. While advancements like AI, IoT, and blockchain are often highlighted for their roles in improving efficiency and predictive maintenance, a quieter but equally critical evo-

DOI: 10.4018/979-8-3373-5457-6.ch009

lution is taking place in the realm of identity and credential management. As energy companies expand across borders and operate in highly regulated environments, the ability to verify and trust workforce credentials in a timely, secure, and compliant manner has become mission-critical. Traditional identity systems—centralized databases, paper-based records, and manual verification processes—are increasingly inadequate for this new landscape. These outdated models are not only inefficient but also vulnerable to fraud, error, and regulatory non-compliance, which can lead to safety risks and operational delays.

In this context, Self-Sovereign Identity (SSI) emerges as a transformative solution. Unlike traditional models where identity data is controlled by centralized authorities such as employers, government bodies, or certification agencies, SSI enables individuals to own and manage their digital credentials directly. Using decentralized identifiers (DIDs) and verifiable credentials (VCs), workers can store proof of training, certifications, medical clearances, and more in secure digital wallets. These credentials are cryptographically signed by trusted issuers and can be verified instantly by employers or site managers—without exposing the full data or relying on third-party databases. For the energy industry, where workforce mobility, safety, and compliance are tightly interlinked, this shift holds enormous promise (Cucko & Turkanovic, 2021). Self-Sovereign Identity (SSI) is an emerging, decentralized identity approach that enables entities (e.g. individuals, organizations, and objects) to fully control their digital identity without reliance on any external authority, eliminating a single point of failure. SSI presents a paradigm shift, a shift in power and control, from identity and service providers to users, who must be central to the administration of identity and information flow during digital interactions

The benefits of SSI in this setting are both operational and strategic. From an operational standpoint, SSI dramatically reduces the time and resources required to verify worker qualifications. This is particularly valuable in dynamic environments like offshore oil platforms or multinational project sites where delays in credential verification can halt workflows or expose companies to legal risks. From a strategic perspective, SSI fosters trust across a distributed and often contract-based workforce. Workers are empowered to carry their credentials throughout their careers, across companies and borders, without the need for redundant re-verification or training. For employers, this translates to faster onboarding, improved safety oversight, and stronger regulatory adherence.

Moreover, SSI supports advanced use cases that further enhance workforce compliance. For example, smart personal protective equipment (PPE) can be linked to a worker's decentralized ID to ensure only qualified personnel access restricted areas. AI-powered systems can integrate with verifiable credentials to build digital twins of workers, dynamically adjusting site permissions based on fatigue levels, certifications, or job roles. Governments and regulators also stand to benefit by harmonizing labor standards and enforcement through interoperable, blockchain-secured identity frameworks.

This article delves into the application of SSI in the energy sector by examining not only the technology behind it but also real-world use cases and research-backed findings. By aligning identity management with the principles of decentralization, security, and privacy, SSI offers a resilient foundation for workforce trust and compliance—at a time when both are more essential than ever.

*Figure 1.*

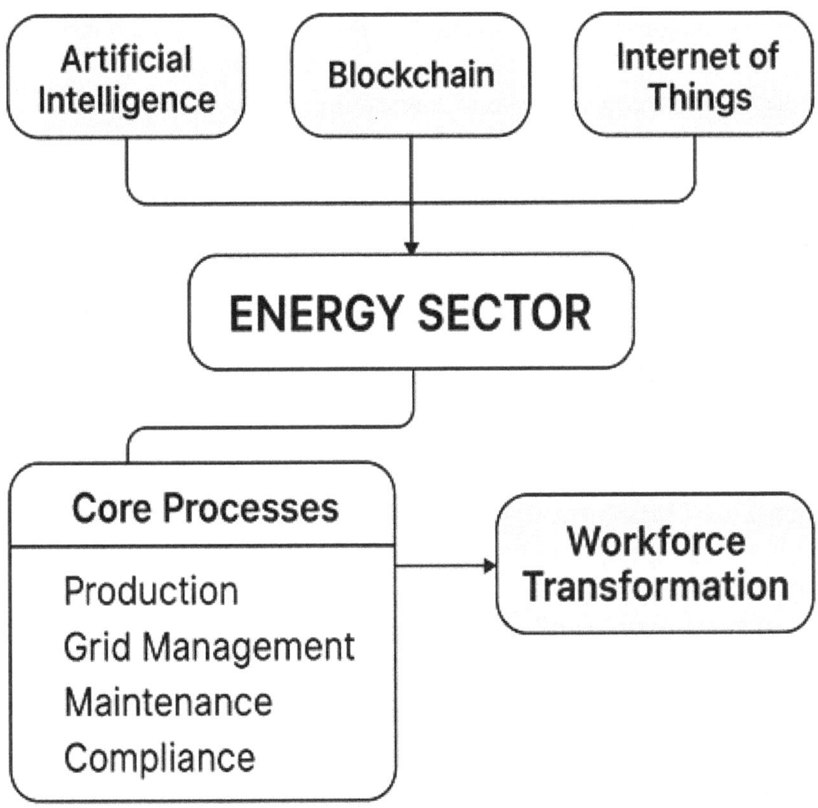


This high-level diagram illustrates how emerging technologies—Artificial Intelligence (AI), Blockchain, and the Internet of Things (IoT)—serve as foundational digital enablers for transformation in the energy sector. The visual flow moves from top to bottom, showing how these technologies impact both core operations and workforce dynamics, signaling a shift not just in tools, but in the very structure and strategy of energy enterprises.

Top Layer: Digital Enablers

- **Artificial Intelligence (AI):** Supports predictive maintenance, demand forecasting, autonomous operations, and data-driven insights.
- **Blockchain:** Enables secure credential verification, decentralized data ownership, tamper-proof audit trails, and trusted energy trading.
- **Internet of Things (IoT):** Connects devices and sensors for real-time monitoring, smart grid optimization, and remote diagnostics.

These technologies feed directly into the energy sector's digital transformation, acting as catalysts for change across all layers of the organization.

Middle Layer: Energy Sector as a Digital Hub

At the center of the diagram lies the energy sector itself, shown not as a static industry but as a dynamic digital hub. This includes:

- Oil and Gas
- Electricity and Power Grids
- Renewables
- Distributed Energy Resources

This layer reflects how digital enablers are reshaping industry-wide infrastructure, introducing agility, transparency, and intelligence into daily operations.

Bottom Layer: Impact Areas

1. Core Operational Domains
    - **Production:** AI/IoT optimize extraction, improve energy generation forecasts, and reduce resource waste.
    - **Grid Management:** Blockchain and IoT support decentralized energy systems, enabling fault detection and load balancing in real time.
    - **Maintenance:** AI-powered predictive systems reduce downtime and cut costs by anticipating failures.
    - **Compliance:** Blockchain offers immutable records for regulatory, safety, and environmental audits.
2. Workforce Transformation

Digitization deeply impacts the workforce, demanding a shift in mindset, skills, and tools:

- **Upskilling and Reskilling:** Workers must adapt to AI- and IoT-integrated environments.
- **Digital Identity:** Blockchain-based Self-Sovereign Identity (SSI) enables workers to manage verifiable credentials securely.
- **Remote Operations:** AI and IoT facilitate control and monitoring from remote or hazardous environments.
- **Cybersecurity Awareness:** As digital systems expand, so does the need for employee fluency in security best practices.

## 2. GAPS IN CURRENT WORKFORCE IDENTITY SYSTEMS

In today's high-speed digital and industrial world, identity is more than a law or administration matter—it's a mission- and business-critical function. The ability to accurately verify "who a person is," "what he or she's credentialed for," and "whether he or she's in compliance" provides the basis for safety, productivity, and regulatory compliance. Current workforce identity infrastructures, however, are rife with deep structural deficiencies that hamstring individual empowerment and business effectiveness.

*Figure 2.*

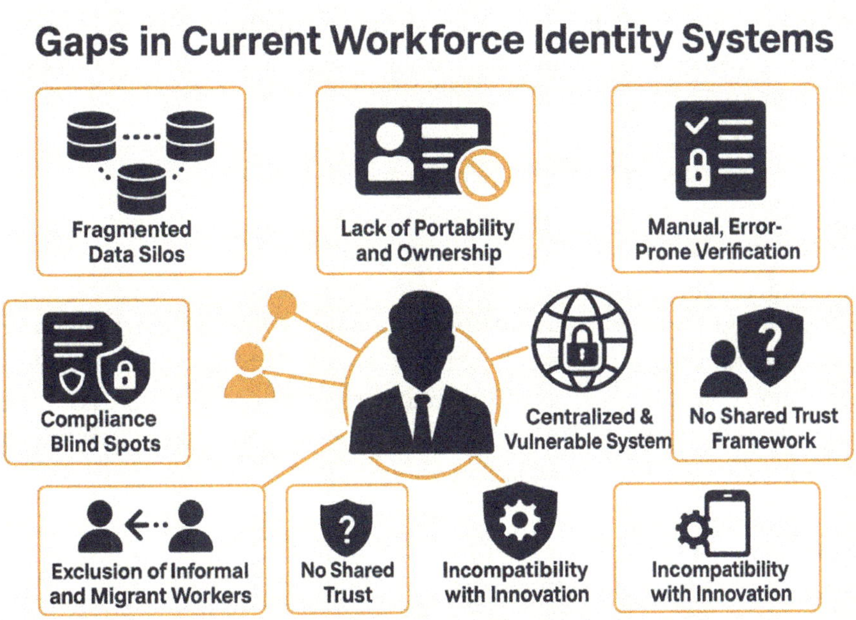

In this section, we explain these system inadequacies and their real-world implications.

1. Fragmented Identity Silos

Workforce identity data is generally maintained in discrete systems—HR databases, contractor sites, compliance sites, training centers, and government registers. The discrete systems do not talk to each other, and the result is data silos that:

- Interfere with seamless verification across projects or employers.
- Lead to repetitive data entry and duplicative background checks.
- Create inconsistencies between real abilities and posted profiles.

An energy technician working on multiple offshore sites may have multiple certifications, yet still find themselves delayed getting into a new site when the databases are isolated (Bai et al., 2022). The proposal of Self-Sovereign Identity (SSI) further emphasizes the user's control over the identity, requiring users to truly own their identities, not just let the user participate in the authentication process

2. Lack of Portability and Worker Control

The majority of workforce credentials are institution-based rather than person-based. It becomes difficult for workers to view or transmit their certifications, performance history, or portfolios of experience when shifting locales or jobs. The implications are:

- Loss of professional experience with each job transition.
- Inability to perform abilities independently of a business system.
- Redundant training and qualification programs.

The digitization technologies are essential elements of the system of digital credentials, underpinning all the other elements (Nita & Mihailescu, 2024a). Despite earlier completion of high-level safety training, repetition became necessary due to missing digital verification. The lack of digital records made repetition of previously completed safety training unavoidable.

3. Laborious and Fraud-Prone Verification Processes

The Proposed Verifiable Credentials Authentication Scheme. Details an authentication process that leverages verifiable credentials to confirm and validate a user's digital identity in a secure, user-friendly manner without excessive disclosure of personal information (Nita & Mihailescu, 2024a). The process of validating the identity and qualification of workers still remains manual—dependent on phone calls, emails, scanned documents, or verbal confirmation. Such outdated procedures are:

- Labor-intensive and time-consuming.
- Subject to forgery and authentication fraud.
- Inefficient when under time-pressured or high-risk applications.

In one major oil pipeline project, the operation was forced to cease when it was found that a subcontractor had fabricated electrical safety certificates—details which had gone unnoticed since they were manually vetted (V. Puri, n.d.). In the authors focus on IoT security requirements, identify key issues, and propose solutions to enhance IoT security.

4. Drawbacks of Auditing and Compliance

Industrial contexts have strict regulatory conditions, yet the vast majority of workforce systems lack the ability for:

- Real-time monitoring of compliance automatically.
- Produce audit-compliant training, access, or safety logs.
- Notify when license expires or standards are violated.

Compliance Gap: A plant was cited on regulatory inspection since it was unable to verify—on request—the fact that all active contract workers had up-to-date hazardous material training.

Ensuring compliance with working hour limits, overtime rules, and rest period requirements across multiple jurisdictions has traditionally been a resource-intensive task prone to human error. A survey conducted by Kronos Incorporated found that 53% of organizations struggle to keep up with changing labor regulations, and 74% report that compliance has become more challenging in recent years

5. Centralized and Vulnerable Architecture

Traditional legacy identity systems are usually centralized, monolithic, and insecure. The resulting design produces:

- Points of failure vulnerable to cyber-attacks.
- Risk of unauthorized access or loss of information.

- Trouble complying with up-to-date data protection laws (e.g., GDPR, India's DPDP).

The GDPR was established to keep pace with the latest technological. Using the GDPR privacy principles, we assess various SSI works and blockchain based solutions.

**Note**: In 2023, a global contractor list for a number of different oilfield companies was hacked, and the names, qualifications, and passport numbers of over 50,000 workers were leaked.

6. Exclusion of Informal, Contractual, and Migrant Labor

Most of the work for industry comes outside the formal or traditional sector—i.e., among short-term contractors, migrant workers, or technically skilled technicians (T. Dara, 2025). Digitalization is facilitating non-traditional forms of employment which provide greater flexibility. The contemporary system usually does not provide for:

- Non-institutional or community-issued credentials.
- More focus on experience than on paper credentials.
- Inclusion of workers without digital access or ID.

Equity Concern: In Africa and Southeast Asia, thousands of qualified technicians are underemployed simply because they cannot account for their prior work experience with conventional methods.

7. No Standardized or Shared Trust Framework

Trust for verification of identities is local, inconsistent, and non-scalable. Every business, locality, or regulating authority employs different parameters for the authentication of workforce credentials. It leads to:

- Redundancy among systems and between jurisdictions.
- Non-recognition on a mutual basis for trusted credentials.
- Increased cost and delay in implementation.

Trust managements are classified into three types (Jovita Nsoh, 2021). Credential-based trust relies on credentials or certified documents to demonstrate the qualifications or status of an individual to perform a task. Reputation-based trust is based on knowledge about the past behavior of an entity and its interactions and relevant events with other entities or service providers. Trust in information resources is a hybrid of the above two trust model concepts, relying not only on credentials but also on the past behavior of entities before granting them trustworthiness.

Global Barrier: German-certified solar engineer should be completely re-verified for job on a Brazil-centric wind power project, although neither certificate adheres to the ISO standard.

8. Incompatibility with Innovation Ecosystems

Rising technologies such as IoT, blockchain, AI, and edge computing are re-designing the workflow within industries. Old identity infrastructure could not be integrated with:

- Worker activity and safety monitoring wristwear.
- Programmable smart contracts for labor authorization.
- Computer tools that match task requirements and skill sets.

Innovation Bottleneck: A building construction site embraced AI-based gate-keeping, but was compelled back to manual gatekeeping as the HR database could not facilitate real-time verification of identity.

## 3. PREVAILING SITUATION OF IDENTITY MANAGEMENT IN THE ENERGY SECTOR

The energy sector—including oil, gas, and utilities—faces unique challenges that set it apart from other industries. Companies operate across remote sites, extreme environments, and high-risk zones where safety and compliance are non-negotiable. While the sector has made significant strides in adopting advanced technologies—like predictive maintenance powered by artificial intelligence, blockchain for carbon tracking, and IoT sensors for real-time monitoring—workforce identity systems have not kept pace. Most work roles will revolve around the three major cyber segments: device, network, and data (Enemosah & Chukwunweike, 2022).

Today's identity and access management practices are still dominated by outdated models, fragmented workflows, and manual processes that create vulnerabilities. These shortcomings not only slow down operations but also expose companies to compliance failures, safety risks, and cybersecurity threats.

Below is a closer look at why traditional identity management is falling short and what this means for the energy industry.

## Reliance on Legacy Identity Systems

Most energy companies still depend on centralized identity management systems—like Microsoft Active Directory or LDAP—that were originally built for static, office-based workforces. For example, an offshore engineer may need to move between rigs in the North Sea, the Gulf of Mexico, and West Africa. Yet, each region's credentialing system often exists in a silo, requiring separate verifications every time the worker transitions to a new site.

Here this practical example of this system is A technician certified in one country may have to revalidate their qualifications in another—even if they're working within the same multinational corporation. The lack of interoperable identity systems creates frustration, delays, and unnecessary duplication of effort. Also, latency is another critical issue, especially in time-sensitive scenarios such as pressure surge management, leak detection, or emergency shutdowns (Pub, 2025).

## A Contractor-Heavy Workforce With Disjointed Identity Protocols

The energy industry relies extensively on third-party contractors, subcontractors, and temporary service providers. Unlike permanent employees, these contractors are rarely onboarded through secure, standardized processes.

In many cases, critical steps like background checks, certification verification, and site access approvals are handled through email chains, PDF attachments, or phone calls. This lack of consistent protocols leaves dangerous gaps in the system.

It is entirely possible for a contractor whose safety training has expired to gain access to a high-risk zone simply because the records were outdated or no automated system flagged the expired credentials.

Leveraging advancements such as blockchain, artificial intelligence (AI), and digital tools for contract management offers significant benefits in ensuring that procurement processes meet regulatory requirements and safety standards (Oluoha et al., 2022).

consider a scenario where a welding contractor's certifications lapse but their access badge remains active. Without real-time revocation, the company faces serious compliance violations and safety hazards. Also, organizations should also engage suppliers and contractors in their safety and compliance efforts (Oluoha et al., 2022).

## Limited Real-Time Verification Capabilities

Many of the current identity management systems operate in batch mode or rely on static records that are updated manually. As a result, companies cannot always validate credentials in real time or ensure that employees access rights reflect their current status.

This shortcoming creates operational inefficiency and increases the risk of insider threats. For example, an employee might leave the company or lose a certification, yet still have access to sensitive control rooms, machinery, or data systems.

A worker's compliance certification may expire, but if the identity system doesn't immediately revoke their access, they can continue to enter restricted areas—putting both safety and regulatory compliance at risk (Tripathi et al., 2025). By integrating identity lifecycle management, real-time risk assessment, dynamic policy enforcement, and regulatory compliance monitoring into a single cohesive system, the framework bridges the longstanding gaps between static access control models and the modern requirements of adaptive, proactive security

## Operations Spanning Multiple Jurisdictions Without Federated Trust

Oil and gas operations are spread across continents, involving joint ventures and partnerships that must comply with different local regulations. This geographic complexity demands federated trust models, which allow credentials issued in one system to be recognized in another. Unfortunately, most organizations operate in isolation, with disconnected systems that cannot share or validate identity information across borders.

A field engineer working for an engineering, procurement, and construction (EPC) contractor in Nigeria might arrive on-site in Norway only to find their qualifications are unrecognized by the local joint venture partner (Ryan Greene, n.d.). This lack of cross-border recognition delays projects and introduces unnecessary risks.

## Growing Cybersecurity Threats Linked to Identity Management

As the industry digitizes more of its operational infrastructure—pipelines, refineries, power grids—identity has become the new security perimeter. If credentials are compromised, attackers can gain access to critical systems with potentially catastrophic results.

Despite this, many companies still rely heavily on weak password-based authentication, outdated access protocols, and misconfigured identity systems.

Industry audits show that nearly 60% of breaches in industrial sectors are linked to compromised credentials—either stolen by attackers or retained by former employees who were never fully offboarded. Industrial networks were first designed as stand-alone systems, quite frequently on proprietary protocols with little exposure to the outside world (Ryan Greene, n.d.).

For Example: A disgruntled former contractor may still have access credentials weeks after leaving a project, because no automated process ensures their permissions are revoked in all connected systems.

## Lack of Worker Control Over Their Own Credentials

Current identity systems do little to empower workers to manage their verified credentials. Employees and contractors have no way to port their records between companies or control how their professional qualifications are shared (Steenholt & Bss, 2023). It is critical that the individual is protected, even in a trust less system. Bad actors in a centralized system can attempt to exploit known cybersecurity weaknesses to gain entry into systems in which they are not permitted.

This shortfall leads to repetitive credentialing, administrative overhead, and lost productivity—especially for specialists whose skills are in high demand.

Vision Gap: Imagine a certified drone inspector who holds flight training records, safety certifications, and equipment clearances. Ideally, they should be able to carry these credentials in a secure digital wallet and present them anywhere. However, under the current systems, this is not possible. Instead, they often must resubmit paperwork and undergo redundant checks every time they start a new contract.

## Cumbersome Audits and Compliance Processes

Energy companies undergo frequent audits to prove compliance with health, safety, environmental, and labor regulations. Yet, because identity records are stored in disconnected systems, generating an audit trail often becomes a labor-intensive process.

With credential verification from an external trustworthy organization, the candidate's training programs and acquired skills could reduce the needed investment (Chanda et al., 2024). Compliance teams must manually cross-reference logs from multiple departments to answer basic questions, like who accessed a control room on a given date or which workers were certified to operate specific equipment.

If an incident occurs, it can take days or even weeks to pull together evidence from disparate logs—wasting valuable time and increasing exposure to regulatory penalties.

## The Cost of Inefficient Identity Systems

The combined effect of all these identity management gaps is far-reaching—and it's costing the energy sector in more ways than many organizations realize.

## Delays in Onboarding Contractors and Employees

Every day a qualified worker sits idle because their credentials can't be verified is a day of lost productivity. Whether it's an offshore engineer waiting for safety clearance or a contractor held back by slow background checks, these delays have ripple effects. Projects get pushed back, critical maintenance is postponed, and teams are forced to work short-staffed. In an industry where timelines are tight and margins are shrinking, even small delays can add up to significant costs and missed targets (Agho & Eyo-Udo, 2023). The use of blockchain-based identity verification in HR management can help streamline the onboarding process by reducing the time and effort required to verify employee identities. This can lead to faster onboarding times and im-proved efficiency.

## Increased Downtime from Slow Verification Processes

When identity systems rely on manual checks, email approvals, or disconnected databases, verifying who can access which site or piece of equipment becomes a bottleneck. This slows everything down—from planned maintenance to emergency response. For example, if a technician needs urgent access to repair a critical system but their clearance isn't updated in real time, operations may be forced to pause. That downtime doesn't just waste time—it can threaten safety and disrupt the entire supply chain. So that by establishing secure data-sharing protocols and ensuring compliance with data protection regulations, energy companies can enhance collaboration and data access across the supply chain, enabling AI systems to work more effectively (Zografopoulos et al., 2023).

## Higher Operational Costs Due to Redundant Credentialing

In many companies, contractors and employees must re-verify the same certifications multiple times. A single qualification might be entered in three or four separate systems—once for HR, again for compliance, again for site access, and again for insurance records. Each duplication means more paperwork, more staff hours, and more opportunities for error. Over time, this redundancy translates into unnecessary administrative costs that eat away at operational budgets.

## Compliance Risks That Lead to Fines and Legal Exposure

Energy companies operate in one of the most heavily regulated environments in the world. Regulations cover everything from health and safety protocols to environmental standards and labor laws. When credential records are incomplete, out of date, or stored in fragmented systems, proving compliance becomes difficult (Zografopoulos et al., 2023). During an audit or investigation, missing or inconsistent records can lead to fines, legal action, or even the suspension of operations. In serious cases, regulatory failures can damage the company's reputation and erode trust with investors, partners, and the public.

### A Weaker Security Posture That Leaves Critical Systems Vulnerable

As operations become more digital, identity is the gateway to nearly everything—from field sensors and control systems to sensitive operational data. If companies can't accurately track who has access to what, they leave themselves open to insider threats, credential theft, and cyberattacks. For example, an outdated record might allow a former employee to keep accessing systems weeks or months after leaving the company. Or an attacker could steal valid credentials and move undetected through critical infrastructure. In industries where an attack can shut down pipelines, disrupt power grids, or create environmental disasters, these security weaknesses are simply too dangerous to ignore (Nita & Mihailescu, 2024b).

### What a Modern Approach Should Look Like

To address these gaps, the industry needs a shift toward decentralized, worker-centric identity models—such as Self-Sovereign Identity (SSI) (Chen et al., 2019). With SSI, credentials are issued as tamper-proof digital records stored in secure wallets controlled by the individual.

Key benefits would include:

- **Real-time verification:** Credentials can be instantly validated on-site, with automatic revocation when they expire or become invalid.
- **Cross-border interoperability:** A credential issued in one jurisdiction can be accepted anywhere, reducing delays and supporting global operations.
- **Stronger security:** Cryptographic protections make it harder for attackers to forge or steal credentials.
- **Worker empowerment:** Employees and contractors can control, share, and reuse their credentials as they move between projects.

## 4. VISUALIZATION SELF-SOVEREIGN IDENTITY (SSI)

Self-Sovereign Identity (SSI) is a transformative approach to digital identity that shifts control from centralized authorities to individuals (Kim et al., 2023a).

To understand SSI fully, visualization tools and conceptual diagrams are critical. They make the abstract concepts of decentralized identifiers, verifiable credentials, and trust frameworks concrete and easier to grasp.

Below is an in-depth breakdown of how SSI is typically visualized, why visualization matters, and what components are commonly represented.

## Key Components of SSI Explained

### 1. Workforce Identity (SSI-Enabled)

At the heart of Self-Sovereign Identity (SSI) is a simple but powerful shift: the worker—whether an employee or contractor—has direct control over their own identity and credentials. Instead of relying on HR departments or external agencies every time they need to prove their qualifications, individuals can store all their certifications, licenses, and compliance records themselves (Mariana Dahan, 2020). When needed, they can present these credentials quickly, confidently, and without waiting for third-party validation.

This model empowers workers to manage their professional identities in a way that is portable, secure, and efficient.

### 2. Digital Wallet

The digital wallet is the interface where credentials are safely stored. This could be a secure app on a smartphone, a protected web platform, or a hardware device.

One of themost important features of a digital wallet is selective disclosure (Yin et al., 2025). For example, if a worker needs to show a supervisor that a certification hasn't expired, they can share just the expiration date—not the entire document. This means workers share only what is necessary and keep everything else private.

### 3. Verifiable Credentials

Verifiable Credentials are digital records that prove something about a person—such as their qualifications, training, or licenses (Moriyama & Otsuka, 2025). These credentials are issued by trusted authorities like training providers, government regulators, or employers and are digitally signed to confirm their authenticity.

What makes them special is that they can be verified without needing to call or email the issuing organization. Instead, the credential itself contains all the cryptographic information needed to confirm it's real (Yin et al., 2025). This cuts down on delays and eliminates a lot of the bureaucracy that slows down traditional verification.

## 4. Decentralized Identifiers (DIDs)

Decentralized identity (DID) is a transformative paradigm that leverages blockchain, decentralized identifiers and verifiable credentials (VCs) to enable self-sovereign and decentralized identity management with various application areas (Kim et al., 2023b). This means no one can revoke, censor, or modify the identifier without the person's consent. DIDs are essential to SSI because they guarantee that the worker has full control over their identity and how it's used

## 5. Relying Parties (Verifiers)

A relying party is any person or organization that needs to validate someone's identity or credentials (Akli & Chougdali, 2025). In the energy sector, this could be a site supervisor checking a safety certification, a compliance officer reviewing licenses, or a contractor manager verifying training records.

With SSI, these verifications happen instantly and securely. The verifier doesn't need an internet connection to call the issuer. Instead, they scan or receive the credential, confirm the cryptographic signature, and record the verification—often within seconds.

## 6. Blockchain/Trust Layer

The blockchain acts as a tamper-proof ledger that records when credentials were issued, revoked, or updated. Importantly, the blockchain doesn't store personal information—only cryptographic proofs that confirm a credential's status.

This design ensures that the system remains private while guaranteeing that records cannot be altered or backdated (Bamakan, 2021). If there is ever a dispute—such as whether a credential was valid at a particular time—the blockchain serves as the ultimate source of truth.

# Benefits of SSI in the Energy Sector

## Security

By eliminating centralized databases—prime targets for hackers—SSI reduces the risk of massive data breaches. Credentials live in workers' wallets, protected by strong encryption.

## Interoperability

A credential issued in one country can be recognized and verified anywhere in the world. This is critical for global operations where contractors and employees frequently cross borders.

## Efficiency

Onboarding times are dramatically shortened. Instead of waiting days for paperwork to clear, site access and compliance checks happen in real time.

## Trust

Immutable records build confidence with regulators, partners, and employees. Everyone can see that credentials are authentic and unchanged.

## Portability

Workers keep their credentials as they move from job to job or project to project, reducing duplicate verifications and saving time.

## Privacy

With selective disclosure, individuals share only the minimum data needed—no more. This strengthens compliance with privacy laws and builds trust with the workforce.

## Real-World Use Case

A geophysicist from Brazil arrives in Abu Dhabi to start work on a new exploration project. Traditionally, they would spend hours or even days presenting paper certificates, waiting for HR staff to verify training records, and revalidating qualifications under local regulations.

With SSI, the process is much simpler. The geophysicist opens their digital wallet app on arrival and scans a QR code provided by the site supervisor (Mazzocca et al., 2025). Instantly, their ISO Health, Safety, and Environment (HSE) certification and radiation safety training credentials are shared and verified through a decentralized trust network.

The supervisor sees that the credentials are authentic, current, and issued by recognized authorities. At the same time, an access log entry is automatically created for audit purposes. There is no need for extra paperwork, no redundant data entry, and no delays.

## 5. LEVERAGING SSI TO STRENGTHEN TRUST AND COMPLIANCE ACROSS ENERGY WORKFORCES

The energy sector relies on a large, dynamic workforce operating in diverse locations—from offshore platforms and remote drilling sites to power generation facilities. Managing identity and credentials in this environment is complex. Traditional identity systems, which often depend on centralized databases, paper certificates, and manual verification processes, are increasingly inadequate. They introduce delays, increase fraud risk, and create compliance gaps.

Self-Sovereign Identity (SSI) offers an innovative approach to overcome these challenges by placing control of identity data directly into the hands of workers themselves (Lemieux et al., 2021). In an SSI framework, each worker holds a digital wallet containing verifiable credentials issued by trusted authorities, such as accredited training providers, regulatory agencies, or previous employers. These credentials can include safety certifications, work permits, employment records, and health clearances.

When workers arrive on-site or apply for access, they can selectively share proofs of these credentials. Employers and site managers use cryptographic verification to instantly confirm authenticity, check expiration or revocation status, and ensure compliance without relying on paper or contacting the issuing body. This process significantly reduces onboarding time, prevents the use of forged documents, and streamlines audits.

By leveraging SSI, energy companies can:

- Strengthen trust by ensuring all workforce credentials are genuine and current.
- Enhance compliance through auditable, tamper-evident records aligned with regulatory standards.
- Protect privacy by allowing workers to disclose only the minimum information required.
- Increase operational efficiency by automating verification and reducing manual administration.

Self-Sovereign Identity (SSI) provides a powerful framework to improve compliance across three critical dimensions: regulatory alignment, auditability, and dynamic revocation.

## Regulatory Alignment (Safety, Labor, Environment)

Energy companies must comply with a wide range of regulations:

- **Safety Standards** – Such as OSHA regulations or ISO 45001 requirements, which demand proof of specific training and certifications before workers can enter hazardous areas.
- **Labor Laws** – Governing worker qualifications, employment rights, and contractual obligations.
- **Environmental Regulations** – Which may require verified authorizations for handling or transporting hazardous materials.

In traditional systems, verifying these requirements typically involves collecting paper documents or PDFs and relying on manual checks. This process is slow, error-prone, and hard to scale.

SSI improves regulatory alignment in several ways:

- Cryptographically verifiable credentials ensure that every claim—like completion of a safety course—is issued by a recognized authority and has not been tampered with.
- Credential schemas can be tailored to contain all necessary regulatory information (e.g., issue date, expiration date, certification level, training provider).
- Selective disclosure allows workers to share only the specific attributes required to prove compliance with a particular regulation, helping protect personal privacy.

For example, a worker can prove they hold an active confined space certification issued by an accredited training body without revealing unrelated personal details. This makes demonstrating compliance faster and more precise.

## Auditability and Transparent Records

Regulatory bodies and internal compliance teams often require evidence trails to show that (Manimaran et al., 2024):

- Workers had the correct certifications before starting work.
- Credentials were valid at the time of verification.
- Processes were followed according to policy.

In conventional systems, collecting this evidence is labor-intensive. HR or compliance staff must retrieve files from multiple systems, validate authenticity, and compile records into an audit report.

SSI makes these processes significantly more efficient and trustworthy:

- Every credential includes a digital signature from the issuer, creating a tamper-evident chain of trust.
- Verification events can be logged securely, providing an auditable record showing when, by whom, and under what circumstances credentials were verified.
- These logs can be used to demonstrate compliance during external inspections or investigations, supporting transparency and accountability.

For example, if a regulator demands proof that all contractors on a particular site were qualified, an employer can generate a report of verification events backed by cryptographic evidence—rather than relying on manual sign-in sheets or unverified records.

## Dynamic Revocation and Expiry

One of the major risks in compliance is that credentials can become invalid over time—such as when certifications expire, training lapses, or authorization is withdrawn. In traditional systems, there is often no reliable way to check whether a credential is still valid without contacting the issuing organization directly, which can be time-consuming or impractical.

SSI solves this problem through dynamic revocation and expiry mechanisms:

- **Revocation Registries** – Issuers can publish revocation information to a distributed ledger or registry. If a credential is revoked (e.g., a worker's license is suspended), any future verification will immediately detect its invalid status (Naik & Jenkins, 2020).
- **Automatic Expiry Dates** – Credentials include embedded expiration timestamps. When a credential is presented, the verifier checks whether it is still within the valid period.
- **Real-Time Verification** – Every time a credential is verified, its current status is checked automatically, reducing the risk of relying on outdated or revoked credentials.

This approach ensures compliance processes remain current and reliable without additional manual effort. For example, if a training certificate expires after 12 months, the worker's credential will automatically fail verification unless a new certificate is issued and presented.

## 6. THE VALUE OF SSI IN BUILDING TRUST AND ENSURING COMPLIANCE

In the energy sector, trust and compliance are essential to running successful operations. Companies not only need to verify that every worker is properly qualified and authorized, but also be able to prove this to regulators, partners, and stakeholders. Traditional identity systems—like paper certificates, spreadsheets, or isolated HR tools—often fall short of delivering the reliability and efficiency needed in today's fast-paced, tightly regulated environment.

Self-Sovereign Identity (SSI) offers a groundbreaking way to strengthen both trust and compliance at the same time. By giving individuals control over their verified credentials and enabling cryptographic validation, SSI creates an ecosystem where identity claims are transparent, tamper-proof, and simple to audit.

### Building Trust Across Stakeholders

One of SSI's main strengths is its ability to create and sustain trust across complex supply chains and widely distributed teams (Manimaran et al., 2024). In traditional setups, companies and regulators have to rely on manual checks or third parties to verify credentials, which causes delays and increases the risk of mistakes or fraud.

With SSI:

- Digital signatures from trusted issuers (like accredited training bodies or regulators) guarantee authenticity.
- Workers retain ownership and control, preventing credentials from being altered or misused without their consent.
- Verification happens instantly, boosting confidence among employers, contractors, and auditors.

For instance, when a subcontractor shows a verifiable credential for a safety certification, the employer can confirm its validity and integrity in seconds. This builds shared trust that everyone on site has been properly vetted and authorized.

## Ensuring Robust Compliance

Beyond building trust, SSI offers strong compliance benefits. Energy companies must meet strict requirements to prove workers are qualified, certifications are up to date, and records are accurate. Failing to do so can lead to fines, project delays, or reputational harm.

SSI helps ensure compliance in several ways:

- **Regulatory Alignment:** Credentials can include all the data required by regulations (such as certification level, issue and expiry dates, and issuer details).
- **Auditability:** Every verification is securely logged, creating an unchangeable record showing that proper checks took place.
- **Dynamic Revocation:** If a certification is suspended or expires, the credential can be flagged or revoked in real time to prevent unauthorized access.
- **Data Minimization:** Workers only share the minimum information needed to prove compliance, reducing privacy risks and supporting GDPR (Fang et al., 2024).

Many current identity systems are based on centralized authorities and rely on established regulations for identity verification. With SSI, compliance moves from a manual, error-prone process to an automated, streamlined workflow backed by cryptographic proofs.

## 7. TECHNICAL IMPLEMENTATION AND ESSENTIAL FEATURES IN THE ENERGY SECTOR

The technical implementation of Self-Sovereign Identity (SSI) within the global energy sector requires an integrated approach that aligns advanced decentralized technologies with the operational realities of petroleum exploration, production, and distribution. Unlike other industries with more uniform work environments, the energy sector's technical landscape is characterized by high-risk sites, remote facilities, mobile and contractual workforces, and stringent safety and compliance requirements. This unique context influences both the design and deployment of SSI solutions.

Below, we explore the key technical components, supporting infrastructure, and essential capabilities that make Self-Sovereign Identity (SSI) practical and effective for energy companies operating in demanding environments.

## Decentralized Identity Infrastructure

At the heart of SSI is a robust architecture that enables credentials to be secure, verifiable, and portable. Each worker receives one or more Decentralized Identifiers (DIDs)—unique, blockchain-anchored IDs that act as cryptographic pointers to their digital credentials. Unlike conventional IDs such as employee numbers or email addresses, DIDs are controlled by the worker and can travel with them as they change roles, employers, or countries.

- Verifiable Credentials (VCs) are the digital records that prove a worker's qualifications, licenses, and training. These are cryptographically signed by trusted issuers—like regulatory agencies, accredited training providers, or corporate HR departments—and formatted using W3C standards to ensure compatibility across verification platforms.
- Blockchain networks such as Ethereum, Hyperledger Indy, or Energy Web Chain serve as the trust layer. They store credential metadata in an immutable ledger so verifiers can instantly confirm whether credentials are authentic and current—without having to contact the issuer each time.
- Digital wallets round out this infrastructure. These secure apps, available on mobile devices and desktops, allow workers to store, organize, and share credentials as needed. Platforms like Trinsic, Dock, or Evernym make it possible to selectively disclose only the information required for a specific verification, giving workers more control over their data.

This combination ensures credentials are tamper-proof, portable, and usable wherever work takes place.

## Credential Lifecycle Management

A successful SSI system requires clear processes to govern how credentials are created, verified, updated, and revoked. It starts with issuance and anchoring, where a credential is digitally signed by the issuer and anchored to a blockchain ledger for transparency and trust.

If a credential expires or is revoked due to non-compliance or updated training, its status is immediately updated on the blockchain so it cannot be misused (Ahmed et al., 2022). Recovery mechanisms are also critical—if a worker loses their device or credentials are compromised, secure processes are in place to help them reclaim their identity without starting from scratch.

This lifecycle approach ensures credentials are always current, valid, and easily verifiable, supporting real-time compliance and reducing the risk of unqualified personnel entering critical environments.

## Integration with Operational Systems

To maximize effectiveness, SSI solutions must seamlessly integrate with existing operational ecosystems deployed by energy enterprises. Integration with Enterprise Resource Planning (ERP) systems such as SAP and Oracle facilitates synchronization of credential data across functions including finance, operations, and HR.

- ERP integration streamlines credential visibility across business processes.
- HRMS interoperability accelerates onboarding workflows.

Human Resource Management Systems (HRMS) can automatically validate worker credentials during onboarding by querying blockchain records in real time. Moreover, access control and safety systems—including AI-enabled cameras, smart personal protective equipment, and secure entry gates—can reference DIDs to determine authorization for specific tasks or zones.

Regulatory reporting and compliance dashboards further benefit from verified credential data, significantly reducing audit preparation times and improving reporting accuracy. This tight integration reduces administrative overhead, eliminates redundant verifications, and reinforces end-to-end compliance (Alex Preukschat, 2021).

## User Experience and Accessibility

To support adoption across diverse field environments:

- **Simplified Mobile Interfaces**
    - Optimized for low-bandwidth conditions
    - Offline verification capability
- **Multilingual Support**
    - Interfaces localized for regional workforces
- **Training Resources**
    - Guides, instructional videos, and help desks to facilitate onboarding and usage

SSI tools must be accessible to all workers, regardless of their location or technical expertise.

Simplified mobile interfaces are essential for field teams who need to manage credentials on the go, especially in low-bandwidth environments (Soltani et al., 2021). Offline capabilities help ensure workers can present credentials even without internet connectivity.

Multilingual support is vital so workers in diverse global teams can interact with the platform in their preferred language.

Training and adoption resources—like clear guides, videos, and help desks—make it easier for employees and contractors to feel comfortable using SSI tools. Prioritizing user experience builds trust and increases adoption across the organization.

## Security and Privacy Safeguards

Given the sensitive nature of workforce and operational data, SSI must adhere to strict security standards.

End-to-end encryption protects all data moving between wallets, verifiers, and blockchain nodes.

Role-based access controls ensure that only authorized individuals can view or act on credential information.

Zero-Knowledge Proofs allow workers to prove qualifications without exposing raw credential data, preserving privacy (Zyskind et al., 2015).

To stay compliant, SSI implementations also align with regulations such as GDPR, CCPA, and local data protection laws. These safeguards collectively build a system where security and transparency can coexist.

## Phased Deployment Strategy

Because rolling out SSI can be complex, most companies avoid trying to implement everything simultaneously. Instead, they start small and proceed incrementally. Typically, they launch pilot programs in areas where the impact will be immediate—such as onboarding contractors or verifying safety certifications. These pilots demonstrate how SSI can address real challenges and establish its value to the business.

Once the initial results are positive, teams advance to integration testing. This phase ensures SSI functions seamlessly with existing systems, including ERP platforms, HR tools, and access control software.

Afterward, companies can gradually expand the program. They may introduce additional types of credentials, involve more departments, or deploy SSI across new sites and countries.

Throughout this process, continuous improvement is essential (Zyskind et al., 2015). Gathering feedback from users and refining policies or workflows helps keep the system reliable, user-friendly, and trusted by all stakeholders.

This phased approach allows organizations to learn, adapt, and build confidence in SSI before committing to a full-scale rollout. It also mitigates risks by resolving challenges early, rather than attempting to tackle them all at once.

### Future-Ready Capabilities

SSI is designed to evolve alongside new operational and technological trends. In the coming years, Decentralized Autonomous Organizations (DAOs) will use smart contracts to automate credential verification, contract management, and payment processing (Chan et al., 2025).

Integration with AI workforce planning tools will allow companies to predict staffing needs and skill gaps more accurately.

Finally, global credential registries will make it easy to recognize professional qualifications across borders, supporting a more mobile and agile workforce (Mukta, 2024).

Together, these capabilities make SSI a scalable, adaptable solution ready to support the energy sector's next decade of transformation.

## 8. IMPLEMENTATION CHALLENGES AND WHAT TO CONSIDER

While Self-Sovereign Identity (SSI) holds transformative promise for workforce credential management in the energy sector, real-world implementation is complex.

Deploying SSI in safety-critical, multinational environments introduces technical, organizational, regulatory, and cultural challenges. This section explores the primary obstacles energy organizations should anticipate—and offers practical considerations for navigating them effectively.

### Credential Lifecycle Flow in a Decentralized System

This diagram walks you through how digital credentials are created, shared, verified, and eventually expired or revoked. It also points out some of the common challenges organizations face when using this approach.

1. **Issuing the Credential**

Everything starts here. A trusted organization, like a training company or certification body, creates a credential for an individual.

2. **Digital Signature by the Issuer**

The issuer then digitally signs the credential. This signature acts as proof that the credential is real and genuinely came from a recognized source.

3. **Anchoring to the Blockchain**

After signing, the credential is recorded on a blockchain. Essentially, this means a record or a secure digital fingerprint of the credential is stored in a decentralized ledger. Anyone can later check this record to verify authenticity without relying on a single organization's database (Garzon et al., 2022). Anchoring registry smart contract periodically stores the hash value of the repository data.

4. **Selective Disclosure With Zero-Knowledge Proofs**

When the holder wants to present their credential—for example, to show they are qualified—they don't have to reveal everything (Khaldy et al., 2024). Using Zero-Knowledge Proofs, they can share only the information needed, proving something is true without exposing all their personal data.

5. **Verification**

A verifier (like an employer or regulator) checks whether the credential is authentic and still valid. They do this by comparing the information with the blockchain record and confirming the proof provided by the holder.

6. **Revocation or Expiration**

Over time, credentials can expire or be revoked if they're no longer valid. For instance, a safety certificate may automatically expire after a year or be canceled if the person no longer meets the criteria.

## Challenges in the Process

On the right side of the diagram, you'll see some typical problems that can come up:

- **Interoperability Issues**: Different systems and software may not work smoothly together, which makes it harder to share and validate credentials across organizations.
- **Unclear Regulations**: Laws and policies may be vague or vary by region, leading to uncertainty about compliance.
- **User Adoption**: Employees and users might be reluctant to adopt new tools or learn unfamiliar technology.
- **Offline Access**: In areas without reliable internet, checking credentials on the blockchain can be difficult or impossible.
- **Governance Challenges**: It can be complex to decide who should manage, update, and oversee the system. Clear rules and cooperation between stakeholders are essential.

Below is an overview of key considerations and strategies to help organizations plan effectively.

## 1. Interoperability Across Platforms and Standards

Challenge:

The SSI ecosystem is diverse. Different blockchain networks (like Ethereum, Hyperledger Indy, and Energy Web Chain), wallet providers, and credential formats often follow different protocols.

Key Issues:

- No universal standards, making it hard to verify credentials across platforms.
- Variations in Decentralized Identifier (DID) methods and Verifiable Credential (VC) schemas can create inconsistencies.
- Integrating SSI with existing HR, ERP, and safety systems may require custom solutions.

What to Consider:

- Adopt W3C standards for DIDs and Verifiable Credentials wherever possible.
- Use interoperability tools like the Decentralized Identity Foundation (DIF) Universal Resolver.
- Develop API middleware to bridge protocol differences.

## 2. Regulatory and Legal Uncertainty

Challenge:

Laws about digital identity on the blockchain are still emerging. Many countries don't clearly define the legal status of decentralized credentials.

Key Issues:

- Liability concerns if credential data is leaked or misused.
- Uncertainty about whether blockchain attestations hold up in court.
- Conflicts with data protection laws like GDPR or CCPA.

What to Consider:

- Work closely with legal and compliance teams to understand local regulations.
- Follow privacy-by-design and data minimization principles.
- Engage with regulators to define acceptable practices.
- Create clear governance policies for issuing, revoking, and recovering credentials.

## 3. Data Privacy and Consent

Challenge:

SSI gives individuals control over their data—but in regulated industries, employers still have record-keeping obligations.

Key Issues:

- Balancing worker privacy with legal and operational needs.
- Ensuring employees fully understand consent when sharing credentials.
- Risks of misuse or over-surveillance if verification logs are not well governed.

What to Consider:

- Provide clear, transparent consent processes in wallet applications.
- Use Zero-Knowledge Proofs to share only necessary information.
- Adopt pseudonymous identifiers to decouple identity from records.
- Develop privacy policies explaining how data is stored, shared, and retained.

## 4. Change Management and Workforce Adoption

Challenge:

Moving to SSI requires a cultural shift for HR teams and field workers with different levels of digital skills.

Key Issues:

- Resistance to change from IT, HR, and compliance stakeholders.
- Worker skepticism about data security and potential job impacts.
- Lack of familiarity with digital wallets and credential management.

What to Consider:

- Launch awareness campaigns to explain SSI's benefits, like faster onboarding and personal data control.
- Develop training and easy-to-follow guides.
- Design mobile interfaces suitable for low-connectivity environments.
- Pilot SSI in smaller, high-impact areas before scaling up.

## 5. Technical Resilience and Availability

Challenge:

Energy operations often occur in remote sites with limited connectivity and harsh conditions.

Key Issues:

- Credential verification may fail without internet access.
- Blockchain transactions can be slow or expensive.
- Recovery procedures are needed if a device is lost or credentials are corrupted.

What to Consider:

- Use wallet apps that support offline caching and delayed sync.
- Consider private or consortium blockchains for better performance.
- Develop backup and recovery protocols.
- Deploy local verification caches for critical systems.

## 6. Credential Revocation and Lifecycle Complexity

Challenge:
Keeping credentials up to date requires constant coordination across decentralized systems.
Key Issues:

- Revocation registries must be accurate and accessible.
- Verifiers need real-time ways to confirm status.
- Lifecycle events like expiry, suspension, and reinstatement must be automated.

What to Consider:

- Use blockchain-based revocation registries for transparency.
- Implement standardized status lists (like W3C Credential Status).
- Automate notifications to all parties about status changes.

## 7. Scalability and Performance

Challenge:
Large energy enterprises manage credentials for thousands of workers.
Key Issues:

- Blockchain networks must handle high volumes of transactions.
- Verification must be fast enough to avoid disrupting operations.
- Issuance and verification costs can be significant at scale.

What to Consider:

- Use layer-2 scaling solutions (sidechains, state channels) to cut costs.
- Build distributed verification caches to reduce delays.
- Batch credentials where possible to ease network load.

## 8. Ethical Considerations

Challenge:
SSI raises important questions about fairness, privacy, and accountability.
Key Issues:

- Risk of discrimination if credential data is misused.

- Potential overreach in tracking worker activities.
- Bias in automated decisions about access or verification.

What to Consider:

- Establish governance frameworks to define responsibilities.
- Apply ethical AI principles to automation.
- Create clear procedures for appeal and redress.

## 9. Vendor Lock-In and Ecosystem Fragmentation

Challenge:
The SSI market is evolving fast, and relying on one vendor can create dependencies.
Key Issues:

- Vendor platforms may become obsolete.
- Switching costs can be high.
- Fragmentation can limit interoperability.

What to Consider:

- Favor open-source and standards-based solutions.
- Develop exit strategies and data portability plans.
- Join industry groups to align on common protocols.

*Table 1. Comparison Table: Centralized vs. Decentralized Identity Risks*

| Risk Area | Traditional Centralized Identity | Self-Sovereign Identity (SSI) |
|---|---|---|
| **Data Breaches** | High risk—centralized HR systems are attractive targets | Lower risk—credentials stored in individual wallets |
| **Onboarding Delays** | Frequent—manual verification from multiple issuers | Reduced—verifiable credentials enable instant validation |
| **Mobility Barriers** | Credentials often not portable across employers or borders | High portability—worker-controlled credentials travel with the holder |
| **Privacy Concerns** | Limited control over what data is shared | High control via selective disclosure (e.g., Zero-Knowledge Proofs) |
| **Interoperability** | Often limited to internal systems | Requires careful planning—ecosystem fragmentation is an emerging risk |

continued on following page

*Table 1. Continued*

| Risk Area | Traditional Centralized Identity | Self-Sovereign Identity (SSI) |
|---|---|---|
| **Governance** | Clear internal policies but opaque processes for workers | Requires new governance models and worker education |
| **Resilience (Dragnoiu & Olimid, 2024)** | Reliant on corporate IT infrastructure | Dependent on blockchain networks and wallet availability |

## 9. FUTURE OUTLOOK FOR SSI IN THE ENERGY WORKFORCE

Self-Sovereign Identity (SSI) is poised to become a key pillar of digital transformation across the energy industry. As regulations grow more complex, technology matures, and companies look for more resilient ways to manage their workforce, SSI offers a compelling path forward. This section explores how SSI is likely to develop, the benefits it can deliver, and the challenges organizations must address to adopt it effectively.

### 1. Regulations Driving Change

In many countries, energy companies face strict rules governing workforce safety, environmental compliance, and labor practices. Meeting these requirements is often time-consuming and prone to errors. SSI provides a new way to handle compliance by using digital credentials that are cryptographically verifiable and anchored on decentralized blockchains.

### Research Perspective

Studies show that verifiable credential systems improve auditability because they create records that cannot be altered Unlike traditional databases, SSI frameworks allow regulators to independently verify credentials and compliance without depending on centralized systems that can be manipulated or hacked.

Consider a large oil and gas company operating across several countries. It can issue digital safety certifications, such as confined space training, to its employees. Regulators can then verify these certifications almost instantly, reducing paperwork and increasing trust in the company's compliance reports.

## 2. Integrating SSI with Workforce Systems

Beyond compliance, SSI has the potential to improve the broader management of people and operations. When SSI is integrated with workforce management platforms, identity and access management (IAM) tools, and IoT-enabled site controls, it can enable:

- Automated validation of credentials when workers arrive on site
- Access permissions that change based on context and role
- Immediate revocation of access if a credential becomes invalid or if there is a security incident

In offshore drilling, a contractor boarding a platform can present their SSI credential at the embarkation point. The system automatically checks their certifications against blockchain records, logs their entry for safety compliance, and grants or denies access on the spot. This reduces manual checks and ensures only properly qualified individuals enter high-risk areas.

## 3. Building Decentralized Reputation Systems

One of the most exciting aspects of SSI is the ability to create decentralized reputation frameworks. Over time, workers will collect attestations—secure records of their experience, safety record, and performance evaluations. Because these credentials are verifiable, they build a portable reputation that the worker controls.

### Research Perspective

Emerging studies suggest that decentralized reputation systems can make labor markets more efficient (Popescu, et al., 2022). They help reduce information gaps between employers and workers, making it easier for skilled professionals to move between companies without having to re-prove their qualifications each time.

### Real-World Example

Imagine a turbine maintenance specialist with a track record of successful projects and endorsements from supervisors. Instead of relying on HR departments to verify their history, the specialist can share a cryptographically signed record of their achievements with any new employer. This speeds up onboarding and supports merit-based hiring.

## 4. Advancing Privacy Protection

A key concern when digitizing identity is privacy (Yildiz et al., 2023). SSI addresses this by using techniques like selective disclosure and Zero-Knowledge Proofs (ZKPs). These allow individuals to prove they have certain qualifications without exposing all their personal details.

Privacy-focused SSI designs are increasingly recognized as essential for compliance with regulations like the General Data Protection Regulation (GDPR).

For example, a field technician may need to show they have a valid medical clearance to work in remote environments. With SSI and ZKPs, they can prove they hold the certificate without revealing sensitive medical data. This approach protects privacy while satisfying compliance rules.

## 5. Standardization and Interoperability

For SSI to reach its full potential, credentials need to work seamlessly across different countries, regulatory frameworks, and technologies. Organizations like the W3C and the Decentralized Identity Foundation are working on shared standards to make this possible.

A technician who receives a credential in Norway under European regulations should be able to present it in the Middle East or North America without issues. This supports global workforce mobility and simplifies contractor engagement.

## 6. Challenges to Widespread Adoption

Despite the promise of SSI, there are several challenges that energy companies must plan for:

### Change Management

Implementing SSI requires shifting from centralized systems to decentralized trust. This can be a big cultural change for organizations used to controlling all data internally. Employees may also resist adopting new processes or tools.

### Governance

Clear rules are needed to define who can issue and revoke credentials, how disputes will be resolved, and what happens if something goes wrong. Without good governance, trust in the system can quickly erode.

### Integration with Legacy Systems

Many companies still rely on older HR and compliance software. Connecting these systems with SSI platforms requires careful planning to avoid disruptions.

### Connectivity Challenges

Energy operations often occur in remote areas with unreliable internet access. SSI solutions will need to combine offline capabilities with eventual blockchain synchronization to remain functional in these environments.

### Research Insight

Experts have emphasized that rolling out SSI is not just about technology—it also demands a mindset shift toward decentralized ways of proving trust.

## 7. Long-Term Strategic Impact

Looking ahead, SSI has the potential to reshape workforce credentialing over the next decade. Some anticipated benefits include:

- **Greater Operational Resilience:**
- Real-time verification of credentials improves safety and ensures only qualified individuals can access critical infrastructure.
- **Lower Administrative Overhead:**
- Automation of credential issuance and verification reduces time spent on paperwork and manual compliance checks.
- **Improved Safety Outcomes:**
- Access controls that adapt dynamically based on valid credentials help keep workers and sites secure.
- **Enhanced Trust:**
- Giving workers ownership of their identity data fosters stronger relationships among employers, contractors, regulators, and employees.

Self-Sovereign Identity is on track to become a cornerstone of the energy sector's digital transformation journey. It promises a future where credentials are portable, verifiable, and secure—helping organizations stay compliant, improve safety, and operate more efficiently. However, realizing this vision will require more than technical solutions. Companies will need to invest in change management, clear governance, and robust integration strategies. By thoughtfully addressing these challenges, energy organizations can build a resilient, trustworthy workforce ecosystem where individuals truly own their professional identities.

## 10. SUMMARY AND CORE INSIGHTS

This chapter takes a close look at why traditional workforce identity management is falling short in the global petroleum industry. Even though companies have poured significant resources into advanced tools—like artificial intelligence for predicting equipment failures, blockchain for tracking carbon emissions, and the Internet of Things for monitoring operations in real time—the way they handle employee credentials and identity has remained outdated and fragmented.

Many organizations still rely on paper records, disconnected HR databases, and repetitive manual checks to verify workers' qualifications. This approach leads to delays, inefficiency, and increased compliance risks. In an industry where safety is critical, regulations are strict, and operations span multiple countries, these shortcomings can weaken a company's resilience and slow its ability to adapt quickly.

Self-Sovereign Identity (SSI) has emerged as a promising solution to these challenges. SSI isn't just another technology—it's also a strategic shift in how identity is managed. Instead of storing credentials in centralized company systems, SSI puts control directly in the hands of workers. With SSI, employees can keep all their professional records—such as certifications, licenses, and medical clearances—in secure digital wallets on their devices.

These credentials are issued as Verifiable Credentials (VCs) and linked to Decentralized Identifiers (DIDs) on blockchains that cannot be tampered with. Because of this setup, credentials are portable and can be instantly verified anywhere in the world. Rather than going through cumbersome document exchanges or waiting for HR to confirm qualifications, employers and regulators can quickly check that credentials are authentic, valid, and up to date. This not only speeds up onboarding but also helps companies stay compliant across different countries and jurisdictions.

The chapter details the complete lifecycle of a credential:

- First, a trusted authority (like a training provider) issue it.
- The credential is securely stored by the worker.
- When needed, the worker can share only the relevant parts of the credential using Zero-Knowledge Proofs (ZKPs), which prove something is true without revealing all personal details.
- Finally, credentials can be revoked or expire when no longer valid.

This process helps protect privacy while making operations more efficient and supporting cross-border work.

Real-world examples show SSI in action:

- Offshore technicians can present blockchain-verified credentials to get onboarded immediately, instead of waiting for paperwork to clear.
- Smart personal protective equipment (PPE) can check whether a worker's qualifications are current before allowing access to restricted areas.
- AI-powered digital twins—virtual models of operations—can use verified credentials to track and manage workforce safety dynamically.

Beyond the technical advantages, SSI delivers clear strategic benefits:

- Project managers and operators can hire faster and cut down on paperwork.
- HR teams have a reliable, current record of everyone's credentials.
- Compliance officers get real-time visibility into workforce qualifications, reducing the risk of non-compliance.
- Regulators gain a transparent framework for enforcing labor standards and supporting secure digital mobility for workers.

At the same time, the chapter doesn't ignore the challenges:

- Different systems and platforms still don't always work well together.
- Standards can be inconsistent, making interoperability difficult.
- Governance—deciding who controls what and how—is complex.
- Some field workers may not have the digital access or skills needed to use SSI right away.

Still, the long-term outlook is very positive. The chapter envisions a future where:

- AI helps companies forecast what skills they will need in advance.
- Decentralized Autonomous Organizations (DAOs) handle tasks like verifying credentials and automating payments to contractors.
- Global SSI registries make it possible to confirm the credentials of energy professionals across borders effortlessly.

This vision reflects a broader transformation where decentralization, digitization, and automation are reshaping not only how equipment and operations are managed but also how people are empowered and supported.

In the end, SSI is presented as a cornerstone of a safer, more transparent, and more agile energy workforce. The underlying message is clear: the future of the industry depends not just on smarter machines but also on smarter, better-supported people.

## DISCLOSURE OF DELEGATION TO GENERATIVE AI

The authors declare the use of generative AI in the research and writing process. According to the GAIDeT taxonomy (2025), the following tasks were delegated to GAI tools under full human supervision:

- Text generation (supportive drafting and refinement only)
- Proofreading and editing
- Summarizing text
- Reformatting

The GAI tool used was: OpenAI ChatGPT (GPT-4).

Responsibility for the final manuscript lies entirely with the authors.

GAI tools are not listed as authors and do not bear responsibility for the final outcomes.

Declaration submitted by: Sonal Parmar

Additional note: I used AI tools in a supportive role to help refine the phrasing, check grammar, and improve the overall flow and readability of the text

## REFERENCES


Agho, M., & Eyo-Udo, N. (2023). Developing a framework for AI-driven optimization of supply chains in energy sector. *Global Journal of Advanced Research and Reviews, 1*, 82–101. DOI: 10.58175/gjarr.2023.1.2.0064

Ahmed, Md. R., Islam, A. K. M. M., Shatabda, S. & Islam, S. (2022). Blockchain-Based Identity Management System and Self-Sovereign Identity Ecosystem: A Comprehensive Survey. *IEEE Access : Practical Innovations, Open Solutions, 10*, 113436–113481. DOI: 10.1109/ACCESS.2022.3216643

Akli, A., & Chougdali, K. (2025). IOTA-Assisted Self-Sovereign Identity Framework for Decentralized Authentication and Secure Data Sharing. *IEEE Access : Practical Innovations, Open Solutions, 13*, 80191–80205. DOI: 10.1109/ACCESS.2025.3567137

Al Khaldy, M., Alshdifat, G., Almalahmeh, T., & Aldweesh, A. (2024). Blockchain as a Resilient Infrastructure for e-Business Transactions. *2024 2nd International Conference on Cyber Resilience (ICCR)*, 1–6. DOI: 10.1109/ICCR61006.2024.10532913

Alex Preukschat, D. R. (2021). *Self-Sovereign Identity: Decentralized Digital Identity and Verifiable Credentials*. Manning Publications.

Bai, Y., Lei, H., Li, S., Gao, H., Li, J., & Li, L. (2022). Decentralized and Self-Sovereign Identity in the Era of Blockchain: A Survey. *2022 IEEE International Conference on Blockchain (Blockchain)*, 500–507. DOI: 10.1109/Blockchain55522.2022.00077

Bamakan, S. M. H., M. A., & B. A. B. (2021). Blockchain in oil and gas industry: Applications, challenges, and future trends. *Computers in Industry, 130*, 103469.

Chan, W., Gai, K., Yu, J., & Zhu, L. (2025). Blockchain-Assisted Self-Sovereign Identities on Education: A Survey. *Blockchains, 3*(1), 3. DOI: 10.3390/blockchains3010003

Chanda, P., Singh, P., Kumar, M., & Bhardwaj, V. (2024). Enhancing Employee Onboarding throughBlockchain-Based Identity Verification in HRManagement. *International Journal of Information Engineering and Electronic Business, 16*(6), 29–41. DOI: 10.5815/ijieeb.2024.06.03

Chen, Y., Cui, Y., & Wu, J. (2019). Image Restoration of Agricultural History Based on Neural Patch Synthesis. *2019 IEEE 11th International Conference on Communication Software and Networks (ICCSN)*, 401–405. DOI: 10.1109/ICCSN.2019.8905400

Cucko, S., & Turkanovic, M. (2021). Decentralized and Self-Sovereign Identity: Systematic Mapping Study. *IEEE Access : Practical Innovations, Open Solutions, 9*, 139009–139027. DOI: 10.1109/ACCESS.2021.3117588

Dara, T. J. N. C. (2025). A Trust Policy Meta-Model for Trustworthy Interoperability. *Procedia Computer Science.*

Dragnoiu, A. E. & Olimid, R. F. (2024). *Towards an identity management solution on Arweave.*

Enemosah, A. & Chukwunweike, J. (2022). *Next-Generation SCADA Architectures for Enhanced Field Automation and Real-Time Remote Control in Oil and Gas Fields*. 514–529. DOI: 10.7753/IJCATR1112.1018

Fang, J., Feng, T., Guo, X., & Wang, X. (2024). Privacy-enhanced distributed revocable identity management scheme based self-sovereign identity. *Journal of Cloud Computing (Heidelberg, Germany), 13*(1), 154. DOI: 10.1186/s13677-024-00715-8

Garzon, S. R., Yildiz, H., & Kupper, A. (2022). Decentralized Identifiers and Self-Sovereign Identity in 6G. *IEEE Network, 36*(4), 142–148. DOI: 10.1109/MNET.009.2100736

Jovita Nsoh. (2021). *Energy transitions and the energy workforce part 2.*

Kim, J., Choi, M., Lee, C., Woo, J., & Hong, J. W.-K. (2023). Service Applicable Blockchain-based Self-Sovereign Identity Management System. *2023 IEEE International Conference on Blockchain and Cryptocurrency (ICBC)*, 1–5. DOI: 10.1109/ICBC56567.2023.10174875

Lemieux, V., Voskobojnikov, A., & Kang, M. (2021). Addressing Audit and Accountability Issues in Self-Sovereign Identity Blockchain Systems Using Archival Science Principles. *2021 IEEE 45th Annual Computers, Software, and Applications Conference (COMPSAC)*, 1210–1216. DOI: 10.1109/COMPSAC51774.2021.00167

Manimaran, P., Da Conceição, A. F., Garrett, T., Raikwar, M., & Vitenberg, R. (2024). Prevoke: Privacy-Preserving Configurable Method for Revoking Verifiable Credentials. *2024 IEEE International Conference on Blockchain (Blockchain)*, 354–361. DOI: 10.1109/Blockchain62396.2024.00053

Mariana Dahan, M. T. J. D. S., & R. M. R. (2020). Self-Sovereign Identity: The Future of Identity—Self-Sovereignity, Digital Wallets, and Blockchain. *Inter-American Development Bank.*

Mazzocca, C., Acar, A., Uluagac, S., Montanari, R., Bellavista, P., & Conti, M. (2025). A Survey on Decentralized Identifiers and Verifiable Credentials. *IEEE Communications Surveys and Tutorials*. DOI: 10.1109/COMST.2025.3543197

Moriyama, K., & Otsuka, A. (2025). Sybil-Resistant Self-Sovereign Identity Utilizing Attested Execution Secure Processors and Zero-Knowledge Membership Proofs. *IEEE Access : Practical Innovations, Open Solutions, 13*, 17919–17944. DOI: 10.1109/ACCESS.2025.3533877

Mukta, R. (2024). *Privacy-Preserving Identity and Credential Management: A Blockchain-Based Solution.*

Naik, N., & Jenkins, P. (2020). Your Identity is Yours: Take Back Control of Your Identity Using GDPR Compatible Self-Sovereign Identity. *2020 7th International Conference on Behavioural and Social Computing (BESC)*, 1–6. DOI: 10.1109/BESC51023.2020.9348298

Nita, S. L., & Mihailescu, M. I. (2024). A Novel Authentication Scheme Based on Verifiable Credentials Using Digital Identity in the Context of Web 3.0. *Electronics (Basel), 13*(6), 1137. DOI: 10.3390/electronics13061137

Oluoha, O. M., Odeshina, A., Reis, O., Okpeke, F., Attipoe, V., & Orieno, O. H. (2022). A Unified Framework for Risk-Based Access Control and Identity Management in Compliance-Critical Environments. *Journal of Frontiers in Multidisciplinary Research, 3*(1), 23–34. DOI: 10.54660/.IJFMR.2022.3.1.23-34

Pub, A. (2025). Ensuring compliance and safety in global procurement operations in the energy industry. *International Journal of Multidisciplinary Research and Growth Evaluation, 05*, 1311–1326. DOI: 10.54660/.IJMRGE.2024.5.4.1311-1326

Puri, V. (n.d.). Detecting Fraud and Enforcing Compliance in Global Time & Attendance Solutions via. *Machine Learning*.

Ryan Greene. (n.d.). *Self-So Self-Sovereign Identity and the Decentralized, Consent-Based Model.*

Soltani, R., Nguyen, U. T., & An, A. (2021). A Survey of Self-Sovereign Identity Ecosystem. *Security and Communication Networks, 2021*, 1–26. DOI: 10.1155/2021/8873429

Steenholt, R., & Bss, A. (2023). *Blockchain: The next revolution for Efficiency, Security, and Privacy in Human Resource Management and Recruitment Master of Science in Strategy, Organisation and Leadership*. DOI: 10.13140/RG.2.2.18365.03046

Tripathi, A., Upadhyay, P., & Goel, P. K. (2025). *Deep Learning for Anomaly Detection in Industrial Networks*. DOI: 10.4018/979-8-3373-3241-3.ch006

Yildiz, H., Küpper, A., Thatmann, D., Göndör, S., & Herbke, P. (2023). Toward Interoperable Self-Sovereign Identities. *IEEE Access : Practical Innovations, Open Solutions, 11*, 114080–114116. DOI: 10.1109/ACCESS.2023.3313723

Yin, J., Xiao, Y., Chen, Q., & Lim, Y., Liu, X., Pei, Q. & Zhou, J. (2025). DP-DID: A Dynamic and Proactive Decentralized Identity System. *IEEE Transactions on Information Forensics and Security, 20*, 4999–5014. DOI: 10.1109/TIFS.2025.3561662

Zografopoulos, I., Hatziargyriou, N. D., & Konstantinou, C. (2023). Distributed Energy Resources Cybersecurity Outlook: Vulnerabilities, Attacks, Impacts, and Mitigations. *IEEE Systems Journal, 17*(4), 6695–6709. DOI: 10.1109/JSYST.2023.3305757

Zyskind, G., Nathan, O. & Pentland, A. (2015). Decentralizing Privacy: Using Blockchain to Protect Personal Data. *2015 IEEE Security and Privacy Workshops*, 180–184. DOI: 10.1109/SPW.2015.27

# Compilation of References

Abd-Elfattah, N., Dahroug, A., Kammar, M. E., & Fahmy, R. (2025). Machine learning and AVO class II workflow for hydrocarbon prospectivity in the Messinian offshore Nile Delta Egypt. *Scientific Reports*, *15*(1), 3566. Advance online publication. DOI: 10.1038/s41598-025-86765-7 PMID: 39875438

Abdullahi Hassan Usman, S., Abdullahi, S., Zakari, A., Abdu, H., Nura, A., Ahmed Zayyad, M., Suleiman, S., Adamu, A., & Samaila Mashasha, A. (2020). Software testing: review on tools, techniques and challenges Software Testing: Review on Tools, Techniques and Challenges. *International Journal of Advanced Research in Technology and Innovation*, *2*(2), 11–18. http://myjms.moe.gov.my/index.php/ijarti

Abdullahi, S., Calem Ambi, Y., & Hali, I. A. Lawal, & Bagiwa, I. (n.d.). *A Radar System For Object And People Detection In Security-Challenged Areas of Katsina State*. Retrieved August 16, 2025, from www.seahipaj.org

Abdullahi, S., Qabasiyu, M. G., Danyaro, K. U., Zakari, A., Maitama, J. Z., & Imam, A. A. (2025). A Systematic Review of Metaheuristic Approaches to the Deployment Problem in Wireless Sensor Networks. [JTEC]. *Journal of Telecommunication, Electronic and Computer Engineering*, *17*(2), 1–14. DOI: 10.54554/jtec.2025.17.02.001

Abdullahi, S., Usman Danyaro, K., Zakari, A., Abdul Aziz, I., Amila Wan Abdullah Zawawi, N., & Adamu, S. (2025). Time-Series Large Language Models: A Systematic Review of State-of-the-Art. *IEEE Access : Practical Innovations, Open Solutions*, *13*, 30235–30261. DOI: 10.1109/ACCESS.2025.3535782

Abdullahi, S., Yusuf, N., Zayyad, M. A., Bagiwa, L. I., Zakari, A., Adamu, A., & Shehu, S. (2020). The Big Data Technology: Assessing the Impact in the Banking Industry. *Open Journal of Science and Technology*, *3*(2), 71–77. DOI: 10.31580/ojst.v3i2.1464

Abdullahi, S., Zakari, A., Nura, A., Mashasha, A. S., Abdu, H., & Suleiman, S. (2020). Criteria for Accepting Software Requirements Negotiation Tools in the Software Industry. *Science Proceedings Series*, *2*(1), 39–45. DOI: 10.31580/sps.v2i1.1241

Abdullahi, S., Zayyad, M. A., Yusuf, N., Bagiwa, L. I., Nura, A., Zakari, A., & Dansambo, B. (2021). Software Requirements Negotiation: A Review on Challenges. *International Journal of Innovative Computing*, *11*(1), 1–6. DOI: 10.11113/ijic.v11n1.264

Abdulrahman, Y., Arnautović, E., Parezanović, V., & Svetinovic, D. (2023). AI and blockchain synergy in aerospace engineering: An impact survey on operational efficiency and technological challenges. *IEEE Access : Practical Innovations, Open Solutions*, *11*, 87790–87804. DOI: 10.1109/ACCESS.2023.3305325

Acemoğlu, D., Autor, D., Hazell, J., & Restrepo, P. (2022). Artificial Intelligence and Jobs: Evidence from Online Vacancies. *Journal of Labor Economics*, *40*(S1), S293–S340. Advance online publication. DOI: 10.1086/718327

Adamu, S., Alhussian, H., Abdulkadir, S. J., Alwadin, A., Khairy, S. O. F., Mamman, H., Abdullahi, S., Yahaya, S., Garba, A., Aliyu, D. A., Yakubu, M. M., & Oyefidein, D. T. (2025). Adaptive hybrid hyperparameter optimization with MRFO and Lévy flight for accurate melanoma classification. *Journal of King Saud University. Computer and Information Sciences*, *37*(4), 1–21. DOI: 10.1007/s44443-025-00078-3

Adebisi, B., Aigbedion, E., Ayorinde, O. B., & Onukwulu, C. (n.d.). *A Conceptual Model for Predictive Asset Integrity Management Using Data Analytics to Enhance Maintenance and Reliability in Oil & Gas Operations*. DOI: 10.54660/.IJMRGE.2021.2.1.534-541

Adisetya, E., & Gunawan, S. (2024, July). The conceptual model of Indonesian palm oil supply chain based on blockchain. [). IOP Publishing.]. *IOP Conference Series. Earth and Environmental Science*, *1377*(1), 012007. DOI: 10.1088/1755-1315/1377/1/012007

Afrin, N., & Pathak, A. (2023). Blockchain-Powered Security and Transparency in Supply Chain: Exploring Traceability and Authenticity through Smart Contracts. *International Journal of Computer Applications*, *185*(49), 975–8887. DOI: 10.5120/ijca2023923318

Aghaei, R., Kiaei, A. A., Boush, M., Vahidi, J., Barzegar, Z., & Rofoosheh, M. (2025). The potential of large language models in supply chain management: advancing decision-making, efficiency, and innovation. *arXiv preprint arXiv:2501.15411*.

Agho, M., & Eyo-Udo, N. (2023). Developing a framework for AI-driven optimization of supply chains in energy sector. *Global Journal of Advanced Research and Reviews*, *1*, 82–101. DOI: 10.58175/gjarr.2023.1.2.0064

Ahmad, R. W., Salah, K., Jayaraman, R., Yaqoob, I., & Omar, M. (2022a). Blockchain in oil and gas industry: Applications, challenges, and future trends. *Technology in Society*, *68*, 101941. DOI: 10.1016/j.techsoc.2022.101941

Ahmed, Md. R., Islam, A. K. M. M., Shatabda, S. & Islam, S. (2022). Blockchain-Based Identity Management System and Self-Sovereign Identity Ecosystem: A Comprehensive Survey. *IEEE Access : Practical Innovations, Open Solutions*, *10*, 113436–113481. DOI: 10.1109/ACCESS.2022.3216643

Ahmed, S. (2025). Enhancing Data Security and Transparency: The Role of Blockchain in Decentralized Systems. *International Journal of Advanced Engineering, Management and Science (IJAEMS). Peer-Reviewed Journal*, *11*(1), 2454–1311. DOI: 10.22161/ijaems.111.12

Aipoh, G., Egbemhenghe, J., Ogunyankinnu, T., Francis Onotole, E., Osunkanmibi, A. A., & Adeoye, Y. (2022). Blockchain and AI synergies for effective supply chain management. *Article in International Journal of Multidisciplinary Research and Growth Evaluation*. DOI: 10.54660/.IJMRGE.2021.2.4-873-876

Akli, A., & Chougdali, K. (2025). IOTA-Assisted Self-Sovereign Identity Framework for Decentralized Authentication and Secure Data Sharing. *IEEE Access : Practical Innovations, Open Solutions*, *13*, 80191–80205. DOI: 10.1109/ACCESS.2025.3567137

Al Khaldy, M., Alshdifat, G., Almalahmeh, T., & Aldweesh, A. (2024). Blockchain as a Resilient Infrastructure for e-Business Transactions. *2024 2nd International Conference on Cyber Resilience (ICCR)*, 1–6. DOI: 10.1109/ICCR61006.2024.10532913

Alali, A. (2023). Modeling CO2 Geologic Storage Using Machine Learning. *SPE Middle East Oil and Gas Show and Conference, MEOS, Proceedings*. DOI: 10.2118/213565-MS

Alazab, M., & Alhyari, S. (2024). Industry 4.0 innovation: A systematic literature review on the role of blockchain technology in creating smart and sustainable manufacturing facilities. *Information (Basel)*, *15*(2), 78. DOI: 10.3390/info15020078

Aldweesh, A., Alshamrani, M., Almuairfi, S., & Alabdulmohsin, I. (2021). AI-based fraud detection and blockchain-powered transactions in banking. *Computers, Materials & Continua*, *69*(2), 2023–2037. DOI: 10.32604/cmc.2021.016618

Alex Preukschat, D. R. (2021). *Self-Sovereign Identity: Decentralized Digital Identity and Verifiable Credentials*. Manning Publications.

Al-Farsi, S., Rathore, M. M., & Bakiras, S. (2021). Security of Blockchain-Based Supply Chain Management Systems: Challenges and Opportunities. *Applied Sciences 2021, Vol. 11, Page 5585, 11*(12), 5585. DOI: 10.3390/app11125585

Alghamedy, F., El-Haggar, N., Alsumayt, A., Alfawaer, Z. M., Alshammari, M., Amouri, L., Aljameel, S. S., & Al-Bassam, S. (2024). Unlocking a Promising Future: Integrating Blockchain Technology and FL-IoT in the Journey to 6G. *IEEE Access : Practical Innovations, Open Solutions, 1*, 115411–115447. Advance online publication. DOI: 10.1109/ACCESS.2024.3435968

Ali Sathio Anwar, A. Mujeeb ur Rehman Shaikh, P., & Javeria Shah, P. (2021). Implementation of ETL Tool for Data Warehousing for Non-Hodgkin Lymphoma (NHL) Cancer in Public Sector, Pakistan. *LC International Journal of STEM (ISSN: 2708-7123), 2*(3), 98–102. DOI: 10.5281/ZENODO.5759519

Ali Sathio Benazir Bhutto Shaheed University Lyari Karachi. (2021). Dynamic Content Enabled Microservice for Business Applications in Distributed Cloudlet Cloud Network. *International Journal of Emerging Trends in Engineering Research, 9*(7), 1035–1039. DOI: 10.30534/ijeter/2021/32972021

Allcott, H., & Gentzkow, M. (2017). Social media and fake news in the 2016 election. *The Journal of Economic Perspectives, 31*(2), 211–236. DOI: 10.1257/jep.31.2.211

Al-okaily, A., & Tbakhi, A. (2024). A novel lossless encoding algorithm for data compression–genomics data as an exemplar. *Frontiers in Bioinformatics, 4*, 1489704. Advance online publication. DOI: 10.3389/fbinf.2024.1489704 PMID: 39917339

Alsultan, A., & Razak, F. A. (2024). *Limitations of Language Models in The Oil & Gas Upstream Operations.* Paper presented at the International Petroleum Technology Conference. DOI: 10.2523/IPTC-23649-EA

Aman, Q. (2024). Adoption of Artificial Intelligence in Accounting and its Impact on Business Performance: Oil and Gas Perspective. *Open Access Organization and Management Review, 3*(1), 66–73. DOI: 10.59644/oagmr.3(1).129

Andoni, M., Robu, V., Flynn, D., Abram, S., Geach, D., Jenkins, D., McCallum, P., & Peacock, A. (2019). Blockchain technology in the energy sector: A systematic review of challenges and opportunities. *Renewable & Sustainable Energy Reviews, 100*, 143–174. DOI: 10.1016/j.rser.2018.10.014

Anikiev, D., Birnie, C., Waheed, U., Alkhalifah, T., Gu, C., Verschuur, D. J., & Eisner, L. (2023). Machine learning in microseismic monitoring. *Earth-Science Reviews, 239*, 104371. DOI: 10.1016/j.earscirev.2023.104371

Antal, C., Cioara, T., Anghel, I., Antal, M., & Salomie, I. (2021). Distributed Ledger Technology Review and Decentralized Applications Development Guidelines. *Future Internet 2021, Vol. 13, Page 62, 13*(3), 62. DOI: 10.3390/fi13030062

Anwar, A., Ali, A., Benazir, S., Shaheed, B., Lyari, U., Bbsul, (, & Karachi,). (2021). *A Review on State of the Art in Flipped Classroom Technology A Blended E-Learning*. DOI: 10.30534/ijeter/2021/22972021

Arafat, M. S., Mirza, J. B., Jony, M. A. M., Islam, R., Rafi, S. S., Jalil, M. S., & Hossen, F. (2024). Blockchain and IoT Integration for Secure Supply Chain Operations: Unlocking Real-Time Transparency and Business Continuity. *AIJMR-Advanced International Journal of Multidisciplinary Research, 2*(6).

Arief, H. A., Wiktorski, T., & Thomas, P. J. (2021). A Survey on Distributed Fibre Optic Sensor Data Modelling Techniques and Machine Learning Algorithms for Multiphase Fluid Flow Estimation. *Sensors 2021, Vol. 21, Page 2801, 21*(8), 2801. DOI: 10.3390/s21082801

Asfha, D. T., Latiff, A. H. A., Otchere, D. A., Tackie-Otoo, B. N., Babikir, I., Rafi, M., Riyadi, Z. A., Putra, A. D., & Adeniyi, B. A. (2024). Mechanisms of sand production, prediction–a review and the potential for fiber optic technology and machine learning in monitoring. *Journal of Petroleum Exploration and Production Technology 2024 14:10, 14*(10), 2577–2616. DOI: 10.1007/s13202-024-01860-1

Ashry, I., Mao, Y., Wang, B., Hveding, F., Bukhamsin, A., Ng, T. K., & Ooi, B. S. (2022). A Review of Distributed Fiber-Optic Sensing in the Oil and Gas Industry. *Journal of Lightwave Technology*, *40*(5), 1407–1431. DOI: 10.1109/JLT.2021.3135653

Asudeh, A., Jin, Z., & Jagadish, H. V. (2020). Assessing and remedying coverage for a given dataset. In *Proceedings of the 2020 ACM SIGMOD International Conference on Management of Data* (pp. 377–392). DOI: 10.1145/3318464.3380598

Attah, R.U., Matthew, B., Garba, P., Gil-Ozoudeh, I., & Iwuanyanwu, O. (2024). Strategic frameworks for digital transformation across logistics and energy sectors: Bridging technology with business strategy. *Open Access Research Journal of Science and Technology*.12(02), 070-80.

Azieva, R. (2020). Blockchain technology as a key element of the development of the oil and gas industry. *Internetjournal «Waste and resources*(2).

Aziz, S., Ahmed, I., Khan, K., & Khalid, M. (2024). Emerging trends and approaches for designing net-zero low-carbon integrated energy networks: A review of current practices. *Arabian Journal for Science and Engineering*, *49*(5), 6163–6185. DOI: 10.1007/s13369-023-08336-0

Babaei, A., Tirkolaee, E. B., & Anka, F. (2024). Efficiency-sustainability models to assess blockchain adoption strategies with uncertainty in the oil and gas sector. *Environment, Development and Sustainability*, ●●●, 1–27. DOI: 10.1007/s10668-024-05604-3

Badshah, A., Daud, A., Alharbey, R., Banjar, A., Bukhari, A., & Alshemaimri, B. (2024). Big data applications: Overview, challenges and future. *Artificial Intelligence Review*, *57*(11), 290. DOI: 10.1007/s10462-024-10938-5

Bai, Y., Lei, H., Li, S., Gao, H., Li, J., & Li, L. (2022). Decentralized and Self-Sovereign Identity in the Era of Blockchain: A Survey. *2022 IEEE International Conference on Blockchain (Blockchain)*, 500–507. DOI: 10.1109/Blockchain55522.2022.00077

Bamakan, S. M. H., M. A., & B. A. B. (2021). Blockchain in oil and gas industry: Applications, challenges, and future trends. *Computers in Industry*, *130*, 103469.

Bamakan, S. M. H., Motavali, A., & Bondori, A. (2021). A review of blockchain-based platforms for sustainable energy and environment. *Journal of Cleaner Production*, *280*, 124461. DOI: 10.1016/j.jclepro.2020.124461

Barnabas, B., & Oloyede, J. (2024). *Cash Flow Optimization: Strategies for Enhancing Short-Term Liquidity*. DOI: 10.2139/ssrn.5004465

Bellagarda, J. S., & Abu-Mahfouz, A. M. (2022). An updated survey on the coverage of distributed ledger technology and artificial intelligence: Current state, major challenges and future direction. *IEEE Access : Practical Innovations, Open Solutions*, *10*, 50774–50793. DOI: 10.1109/ACCESS.2022.3173297

Bello, A. D., Adeoye, Y., Osunkanmibi, A. A., Onotole, E. F., Ogunyankinnu, T., Ederhion, J., & Abubakar, A. (2025). Blockchain and Global Trade: Streamlining Cross Border Transactions with Blockchain. *Article in International Journal of Multidisciplinary Research and Growth Evaluation*. DOI: 10.54660/.IJMRGE.2025.6.2.253-265

Bendiab, G., Hameurlaine, A., Germanos, G., Kolokotronis, N., & Shiaeles, S. (2023, April). Autonomous vehicles security: Challenges and solutions using blockchain and artificial intelligence. *IEEE Transactions on Intelligent Transportation Systems*, *24*(4), 3614–3637. DOI: 10.1109/TITS.2023.3236274

Benedetti, H., & Rodriguez-Garnica, G. (2023). Tokenized Assets and Securities. *The Emerald Handbook on Cryptoassets: Investment Opportunities and Challenges*, 107–121. DOI: 10.1108/978-1-80455-320-620221008

Bensonch, C., Argyropoulos, C. D., Dimopoulos, C., Mikellidou, C. V., & Boustras, G. (2022). Analysis of safety climate factors and safety compliance relationships in the oil and gas industry. *Safety Science*, *151*, 105744. DOI: 10.1016/j.ssci.2022.105744

Berger, A., Hillebrand, L., Leonhard, D., Deußer, T., De Oliveira, T. B. F., Dilmaghani, T., . . . Bauckhage, C. (2023). *Towards automated regulatory compliance verification in financial auditing with large language models.* Paper presented at the 2023 IEEE International Conference on Big Data (BigData). DOI: 10.1109/BigData59044.2023.10386518

Berkani, A.-S., Moumen, H., Benharzallah, S., Kechadi, M. T., & Bounceur, A. (2025). PrGChain: A privacy-preserving blockchain-enabled energy trading system. *Computers & Electrical Engineering*, *123*, 110289. DOI: 10.1016/j.compeleceng.2025.110289

Bilal, M., Ali, G., Iqbal, M. W., Anwar, M., Malik, M. S. A., & Kadir, R. A. (2022). Auto-Prep: Efficient and Automated Data Preprocessing Pipeline. *IEEE Access : Practical Innovations, Open Solutions*, *10*, 107764–107784. DOI: 10.1109/ACCESS.2022.3198662

Blockis, M. (2025). *The role of stakeholder engagement in business process performance.*

Bodensohn, J.-M., Brackmann, U., Vogel, L., Sanghi, A., & Binnig, C. (2025). Unveiling challenges for llms in enterprise data engineering. *arXiv preprint arXiv:2504.10950.*

Boggio Viola, A. (2024). *The Tokenization of Assets: Analysing the Emergence of a New Market Trend.*

Borade, S. A., Bansod, S., Hati, A. J., & Singh, S. K. (2025, May). AI Edge Processor Using RISC-V Instruction Set Architecture Design. In *2025 Global Conference in Emerging Technology (GINOTECH)* (pp. 1-8). IEEE. DOI: 10.1109/GINOTECH63460.2025.11076631

Boston Consulting Group. (2021). *How Digital Technologies Can Drive a Faster Energy Transition.* https://www.bcg.com

Boukredera, F. S., Hadjadj, A., Youcefi, M. R., & Ouadi, H. (2025). AI-Driven Optimization of Drilling Performance Through Torque Management Using Machine Learning and Differential Evolution. *Processes (Basel, Switzerland)*, *13*(5), 1472. DOI: 10.3390/pr13051472

Brennan, B., & Schafer, L. (n.d.). *Harness Oil and Gas Big Data with Analytics Wiley & SAS Business Series*. Retrieved August 15, 2025, from https://books.google.com/books/about/Harness_Oil_and_Gas_Big_Data_with_Analyt.html?id=imdiAwAAQBAJ

Burger, M., Taken, K., Smith, S. L. M., & Wood, J. (n.d.). An Examination of Fraud Risk at Oil and Gas Companies. *Journal of Forensic & Investigative Accounting*, *14*(1).

Butcher, A., Hudson, T., Baird, A., & Mellors, R. (2020). DAS Preprocessing Workflow. *18*. https://norceresearch.brage.unit.no/norceresearch-xmlui/handle/11250/3069183

Butcher, A., Zhou, W., Vandeweijer, V., Lapins, S., Kendall, J.-M., Boullenger, B., Paap, B., Broman, B., Stork, A., & Macquet, M. (2022). Monitoring CO2 injection at CAMI FRS using Distributed Acoustic Sensing networks. SSRN *Electronic Journal*. https://doi.org/DOI: 10.2139/SSRN.4286315

Campanella, F., Serino, L., Battisti, E., Giakoumelou, A., & Karasamani, I. (2023). FinTech in the financial system: Towards a capital-intensive and high competence human capital reality? *Journal of Business Research*, *155*, 113376. DOI: 10.1016/j.jbusres.2022.113376

Carpentieri, B. (2025). Data Compression with a Time Limit. *Algorithms 2025, Vol. 18, Page 135, 18*(3), 135. DOI: 10.3390/a18030135

Casino, F., Dasaklis, T. K., & Patsakis, C. (2019). A systematic literature review of blockchain-based applications: Current status, classification and open issues. *Telematics and Informatics*, *36*, 55–81. DOI: 10.1016/j.tele.2018.11.006

Cath, C., Wachter, S., Mittelstadt, B., Taddeo, M., & Floridi, L. (2018). Artificial intelligence and the 'good society': The US, EU, and UK approach. *Science and Engineering Ethics*, *24*(2), 505–528. DOI: 10.1007/s11948-017-9901-7 PMID: 28353045

Chai, S., Zhang, X., Abedin, M. Z., Chen, H., Lucey, B., & Hajek, P. (2023). An optimized GRT model with blockchain digital smart contracts for power generation enterprises. *Energy Economics*, *128*, 107153. DOI: 10.1016/j.eneco.2023.107153

Chanda, P., Singh, P., Kumar, M., & Bhardwaj, V. (2024). Enhancing Employee Onboarding throughBlockchain-Based Identity Verification in HRManagement. *International Journal of Information Engineering and Electronic Business*, *16*(6), 29–41. DOI: 10.5815/ijieeb.2024.06.03

Chandio, S. A., Mahar, J. A., & Shaikh, M. U. R. (2017). Gadget improved security alert monitoring, management and mitigation system to control the crowded occasions. *ICIEECT 2017 - International Conference on Innovations in Electrical Engineering and Computational Technologies 2017, Proceedings*. DOI: 10.1109/ICIEECT.2017.7916557

Chang, V., Baudier, P., Zhang, H., Xu, Q., Zhang, J., & Arami, M. (2020). How Blockchain can impact financial services – The overview, challenges and recommendations from expert interviewees. *Technological Forecasting and Social Change*, *158*, 120166. DOI: 10.1016/j.techfore.2020.120166

Chan, W., Gai, K., Yu, J., & Zhu, L. (2025). Blockchain-Assisted Self-Sovereign Identities on Education: A Survey. *Blockchains*, *3*(1), 3. DOI: 10.3390/blockchains3010003

Chen, F., Sun, L., Jian, S., Huo, X., Pan, X., Feng, C., & Zhang, Z. (2025). A Review of AI Applications in Unconventional Oil and Gas Exploration and Development [Review of A Review of AI Applications in Unconventional Oil and Gas Exploration and Development]. Energies, 18(2), 391. Multidisciplinary Digital Publishing Institute. DOI: 10.3390/en18020391

Chen, Y., Cui, Y., & Wu, J. (2019). Image Restoration of Agricultural History Based on Neural Patch Synthesis. *2019 IEEE 11th International Conference on Communication Software and Networks (ICCSN)*, 401–405. DOI: 10.1109/ICCSN.2019.8905400

Chen, G.. (2018). *Exploring blockchain technology and its potential applications for education*. Smart Learning Environments., DOI: 10.1186/s40561-017-0050-x

Cheng, L., Liu, F., & Yao, D. D. (2017). Enterprise data breach: Causes, challenges, prevention, and future directions. *Wiley Interdisciplinary Reviews. Data Mining and Knowledge Discovery*, *7*(5), e1211. DOI: 10.1002/widm.1211

Chen, L., Baird, A., & Straub, D. (2022). The impact of hierarchical privilege levels and non-hierarchical incentives on continued contribution in online Q&A communities: A motivational model of gamification goals. *Decision Support Systems*, *153*, 113667. DOI: 10.1016/j.dss.2021.113667

Chen, M., Tang, J., Zhu, D., & Hill, A. (2022). Classification and Localization of Fracture-Hit Events in Low-Frequency Distributed Acoustic Sensing Strain Rate with Convolutional Neural Networks. *SPE Journal*, *27*(2), 1341–1353. DOI: 10.2118/205136-PA

Chen, S., You, H., Xu, J., Wei, M., Xu, T., & Wang, H. (2024). *Leakage monitoring of carbon dioxide injection well string using distributed optical fiber sensor.* Petroleum Research., DOI: 10.1016/j.ptlrs.2024.08.003

Chen, W., Men, Y., Fuster, N., Osorio, C., & Juan, A. A. (2024). Artificial intelligence in logistics optimization with sustainable criteria: A review. *Sustainability (Basel)*, *16*(21), 9145. DOI: 10.3390/su16219145

Choubey, S., & Karmakar, G. (2021). Artificial intelligence techniques and their application in oil and gas industry. *Artificial Intelligence Review*, *54*(5), 3665–3683. DOI: 10.1007/s10462-020-09935-1

Choudhary, A., Pawar, S., & Haribhakta, Y. (2025). Efficient Malware Detection with Optimized Learning on High-Dimensional Features. DOI: 10.1109/ISAC364032.2025.11156575

Chourasiya, R., & Malviya, R. K. (2025). Unlocking Circular Potential and Empowering Circularity: Paving the Path for Circular Supply Chain Enablement in Indian Textile Industries. *Business Strategy and the Environment*, *34*(7), 9441–9462. Advance online publication. DOI: 10.1002/bse.70081

Chowdhury, M. T. A., & Islam, M. A. (1 C.E.). Blockchain Synergies With the Internet of Everything (IoE). Https://Services.Igi-Global.Com/Resolvedoi/Resolve.Aspx?Doi=10.4018/979-8-3373-1424-2.Ch001, 1–38. DOI: 10.4018/979-8-3373-1424-2.ch001

Chowdhury, M. T. A., & Islam, M. A. (2025). Blockchain Synergies With the Internet of Everything (IoE). In *Convergence of Blockchain, Internet of Everything, and Federated Learning for Security* (pp. 1-38): IGI Global Scientific Publishing.

Conti, M., Dehghantanha, A., Franke, K., & Watson, S. (2018). Internet of Things security and forensics: Challenges and opportunities. *Future Generation Computer Systems*, *78*, 544–546. DOI: 10.1016/j.future.2017.07.060

Cordes, E. E., Jones, D. O. B., Schlacher, T. A., Amon, D. J., Bernardino, A. F., Brooke, S., Carney, R., DeLeo, D. M., Dunlop, K. M., Escobar-Briones, E. G., Gates, A. R., Génio, L., Gobin, J., Henry, L. A., Herrera, S., Hoyt, S., Joye, M., Kark, S., Mestre, N. C., & Witte, U. (2016). Environmental impacts of the deep-water oil and gas industry: A review to guide management strategies. *Frontiers in Environmental Science*, *4*(SEP), 207190. DOI: 10.3389/fenvs.2016.00058

Crawford, K., & Calo, R. (2016). There is a blind spot in AI research. *Nature*, *538*(7625), 311–313. DOI: 10.1038/538311a PMID: 27762391

Cucko, S., & Turkanovic, M. (2021). Decentralized and Self-Sovereign Identity: Systematic Mapping Study. *IEEE Access : Practical Innovations, Open Solutions*, *9*, 139009–139027. DOI: 10.1109/ACCESS.2021.3117588

Cui, L., Gao, M., Dai, J., & Mou, J. (2022). Improving supply chain collaboration through operational excellence approaches: An IoT perspective. *Industrial Management & Data Systems*, *122*(3), 565–591. DOI: 10.1108/IMDS-01-2020-0016

Cynthia Onukwulu, E., Efekpogua Fiemotongha, J., Ngochindo Igwe, A., Paul-Mikki Ewim, C., & Author, C. (2025). The Role of Blockchain and AI in the Future of Energy Trading: A Technological Perspective on Transforming the Oil & Gas Industry by 2025. *Int. j. Adv. Multidisc. Res. Stud*, *5*(2), 48–65. DOI: 10.62225/2583049X.2025.5.2.3809

Dara, T. J. N. C. (2025). A Trust Policy Meta-Model for Trustworthy Interoperability. *Procedia Computer Science*.

Das, S., Dey, A., Pal, A., & Roy, N. (2023). Applications of Artificial Intelligence in Machine Learning: Review and prospect. *International Journal of Computer Applications*, *115*(9), 31–41. DOI: 10.5120/20182-2402

De Filippi, P. (2016). The interplay between decentralization and privacy: the case of blockchain technologies. *Technologies. Journal of Peer Production*. https://hal.science/hal-01382006v1

De Filippi, P., & Wright, A. (2018). *Blockchain and the law: The rule of code*. Harvard University Press.

De Mauro, A., Greco, M., & Grimaldi, M. (2016). A formal definition of Big Data based on its essential features. *Library Review*, *65*(3), 122–135. DOI: 10.1108/LR-06-2015-0061

Deshpande, A. V. (2025). *Enhancing Cross-Border Payment Efficiency with Stablecoins: Reducing Costs and Settlement Delays*. DOI: 10.2139/ssrn.5337435

Dev, N. K., Shankar, R., & Qaiser, F. H. (2020). Industry 4.0 and circular economy: Operational excellence for sustainable reverse supply chain performance. *Resources, Conservation and Recycling, 153*, 104583. DOI: 10.1016/j.resconrec.2019.104583

Dhayal, K. S., Giri, A. K., Esposito, L., & Agrawal, S. (2023). Mapping the significance of green venture capital for sustainable development: A systematic review and future research agenda. *Journal of Cleaner Production, 396*, 136489. DOI: 10.1016/j.jclepro.2023.136489

Di Silvestre, M. L., Gallo, P., Luna, A. C., Sanseverino, E. R., & Zobaa, A. F. (2020). Blockchain for power systems: Current trends and future applications. *Renewable & Sustainable Energy Reviews, 119*, 109585. DOI: 10.1016/j.rser.2019.109585

*Distributed Acoustic Sensing | EarthScope Consortium*. (n.d.). Retrieved July 17, 2025, from https://www.earthscope.org/what-is/das/

Dong, B., Tribaldos, V. R., Xing, X., Byna, S., Ajo-Franklin, J., & Wu, K. (2020). DASSA: Parallel das Data Storage and Analysis for Subsurface Event Detection. *Proceedings - 2020 IEEE 34th International Parallel and Distributed Processing Symposium, IPDPS 2020*, 254–263. DOI: 10.1109/IPDPS47924.2020.00035

Dong, B., Popescu, A., Tribaldos, V. R., Byna, S., Ajo-Franklin, J., & Wu, K. (2022). Real-time and post-hoc compression for data from Distributed Acoustic Sensing. *Computers & Geosciences, 166*, 105181. DOI: 10.1016/j.cageo.2022.105181

Dong, Z., Yan, X., Zhang, J., Chen, Z., & Ma, H. (2025). Reservoir Characterization of Tight Sandstone Gas Reservoirs: A Case Study from the He 8 Member of the Shihezi Formation, Tianhuan Depression, Ordos Basin. *Processes (Basel, Switzerland), 13*(5), 1355. DOI: 10.3390/pr13051355

Doshi-Velez, F., & Kim, B. (2017). Towards a rigorous science of interpretable machine learning. arXiv preprint arXiv:1702.08608. https://arxiv.org/abs/1702.08608

Dragnoiu, A. E. & Olimid, R. F. (2024). *Towards an identity management solution on Arweave*.

Dubovitskaya, A., Xu, Z., Ryu, S., Schumacher, M., & Wang, F. (2018). Secure and trustable electronic medical records sharing using blockchain. *AMIA Annual Symposium Proceedings*, 650–659.

Durán, C., Yazdi, A. K., Derpich, I., & Tan, Y. (2024). Leveraging blockchain for maritime port supply chain management through multicriteria decision making. *Mathematics, 12*(10), 1511. DOI: 10.3390/math12101511

Du, S., Huang, Z., Jin, L., & Wan, X. (2024). Recent Progress in Data-Driven Intelligent Modeling and Optimization Algorithms for Industrial Processes. *Algorithms*, *17*(12), 569. DOI: 10.3390/a17120569

Dutta, S. K. (2020). Smart Contracts. *The Definitive Guide to Blockchain for Accounting and Business: Understanding the Revolutionary Technology*, 61–78. DOI: 10.1108/978-1-78973-865-020201005

Ebrahimi, S. M., Koh, S. C. L., Genovese, A., & Kumar, N. (2018). Structure-integration relationships in oil and gas supply chains. *International Journal of Operations & Production Management*, *38*(2), 424–445. DOI: 10.1108/IJOPM-02-2016-0089

Eckroth, J., Gipson, M., Boden, J., Hough, L., Elliott, J., & Quintana, J. (2023). Answering Natural Language Questions with OpenAI's GPT in the Petroleum Industry. Paper presented at the *SPE Annual Technical Conference and Exhibition*.

Egbumokei, P. I., Dienagha, I. N., Digitemie, W. N., Onukwulu, E. C., & Oladipo, O. T. (2024). The role of digital transformation in enhancing sustainability in oil and gas business operations. *International Journal of Multidisciplinary Research and Growth Evaluation*, *5*(5), 2582–7138. DOI: 10.54660/.IJMRGE.2024.5.5.1029-1041

Egelund-Müller, B., Elsman, M., Henglein, F., & Ross, O. (2017). Automated Execution of Financial Contracts on Blockchains. *Business & Information Systems Engineering*, *59*(6), 457–467. DOI: 10.1007/s12599-017-0507-z

El Khatib, , MAl Hammadi, , AOraby, , KAl Hamar, , A. (2023). A Functional vs Projectized approach in Oil and Gas Industry: The added value of Projectized approach. [IJTOP]. *International Journal of Theory of Organization and Practice*, *3*(2), 197–209.

Enemosah, A. & Chukwunweike, J. (2022). *Next-Generation SCADA Architectures for Enhanced Field Automation and Real-Time Remote Control in Oil and Gas Fields*. 514–529. DOI: 10.7753/IJCATR1112.1018

English, J. M., & English, K. L. (2022). An overview of carbon capture and storage and its potential role in the energy transition. *First Break*, *40*(4), 35–40. DOI: 10.3997/1365-2397.fb2022028

European Commission. (2020). *Clean Energy for All Europeans Package*. https://energy.ec.europa.eu

Faccia, A., & Petratos, P. (2021). Blockchain, Enterprise Resource Planning (ERP) and Accounting Information Systems (AIS): Research on e-Procurement and System Integration. *Applied Sciences 2021, Vol. 11, Page 6792, 11*(15), 6792. DOI: 10.3390/app11156792

Fang, J., Feng, T., Guo, X., & Wang, X. (2024). Privacy-enhanced distributed revocable identity management scheme based self-sovereign identity. *Journal of Cloud Computing (Heidelberg, Germany), 13*(1), 154. DOI: 10.1186/s13677-024-00715-8

Farooqi, A., Das, D., Tripathi, M., Dutta, R., Goyal, N. K., & Sheikh, M. F. (2026). Navigating Ethical Frontiers in AI-Driven Geriatric Care. In Stolakis, K., & Efthymiou, I. (Eds.), *AI for Geriatric Care in an Aging Society: Ethical, Clinical, and Policy Challenges* (pp. 243–266). IGI Global Scientific Publishing., DOI: 10.4018/979-8-3373-5462-0.ch009

Farshidi, S., Jansen, S., Espana, S., & Verkleij, J. (2020). Decision Support for Blockchain Platform Selection: Three Industry Case Studies. *IEEE Transactions on Engineering Management, 67*(4), 1109–1128. DOI: 10.1109/TEM.2019.2956897

Fatorachian, H., Kazemi, H., & Pawar, K. S. (2025). Digital Technologies in Food Supply Chain Waste Management: A Case Study on Sustainable Practices in Smart Cities. *Sustainability (Basel), 17*(5), 1996. DOI: 10.3390/su17051996

Fejjari, A., Delavault, A., Camilleri, R., & Valentino, G. (2025). A Review of Anomaly Detection in Spacecraft Telemetry Data [Review of A Review of Anomaly Detection in Spacecraft Telemetry Data]. Applied Sciences, 15(10), 5653. Multidisciplinary Digital Publishing Institute. DOI: 10.3390/app15105653

Finck, M. (2019). Blockchain and the General Data Protection Regulation: Can distributed ledgers be squared with European data protection law? European Parliamentary Research Service. https://www.europarl.europa.eu/thinktank

Floridi, L. (2019). *The logic of information: A theory of philosophy as conceptual design*. Oxford University Press. DOI: 10.1093/oso/9780198833635.001.0001

Gajjar, T., Parikh, S., & Shekokar, K. (2025). *Integrating blockchain technology with AI to enhance security measure*. Paper presented at the IET Conference Proceedings CP920.

Gamal, H., Omotunde, O., Duarte, M., Mohamed, O., & Elkatatny, S. (2024). *How complex lithology schemes affect drilling rate prediction: machine learning study*. Paper presented at the International Petroleum Technology Conference. DOI: 10.2523/IPTC-23898-MS

Gamso, J., Inkpen, A., & Ramaswamy, K. (2024). Managing geopolitical risks: The global oil and gas industry plays a winning game. *The Journal of Business Strategy*, *45*(3), 190–198. DOI: 10.1108/JBS-04-2023-0081

Ganesh, P. R., Kelley, M., Tamrakar, S., Hill, B., Schuetter, J., Tribaldos, V. R., & Omosebi, O. (2022). *Machine Learning-Based, Near Real-time Leakage Detection for Caprock Integrity Monitoring using Distributed Acoustic Sensing (DAS) Data from Carbon Capture and Sequestration (CCS) Operations*. https://ssrn.com/abstract=4281129

Gao, S., Wang, X., Xia, Z., Zhang, H., Yu, J., & Yang, F. (2025). Artificial Intelligence in Dentistry: A Narrative Review of Diagnostic and Therapeutic Applications [Review of Artificial Intelligence in Dentistry: A Narrative Review of Diagnostic and Therapeutic Applications]. Medical Science Monitor, 31. International Scientific Information Inc. DOI: 10.12659/MSM.946676

Gardas, B. B., Raut, R. D., & Narkhede, B. (2019). Determinants of sustainable supply chain management: A case study from the oil and gas supply chain. *Sustainable Production and Consumption*, *17*, 241–253. DOI: 10.1016/j.spc.2018.11.005

Garzali Qabasiyu, M., Ahmed Zayyad, M., & Abdullahi, S. (2023). Systematic Literature Review on Sentence Level Sentiment Analysis. [IJMRAP]. *International Journal of Multidisciplinary Research and Publications*, *6*(5), 1–8. http://scholars.google.com/

Garzon, S. R., Yildiz, H., & Kupper, A. (2022). Decentralized Identifiers and Self-Sovereign Identity in 6G. *IEEE Network*, *36*(4), 142–148. DOI: 10.1109/MNET.009.2100736

Ghadge, N. (2024). Analyzing the Role of Blockchain in Identity and Access Management Systems. SSRN *Electronic Journal*. https://doi.org/DOI: 10.2139/SSRN.4872028

Ghinadya, N., & Suyanto, S. (2020). Synonyms-Based Augmentation to Improve Fake News Detection using Bidirectional LSTM. DOI: 10.1109/ICoICT49345.2020.9166230

Ghoddusi, H., Moghaddam, H., & Wirl, F. (2022). Going downstream – An economical option for oil and gas exporting countries? *Energy Policy*, *161*, 112487. DOI: 10.1016/j.enpol.2021.112487

Gonen, L. D., Tavor, T., & Spiegel, U. (2024). Unlocking Market Potential: Strategic Consumer Segmentation and Dynamic Pricing for Balancing Loyalty and Deal Seeking. *Mathematics*, *12*(21), 3364. DOI: 10.3390/math12213364

Gong, J., Yan, P., Zhang, Y., An, H., & Liu, L. (2024). Blockchain Meets LLMs: A Living Survey on Bidirectional Integration. *arXiv preprint arXiv:2411.16809.*

Google, A. I. (2019). *Federated Learning: Collaborative Machine Learning without Centralized Training Data.* https://ai.googleblog.com/2017/04/federated-learning-collaborative.html

Goyal, N. K. (2025). Security and Privacy in IoT, Fog, and Blockchain Networks. In Sathio, A., Rind, M., Awan, S., & Junejo, A. (Eds.), *Energy-Efficient Deep Learning Approaches in IoT, Fog, and Green Blockchain Revolution* (pp. 371–398). IGI Global Scientific Publishing., DOI: 10.4018/979-8-3373-0300-0.ch015

Goyal, N. K. (2025). Weaponizing Misinformation and Cyberattacks on Supply Chains. In Bukhari, S., & Zafar, I. (Eds.), *Mass Media and Impact of Fake News on Supply Chains* (pp. 177–210). IGI Global Scientific Publishing., DOI: 10.4018/979-8-3373-2175-2.ch007

Goyal, N. K., Dandotiya, M., Kumari, M., Kaloria, S., & Anushya, A. (2025). AI-Powered Haptic Devices for Patient Rehabilitation. In Mamodiya, U., Kalam, A., Bossoufi, B., Awad, M., & Somwanshi, D. (Eds.), *Integrating AI With Haptic Systems for Smarter Healthcare Solutions* (pp. 143–170). IGI Global Scientific Publishing., DOI: 10.4018/979-8-3373-2307-7.ch007

Goyal, N. K., Dandotiya, M., Kumari, M., Sheikh, M. F., & Sharma, S. (2025). Emerging Job Roles in the Tourism Sector Leveraging Artificial Intelligence. In Silic, M., Luthia, M., Ahmad, F., & Chakraborty, P. (Eds.), *Empowering Sustainable Performance and Competitive Advantage in Tourism* (pp. 89–126). IGI Global Scientific Publishing., DOI: 10.4018/979-8-3373-4546-8.ch004

Goyal, N. K., Dandotiya, M., Qurashi, J. A., Kumari, M., & Sharma, S. (2025). AI-Driven Predictive Analytics for Disease Management. In Ouaissa, M., Ouaissa, M., Imad, M., Qurashi, J., & Farooq, M. (Eds.), *Utilizing AI of Medical Things for Healthcare Security and Sustainability* (pp. 231–276). IGI Global Scientific Publishing., DOI: 10.4018/979-8-3373-0690-2.ch008

Goyal, N. K., Kumari, M., Kushwah, V., Dandotiya, M., & Vijay, A. (2025). Evaluating blockchain security: Trade-offs in consensus mechanisms. *IET Conference Proceedings*, 2024(38), 80–88. DOI: 10.1049/icp.2025.0775

Gumut, G., Umar, B. U., Abdullahi, I. M., Ajao, L. A., Olaniyi, O. M., & Adeniyi, S. (2024). *A Real-Time Secure-Based Oil and Gas Supply Chain Management using Blockchain.* Paper presented at the 2024 IEEE 5th International Conference on Electro-Computing Technologies for Humanity (NIGERCON). DOI: 10.1109/NIGERCON62786.2024.10927207

Hader, M., Tchoffa, D., El Mhamedi, A., Ghodous, P., Dolgui, A., & Abouabdellah, A. (2022). Applying integrated Blockchain and Big Data technologies to improve supply chain traceability and information sharing in the textile sector. *Journal of Industrial Information Integration*, *28*, 100345. DOI: 10.1016/j.jii.2022.100345

Hasan, K. M. B., Sajid, M., Lapina, M. A., Shahid, M., & Kotecha, K. (2024). Blockchain technology meets 6 G wireless networks: A systematic survey. *Alexandria Engineering Journal*, *92*, 199–220. DOI: 10.1016/j.aej.2024.02.031

Hassani, H., Huang, X., & Silva, E. (2018). Big-crypto: Big data, blockchain and cryptocurrency. *Big Data and Cognitive Computing*, *2*(4), 34. DOI: 10.3390/bdcc2040034

Hassani, M., Bazaeeand, G., & Shahmansouri, A. (2020). Identifying Blockchain Technology Maturity's Levels in the Oil and Gas Industry. *Petroleum Business Review*, *4*(3), 43–61. DOI: 10.22050/PBR.2020.256181.1138

Hassan, M. F., Akbar, R., Ullah, R., Savita, K., Rehman, U., & Yalli, J. S. (2024). Pre-Encryption Ransomware Detection (PERD) Taxonomy, and Research Directions: Systematic Literature Review. *International Journal of Advanced Computer Science and Applications*, *15*(9).

Hassan, M. U., Rehmani, M. H., & Chen, J. (2019). Privacy preservation in blockchain-based IoT systems: Integration issues, prospects, challenges, and future research directions. *Future Generation Computer Systems*, *97*, 512–529. DOI: 10.1016/j.future.2019.02.060

Hassija, V., Chamola, V., Gupta, V., Jain, S., & Guizani, N. (2021). A Survey on Supply Chain Security: Application Areas, Security Threats, and Solution Architectures. *IEEE Internet of Things Journal*, *8*(8), 6222–6246. DOI: 10.1109/JIOT.2020.3025775

HASSOUNI, L. EL, & OUCHEKKIR, A. (2024). Revolutionizing Financial Markets: The Role of Distributed Ledger Technology in Payments, Clearing, and Settlements. *International Journal of Accounting Finance Auditing Management and Economics*, *5*(10), 198–226. DOI: 10.5281/zenodo.13907838

Hosmer, D. W., Lemeshow, S., & Sturdivant, R. X. (2013). *Applied logistic regression* (3rd ed.). Wiley., DOI: 10.1002/9781118548387

Hossain, M. D., Faruk, M. I., Plabon, F. W., & Jyoti, J. S.Mohammad Didar Hossain-Md Imtiaz FarukFatin Wahab PlabonJeba Sadia Jyoti. (2025). Sustainable Supply Chain Project Management: Strategies for Reducing Carbon Footprints. *Journal of Business and Management Studies*, *7*(2), 78–90. DOI: 10.32996/jbms.2025.7.2.7

Hu, J., Wang, X., Shao, F., & Jiang, Q. (2020). TSPR: Deep network-based blind image quality assessment using two-side pseudo reference images. *Digital Signal Processing*, *106*, 102849. DOI: 10.1016/j.dsp.2020.102849

Hussain, M. I., Bhuiyan, M. K. I., Sumon, S. A., Akter, S., Hossain, M. I., & Akther, A. (2024). Enhancing Data Integrity and Traceability in Industry Cyber Physical Systems (ICPS) through Blockchain Technology: A Comprehensive Approach. *Advances in Artificial Intelligence and Machine Learning*, *4*(4), 2883–2907. DOI: 10.54364/AAIML.2024.44168

IBM. (2020). *TenneT and IBM Use Blockchain to Balance the Power Grid*. Retrieved from https://www.ibm.com

Ibrahim Shelash, S., & Ibrahim Al-Daoud, K. (2025). Impact of crude oil price volatility on procurement and inventory strategies in the Middle East International Journal of Energy Economics and Policy Impact of Crude Oil Price Volatility on Procurement and Inventory Strategies in the Middle East. *International Journal of Energy Economics and Policy*, *15*(2), 715–727. DOI: 10.32479/ijeep.18950

Idris, M. A., & Alsultan, H. (2023). *Smart knowledge submission system based on natural language processing (NLP) leveraging on language modelling approach.* Paper presented at the SPE Gas & Oil Technology Showcase and Conference.

IEA. (2021). *Digitalization and Energy*. International Energy Agency. https://www.iea.org/reports/digitalisation-and-energy

Ilesanmi, A. E., & Ilesanmi, T. O. (2021). Methods for image denoising using convolutional neural network: A review. *Complex & Intelligent Systems*, *7*(5), 2179–2198. DOI: 10.1007/s40747-021-00428-4

Imbwaga, J. L., Chittaragi, N., & Koolagudi, S. G. (2022). Fake news detection using machine learning algorithms. In *Proceedings of the 2022 Fourteenth International Conference on Contemporary Computing*. DOI: 10.1145/3549206.3549256

Ioannou, I., & Demirel, G. (2022). *Blockchain and supply chain finance: a critical literature review at the intersection of operations, finance and law. 6*, 83–107. DOI: 10.1007/s42786-022-00040-1

Islam, M. J., Pathan, M. N., Rahman, A., Islam, S., Sultana, A., & Das, S. C. "Priority-based Traceability in Crude Oil Refined Products Supply Chain Through Blockchain." In *2024 6th International Conference on Sustainable Technologies for Industry 5.0 (STI)*, pp. 1-6. IEEE, 2024. DOI: 10.1109/STI64222.2024.10951058

ISO. (2023). Information technology—Artificial Intelligence—Overview of trustworthiness in AI. International Organization for Standardization. https://www.iso.org

Javed, I. T., Alharbi, F., Margaria, T., Crespi, N., & Qureshi, K. N. (2021). PETchain: A Blockchain-Based Privacy Enhancing Technology. *IEEE Access : Practical Innovations, Open Solutions*, *9*, 41129–41143. DOI: 10.1109/ACCESS.2021.3064896

Jehad, R., & Yousif, S. A. (2020). Fake news classification using random forest and decision tree (J48). *Al-Nahrain Journal of Science*, *23*, 49–55. DOI: 10.22401/ANJS.23.4.09

Ji, Z., Yu, T., Xu, Y., Lee, N., Ishii, E., & Fung, P. (2023). *Towards mitigating LLM hallucination via self reflection.* Paper presented at the Findings of the Association for Computational Linguistics: EMNLP 2023. DOI: 10.18653/v1/2023.findings-emnlp.123

Jin, Y., Li, C., Fan, P., Liu, P., Li, X., Liu, C., & Qiu, W. (2025). LLM-BSCVM: An LLM-Based Blockchain Smart Contract Vulnerability Management Framework. *arXiv preprint arXiv:2505.17416.*

Jolly, A., & Kumar, S. (2022). Fake news detection in different applications: State-of-the-art and future directions. *Research Square*. DOI: 10.21203/rs.3.rs-2024922/v1

Jovita Nsoh. (2021). *Energy transitions and the energy workforce part 2.*

Jung, H., Subban, C. V., McTigue, J. D., Martinez, J. J., Copping, A. E., Osorio, J., Liu, J., & Deng, Z. D. (2022). Extracting energy from ocean thermal and salinity gradients to power unmanned underwater vehicles: State of the art, current limitations, and future outlook. *Renewable & Sustainable Energy Reviews*, *160*, 112283. DOI: 10.1016/j.rser.2022.112283

Jurafsky, D., & Martin, J. H. (2024). Speech and language processing (3rd ed. draft). Retrieved from https://web.stanford.edu/ jurafsky/slp3/

Kaliyar, R. K. (2020). Fake News Detection Using A Deep. *Neural Networks*. Advance online publication. DOI: 10.1109/CCAA.2020.8777343

Kaluvakuri, S., & Amin, R. (2018). From Paper Trails to Digital Success: The Evolution of E-Accounting. *Asian Accounting and Auditing Advancement, 9*(1).

Kanka, V. (2024). *Scaling Big Data: Leveraging LLMs for Enterprise Success.* Libertatem Media Private Limited.

Kaplan, A., & Haenlein, M. (2019). Siri, Siri, in my hand: Who's the fairest in the land? On the interpretations, illustrations, and implications of artificial intelligence. *Business Horizons*, *62*(1), 15–25. DOI: 10.1016/j.bushor.2018.08.004

Karisma, K., & Moslemzadeh Tehrani, P. (2023). Blockchain: Legal and Regulatory Issues. *Lecture Notes in Energy*, *98*, 75–118. DOI: 10.1007/978-3-031-30697-6_4

Kasych, A., Yakovenko, Y., & Tarasenko, I. (2019, September). *Optimization of business processes with the use of industrial digitalization. In 2019 ieee international conference on modern electrical and energy systems (mees).* IEEE.

Kelvin Chima, O., Orobosa Ikponmwoba, S., Jacqueline Ezeilo, O., Monday Ojonugwa, B., Olumuyiwa Adesuyi, M., & Author, C. (2020). Advances in Cash Liquidity Optimization and Cross-Border Treasury Strategy in Sub-Saharan Energy Firms. *Journal of Frontiers in Multidisciplinary Research.* DOI: 10.54660/.IJFMR.2020.1.1.44-56

Kesarwani, S., Chauhan, S. S., & Nair, A. R. (2020). Fake News Detection on Social Media using K-Nearest Neighbor Classifier. DOI: 10.1109/ICACCE49060.2020.9154997

Khan, N., Hossain, S., Khadka, U., & Sarkar, S. (2024). Blockchain in Supply Chain Management: Enhancing Transparency, Efficiency, and Trust. *AIJMR-Advanced International Journal of Multidisciplinary Research, 2*(5).

Khanam, Z., Alwasel, B. N., Sirafi, H., & Rashid, M. (2021). Fake news detection using machine learning approaches. *IOP Conference Series. Materials Science and Engineering*, *1099*(1), 012040. DOI: 10.1088/1757-899X/1099/1/012040

Khan, D., Jung, L. T., & Hashmani, M. A. (2021). Systematic literature review of challenges in blockchain scalability. *Applied Sciences (Basel, Switzerland)*, *11*(20), 9372. DOI: 10.3390/app11209372

Khan, M., & Salah, K. (2018). IoT security: Review, blockchain solutions, and open challenges. *Future Generation Computer Systems*, *82*, 395–411. DOI: 10.1016/j.future.2017.11.022

Khurram, M., Wu, C., Muhammad, S. M., Kishnani, H., An, K. R., Abeywardena, K., Chadha, U., & Behdinan, K. (2025). Artificial Intelligence in Manufacturing Industry Worker Safety: A New Paradigm for Hazard Prevention and Mitigation. *Processes (Basel, Switzerland)*, *13*(5), 1312. DOI: 10.3390/pr13051312

Kim, G. W., Kim, T. H., Lee, J., & Lee, K. S. (2018). Coupled Geomechanical-Flow Assessment of CO2 Leakage through Heterogeneous Caprock during CCS. *Advances in Civil Engineering*, *2018*(1), 1474320. Advance online publication. DOI: 10.1155/2018/1474320

Kim, J., Choi, M., Lee, C., Woo, J., & Hong, J. W.-K. (2023). Service Applicable Blockchain-based Self-Sovereign Identity Management System. *2023 IEEE International Conference on Blockchain and Cryptocurrency (ICBC)*, 1–5. DOI: 10.1109/ICBC56567.2023.10174875

Kishnani, U., Madabhushi, S., & Das, S. (2023, July). Blockchain in oil and gas supply chain: a literature review from user security and privacy perspective. In *International Symposium on Human Aspects of Information Security and Assurance* (pp. 296-309). Cham: Springer Nature Switzerland. DOI: 10.1007/978-3-031-38530-8_24

Klems, M., Eberhardt, J., Tai, S., Härtlein, S., Buchholz, S., & Tidjani, A. (2017). Trustless intermediation in blockchain-based decentralized service marketplaces. *Lecture Notes in Computer Science (Including Subseries Lecture Notes in Artificial Intelligence and Lecture Notes in Bioinformatics), 10601 LNCS*, 731–739. https://doi.org/DOI: 10.1007/978-3-319-69035-3_53/FIGURES/2

Ko, T., Lee, J., & Ryu, D. (2018). Blockchain Technology and Manufacturing Industry: Real-Time Transparency and Cost Savings. *Sustainability 2018, Vol. 10, Page 4274, 10*(11), 4274. DOI: 10.3390/su10114274

Kostadimas, D., Kasapakis, V., & Kotis, K. (2025). A Systematic Review on the Combination of VR, IoT and AI Technologies, and Their Integration in Applications [Review of A Systematic Review on the Combination of VR, IoT and AI Technologies, and Their Integration in Applications]. Future Internet, 17(4), 163. Multidisciplinary Digital Publishing Institute. DOI: 10.3390/fi17040163

Kozman, J., Lowery, S., & Lamb, J. (2024). End-to-End Workflow for Managing Large Volume Data from CCUS. *Society of Petroleum Engineers - SPE/AAPG/SEG Carbon, Capture, Utilization, and Storage Conference and Exhibition. CCUS, 2024.* Advance online publication. DOI: 10.15530/ccus-2024-4014747

Krishna, V. V. (n.d.) Economic development of Tamil Nadu (1956-2025): agricultural transformation, industrialization, rise of the service sector, infrastructure development, and the state's role in exports-an overview.

Ktari, J., Frikha, T., Hsairi, M. M., Lakhal, I. B., Naifar, F., & Bouaziz, A. (2024, May). Development of a Decentralized Application for Managing Food Supply Chain Based on Blockchain. In *2024 IEEE 4th International Maghreb Meeting of the Conference on Sciences and Techniques of Automatic Control and Computer Engineering (MI-STA)* (pp. 36-40). IEEE. DOI: 10.1109/MI-STA61267.2024.10599659

Kuang, L., Liu, H., Ren, Y., Luo, K., Shi, M., Su, J., & Li, X. (2021). Application and development trend of artificial intelligence in petroleum exploration and development. *Petroleum Exploration and Development, 48*(1), 1–14. DOI: 10.1016/S1876-3804(21)60001-0

Kumari, A., Gupta, R., Tanwar, S., & Kumar, N. (2020, September). Blockchain and AI amalgamation for energy cloud management: Challenges, solutions, and future directions. *Journal of Parallel and Distributed Computing*, *143*, 148–166. DOI: 10.1016/j.jpdc.2020.05.004

Kumari, M., & Goyal, N. K. (2026). Artificial Intelligence in the Cryptocurrency Ecosystem: Crime Mechanisms, Detection Strategies, and Legal Perspectives. In Lin, L. (Ed.), *Innovations in Cryptocrime and Financial Fraud* (pp. 245–282). IGI Global Scientific Publishing., DOI: 10.4018/979-8-3373-0675-9.ch007

Kumari, M., Kumawat, R., Tripathi, M., Suganthi, K., Goyal, N. K., & Sheikh, M. F. (2026). Blockchain for Transparency and Traceability in Supply Chains. In Khan, M., Mehmood, T., & Rao, M. (Eds.), *Maximizing Operational Efficiency at the Intersection of Supply Chain Management and Marketing* (pp. 35–64). IGI Global Scientific Publishing., DOI: 10.4018/979-8-3373-3109-6.ch002

Kumar, N., & Mallick, P. K. (2018). Blockchain technology for security issues and challenges in IoT. *Procedia Computer Science*, *132*, 1815–1823. DOI: 10.1016/j.procs.2018.05.140

Kumar, S., Lim, W. M., Sivarajah, U., & Kaur, J. (2023). Artificial intelligence and blockchain integration in business: Trends from a bibliometric-content analysis. *Information Systems Frontiers*, *25*(2), 871–896. PMID: 35431617

Labonno, S. I., & Chowdhury, M. T. A. (1 C.E.). Blockchain and IoE Transforming Industry Applications. Https://Services.Igi-Global.Com/Resolvedoi/Resolve.Aspx?Doi=10.4018/979-8-3373-1424-2.Ch007, 177–208. DOI: 10.4018/979-8-3373-1424-2.ch007

Lahami, M., & Chaabane, F. (2023, November). Improving the supply chain management via Blockchain: an olive oil case study. In *TACC* (pp. 182-193).

Lakhanpal, V., & Samuel, R. (2018). Implementing blockchain technology in oil and gas industry: A review. Paper presented at the *SPE Annual Technical Conference and Exhibition.*

Landrø, M., Ringrose, P., & Wienecke, S. (2024). Using DAS for CO2-Monitoring – Possibilities and Limitations. *Fifth EAGE Global Energy Transition Conference & Exhibition (GET 2024),* 2024(1), 1–5. DOI: 10.3997/2214-4609.202421042

Lapins, S., Butcher, A., Kendall, J. M., Hudson, T. S., Stork, A. L., Werner, M. J., Gunning, J., & Brisbourne, A. M. (2023). DAS-N2N: Machine learning distributed acoustic sensing (DAS) signal denoising without clean data. *Geophysical Journal International*, *236*(2), 1026–1041. DOI: 10.1093/gji/ggad460

Lashkari, B., & Musilek, P. (2021). A Comprehensive Review of Blockchain Consensus Mechanisms. *IEEE Access : Practical Innovations, Open Solutions*, *9*, 43620–43652. DOI: 10.1109/ACCESS.2021.3065880

Lazer, D. M., Baum, M. A., Benkler, Y., Berinsky, A. J., Greenhill, K. M., Menczer, F., Metzger, M. J., Nyhan, B., Pennycook, G., Rothschild, D., Schudson, M., Sloman, S. A., Sunstein, C. R., Thorson, E. A., Watts, D. J., & Zittrain, J. L. (2018). The science of fake news. *Science*, *359*(6380), 1094–1096. DOI: 10.1126/science.aao2998 PMID: 29590025

Lee, J., Bagheri, B., & Kao, H. A. (2015). A cyber-physical systems architecture for industry 4.0-based manufacturing systems. *Manufacturing Letters*, *3*, 18–23. DOI: 10.1016/j.mfglet.2014.12.001

Lellouch, A., Lindsey, N. J., Ellsworth, W. L., & Biondi, B. L. (2020). Comparison between Distributed Acoustic Sensing and Geophones: Downhole Microseismic Monitoring of the FORGE Geothermal Experiment. *Seismological Research Letters*, *91*(6), 3256–3268. DOI: 10.1785/0220200149

Lemieux, V., Voskobojnikov, A., & Kang, M. (2021). Addressing Audit and Accountability Issues in Self-Sovereign Identity Blockchain Systems Using Archival Science Principles. *2021 IEEE 45th Annual Computers, Software, and Applications Conference (COMPSAC)*, 1210–1216. DOI: 10.1109/COMPSAC51774.2021.00167

Leng, , JZhu, , XHuang, , ZXu, , KLiu, , ZLiu, , QChen, , X. (2023). ManuChain II: Blockchained smart contract system as the digital twin of decentralized autonomous manufacturing toward resilience in industry 5.0. *IEEE Transactions on Systems, Man, and Cybernetics. Systems*, *53*(8), 4715–4728.

Li, J., & Maiti, A. (2025). Applying Large Language Model Analysis and Backend Web Services in Regulatory Technologies for Continuous Compliance Checks. *Future Internet*, *17*(3), 100. DOI: 10.3390/fi17030100

Lin, B., Jin, Y., Cao, Q., Meng, H., Pang, H., & Wei, S. (2025). Developing a large language model for oil-and gas-related rock mechanics: Progress and challenges. *Natural Gas Industry B*, *12*(2), 110–122. DOI: 10.1016/j.ngib.2025.03.007

Ling, Q. (2023). Machine learning algorithms review. *Applied and Computational Engineering*, *4*(1), 91–98. DOI: 10.54254/2755-2721/4/20230355

Li, T., Sahu, A. K., Talwalkar, A., & Smith, V. (2020). Federated learning: Challenges, methods, and future directions. *IEEE Signal Processing Magazine*, *37*(3), 50–60. DOI: 10.1109/MSP.2020.2975749

Liu, W., Wang, Y., Shi, Q., Wan, H., & Fu, M. (2022). Optimization of decentralized control strategies of distributed resources under cyber failures in flexible distribution network. *International Journal of Electrical Power & Energy Systems*, *142*, 108320. DOI: 10.1016/j.ijepes.2022.108320

Liu, Y. M., Xie, W., Guo, Q., & Wang, S. (2025). Enhancing Pipeline Leakage Detection Through Multi-Algorithm Fusion with Machine Learning. *Processes (Basel, Switzerland)*, *13*(5), 1519. DOI: 10.3390/pr13051519

Liu, Y. P., & Wu, Y. F. B. (2018). Early detection of fake news on social media through propagation path classification with recurrent and convolutional networks. *AAAI Conference Proceedings*. DOI: 10.1609/aaai.v32i1.11268

Li, X., Li, J., Zhao, P., Feng, G., & Lei, Z. (2025). Overview of the Progress in Practice and Experimental Research in Petroleum and Natural Gas Engineering. *Energies*, *18*(11), 2738. DOI: 10.3390/en18112738

Li, Z. (2021). Recent advances in earthquake monitoring I: Ongoing revolution of seismic instrumentation. *Earth Science*, *34*(2), 177–188. DOI: 10.29382/eqs-2021-0011

Lodhi, S. K., & Zeb, S. (2025). The Role of AI in Circular Manufacturing: Towards a Zero-Waste Economy Provides its Headings. *Enrichment: Journal of Multidisciplinary Research and Development*, *3*(1), 124–134. DOI: 10.55324/enrichment.v3i1.339

Logistic regression in medical research. (2021). Retrieved from https://www.anesthesia-analgesia.org

Lokhande, A., Pillai, P., & Mangsuli, P. (2023). *Enabling Contextual Natural Language Search on Oil and Gas Databases.* Paper presented at the Abu Dhabi International Petroleum Exhibition and Conference. DOI: 10.2118/216349-MS

Luger, G. F. (2022). Artificial Intelligence (Structure and strategies for complex problem solving) (6th ed.).

Lu, H., Huang, K., Azimi, M., & Guo, L. (2019a). Blockchain technology in the oil and gas industry: A review of applications, opportunities, challenges, and risks. *IEEE Access : Practical Innovations, Open Solutions*, *7*, 41426–41444. DOI: 10.1109/ACCESS.2019.2907695

Lu, Y., Huang, X., Dai, Y., Maharjan, S., & Zhang, Y. (2020). Blockchain and federated learning for privacy-preserved data sharing in industrial IoT. *IEEE Transactions on Industrial Informatics*, *16*(6), 4177–4186. DOI: 10.1109/TII.2019.2942190

Lyu, J., Qiu, M., Yang, H., Zhou, D., & Liu, J. (2020). Blockchain Applications in Midstream Oil and Gas Industry. *Society of Petroleum Engineers - Abu Dhabi International Petroleum Exhibition and Conference 2020, ADIP 2020*. DOI: 10.2523/IPTC-19937-Abstract

Madine, M., Salah, K., Jayaraman, R., Al-Hammadi, Y., Arshad, J., & Yaqoob, I. (2021). appxchain: Application-level interoperability for blockchain networks. *IEEE Access : Practical Innovations, Open Solutions*, *9*, 87777–87791. DOI: 10.1109/ACCESS.2021.3089603

Mahal, Z. (2024). Exploring the Impact of Attention Mechanisms in Big Data Analysis and Large Language Models. *American-Eurasian Journal of Scientific Research*, *11*(06), 68–76.

Malhotra, A., O'Neill, H., & Stowell, P. (2022). Thinking strategically about blockchain adoption and risk mitigation. *Business Horizons*, *65*(2), 159–171. DOI: 10.1016/j.bushor.2021.02.033

Manimaran, P., Da Conceição, A. F., Garrett, T., Raikwar, M., & Vitenberg, R. (2024). Prevoke: Privacy-Preserving Configurable Method for Revoking Verifiable Credentials. *2024 IEEE International Conference on Blockchain (Blockchain)*, 354–361. DOI: 10.1109/Blockchain62396.2024.00053

Mariana Dahan, M. T. J. D. S., & R. M. R. (2020). Self-Sovereign Identity: The Future of Identity—Self-Sovereignity, Digital Wallets, and Blockchain. *Inter-American Development Bank*.

Marlot, M., Srivastava, D. N., Wong, F. K., & Lee, M. X. (2023). *Unsupervised multitask learning for oil and gas language models with limited resources*. Paper presented at the Abu Dhabi International Petroleum Exhibition and Conference. DOI: 10.2118/216402-MS

Martin, J. L., Zanuri, M. N. A., Sockalingam, M. K., & Andersen, E. (2024). *LLMs, Embeddings and Indexing Pipelines to Enable Natural Language Searching on Upstream Datasets*. Paper presented at the International Petroleum Technology Conference. DOI: 10.2523/IPTC-23626-EA

Mas' ud, A., Yusuf, R., Udin, N. M., & Al-Dhamari, R. (2020). Enforce environmental tax compliance model for the oil and gas industry. *International Journal of Energy Sector Management, 14*(6), 1073-1088.

Mazzocca, C., Acar, A., Uluagac, S., Montanari, R., Bellavista, P., & Conti, M. (2025). A Survey on Decentralized Identifiers and Verifiable Credentials. *IEEE Communications Surveys and Tutorials*. DOI: 10.1109/COMST.2025.3543197

Mehnert, E., Damico, J., Frailey, S., Leetaru, H., Okwen, R., Storsved, B., & Valocchi, A. (2014). Basin-scale modeling for CO2 sequestration in the basal sandstone reservoir of the Illinois Basin—Improving the geologic model. *Energy Procedia*, *63*, 2949–2960. DOI: 10.1016/j.egypro.2014.11.317

Mengelkamp, E., Gärttner, J., Rock, K., Kessler, S., Orsini, L., & Weinhardt, C. (2018). Designing microgrid energy markets: A case study: The Brooklyn Microgrid. *Applied Energy*, *210*, 870–880. DOI: 10.1016/j.apenergy.2017.06.054

Mhlanga, D. (2025). Leveraging Blockchain for Sustainable Finance: Insights, Challenges, and Opportunities for Africa. *Financial Inclusion and Sustainable Development in Sub-Saharan Africa*, 52–73. https://doi.org/DOI: 10.4324/9781003515715-4/LEVERAGING-BLOCKCHAIN-SUSTAINABLE-FINANCE-DAVID-MHLANGA

Miller, T., Durlik, I., Kostecka, E., Kozlovska, P., Łobodzińska, A., Sokołowska, S., & Nowy, A. (2025). Integrating Artificial Intelligence Agents with the Internet of Things for Enhanced Environmental Monitoring: Applications in Water Quality and Climate Data. *Electronics (Basel)*, *14*(4), 696. DOI: 10.3390/electronics14040696

Mitchell, T. (2015). *Machine Learning*. McGraw Hill.

Mohammed, A. S., Reinecke, P., Burnap, P., Rana, O., & Anthi, E. (2022). Cybersecurity Challenges in the Offshore Oil and Gas Industry: An Industrial Cyber-Physical Systems (ICPS) Perspective. *ACM Transactions on Cyber-Physical Systems*, *6*(3), 1–27. Advance online publication. DOI: 10.1145/3548691

Molenaar, M. M., Hill, D. J., Webster, P., Fidan, E., & Birch, B. (2011). First downhole application of Distributed Acoustic Sensing (DAS) for hydraulic fracturing monitoring and diagnostics. *Society of Petroleum Engineers - SPE Hydraulic Fracturing Technology Conference 2011*, 751–759. DOI: 10.2118/140561-MS

Moriyama, K., & Otsuka, A. (2025). Sybil-Resistant Self-Sovereign Identity Utilizing Attested Execution Secure Processors and Zero-Knowledge Membership Proofs. *IEEE Access : Practical Innovations, Open Solutions*, *13*, 17919–17944. DOI: 10.1109/ACCESS.2025.3533877

Mukta, R. (2024). *Privacy-Preserving Identity and Credential Management: A Blockchain-Based Solution.*

Munim, Z. H., Balasubramaniyan, S., Kouhizadeh, M., & Hossain, N. U. I. (2022). Assessing blockchain technology adoption in the Norwegian oil and gas industry using Bayesian Best Worst Method. *Journal of Industrial Information Integration*, *28*, 100346. DOI: 10.1016/j.jii.2022.100346

Murroni, M., Anedda, M., Fadda, M., Ruiu, P., Popescu, V., Zaharia, C., & Giusto, D. (2023). 6G—Enabling the New Smart City: A Survey [Review of 6G—Enabling the New Smart City: A Survey]. Sensors, 23(17), 7528. Multidisciplinary Digital Publishing Institute. DOI: 10.3390/s23177528

Naik, N., & Jenkins, P. (2020). Your Identity is Yours: Take Back Control of Your Identity Using GDPR Compatible Self-Sovereign Identity. *2020 7th International Conference on Behavioural and Social Computing (BESC)*, 1–6. DOI: 10.1109/BESC51023.2020.9348298

Nakamoto, S. (2008). Bitcoin: A peer-to-peer electronic cash system. https://bitcoin.org/bitcoin.pdf

Nanayakkara, S., Perera, S., Senaratne, S., Weerasuriya, G. T., & Bandara, H. M. N. D. (2021). Blockchain and Smart Contracts: A Solution for Payment Issues in Construction Supply Chains. *Informatics 2021, Vol. 8, Page 36, 8*(2), 36. DOI: 10.3390/informatics8020036

Nasteski, V. (2019). An overview of the supervised machine learning methods. Horizonti. *Serija B, 4*, 51–62. DOI: 10.20544/HORIZONS.B.04.1.17.P05

Natekin, A., & Knoll, A. (2013). Gradient boosting machines, a tutorial. *Frontiers in Neurorobotics, 7*, 21. DOI: 10.3389/fnbot.2013.00021 PMID: 24409142

Naveena, M., Ellaturu, N., Kumari, T. L., Bambuwala, S., & Rajalakshmi, M. (2024). Ai-Driven Solutions for Supply Chain Management. *Journal of Informatics Education and Research, 4*, 861–868.

Nguyen, D. C., Ding, M., Pathirana, P. N., & Seneviratne, A. (2021). Federated learning with blockchain for privacy-preserving and secure communications. *IEEE Communications Surveys and Tutorials, 23*(2), 1336–1382. DOI: 10.1109/COMST.2021.3065060

Nguyen, T., Gosine, R. G., & Warrian, P. (2020). A Systematic Review of Big Data Analytics for Oil and Gas Industry 4.0. *IEEE Access : Practical Innovations, Open Solutions, 8*, 61183–61201. DOI: 10.1109/ACCESS.2020.2979678

Nie, A., Su, Y., Chang, B., Lee, J. N., Chi, E. H., Le, Q. V., & Chen, M. (2024). Evolve: Evaluating and optimizing llms for exploration. *arXiv preprint arXiv:2410.06238.*

Nita, S. L., & Mihailescu, M. I. (2024). A Novel Authentication Scheme Based on Verifiable Credentials Using Digital Identity in the Context of Web 3.0. *Electronics (Basel), 13*(6), 1137. DOI: 10.3390/electronics13061137

Nkeonadi, O. P., Kingsley Egbuna, I., Adjei, K. Y., Chukwuma, E. O., Davison Dirisu, C., & Ekechi, C. C.Obinna Paschal NkeonadiIfeanyi Kingsley EgbunaKofi Yeboah AdjeiEmmanuel Onyemeachi ChukwumaChristian Davison DirisuChi-jioke Cyriacus Ekechi. (2025). Corresponding author: Obinna Paschal Nkeonadi Blockchain technology for secure and transparent oil and gas supply chains. *World Journal of Advanced Research and Reviews, 2025*(03), 1818–1830. DOI: 10.30574/wjarr.2025.26.3.2308

Nura, A., & Abdullahi, S. aa systematic Literature Review and Meta-E3E.

Nura, A., & Abdullahi, S. (2022). A systematic review of multi-depot vehicle routing problems. *Systematic Literature Review and Meta-Analysis Journal, 3*(2), 51–60. DOI: 10.54480/slrm.v3i2.37

Nwankwo, C. B., & Emmanuel, O. K. (2025). The Role of Blockchain Technology in Enhancing Tax Transparency and Revenue Collection in Nigeria's Oil and Gas Sector. *Journal of Customary and Religious Law, 2*(2), 97–110. https://journals.unizik.edu.ng/jocarl/article/view/6494

Nwulu, E. O., Elete, T. Y., Erhueh, O. V., Akano, O. A., & Omomo, K. O. (2024). Leveraging predictive modelling to enhance equipment reliability: A generic approach for the oil and gas industry. *International Journal of Engineering Research and Development, 20*(11), 951–969.

Odimarha, A. C., Ayodeji, S. A., & Abaku, E. A.Agnes Clare OdimarhaSodrudeen Abolore AyodejiEmmanuel Adeyemi Abaku. (2024). Machine learning's influence on supply chain and logistics optimization in the oil and gas sector: A comprehensive analysis. *Computer Science & IT Research Journal, 5*(3), 725–740. DOI: 10.51594/csitrj.v5i3.976

Ogunsuyi, O. J., & Ojo, K. O. (2022). K-nearest neighbors Bayesian approach to false news detection from text on social media. *International Journal of Education and Management Engineering, 12*(4), 22–32. . Manzoor, S. I., Singla, J., & Nikita, N. (2019). Fake News Detection Using Machine Learning approaches: A systematic Review. In 2019 3rd International Conference on Trends in Electronics and Informatics (ICOEI). https://doi.org/DOI: 10.5815/ijeme.2022.04.03

Okah Elumah, L., & Sopelola, T. A. (2025). Exploring Financing Strategies in Oil and Gas Industry: Lessons from Nigeria. *Oil and Gas Economics and Management Research Article Petroleum Business Review, 9*(1), 1–12. DOI: 10.22050/pbr.2025.502211.1380

Okedele, P. O., Aziza, O. R., Oduro, P., & Ishola, A. O. (2024). Renewable Energy Policies and Global Socioeconomic Impacts: A Comparative Study of Policy Implementation and Outcomes.

Okoh, C. I., & Odorikpe, V. O. (2025). Smart Contracts and Secure Chains: Optimizing Oil and Gas Logistics in a Digital Age. *SPE Nigeria Annual International Conference and Exhibition*. DOI: 10.2118/228706-MS

Okoro, E., Abara, B. A., Umagba, A. O., Ajonye, A. A., & Isa, Z. S. (2018). A hybrid approach to fake news detection on social media. *Nigerian Journal of Technology*, *37*(2), 454. DOI: 10.4314/njt.v37i2.22

Olsen, B. E., Haugland, S. A., Karlsen, E., & Husøy, G. J. (2005). Governance of complex procurements in the oil and gas industry. *Journal of Purchasing and Supply Management*, *11*(1), 1–13. DOI: 10.1016/j.pursup.2005.03.003

Oluoha, O. M., Odeshina, A., Reis, O., Okpeke, F., Attipoe, V., & Orieno, O. H. (2022). A Unified Framework for Risk-Based Access Control and Identity Management in Compliance-Critical Environments. *Journal of Frontiers in Multidisciplinary Research*, *3*(1), 23–34. DOI: 10.54660/.IJFMR.2022.3.1.23-34

Omar, I. A., Jayaraman, R., Salah, K., Debe, M., & Omar, M. (2020). Enhancing vendor managed inventory supply chain operations using blockchain smart contracts. *IEEE Access : Practical Innovations, Open Solutions*, *8*, 182704–182719. DOI: 10.1109/ACCESS.2020.3028031

Onukwulu, E. C., Agho, M. O., Eyo-Udo, N. L., Sule, A. K., & Azubuike, C. (2024). Advances in automation and AI for enhancing supply chain productivity in oil and gas. *International Journal of Research and Innovation in Applied Science*, *9*(12), 654–687.

Onukwulu, E. C., Fiemotongha, J. E., Igwe, A. N., & Ewim, C. P.-M. (2023). Transforming supply chain logistics in oil and gas: Best practices for optimizing efficiency and reducing operational costs. *Journal of Advance Multidisciplinary Research*, *2*(2), 59–76. DOI: 10.54660/.JAMR.2023.2.2.59-76

Onukwulu, E. C., Fiemotongha, J. E., Igwe, A. N., & Paul-Mikki, C. (2023). The role of blockchain and AI in the future of energy trading: A technological perspective on transforming the oil & gas industry by 2025. *Methodology: European Journal of Research Methods for the Behavioral and Social Sciences*, *173*, 1–15.

Osman, Y. I. A., Li, J. P., Zhen, X. F., & Yang, A. R. (2018). Experimental Study of the Cloud Influence on PV Grid Connected System. *Smart Grid and Renewable Energy*, *9*(1), 1–15. DOI: 10.4236/sgre.2018.91001

Otchere, D. A., Latiff, A. H., & Tackie-Otoo, B. N. (2024). Distributed acoustic sensing in subsurface applications – Review and potential integration with artificial intelligence for an intelligent CO2 storage monitoring system. *Geoenergy Science and Engineering*, *237*, 212818. DOI: 10.1016/j.geoen.2024.212818

Pacis, F., Alyaev, S., Pelfrene, G., & Wiktorski, T. (2024). *Enhancing Information Retrieval in the Drilling Domain: Zero-Shot Learning with Large Language Models for Question-Answering*. Paper presented at the SPE/IADC Drilling Conference and Exhibition. DOI: 10.2118/217671-MS

Padhy, N., Suman, S., Priyadarshini, T. S., & Mallick, S. (2024). A Recommendation System for E-Commerce Products Using Collaborative Filtering Approaches. 50. DOI: 10.3390/engproc2024067050

Pandey, Y. N., Rastogi, A., Kainkaryam, S., Bhattacharya, S., & Saputelli, L. (2020). Opportunities, Challenges, and Future Trends. In Apress eBooks (p. 259). DOI: 10.1007/978-1-4842-6094-4_8

Panhwar, A. O., Sathio, A. A., Shaikh, M. R., Lakhan, A., Umer, M., Mithiani, R. M., & Khan, S. (2022). Plant Health Detection Enabled CNN Scheme in IoT Network. *International Journal of Computing and Digital Systems*, *12*(1), 335–344. DOI: 10.12785/ijcds/120127

Pavan, T. N. V., Devarapu, S. R., & Govindarajan, S. K. (2024). Characterization of Leaky Deep Saline Aquifer for Storing sc-CO2. *Energy & Fuels*, *38*(12), 11051–11063. DOI: 10.1021/acs.energyfuels.4c01599

Peng, Z. (2025). Transforming Energy Resilience through Supply Chain Digitization: Risk Management as a Mediator. *International Review of Economics & Finance*, *102*, 104293. DOI: 10.1016/j.iref.2025.104293

Periodicals of Engineering and Natural Sciences. (n.d.). Retrieved from https://pen.ius.edu.ba/

Piana Agostinetti, N., Villa, A., & Saccorotti, G. (2021). *Distributed acoustic sensing as a tool for exploration and monitoring: a proof-of-concept*. DOI: 10.5194/se-2021-37

Pillai, P., Ryali, S., Maniar, H., Mangsuli, P., & Abubakar, A. (2022). *NLP applications in the oil and natural gas industry.* Paper presented at the SEG/AAPG International Meeting for Applied Geoscience & Energy. DOI: 10.1190/image2022-3739659.1

Politou, E., Casino, F., Alepis, E., & Patsakis, C. (2021). Blockchain Mutability: Challenges and Proposed Solutions. *IEEE Transactions on Emerging Topics in Computing*, *9*(4), 1972–1986. DOI: 10.1109/TETC.2019.2949510

Popa, I.,  tefan, S. C., Josan, A., Mircioiu, C.-E., & Căruceru, N. (2025). Artificial Intelligence as a Catalyst for Management System Adaptability, Agility and Resilience: Mapping the Research Agenda. *Systems*, *13*(1), 47. DOI: 10.3390/systems13010047

Power Ledger. (2022). *Powering the Future of Energy*. Retrieved from https://www.powerledger.io

Prestidge, K. L. (2022). *Digital Transformation in the Oil and gas industry: Challenges and potential solutions*. Massachusetts Institute of Technology.

Pub, A. (2025). Ensuring compliance and safety in global procurement operations in the energy industry. *International Journal of Multidisciplinary Research and Growth Evaluation*, *05*, 1311–1326. DOI: 10.54660/.IJMRGE.2024.5.4.1311-1326

Puri, V. (n.d.). Detecting Fraud and Enforcing Compliance in Global Time & Attendance Solutions via. *Machine Learning*.

Qabasiyu, , M. GZayyad, , M. AAbdullahi, , S. (2023a). An ensembled based machine learning technique of sentiment analysis. [JTEC]. *Journal of Telecommunication, Electronic and Computer Engineering*, *15*(1), 23–28.

Qabasiyu, M. G., Zayyad, M. A., & Abdullahi, S. (2023). An Ensembled Based Machine Learning Technique of Sentiment Analysis. [JTEC]. *Journal of Telecommunication, Electronic and Computer Engineering*, *15*(1), 23–28. DOI: 10.54554/jtec.2023.15.01.004

Qi, M., Wu, T., Duan, W., & Li, S. (2025). Effects of Employee–Artificial Intelligence (AI) Collaboration on Counterproductive Work Behaviors (CWBs): Leader Emotional Support as a Moderator. *Behavioral Sciences (Basel, Switzerland)*, *15*(5), 696. DOI: 10.3390/bs15050696 PMID: 40426473

Qiu, Z., Kownatzki, C., Scalzo, F., & Sang, E. (2025). Historical Perspectives in Volatility Forecasting Methods with Machine Learning. *Risks*, *13*(5), 98. DOI: 10.3390/risks13050098

Qothrunada, N., & Handayani, W. (2023). Does Environmental Disclosure of the Oil and Gas Industry Comply with the GRI? Evidence from Indonesia. *Journal of Business Management and Accounting*, *13*(2), 153–180. DOI: 10.32890/jbma2023.13.2.1

Quinlan, J. R. (1993). *C4.5: Programs for machine learning*. Morgan Kaufmann., DOI: 10.1016/C2009-0-06116-2

Rajasekaran, A. S., Azees, M., & Al-Turjman, F. (2022). A comprehensive survey on blockchain technology. *Sustainable Energy Technologies and Assessments*, *52*, 102039. DOI: 10.1016/j.seta.2022.102039

Ramy, C., Rîpeanu, R. G., Nassreddine, S., Tănase, M., Zouein, E. Y., Dini ă, A., & Muresan, C. C. (2025). Recent Advances in Stimulation Techniques for Unconventional Oil Reservoir and Simulation of Fluid Dynamics Using Predictive Model of Flow Production. *Processes (Basel, Switzerland), 13*(4), 1138. DOI: 10.3390/pr13041138

Rane, S. B., & Narvel, Y. A. M. (2021). Re-designing the business organization using disruptive innovations based on blockchain-IoT integrated architecture for improving agility in future Industry 4.0. *Benchmarking*, *28*(5), 1883–1908. DOI: 10.1108/BIJ-12-2018-0445

Rauniyar, K., Wu, X., Gupta, S., Modgil, S., & Lopes De Sousa Jabbour, A. B. (n.d.). *Risk management of supply chains in the digital transformation era: contribution and challenges of blockchain technology*. DOI: 10.1108/IMDS-04-2021-0235

Ravi Ganesh, P., Kelley, M., Tamrakar, S., Hill, B., Schuetter, J., Rodriguez Tribaldos, V., & Omosebi, O. (2022). Machine Learning-Based, Near Real-time Leakage Detection for Caprock Integrity Monitoring using Distributed Acoustic Sensing (DAS) Data from Carbon Capture and Sequestration (CCS) Operations. SSRN *Electronic Journal*. https://doi.org/DOI: 10.2139/SSRN.4281129

Raza, J. (2020). *From Prevent to "Predict & Prevent (PnP)": Optimizing Oil and Gas Asset Integrity Decisions*. Paper presented at the Engineering Assets and Public Infrastructures in the Age of Digitalization: Proceedings of the 13th World Congress on Engineering Asset Management. DOI: 10.1007/978-3-030-48021-9_57

Raza, M., Jahangir, Z., Riaz, M. B., Saeed, M. J., & Sattar, M. A. (2025). Industrial applications of large language models. *Scientific Reports*, *15*(1), 13755. Advance online publication. DOI: 10.1038/s41598-025-98483-1 PMID: 40258923

Rehman, M. u., Akbar, R., Omar, M., & Gilal, A. R. (2023). *A Systematic Literature Review of Ransomware Detection Methods and Tools for Mitigating Potential Attacks*. Paper presented at the International Conference on Computing and Informatics.

Rehman, M. ur, Akbar, R., Omar, M., & Gilal, A. R. (2024). A Systematic Literature Review of Ransomware Detection Methods and Tools for Mitigating Potential Attacks. *Communications in Computer and Information Science, 2001 CCIS*, 80–95. DOI: 10.1007/978-981-99-9589-9_7

Rehman, M. ur, Hassan, M. F., Akbar, R., Al-rimy, B. A. S., Savita, K. S., Ullah, R., & Zafar, Z. (2025). *Analyzing Early Indicators of Ransomware: Pre-encryption Behavior Patterns*. 566–578. DOI: 10.1007/978-981-96-5848-0_46

Revelou, P., Tsakali, E., Batrinou, A., & Strati, I. F. (2025). Applications of Machine Learning in Food Safety and HACCP Monitoring of Animal-Source Foods [Review of Applications of Machine Learning in Food Safety and HACCP Monitoring of Animal-Source Foods]. Foods, 14(6), 922. Multidisciplinary Digital Publishing Institute. DOI: 10.3390/foods14060922

Rojas, L., Peña, Á., & García, J. (2025). AI-Driven Predictive Maintenance in Mining: A Systematic Literature Review on Fault Detection, Digital Twins, and Intelligent Asset Management. *Applied Sciences (Basel, Switzerland)*, *15*(6), 3337. DOI: 10.3390/app15063337

Rouf, N., Malik, M. B., Arif, T., Sharma, S., Singh, S., Aich, S., & Kim, H. (2021). Stock Market Prediction Using Machine Learning Techniques: A Decade Survey on Methodologies, Recent Developments, and Future Directions. *Electronics (Basel)*, *10*(21), 2717. DOI: 10.3390/electronics10212717

Rubin, V. L., Conroy, N. J., Chen, Y., & Cornwell, S. (2016). Fake news or truth? Using satirical cues to detect potentially misleading news. *Proceedings of the Second Workshop on Computational Approaches to Deception Detection*, 7–17. DOI: 10.18653/v1/W16-0802

Russell, S., & Norvig, P. (2021). *Artificial Intelligence: A modern approach* (4th ed.). Pearson.

Ryan Greene. (n.d.). *Self-So Self-Sovereign Identity and the Decentralized, Consent-Based Model.*

Sahoo, S. R., & Gupta, B. B. (2021). Multiple features based approach for automatic fake news detection on social networks using deep learning. *Applied Soft Computing*, *100*, 106983. DOI: 10.1016/j.asoc.2020.106983

Saka, B. (2024). *Trade Finance and Blockchain Technology: Opportunities to Scale for Big, Small and Medium Enterprises*. https://papers.ssrn.com/abstract=4878957

Sathio, A. A., Ali Dootio, M., Lakhan, A., Rehman, M. U., Orangzeb Pnhwar, A., & Sahito, M. A. (2021). Pervasive Futuristic Healthcare and Blockchain enabled Digital Identities-Challenges and Future Intensions. *Proceedings - 2021 International Conference on Computing, Electronics and Communications Engineering, ICCECE 2021*, 30–35. DOI: 10.1109/iCCECE52344.2021.9534846

Shah, M., Wever, M., & Espig, M. (2025). A Framework for Assessing the Potential of Artificial Intelligence in the Circular Bioeconomy. *Sustainability (Basel)*, *17*(8), 3535. DOI: 10.3390/su17083535

Sharma, P., Kumawat, R., Jain, G., Keswani, G., Goyal, N. K., & Sheikh, M. F. (2026). Machine Learning-Based Intrusion Detection Systems for Healthcare Internet of Things (HIoT). In Shieh, C., Goel, P., Horng, M., & Pandey, H. (Eds.), *Resilient Healthcare Internet of Things Systems: Architectures, Security, and Trust* (pp. 185–214). IGI Global Scientific Publishing., DOI: 10.4018/979-8-3373-7610-3.ch007

Sharma, S., Goyal, N. K., Dandotiya, M., & Sharma, V. P. (2026). An Intelligent Data Encryption Approach with the Entangled Mermin-Based Qkd Protocol for Secure Quantum Communications. In Nayak, R., Mittal, N., Khunteta, A., & Kumar, M. (Eds.), *Recent Advancements in Artificial Intelligence. ICRAAI 2025. Lecture Notes in Networks and Systems* (Vol. 1468). Springer., DOI: 10.1007/978-981-96-7760-3_9

Shehu Yalli, J., Hilmi Hasan, M., Samiha Haron, N., Ur Rehman Shaikh, M., Yousuf Murad, N., & Lawal Bako, A. (n.d.). Quality of Data (QoD) in Internet of Things (IOT): An Overview, State-of-the-Art, Taxonomy and Future Directions. *IJACSA) International Journal of Advanced Computer Science and Applications, 14*(12), 2023. Retrieved August 16, 2025, from www.ijacsa.thesai.org

Sheikh, M. F. A., Kapoor, S. K., Goyal, N. K., & Tuba, E. rao, A. (2026). Enhancing Healthcare Security with Fog Computing and Blockchain Technology. In: Nayak, R., Mittal, N., Khunteta, A., Kumar, M. (eds) Recent Advancements in Artificial Intelligence. ICRAAI 2025. Lecture Notes in Networks and Systems, vol 1468. Springer, Singapore. DOI: 10.1007/978-981-96-7760-3_38

Siano, P. (2014). Demand response and smart grids—A survey. *Renewable & Sustainable Energy Reviews, 30*, 461–478. DOI: 10.1016/j.rser.2013.10.022

Siddique, M. T., Jamee, S. S., Sajal, A., Mou, S. N., Mahin, M. R. H., Obaid, M. O., & Hasan, M. (2025). Enhancing Automated Trading with Sentiment Analysis: Leveraging Large Language Models for Stock Market Predictions. *The American Journal of Engineering and Technology, 7*(03), 185–195. DOI: 10.37547/tajet/Volume07Issue03-16

Singh, S., & Vorster, L. (2024). *LLM Supply Chain Provenance: A Blockchain-Based Approach.* Paper presented at the Proceedings of the International Conference on AI Research. DOI: 10.34190/icair.4.1.3128

Singh, S., Sharma, P. K., Yoon, B., Shojafar, M., Cho, G. H., & Ra, I.-H. (2020). Convergence of blockchain and artificial intelligence in IoT network for the sustainable smart city. *Sustainable Cities and Society, 63*, 102364. DOI: 10.1016/j.scs.2020.102364

Sircar, A., Yadav, K., Rayavarapu, K., Bist, N., & Oza, H. (2021). Application of machine learning and artificial intelligence in oil and gas industry. *Petroleum Research, 6*(4), 379–391. DOI: 10.1016/j.ptlrs.2021.05.009

Soltani, R., Nguyen, U. T., & An, A. (2021). A Survey of Self-Sovereign Identity Ecosystem. *Security and Communication Networks, 2021*, 1–26. DOI: 10.1155/2021/8873429

Song, Y., Sung, W., Jang, Y., & Jung, W. (2020). Application of an artificial neural network in predicting the effectiveness of trapping mechanisms on CO2 sequestration in saline aquifers. *International Journal of Greenhouse Gas Control, 98*, 103042. DOI: 10.1016/j.ijggc.2020.103042

Sousa, A. L., Ribeiro, T. P., Relvas, S., & Barbosa-Póvoa, A. (2019). Using machine learning for enhancing the understanding of bullwhip effect in the oil and gas industry. *Machine Learning and Knowledge Extraction, 1*(3), 57. DOI: 10.3390/make1030057

Steenholt, R., & Bss, A. (2023). *Blockchain: The next revolution for Efficiency, Security, and Privacy in Human Resource Management and Recruitment Master of Science in Strategy, Organisation and Leadership*. DOI: 10.13140/RG.2.2.18365.03046

Stoll, C., Klaaßen, L., & Gallersdörfer, U. (2019). The carbon footprint of bitcoin. *Joule, 3*(7), 1647–1661. DOI: 10.1016/j.joule.2019.05.012

Suhail, S., Malik, S. U. R., Jurdak, R., Hussain, R., Matulevičius, R., & Svetinovic, D. (2022). Towards situational aware cyber-physical systems: A security-enhancing use case of blockchain-based digital twins. *Computers in Industry, 141*, 103699. DOI: 10.1016/j.compind.2022.103699

Sulkowski, A. (2018). Blockchain, Business Supply Chains, Sustainability, and Law: The Future of Governance, Legal Frameworks, and Lawyers. *Delaware Journal of Corporate Law, 43*. https://heinonline.org/HOL/Page?handle=hein.journals/decor43&id=311&div=&collection=

Sun, J., Zhao, G., & Wang, R. (2021). *Application of Blockchain Technology in Oil and Gas Industry*. Paper presented at the Proceedings of the 2021 3rd International Conference on Blockchain Technology. DOI: 10.1145/3460537.3460538

Sun, Y., Liu, J., Xue, Z., Li, Q., Fan, C., & Zhang, X. (2021). A critical review of distributed fiber optic sensing for real-time monitoring geologic CO2 sequestration. *Journal of Natural Gas Science and Engineering, 88*, 103751. DOI: 10.1016/j.jngse.2020.103751

Swan, M. (2015). *Blockchain: Blueprint for a new economy*. O'Reilly Media.

Tacchini, E., Ballarin, G., Della Vedova, M. L., Moret, S., & de Alfaro, L. (2017). *Some like it hoax: Automated fake news detection in social networks*. arXiv preprint arXiv:1704.07506. https://doi.org//arXiv.1704.07506.DOI: 10.48550

Taiwo, T. O. (2020). *An evaluation of contractual clauses used to mitigate risks in long term oil and gas agreements*.

Tamtam, F., & Tourabi, A. (2025). Advancing Digital Supply Chains through Generative AI: A Strategic Framework with the ELECTRE III Method. *Complex Systems Informatics and Modeling. Quarterly*, *43*, 17–33.

Tapscott, D., & Tapscott, A. (2016). *Blockchain revolution: How the technology behind Bitcoin is changing money, business, and the world*. Penguin.

Tariq, M. U. (2025). The Role of AI-Powered Learning Analytics in Enhancing Student Engagement and Performance. In J. Moore, S. Gupta, M. Sharma, A. Garg, & H. Josephine V. L. (Eds.), *Transforming Education With Data Science in the AI Era* (pp. 123-148). IGI Global Scientific Publishing. DOI: 10.4018/979-8-3373-2185-1.ch005

Tariq, M. (Ed.). (2025). *Emerging Multisector Applications of AI and IoT*. IGI Global., DOI: 10.4018/979-8-3373-4332-7

Tariq, M. (Ed.). (2025). *Merging Artificial Intelligence With the Internet of Things*. IGI Global., DOI: 10.4018/979-8-3693-8547-0

Tariq, M. U. (2025). *AI-Driven Learning and Engagement in Higher Education*. IGI Global., DOI: 10.4018/979-8-3693-4074-5

Tariq, M. U. (2025). Integration of Artificial Intelligence and Machine Learning in Business Intelligence: Enhancing Decision Making and Operational Efficiency. In Ishtaiwi, A., Al-Qerem, A., Al Khaldy, M., & Alauthman, M. (Eds.), *Driving Modern Business Intelligence Architecture for Operational Efficiency* (pp. 279–306). IGI Global Scientific Publishing., DOI: 10.4018/979-8-3373-2125-7.ch009

Tavakoli, P., Yitmen, I., Sadri, H., & Taheri, A. (2024). Blockchain-based digital twin data provenance for predictive asset management in building facilities. *Smart and Sustainable Built Environment*, *13*(1), 4–21. DOI: 10.1108/SASBE-07-2023-0169

Tiwari, G., Channakkalavara, P., Singh, G., & Sarella, P. N. K. (2024). Enhancing Security, Transparency, and Efficiency of Blockchain Technology in Pharmaceutical Supply Chain. *Int. J. Pharm. Qual. Assur*, *15*(02), 1009–1016. DOI: 10.25258/ijpqa.15.2.71

Trautz, R., Daley, T., Miller, D., Robertson, M., & Koperna, G. (n.d.). *Geophysical Monitoring Using Active Seismic Techniques at the Citronelle Alabama CO2 Storage 1 Demonstration Site 2 3.*

Tripathi, A., Upadhyay, P., & Goel, P. K. (2025). *Deep Learning for Anomaly Detection in Industrial Networks*. DOI: 10.4018/979-8-3373-3241-3.ch006

Trueman, T. E., Kumar, A., Narayanasamy, P., & Vidya, J. (2021). Attention-based C-BiLSTM for fake news detection. *Applied Soft Computing*, *110*, 107600. DOI: 10.1016/j.asoc.2021.107600

Tsallis, C., Papageorgas, P., Piromalis, D., & Munteanu, R. (2025). Application-Wise Review of Machine Learning-Based Predictive Maintenance: Trends, Challenges, and Future Directions. *Applied Sciences (Basel, Switzerland)*, *15*(9), 4898. DOI: 10.3390/app15094898

Turov, A. T., Konstantinov, Y. A., Barkov, F. L., Korobko, D. A., Zolotovskii, I. O., Lopez-Mercado, C. A., & Fotiadi, A. A. (2023). Enhancing the Distributed Acoustic Sensors' (DAS) Performance by the Simple Noise Reduction Algorithms Sequential Application. *Algorithms 2023, Vol. 16, Page 217*, *16*(5), 217. DOI: 10.3390/a16050217

Tyagi, N. (n.d.). 6 Major Branches of Artificial intelligence (AI) — Analytics Steps. Retrieved from https://www.analyticssteps.com/blogs/6-major- branches-artificial-intelligence-ai

Ullah, A., Qi, G., Hussain, S., Ullah, I., & Ali, Z. (2024). The role of llms in sustainable smart cities: Applications, challenges, and future directions. *arXiv preprint arXiv:2402.14596*.

Ullah, F., & Chowdhury, M. T. A. (1 C.E.). Leveraging Smart Contracts for Enhanced IoE Security. Https://Services.Igi-Global.Com/Resolvedoi/Resolve.Aspx?Doi=10.4018/979-8-3373-1424-2.Ch005, 115–154. DOI: 10.4018/979-8-3373-1424-2.ch005

ur Rehman Shaikh, M., Fadzil Hassan, M., Akbar, R., Ullah, R., Savita, K., Rehman, U., & Shehu Yalli, J. (2024). Pre-Encryption Ransomware Detection (PERD) Taxonomy, and Research Directions: Systematic Literature Review. *IJACSA) International Journal of Advanced Computer Science and Applications*, *15*(9). www.ijacsa.thesai.org

ur Rehman, M., Akbar, R., Mujeeb, S., & Janisar, A. A. (2024). Deep-learning enabled early detection of COVID-19 infection in IoMT fog-cloud healthcare in LPWAN. *Low-Power Wide Area Network for Large Scale Internet of Things: Architectures, Communication Protocols and Recent Trends*, 235–257. https://doi.org/DOI: 10.1201/9781003426974-13/DEEP-LEARNING-ENABLED-EARLY-DETECTION-COVID-19-INFECTION-IOMT-FOG-CLOUD-HEALTHCARE-LPWAN-MUJEEB-UR-REHMAN-REHAN-AKBAR-SHAGUFTA-MUJEEB-AFTAB-ALAM-JANISAR

Ur, M., Shaikh, R., Ullah, R., Akbar, R., Savita, K. S., & Mandala, S. (2024). Fortifying Against Ransomware. *International Journal of Academic Research in Business & Social Sciences*, *14*(1). Advance online publication. DOI: 10.6007/IJARBSS/v14-i1/20566

Valliyatt, M. P., Tharayil, S. M., Razhi, A. A., AlQarni, S., & AlThubaiti, L. (2024). AI-Driven Optimization of Refinery Configurations: A Novel Approach to Predicting Production Outputs and Capacities. Paper presented at the *SPE Annual Technical Conference and Exhibition*. DOI: 10.2118/220241-MS

Vandeweijer, V., Candela, T., Lien, M., Koedel, U., Fechner, T., Bond, T., Zhou, W., Butcher, A., Kendall, M., Stork, A., & Mellors, R. (2022). *A technology readiness assessment for CCS site monitoring systems.*

Varriale, V., Cammarano, A., Michelino, F., & Caputo, M. (2021). New organizational changes with blockchain: A focus on the supply chain. *Journal of Organizational Change Management*, *34*(2), 420–438. DOI: 10.1108/JOCM-08-2020-0249

Vaswani, A., Shazeer, N., Parmar, N., Uszkoreit, J., Jones, L., Gomez, A. N., . . . Polosukhin, I. (2017). Attention is all you need. *Advances in Neural Information Processing Systems, 30.*

Veale, M., & Borgesius, F. Z. (2021). Demystifying the draft EU Artificial Intelligence Act. *Computer Law Review International*, *22*(4), 97–112. DOI: 10.9785/cri-2021-220402

von Schwerin, M., & Reichert, M. (2024). A systematic comparison between open- and closed-source large language models in the context of generating gdpr-compliant data categories for processing activity records. *Future Internet*, *16*(12), 459. DOI: 10.3390/fi16120459

Wang, H., Chen, J., Zheng, Y., & Song, X. (2025). Accelerating flood warnings by 10 hours: The power of river network topology in AI-enhanced flood forecasting. *Npj Natural Hazards*, *2*(1), 45. Advance online publication. DOI: 10.1038/s44304-025-00083-6

Wang, J., Luo, X., Zhang, X., & Du, S. (2025). Artificial General Intelligence (AGI) Applications and Prospect in Oil and Gas Reservoir Development. *Processes (Basel, Switzerland), 13*(5), 1413. DOI: 10.3390/pr13051413

Wang, Y.. (2019). Blockchain for industrial manufacturing: Security and trust issues. *Computers in Industry*. Advance online publication. DOI: 10.1016/j.compind.2019.103120

Wang, Z., Yu, L., & Zhou, L. (2024). Navigating the Blockchain-Driven Transformation in Industry 4.0: Opportunities and Challenges for Economic and Management Innovations. *Journal of the Knowledge Economy*, *16*(1), 3507–3549. DOI: 10.1007/s13132-024-02007-7

Waqar, A., Othman, I., Shafiq, N., & Mansoor, M. S. (2023). Applications of AI in oil and gas projects towards sustainable development: A systematic literature review. *Artificial Intelligence Review*, *56*(11), 12771–12798. DOI: 10.1007/s10462-023-10467-7 PMID: 37362898

Weijermars, R. (2011). Credit Ratings and Cash-Flow Analysis of Oil and Gas Companies: Competitive Disadvantage in Financing Costs for Smaller Companies in Tight Capital Markets. *SPE Economics & Management*, *3*(02), 54–67. DOI: 10.2118/144489-PA

Wen, G., Hay, C., & Benson, S. M. (2021). CCSNet: A deep learning modeling suite for CO2 storage. *Advances in Water Resources*, *155*, 104009. Advance online publication. DOI: 10.1016/j.advwatres.2021.104009

Wright, A., & De Filippi, P. (2015). Decentralized blockchain technology and the rise of lex cryptographia. Social Science Research Network. DOI: 10.2139/ssrn.2580664

Wu, H., Li, G., & Zheng, H. (2024). How does digital intelligence technology enhance supply chain resilience? Sustainable framework and agenda. *Annals of Operations Research*, •••, 1–23.

Wu, J., Yuan, L., Xie, T., & Dai, H. (2024). A sharding blockchain protocol for enhanced scalability and performance optimization through account transaction reconfiguration. *Journal of King Saud University. Computer and Information Sciences*, *36*(8), 102184. DOI: 10.1016/j.jksuci.2024.102184

Xu, L., Li, Q., Tan, Y., & Li, X. (2022). Characterization of carbon dioxide leakage process along faults in the laboratory. *Journal of Rock Mechanics and Geotechnical Engineering*, *14*(3), 674–688. DOI: 10.1016/j.jrmge.2021.12.019

Xu, X.. (2021). *Blockchain-based decentralized data storage and access control for edge computing*. IEEE IoT Journal., DOI: 10.1109/JIOT.2021.3060894

Yalli, J. S., Hasan, M. H., Haron, N. S., Shaikh, M. U. R., Murad, N. Y., & Bako, A. L. (2023). Quality of Data (QoD) in Internet of Things (IOT): An Overview, State-of-the-Art, Taxonomy and Future Directions. *International Journal of Advanced Computer Science and Applications*, *14*(12), 1075–1091. DOI: 10.14569/IJACSA.2023.01412110

Yalli, J. S., Hilmi Hasan, M., Tang Jung, L., Ibrahim Yerima, A., Adamu Aliyu, D., Danjuma Maiwada, U., Mahmood Al-Selwi, S., & Ur Rehman Shaikh, M. (2025). A Systematic Review for Evaluating IoT Security: A Focus on Authentication, Protocols and Enabling Technologies. *IEEE Internet of Things Journal*, *12*(12), 18908–18928. DOI: 10.1109/JIOT.2025.3545737

Yang, H., Shang, G., Li, X., & Feng, Y. (2023). Application of Artificial Intelligence in Drilling and Completion. In *IntechOpen eBooks*. IntechOpen., DOI: 10.5772/intechopen.112298

Yan, Y., Borhani, T. N., Subraveti, S. G., Pai, K. N., Prasad, V., Rajendran, A., Nkulikiyinka, P., Asibor, J. O., Zhang, Z., Shao, D., Wang, L., Zhang, W., Yan, Y., Ampomah, W., You, J., Wang, M., Anthony, E. J., Manovic, V., & Clough, P. T. (2021a). Harnessing the power of machine learning for carbon capture, utilisation, and storage (CCUS) – a state-of-the-art review. *Energy & Environmental Science*, *14*(12), 6122–6157. DOI: 10.1039/D1EE02395K

Yildiz, H., Küpper, A., Thatmann, D., Göndör, S., & Herbke, P. (2023). Toward Interoperable Self-Sovereign Identities. *IEEE Access : Practical Innovations, Open Solutions*, *11*, 114080–114116. DOI: 10.1109/ACCESS.2023.3313723

Yin, H., Yu, J., Qu, H., & Siqi, Y. (2025). A Novel Approach to Waterflooding Optimization in Irregular Well Patterns Using Streamline Simulation and 3D Visualization. *Processes (Basel, Switzerland)*, *13*(4), 1114. DOI: 10.3390/pr13041114

Yin, J., Xiao, Y., Chen, Q., & Lim, Y., Liu, X., Pei, Q. & Zhou, J. (2025). DP-DID: A Dynamic and Proactive Decentralized Identity System. *IEEE Transactions on Information Forensics and Security*, *20*, 4999–5014. DOI: 10.1109/TIFS.2025.3561662

Yu, P., Zhu, T., Marone, C., Elsworth, D., & Yu, M. (2024). DASEventNet: AI-Based Microseismic Detection on Distributed Acoustic Sensing Data From the Utah FORGE Well 16A (78)-32 Hydraulic Stimulation. *Journal of Geophysical Research: Solid Earth, 129*(9), e2024JB029102. DOI: 10.1029/2024JB029102

Yurikov, A., Tertyshnikov, K., Yavuz, S., Shashkin, P., Isaenkov, R., Sidenko, E., Glubokovskikh, S., Barraclough, P., & Pevzner, R. (2022). Seismic monitoring of CO2 geosequestration using multi-well 4D DAS VSP: Stage 3 of the CO2CRC Otway project. *International Journal of Greenhouse Gas Control*, *119*, 103726. DOI: 10.1016/j.ijggc.2022.103726

Yu, S., Wang, K., Dong, H., Tai, Y., Chen, Z., Zhou, D., & Sun, S. (2025). Optimized Economic Evaluation Model for Intensive Drilling in Unconventional Oil and Gas Development. *Processes (Basel, Switzerland)*, *13*(5), 1579. DOI: 10.3390/pr13051579

Zakari, A., Modi Shagari, N., & Sofian, H. (2021). *Systematic Literature Review in Software Testing*. https://www.researchgate.net/publication/354632499

Zakari, A., Abdullahi, S., Shagari, N., Bello Tambawal, A., Musa Shanono, N., Zubairu Maitama, J., Abubakar Rasheed, R., Adamu, A., Mamman Abdulrahman, S., & Abubakar Zakari, B., Zakari α, A., Abdullahi σ, S., Shagari ρ, N., Bello Tambawal , A., Abubakar Rasheed χ Alhassan Adamu ν, R., & Mamman Abdulrahman Θ, S. (2020). Spectrum-based Fault Localization Techniques Application on Multiple-Fault Programs. *RE:view*.

Zakari, A., Abdullahi, S., Shagari, N., Tambawal, A. B., Shanono, N. M., Maitama, J. Z., Rasheed, R. A., Adamu, A., & Abdulrahman, S. M. (2020). Spectrum-based fault localization techniques application on multiple-fault programs: A review. *Global Journal of Computer Science and Technology*, *20*, 41–48. DOI: 10.34257/GJCSTGVOL20IS2PG41

Zakizadeh, M., & Zand, M. (2024). *Revolutionizing Oil & Gas: A Comprehensive Review of Smartening Technologies in the oil & Gas Industry.* Paper presented at the Proceedings of the International Conference of New Technologies in Oil, Gas and Petrochemical Engineering in Iran, Tehran, Iran.

Zarrin, J., Wen Phang, H., Babu Saheer, L., & Zarrin, B. (2021). Blockchain for decentralization of internet: Prospects, trends, and challenges. *Cluster Computing*, *24*(4), 2841–2866. DOI: 10.1007/s10586-021-03301-8

Zhang, X., Qi, J., Liang, X., Guan, Z., Liu, Z., Zhang, C., Chen, D., Deng, W., Xu, C., Wang, X., & Liu, H. (2024). Fiber-Optic Distributed Acoustic Sensing for Smart Grid Application. *Photonics 2025, Vol. 12, Page 7, 12*(1), 7. DOI: 10.3390/photonics12010007

Zhang, C., Wu, J., Zhou, Y., Cheng, M., & Long, C. (2018). Peer-to-peer energy trading in a microgrid. *Applied Energy*, *220*, 1–12. DOI: 10.1016/j.apenergy.2018.03.010

Zhang, Y., & Jacobsen, H. A. (2018). Towards dependable, scalable, and pervasive distributed ledgers with Blockchains. *Proceedings of the VLDB Endowment International Conference on Very Large Data Bases, 10*(4), 385–386. DOI: 10.14778/3159176.3159184

Zhang, Y., & Lee, J. (2020). Data security and trust in hybrid blockchain and machine learning systems: A review. *Future Generation Computer Systems, 108*, 1106–1120. DOI: 10.1016/j.future.2019.11.014

Zhan, Y., Zhang, W., Wang, Z., Yang, J., Li, K., Liu, L., & Ye, Q. (2024). Fast earthquake recognition method based on DAS and one dimensional QRE-net. *Optics Communications, 559*, 130382. DOI: 10.1016/j.optcom.2024.130382

Zhao, A., Yu, Y., Wang, B., Liu, Y., Liu, J., Fu, X., Zheng, W. J., & Tian, F. (2025). Real-Time Intelligent Recognition and Precise Drilling in Strongly Heterogeneous Formations Based on Multi-Parameter Logging While Drilling and Drilling Engineering. *Applied Sciences (Basel, Switzerland), 15*(10), 5536. DOI: 10.3390/app15105536

Zhao, Z., Xie, X., Wu, Y., Liu, Y., & Yin, H. (2021). Federated learning with blockchain: A new architecture for industrial AI. *IEEE Transactions on Industrial Informatics, 17*(11), 7778–7787. DOI: 10.1109/TII.2021.3060996

Zhong, Z., Sun, A. Y., Yang, Q., & Ouyang, Q. (2019). A deep learning approach to anomaly detection in geological carbon sequestration sites using pressure measurements. *Journal of Hydrology (Amsterdam), 573*, 885–894. DOI: 10.1016/j.jhydrol.2019.04.015

Zhou, Q., Huang, H., Zheng, Z., & Bian, J. (2020). Solutions to scalability of blockchain: A survey. *IEEE Access : Practical Innovations, Open Solutions, 8*, 16440–16455. DOI: 10.1109/ACCESS.2020.2967218

Zhou, X., & Zafarani, R. (2020). A survey of fake news. *ACM Computing Surveys, 53*(5), 1–40. DOI: 10.1145/3395046

Zhuang, X., Wang, W., Su, Y., Li, Y., Dai, Z., & Yuan, B. (2024). Spatio-temporal sequence prediction of CO2 flooding and sequestration potential under geological and engineering uncertainties. *Applied Energy, 359*, 122691. DOI: 10.1016/j.apenergy.2024.122691

Zhu, L., Han, R., Zhang, Y., Fu, H., Luo, J., & Luo, Y. (2025). Enhancing Prospecting Target Prediction Precision: A Multi-Source Data Mining Approach in Gansu's Beishan Area. *Applied Sciences (Basel, Switzerland), 15*(10), 5430. DOI: 10.3390/app15105430

Ziegeldorf, J. H., Grossmann, F., Roth, J., & Wehrle, K. (2022). Transparent experimentation with regulatory sandboxes for AI and blockchain: A framework for co-creation. *Technology in Society*, *69*, 101885. DOI: 10.1016/j.techsoc.2022.101885

Zografopoulos, I., Hatziargyriou, N. D., & Konstantinou, C. (2023). Distributed Energy Resources Cybersecurity Outlook: Vulnerabilities, Attacks, Impacts, and Mitigations. *IEEE Systems Journal*, *17*(4), 6695–6709. DOI: 10.1109/JSYST.2023.3305757

Zubiaga, A., Liakata, M., Procter, R., Hoi, G. W. S., & Tolmie, P. (2018). Detection and resolution of rumours in social media: A survey. *ACM Computing Surveys*, *51*(2), 1–36. DOI: 10.1145/3161603

Zuboff, S. (2019). *The age of surveillance capitalism: The fight for a human future at the new frontier of power, edn*. PublicAffairs.

Zuo, Y., & Qi, Z. (2022). A Blockchain-Based IoT Framework for Oil Field Remote Monitoring and Control. *IEEE Access : Practical Innovations, Open Solutions*, *10*, 2497–2514. DOI: 10.1109/ACCESS.2021.3139582

Zyskind, G., Nathan, O., & Pentland, A. S. (2015). Decentralizing privacy: Using blockchain to protect personal data. *Proceedings - 2015 IEEE Security and Privacy Workshops. SPW*, *180–184*, 180–184. Advance online publication. DOI: 10.1109/SPW.2015.27

# About the Contributors

**Shashi Bhushan**, a PhD in Computer Science & Engineering has over 15 years of experience in academics and research. Currently working as Professor & Associate Dean, School of Computing Science and Engineering, Galgotias University, Greater Noida, India. Area of specialization includes but not limited to Wireless Sensor Network, IoT, AIML, Deep Learning. He has delivered several guest lectures, seminars and chaired the session at various reputed international conferences. He has published more than 60 research articles and books in indexed journals and reputed conferences. He edited several journal issues from the most famed publishers like Springer, Bentham Science, Taylor & Francis, and Elsevier, etc. He is also serving as a Reviewer and Editorial Board Member of many reputed Journals.

**Fasee Ullah** is currently working as an Associate Professor with the Department of Computing, Universiti Teknologi PETRONAS, Seri Iskandar, Perak Darul Ridzuan, Malaysia. He received a Ph.D. degree from the Faculty of Computing, Universiti Teknologi Malaysia (UTM), Malaysia. He has also completed the postdoctoral fellowship from the University of Macau, Macao, the academic talented program of the Government of Macau. He has published many research papers in reputed impact factor journals and conferences. He was a recipient of the Chancellor Award and the Best Student Award at UTM during his Ph.D. degree. His research interests include cloud security, cybersecurity, Computer Forensics, information security, smart hash security designing, cognitive smart cities, big data analytics, WBAN, deep learning, and IoT. He is currently providing reviewing services to IEEE Transactions journals, IEEE Access, ACM, Scientific Reports, and so on.

**Mohd Hilmi Hasan** is an Associate Professor and Chair of the Department of Computing at Universiti Teknologi PETRONAS (UTP). He earned his PhD in Information Technology from UTP in 2017, a Master's degree in Information Technology from the Australian National University in 2004, and a Bachelor of Technology (Hons.) in Information Technology from UTP in 2002. His research interests include Artificial Intelligence, Machine Learning, Fuzzy Logic, and Data Analytics, with emphasis on modelling and system development. He is a Professional Technologist registered with the Malaysia Board of Technologists, an active member of international professional bodies, and a reviewer for reputable academic journals. He has published widely in journals and conferences, particularly in AI, fuzzy logic interpretability, and anomaly detection in oil well surveillance. His teaching focuses on active learning, student engagement, and adapting to emerging technologies.

***

**Mohd Hafizul Afifi bin Abdullah** specializes in Information Extraction, Big Data Analytics, Artificial Intelligence, Machine Learning, and Deep Learning. He holds a Bachelor of Science in Computer Science and a Master of Science in Information Technology from Universiti Tun Hussein Onn Malaysia, as well as a Ph.D. from Universiti Teknologi PETRONAS. Hafizul has 8 years of research experience and 5 years of teaching experience. He is a certified Graduate Technologist by MBOT and an IEEE Graduate Student Member. His recent development includes continuous improvement in teaching methods. Additionally, Hafizul serves as a reviewer for leading academic journals in the field of computer science and information technology.

**Kamaluddeen Usman Danyaro** is currently a Postdoctoral / Data Engineer at Offshore Engineering Center, Universiti Teknologi PETRONAS. He received his Ph.D. from Universiti Teknologi PETRONAS, Malaysia. He obtained his M.Sc. in Business IT from Northumbria University, UK. His B.Sc. is in Mathematical Science from Bayero University, Kano. Danyaro's PhD research focused on the development of Semantic Web in oil and gas sector. His research interests include: Computing Intelligence, Machine Learning, Semantic Web, Web Intelligence, Big Data, Linked Data, Web 2.0, Fuzzy Logic Systems, Description Logics, Web Development, Database Design, Knowledge Representation. He is a reviewer in many conferences and journals. He also involves in many Web and software development projects.

**Shahab Haider** is working as Assistant Professor of Cyber Security. His field of interests include Wireless sensor networks, Software engineering, and MANETs.

**Hamza Khan** is a computer science professional from Khyber Pakhtunkhwa, Pakistan, currently serving as an Office/IT Assistant at Ghulam Ishaq Khan Institute of Engineering Sciences and Technology. He holds a BS in Computer Science and is pursuing his MS in the same field at Qurtuba University of Science and Technology. His expertise includes Python programming, Object-Oriented Programming,

Machine Learning, ERP systems, and web development. With prior experience as a Computer Instructor and Senior Web Developer, he has been actively involved in teaching, curriculum design, and applied IT solutions. His research interests center around fake news detection using supervised machine learning techniques, with a passion for bridging academic research and real-world applications.

**Damodharan Palaniappan** works as a Professor & Head in the Department of Information Technology, Marwadi University, Rajkot, Gujarat. He completed his Ph.D. at Anna University, Chennai, M.E. in Computer Science and Engineering at C.I.E.T, Coimbatore and B.E. in Computer Science and Engineering at CSI College of Engineering, Ketty, Nilgiri. He has 19 years' experience of teaching and research. Currently, he guides 6 Ph.D. research scholars. He has authored 8 book chapters, and he has published research papers in reputed journals. His interested areas of research are Data Mining, Image Processing, Software, Machine Learning and Deep Learning.

**Premavathi T** is an Assistant Professor in the Department of Computer Engineering – Artificial Intelligence at Marwadi University, Rajkot, Gujarat. She earned her M.E. in Software Engineering with Distinction from Anna University and is currently pursuing her Ph.D. at Marwadi University. With over 15 years of academic experience, Prof. Premavathi specializes in Machine Learning, Deep Learning, and core programming subjects. She actively mentors students, supervises academic projects, and plays a key role in guiding research and innovation. Her academic portfolio includes 23 book chapters, 5 patents, and 5 research articles, including 1 publication in an SCI-indexed journal. She has also presented papers at 5 national and international conferences.

**Muhammad Usman Tariq** is a strategic higher education leader and scholar with more than 17 years of international experience across academia, research, and industry. He holds dual doctorates, a PhD in Artificial Intelligence and a Doctorate in Business Administration and has published extensively as the author of research articles, case studies, book chapters, and academic texts. His contributions also include several patents, reflecting his applied research in technology, business, and education. He is the Founder and CEO of TheCaseHQ.com, a global hub for professional certification programmes, narrative and video case studies, and digital learning innovation. In addition, he serves as President of the Gulf Higher Education Network (Gulf HE), an initiative dedicated to advancing academic practice, faculty development, and institutional collaboration across the region. He is a Principal Fellow of Advance HE (UK), Chartered Fellow of the CIPD (UK), Senior Fellow of SEDA (UK), and a Senior Member of IEEE, reflecting his standing as both an academic innovator and a global professional leader.

**Ashutosh Verma** is a seasoned Human Resource professional with over 18 years of diverse experience spanning both academia and the corporate sector. He completed his Doctorate from Himachal Pradesh University, Shimla (India) and is currently serving as an Associate Professor at the Parul Institute of Management & Research, Parul University, Gujarat, India. Dr. Verma has worked with reputed organizations across the pharmaceutical, financial services, and life sciences industries, gaining extensive hands-on expertise in various HR functions. A dedicated lifelong learner, he has actively participated in and contributed to numerous seminars, conferences, and workshops at national and international levels. He has several scholarly publications to his credit, including journal articles and book chapters. His current research interests lie at the intersection of human resource development and emerging technologies.

**Muhammad Yahaya** received the B.Engr. computer engineering from University of Maiduguri, Borno, Nigeria, class of 2018. He is currently pursuing his MSc. Degree in information technology with the Department of Computing, Universiti Teknologi PETRONAS (UTP), Malaysia. His research focused on software quality specifically software testing.

# Index

## A



## B



## C



## D



## E

## F



## G



## H



## I



## L



## M



## N



## O



## P



## R



## S

## T



## U



## V



## W



## Z

www.ingramcontent.com/pod-product-compliance
Lightning Source LLC
LaVergne TN
LVHW081529300926
849161LV00006B/1355